Moving in on Occupational Injury

Edited by

David R. Worth

Physiotherapist and Senior Consultant,
Rankin Occupational Safety and Health,
Mile End, South Australia

Physiotherapy Research Foundation

APA
AUSTRALIAN PHYSIOTHERAPY ASSOCIATION

BUTTERWORTH
HEINEMANN

OXFORD AUCKLAND BOSTON JOHANNESBURG MELBOURNE NEW DELHI

Butterworth-Heinemann
Linacre House, Jordan Hill, Oxford OX2 8DP
225 Wildwood Avenue, Woburn, MA 01801-2041
A division of Reed Educational and Professional Publishing Ltd

A member of the Reed Elsevier plc group

First published 2000

British Library Cataloguing in Publication Data
Moving in on occupational injury
1. Industrial accidents – Congresses 2. Industrial safety – Congresses
I. Worth, David R.
363.1′16

Library of Congress Cataloguing in Publication Data
A catalogue record of this book is available from the Library of Congress

ISBN 0 7506 4198 3

Typeset by Techset Composition Ltd, Salisbury, Wiltshire
Printed and bound in Great Britain by Biddles Ltd, Guildford and Kings Lynn

Contents

List of main contributors

Christine Aickin, BAppSc (Physio) MPH (OH), Managing Director, Workability, East Balmain, NSW, Australia

N Ayres, Combrook Pty Ltd, Sydney, NSW, Australia

J S Baines, Dip Phty, Grad Dip Adv Manip Therapy, Grad Dip OH&S, Principal, Paradise Health Clinic, Paradise, SA, Australia

T Becht, BPhty, M Hum Serv, Rehabilitation Officer, 2nd Field Hospital Rehabilitation Unit, Gallipoli Barracks, Enoggera, Qld, Australia

Jane Bell, Grad Dip Phys, MCSP, MAPA, J C Bell & Associates Pty Ltd

Margaret Bullock, AM, FTSE, PhD, BSc App, Professor, The University of Queensland, Brisbane, Qld, Australia

Kerry Butler, Dip Phys, Grad Dip Health Sc, Health Dynamics, WA, Australia

David Caple, BSc (Hons), Dip Ed, MSc (Erg), Director, David Caple & Associates P/L, East Ivanhoe, Vic, Australia

Heather Dale, PO Box 142, Thuringowa Central, Qld, Australia

J J Ford, School of Physiotherapy, Melbourne University, Carlton, Vic, Australia

Dr Ian Gardner, MBBS, MPH, FAFOM, FACOEM, Consultant Occupational Physician, Lindfield, NSW, Australia

Ann Grant, BAppSc (Physio), Grad Dip Rehab Studies, Grad Dip Health Admin, Occupational Health and Rehabilitation Manager, Royal & Sun Alliance Workers Compensation Ltd, Melbourne, Vic, Australia

E Innes, BAppSc (OT), MHPEd, Lecturer in Occupational Therapy, School of Occupation and Leisure Sciences, University of Sydney, NSW, Australia

Åsa Kilbom, Swedish National Institute for Working Life, Solna, Sweden

E D Marshall, BAppSc (Phty), Grad Dip Paed Phty, MPH, Senior Lecturer, School of Physiotherapy, The University of Sydney, Lidcombe, NSW, Australia

Barbara McPhee, MPH (OH), Dip Phty, Cert Erg, FESA, MAPA, Principal, The OH & S Services Network P/L, Ryde, NSW, Australia

M McKie, BA(Hons Psy), State Manager, IRS – Total Injury Management, Melbourne, Vic, Australia

Libby MacWhirter, Grad Dip Phty, Manager, Health and Safety Strategy, South Pacific Tyres, Somerton, Vic, Australia

Steve Milanese, BAppSc, MAppSc (Man Phty) Grad Dip (Erg), Industrial Physiotherapist, Centre for Physiotherapy Research, University of South Australia, Adelaide, SA, Australia

Ruth Mitchell, Consultant in Injury Management and Occupational Safety and Health, Pyrmont, NSW, Australia

Dr Maurice Oxenburgh, BSc, PhD, CPE, MAIOH, Occupational Health and Ergonomics Consultant

R Pashen, State Insurance Manager, Woolworths, Qld, Australia

Robyn Rankin, MSc, BAppSc (Physio), Director, Rankin Occupational Safety & Health, Mile End, SA, Australia

Paul Rothmore, BAppSc Phty (Hons), Grad Cert Workplace Erg, Consultant Physiotherapist (OH & S), Repatriation General Hospital, Daw Park, Adelaide, SA, Australia

Eva Schonstein, BAppSc (Phty), MHPEd (UNSW), Lecturer, Department of Behavioural Sciences and School of Physiotherapy, Faculty of Health Sciences, Cumberland Campus, The University of Sydney, NSW, Australia

Robert Sellars, Director, FCE Systems (NZ) Ltd, Newmarket, Auckland, New Zealand

Pat Smart, Resolutions Pty Ltd, Toorak,Vic, Australia

Leon Straker, BAppSc (Physio), MSc (Erg), PhD (Erg), Senior Lecturer in Ergonomics, School of Physiotherapy, Curtin University of Technology, Perth, WA, Australia

N Sulley, BAppSc (Physio), Grad Dip Soc Sc (Rehab), Royal District Nursing Service, St Kilda, Vic, Australia

S A Sypek, School of Physiotherapy, University of South Australia, Adelaide, SA, Australia

Grace Szeto, Department of Rehabilitation Sciences, Hong Kong Polytechnic University, Kowloon, Hong Kong

Pamela Veal, Mercantile Mutual Insurance, NSW Workers Compensation Ltd, Strathfield, NSW, Australia

D R Worth, PhD, MAppSc, BAppSc (Physio), Dip Physio, Physiotherapist and Senior Consultant, Rankin Occupational Safety & Health, Mile End, SA, Australia

Editorial

This book contains some of the papers from the multidisciplinary international conference Moving in on Occupational Injury held in Cairns, Queensland, Australia, 2–5 June 1999. The conference was convened by the Australian Physiotherapy Association, its Physiotherapy Research Foundation and the Ergonomics and Occupational Health Group. The conference and this publication are the second of their type, the first being *Moving in on Pain* (Butterworth-Heinemann, 1995).

Whilst not all of the papers, seminar discussions and workshops from the conference are included, the contents reflect the breadth of interest in occupational injury. The papers not in this book are on the publisher's Website.

Prevention and management of occupational injury involve employers, employees, governments, government workers, compensation authorities, medical practitioners and specialists, physiotherapists, occupational therapists, occupational hygienists, psychologists, occupational health, safety and welfare experts, insurance companies, public health experts, rehabilitation consultants, ergonomists, university academics and researchers, unions, line managers, supervisors and leading hands, occupational health nurses and design engineers. Each of these experts approaches occupational injury from their own perspective. This tends to lead to a fragmented approach, diluting the effect of intervention.

This book brings together the views of a number of such individuals who are experts within their own fields, indicating the potential for more cohesiveness amongst the experts and stakeholders so that, working together, the measurable outcomes are likely to be greater than the sum of the individual outcomes.

Despite the wide-ranging interests of conference delegates and speakers, in the short space of time these people were together, a common thread appeared to emerge. This was the need to approach injury prevention from its source 'upstream' rather than intervening after the event in order to prevent it from happening again or to lessen the effect after injury or illness recovery and rehabilitation. This requires an attitude shift amongst all experts and stakeholders to emphasise the significance of work-related injury and illness prevention. There does not appear to be the same urgency or emphasis on occupational injury and illness prevention as there is on prevention of road traffic accidents or the reduction of disease and death due to smoking or other substance abuse. Likewise, there does not appear to be the same national investment in advertising campaigns or physical programmes directed towards prevention of occupational injury and disease as for the other categories, despite the frightening statistics presented in several of the papers in this book.

It is therefore my hope that the groundswell of support for strategic alliances and further action in this field will flourish.

I wish to thank the members of the Organising and Scientific Committees for the Moving in on Occupational Injury Conference including Charles Flynn, Annette Cursley, Suzanne Jones, Kerry Butler, Glenn Ruscoe, Elfreda Marshall, Margaret Bullock, Trish Kemp, Barbara McPhee, Jean Cromie, Jane Bell and Rose Boucaut. Special thanks go to Melinda Huntley, Suzanne Moreland, Mina Softich, Jenny Donithorne, Deb Schneider (for her clerical support) and Butterworth-Heinemann for publishing the book. I have greatly enjoyed the privilege of editing this book and sincerely thank all of the presenters and authors for their work. I am confident you will find this book valuable.

David R. Worth

Chapter 1

Perspectives on occupational injury

Occupational injury today: options for workers' compensation reform

Ian Gardner

The USA has done some excellent statistical analyses of its workplace accidents and injury data. The Occupational Health and Safety Administration (USA) (OSHA) figures for the year 1997 show that there was a fatal injury every six minutes. Although everyone focuses on AIDS and all kinds of other chronic diseases, it must be remembered that preventable injuries are the fifth leading cause of death in the USA.

How much do these preventable injuries cost? If you can't quantify it with a cost figure, you will not get the key manager's attention. Unfortunately the most recently available quality cost figures for the USA are only for the year 1992 (see Table 1.1). These figures show the size of the costs of occupational injury in the USA compared to the things that we hear about every day. Occupational injury and ill health cost more than cancer, more than heart disease and more than the arthritic diseases, and are nearly six times more costly than the economic impact of HIV/AIDS.

In 1997, OSHA undertook a major review of 80,000 workplaces in the USA (see Table 1.2). As a result of this survey, they identified 12,500 employers who

Table 1.1 Occupational injury costs for the USA (1992 figures)

	Billions of US$
Occupational injury/illness	171
Cancer	170.7
Heart/blood vessel	164.3
Arthritis/musculoskeletal	149
Alzheimer's	67.3
AIDS	30

statistically had abnormal patterns of illness and injury, that is these 12,500 workplaces had an average of 8.0 lost time or other restricted day injuries compared to the national average of 3.3.

Now just think for a minute – how would we respond to that kind of thing in Australia? Do you think anything would be done?

The short answer is that there may be an editorial written in 'The Australian', and possibly an article in the Worksafe magazine. But in the USA, Charles Jeffress, the Assistant Secretary for Occupational Safety and Health, sent a personal letter to the managing directors of each of these 12,500 'felon companies' telling them that they were statistically abnormal and well outside the parameters of a good corporation. He also included in the letter data for their industry groups. This showed the kinds of accidents and injuries and average performance figures that were being achieved, as well as that industry's most commonly violated OSHA standards.

His letter also included a recommendation that they get some advice from a variety of sources. OSHA has a free consultation programme, which basically guarantees an employer who participates protection from prosecution for the duration of the consultation. A nice little twist at the end of his letter implied that, if they chose not to take up the 'offer', the OSHA were likely to visit the workplace involved and give them a citation. And then, to really rub it in, not only was his letter sent to and published by the press, but the list of every one of these 12,500 'bad' employers was put on a publicly accessible Website. The relevant Web address is http://www.osha-slc.gov/html/hot_2.html

Another US survey which has been very useful is the annual one produced by the US Bureau of Labor Statistics (BLS). Although published every year, the most recently available is only from 1997. It was released in three tranches, in August 1998, December 1998 and April 1999. However, it is important to realise a couple of things when you read these US data surveys. One has to remember the source of the data, i.e. it comes from employer-provided and employer-classified information. So, if the employer does not think that something is an OSHA-recordable injury, it does not show up in the statistics. In addition, it excludes large numbers and different classes of persons – in particular self-employed people, workers on farms employing less than eleven people, those in private households and all government employees.

Table 1.2 Recent activities of the OSHA

- OSHA 1997 survey of 80,000 workplaces
- 12,500 employers with 8 or more lost time injuries or illnesses per 100 workers
- National average is 3.3
- Charles Jeffress, Assistant Secretary of Labor for OSH, sending letters to employers including industry data and the most frequently violated OSHA standards

The average US injury and illness rate per 100 full-time workers for 1997 was 7.1; for manufacturing industry it was 9.9; and for the services industry 5.9. The top line says 8.5, 8.4 etc. and indicates a steady downward movement. In fact some of this is an artefact due to the fact that, whilst the denominator (i.e. 100 full-time workers) is the same, the number of hours worked by those full-time workers has actually increased by about 3 per cent. Therefore, in the last few years there has been no real improvement in worker safety in the USA.

Also in the USA in 1997, there were 6.1 million lost time injuries or illnesses, and 2.9 million restricted workday injuries. These latter injuries are ones where a person is injured and returns to work but not to their normal job. Interestingly, fewer and fewer people are taking time off work for any reason. This is clearly associated with the economic changes that are happening in the USA. Unionism in the USA is almost dead, except in federal and state government employment. Very few private employees are in a union and there are relatively few protections for injured workers in the US system.

Very importantly, if you look at the figures not just in the USA but also in Australia, there is a massive under-reporting of occupational diseases. Occupational fatalities and major injuries are easy to count (and accurate) because there is blood on the floor and a coronial inquest. But when somebody dies slowly over thirty or forty years due to an industrial disease, this is often not captured in any government or private statistics. The Web and FTP addresses of the full BLS Report:

ftp://146.142.4.23/pub/news.release/osh.txt
http://stats.bls.gov/oshhome.htm

Interestingly, and of great importance to people in the physiotherapy and other therapy professions, repeated (cumulative) trauma in the USA is almost non-existent. The figures from the USA showed that cumulative trauma disorders made up only 4 per cent of the 6.1 million cases in 1997. However, the real prevalence is much higher than might be suggested just by looking at lost time estimates. Interestingly, compared to operations in Australia and New Zealand, where the bulk of the repetitive strain injury (RSI) and cumulative trauma disorder (CTD) claims were in non-manufacturing service industries, in the USA such claims have always been most common in manufacturing. In 1997, 72 per cent of these cases were in the manufacturing industry.

WHAT AUSTRALIAN DATA SOURCES CAN WE RELY ON FOR QUALITY INFORMATION?

In the past, of course, it has been Worksafe Australia. More recently the state-based WorkCover Authorities are finally getting their acts together and are starting to produce very high quality data. The Heads of Workers' Compensation Authorities meet three or four times a year to promote co-ordination and uniformity between the disparate workers' compensation systems in the ten jurisdictions that make up the Australian scene. In addition, the Labour Ministers' Council functions at a federal and state government level. The Labour Ministers' Council has now started requiring the states, including the ACT, to provide occupational injury data for a series of studies called 'Comparative Performance Monitoring'. For the first time ever in Australia, we really can look at injury data by state, by industry, by sex – and the information is all being consistently coded and classified.

Before Worksafe Australia was marginalised, they produced some excellent research material. In particular, their study of work-related traumatic fatalities covering the period 1989–92 was recently released. Even though it is now old data, this was the first really good look at workplace fatalities in Australia. It was accurate because its source of data was coronial inquests. If we look at the latest WorkCover data from all the states, there has been little subsequent change in the frequencies of *non-fatal work-related accidents*. Therefore we can assume that occupational fatalities in Australia today are still roughly the same as they were back in 1992 when Worksafe did this landmark study.

In Australia, Worksafe found that there were more than 440 major traumatic deaths per year. If you bring this down to the data denominator that they use, the fatality rate was 5.5 per 100,000 workers. Every time you see a semitrailer on the road, remember that it is also a workplace. Every time you see an accident on the road, in many cases these are occupational accidents. Surprisingly, only forty people were killed travelling to or from work each year, whereas the other ninety motor vehicle related occupational fatalities occurred at the workplace. Other common ways of getting killed at work in Australia are listed in Table 1.3.

WHAT WERE THE MOST DANGEROUS JOBS?

We have known for a long time that occupations involving certain types of flying such as crop-dusting and offshore fishing were very dangerous. Table 1.4 lists these dangerous occupations in order of frequency of incident, from worst to (almost) best. If you look at tractors and farmers, a frequently forgotten sector of the workforce, there are somewhere between forty and sixty people killed in farm-related tractor accidents every year in Australia. This is in spite of having roll-over protection cages on newer tractors. Many tractor fatalities result from the operators trying to jump clear to escape a tipping incident, and ending up being crushed by the cage that is meant to protect them. Also, a lot of Australian farm

Table 1.3 Worksafe data on traumatic deaths at work

440 traumatic deaths per year
5.5 deaths/100,000 workers
135 deaths per year in work-related MVA (includes semitrailers, trucks, minesites etc.)
40 deaths per year in travelling to/from work
Others: hit by falling objects, hit by vehicles, falls from a height, electrocution, drowning

Table 1.4 Worksafe data on the most dangerous jobs

Crop dusters – accident/low power lines
Offshore fishing – drowning
Forestry workers – hit by falling trees
Mining – rock falls, hit by vehicles
Truck drivers – head-on accidents
Farmers – tractors
200 non-working people died each year as the result of the work activity of others!

children are killed in tractor accidents from falls and crush injuries, as well as from the ever lethal power take-off shafts.

Another interesting statistic is that there were an average of 200 other people a year, *not workers*, who were killed as the result of workplace accidents. These are passers-by who happen to be in the wrong place at the wrong time: hit by bits of concrete falling from a construction site, being involved in a car crash with a semitrailer on the wrong side of the road, or passing a truck that loses its load and rolls over and crushes them.

Figure 1.1 shows a schematic diagram taken from the Australian Labour Ministers' Council Website at http://www.dewrsb.gov.au/group_rd/lmc/cpm/reports/

The high level objective of the Labour Ministers' Council is to reduce the incidence, severity and cost of workplace injury and disease through two separate

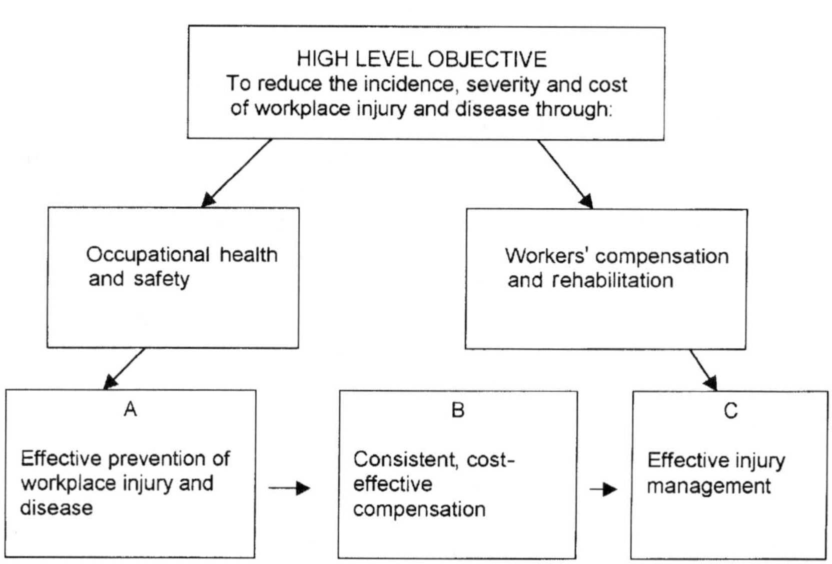

Figure 1.1 Australian Labour Ministers' objectives toward reduction of workplace injury and disease

actions. One is occupational health and safety and the other is workers' compensation and rehabilitation. At the bottom of Figure 1.1 are their outcome measurements: effective prevention of workplace injury, consistent cost effective compensation, and effective injury management.

The bulk of Australian workplaces are run by small employers employing less than twenty-five people. A small employer who is only paying $5000 a year in compensation premiums will statistically only have one serious (meaning one lost time) accident every ten years. What this means is that, for the ordinary small employer, health and safety doesn't count, doesn't matter, doesn't affect his bottom line – and in his or her lifetime as a manager, he/she is unlikely to see the bad outcome of even a single serious occupational accident.

The cost data show that there are a lot of people receiving weekly payments, but the largest amount is actually paid to people who are chronically injured and those with long term injuries. What about injuries from a physiotherapy perspective? What about backs and strains and sprains? Table 1.5 gives some relevant information.

Workers' compensation claims in NSW have been rocketing up in the last few years, increasing at a 7 per cent compound annual growth rate – way above the rate of inflation. Strains and sprains are important and cost the country a lot of money. However, concussion or brain injuries and multiple injuries – especially high impact ones such as car accidents and the like – have the biggest individual costs even though fractures and dislocations have the longest time off work.

Nationally, for the most recent years that data are available (1995/96), the Australian average was twenty days lost per 1000 employees. NSW, QLD, WA and SA were better than the national average. If you look at the national Labour Ministers' Council data, re-analyse them and standardise them for industry mix, then the national average becomes nineteen days, and NSW, WA and SA become relatively worse.

What about the people who are off work long term – thirty or more days? Again, if we look, the average across the country was seven days' lost time. Two states stand out: SA and NSW. Again, because of the larger number of people in NSW, if that state's system is not working well, then the whole of the Australian compensation and injury management system will be poor.

Throughout Australia, most of the states have a state-based WorkCover system. In many, the WorkCover system acts as the sole workers' compensation insurer. Private insurance companies may act as agents for the WorkCover Authority, but do not really take any risk and don't underwrite the business themselves. Let us briefly focus on NSW and have a look at the problems there

Table 1.5 Facts about backs and sprains and strains

Sprains and strains, especially of the back, have been increasing in cost at 7% compound annual growth rate (CAGR) over the last 5 years in NSW
However, concussion and multiple injury have the biggest individual costs
Fractures and dislocations have the highest average claim for lost days

Table 1.6 Representative costs for NSW from WorkCover

Assets: \$5.7 billion
Liabilities: \$7.4 billion
Deficit \$1.675 billion (early 1999)
Costs have exceeded premiums since 1990
Currently 3.3% versus funding of 2.8%

(see Table 1.6). In NSW at the start of 1999 the workers' compensation system had \$5.7 billion in assets. Their liabilities were \$7.4 billion! This decline has been happening for the last nine years. The genesis of this problem is very simple. The cost of the current NSW workers' compensation system is 3.3 per cent of wages, and we are only taking in 2.8 per cent in premiums. Governments have said that they don't want to increase the cost to employers. Each individual state doesn't want to have a higher rate of premiums in their state because they are worried about business moving from a high tariff state to a low tariff state. Inevitably, the result is a burgeoning deficit.

WHY HAVE THE COSTS INCREASED?

In spite of a gentle decline over time in many types of injuries in NSW, the numbers of claims have been very stable over the last seven or eight years. They have been hovering around 120,000 claims plus or minus 10,000 per year. The two key drivers have been:

1. the fact that the numbers of people on long term benefits have doubled from 6 to 12 per cent in the last six years; and
2. the costs of rehabilitation have quadrupled even though the numbers involved have only doubled (see Table 1.7).

Let's look at some US figures. The Unum Life Insurance Company, which is based in the north eastern part of the United States, has done some excellent work on the true cost of disability. What they have done is to look at all the costs that can be measured, both the direct costs and all the indirect costs. They show that,

Table 1.7 Why claims costs have increased in NSW

Claim *numbers* have *not* increased
120,000 ± 10,000 per year
BUT:
Number on *long term benefits* for more than 6 months has *doubled* from 6 to 12% in the last 6 years
AND:
Rehabilitation costs have nearly *quadrupled*

Table 1.8 True cost of disability

4 %:	Direct costs
3 %:	Hidden costs
1 %:	Risk management
8 % of payroll	
Australian estimate = 6.5–7 %	

Source: Unum Life, USA.

for a major manufacturing company, the true cost of disability is about 8 per cent of payroll (see Table 1.8).

There are no exact figures from Australia, but using the Australian labour statistics, WorkCover figures, and Heads of WorkCover Authorities figures, estimates have been made that the Australian true cost of disability is probably in the range of 6.5–7.5 per cent of payroll.

Table 1.9, developed from the 1994 Industry Commission Inquiry, shows that the estimated average total cost of a workplace illness or injury was $27,000 per injury. However, for people who were off work for less than five days, the cost is only $1000. For those off greater than five days, you can see how it rockets up to between $8500 and $28,000.

Table 1.10 shows the costs of long term injuries and fatalities. It is evident that the cheapest way to kill someone is to kill them outright. For traumatic deaths, the cost is only $400,000 all up. If they get asbestosis, mesothelioma or some long lingering death, then the costs go up again to $450,000. Absolutely the worst is where you get someone chronically disabled but with a lifetime ahead of them.

Table 1.9 Australian cost data: estimated total average costs

Average *total* cost of a workplace injury or illness: $27,000

Source: Industry Commission Inquiry, 1994.

Table 1.10 Australian cost data: long term injuries and fatalities

< 5 days	$1000
> 5 days	$8500–28,000
Traumatic fatality	$400,000
Chronic fatality	$450,000
Permanent incapacity	$600,000

Source: Industry Commission Inquiry, 1994.

These cases average costs of $600,000 – nearly 50 per cent higher than for a neat, clean, fatal injury!

One of the major reasons why the costs are higher for the long term cases is because of our legal system. In fact, in the NSW workers' compensation system, one of the questions they ask claimants is 'Do you have legal representation?'. If that box is ticked, the insurers add an automatic $15,000 to their estimate of the claim cost. If lawyers are involved in workers' compensation claims, it pushes up the cost without any measured improvement in the health outcomes for the injured worker.

Can we improve safety at the workplace, and are safety statistics useful in comparing the safety performance of different companies? Many people are wary about their use. However, safety statistics can be regarded as a 'leading indicator' of the likely ultimate cost of claims, and as such are worth collecting and analysing.

However, many of the things that we do in the name of safety are a waste of time and money when evaluated according to evidence-based criteria. Table 1.11 shows three activities that have been shown globally to positively impact safety performance.

The first, and most effective, is changing the safety culture. However, it is probably the hardest of all to do, as it requires senior management leadership and direction. The aim is to establish safety as part of a culture that says 'we live safely round here'. Secondly, by implementing appropriate return to work strategies, most injuries can be safely and effectively treated in the workplace. Except in rare cases when an injured worker needs to be confined to bed, the workplace is the best place to help them rehabilitate back to their full normal duties. If an employer has active, appropriately set up return to work strategies, significant improvement in lost time and therefore total injury costs will result. The third effective strategy shown to improve safety performance is safety training. Deficiencies in safety training and safety systems were highlighted in the recent Longford Royal Commission in Victoria, and international studies show that investments in safety training have a pay-back of between two and seven times per dollar depending on the country and the legislative environment.

Unfortunately, office ergonomics is almost useless unless it focuses on the whole 'system of work' rather than the all too common 'fix-it' solution of buying

Table 1.11 How to influence safety

Effective:
1. Safety culture
2. RTW strategies
3. Safety training
Not effective:
Office ergonomics?? Wellness/People focus/Case monitoring

Table 1.12 Paradigm shift

Compensation	⟶	Wellness
Output driven	⟶	Outcomes driven

Source: G. Sartorel, MMI, 1999.

Table 1.13 Moves to create a safer workplace

Prevention:		Mitigation and management:
Safety culture		Early intervention
Safety training	⟶	RTW programmes
? Health and wellness		Integrated rehabilitation

new ergonomic furniture, adjusting computer screens and heights and getting low profile keyboards and non-glare monitors.

Similarly, a focus just on 'wellness' by itself has not proven to be effective from a safety viewpoint. However, it may indirectly have benefits from an employee morale point of view. And simple 'case monitoring' is also useless. This is not referring to 'case management' which embodies the active management of injured workers through a co-ordinated programme involving rehabilitation with an integrated return to work strategy. This is very effective. But just keeping a track of the numbers of injured workers, and maybe giving them a phone call once a week, has not been shown consistently to work anywhere in the world.

George Sartorell, the new General Manager, Privatisation for the MMI Group in Australia, gave an excellent presentation on workers' compensation drivers recently at one of the Institute for International Reasearch (IIR) Industry Conferences. He claimed that we need to have a paradigm shift which moves from a compensation focus looking at outputs after injury, to a wellness or holistic focus which looks at keeping people safe at work. Tables 1.12 and 1.13 show this model.

In his integrated model, items to the left are things you can do to improve **prevention**, and on the right of the vertical line are the things you can do **after** the accident. Clearly, early intervention is one of the key programmes. Most of the developed world's safety figures show that, if you don't get to an injured worker within twenty-four hours post-injury, you have lost control of the industrial injury consequences. On average, his or her outcomes will be much worse than they would have been if you had been able to implement early assessment, early intervention and early rehabilitation right from the start.

CHANGES TO AUSTRALIA'S WORKERS' COMPENSATION SYSTEM IN MID–1999

Most states are changing their workers' compensation systems and, in the opinion of some, they are not being changed for the better. They are being changed only to save money. States are doing this by decreasing benefits, limiting access to common law, and by excluding certain conditions such as stress and journey accidents.

For many years, the NSW system has had a focus on providing services to injured workers through rehabilitation co-ordinators. But in spite of some good data showing cost savings from such interventions, the overall system costs have been increasing. The focus of the new system is on an **early and durable return to work**. The new workers' compensation system is now experimenting with using a 'nominated treating doctor' in an attempt to ensure that the local doctor keeps some control of the case, manages the person's injury, and is aware of what is happening. It is also an attempt to stop 'doctor shopping' by patients. The WorkCover Authority in NSW will now no longer accept any workers' compensation certificates other than those from the nominated treating doctor. However, no one really knows if this new system of control is going to work or not. In addition, there are now also 'injury management consultants' and 'authorised medical specialists'. If you are not on the authorised medical specialist list, you won't get any referred compensation work in future (Table 1.14).

The NSW government is also hoping that they will soon get rid of this huge workers' compensation financial deficit by privatising it. A major problem here is that for the last fifteen years in most Australian states, all insurers of workers' compensation have been acting only as 'agents' for WorkCover. They get a handling fee and a percentage of profits, and have not underwritten any of the risk themselves. Their previous expert knowledge in managing workers' compensation insurance has been lost. Similarly, across the Tasman where the Accident Compensation Commission (NZ) (ACC) has been the sole insurer for many years, the New Zealand Government wants to privatise the workers' compensation system early in 2000. If we look overseas to the USA, workers' compensation insurance is the second most profitable area of insurance for insurance companies. It is the belief of some that this doesn't necessarily bode well for injured Australian workers.

Table 1.14 New structures

New Workers' Compensation Acts
Decreased benefits
Limited access to common law
Excluded conditions, e.g. stress
Greater role for treating doctor
Rehabilitation/injury management plans
Focus on early and durable RTW
Privatisation of workers' compensation system

References

http://www.dewrsb.gov.au/group_rd/lmc/cpm/reports

http://www.worksafe.gov.au

http://stats.bls.gov/oshhome

ACOEM (1998). BLS Issues Annual Survey of Workplace Injuries. ACOEM Report, December 1998, pp. 1–2. ACOEM, Chicago.

Poole, L. (1999). CPM – can jurisdictions be fairly compared? *Inside OHS*, **1**, February.

Safety WA (1999). *Focus on hazards casts light on all hazards*. February. Worksafe WA, Perth, WA.

Occupational injury: the employer's perspective

Rhonda Pashen

INTRODUCTION

This paper outlines one employer's recent programmes introduced to improve the delivery of Occupational Health and Safety (OHS) services, including injury management and rehabilitation. It highlights some of the issues that are critical in the delivery of effective OHS/Workers' Compensation services at the workplace. To indicate some of the areas where service providers can assist employers in delivery of OHS services.

Woolworths' operations in Queensland encompass several different types of retail outlets, as well as Chisholm Manufacturing – a small-goods manufacturing business. Under the provisions of the WorkCover Queensland Act 1996, to obtain a self-insurance licence for workers' compensation, all wholly owned companies operating in the state must be covered by the licence.

Hence, as State Insurance Manager for Woolworths Queensland, the author has a role in delivering a certain level of occupational health-related services to all divisions, which employ 27,000 workers, at approximately 300 workplaces. The Supermarket Division is by far the largest, employing approximately 21,000 staff throughout the state.

Since the beginning of 1998 Woolworths have made significant changes to the way their occupational health services are delivered. Before discussing WHAT these changes were, it is interesting first to consider WHY the Executive in Queensland took the decision to place such focus on occupational health at that time.

In 1997 the workers' compensation premium rating system in Queensland changed. From July 1997 an experience-based rating system was introduced into the workers' compensation scheme in Queensland. This meant that an employer the size of Woolworths would have their premium calculated almost entirely on their own claims performance over the previous five years. Previously the calculation was based on an industry rate – with some adjustment for claims performance over the preceding year.

In late 1997 WorkCover presented Woolworths with an analysis of their premium under the new system, and management realised there was considerable room for improvement. This provided the stimulus for the company to conduct a full review of all services involved in the delivery of its occupational health programme.

The reaction of Woolworths to the impending cost issues at this time was similar to many other large organisations and highlights one important principle for employers in addressing OHS issues – namely the need to understand the real financial impact of occupational injury.

This is therefore obviously an important issue for any service provider assisting employers in this area. The more detailed an understanding providers have of the way costs are incurred in respect to occupational injury, the better they can tailor their services to address the critical areas and present relevant cost–benefit analyses. However, from past experience in Queensland, this is not something that is well done by many providers.

So now – WHAT was done differently? There are four areas to address:

- insurance position
- structure and resources
- systems improvement
- skills development.

INSURANCE POSITION

The ability to self-insure for workers' compensation purposes was introduced in Queensland from July 1997. The management of Woolworths decided to investigate the benefits of applying for a licence as a key initiative in improving their occupational health and safety performance.

After considerable research it was decided that there could be considerable benefits obtained from self-insurance in a company like Woolworths – and the application was lodged. Management considered that the improved services that could be offered to staff, particularly in respect to rehabilitation programmes, were some of the key benefits that could be gained. It must also be stated that the analysis of the cost of self-insurance versus staying with WorkCover was also very appealing.

Now that implementation is complete, one of the most important benefits that has been realised is the ownership of the organisation's own database in respect to occupational injury. The on-line ability to analyse all indicators whenever considered necessary has presented an enormous advantage. Managers can now identify which departments are the most costly, which injuries are the most common, and which incidents result in the most injuries. The ability to use this information to educate management at all levels in the need for greater attention to prevention programmes has been invaluable.

Another important change that was facilitated by the introduction of self-insurance was the ability to charge back the cost of each statutory claim to the actual work units where the incident occurred. This inherently means that individual bonuses paid to managers at all levels in the organisation are impacted by the occupational health performance of their unit. Each unit is provided with a budget for workers' compensation based on the average anticipated expenditure. Hence a nil claims performance will assist in increasing individual bonuses and a poor performance will detract. This approach has contributed substantially to an improved culture in respect to prevention of injuries.

STRUCTURE AND RESOURCES

A new Insurance Department was created – and staff numbers increased from four to fifteen. The functions which were brought together were:

- workers' compensation claims
- rehabilitation
- OHS
- public liability
- administration.

The links between most of these areas are obvious and the benefits of constant communication between the groups are being realised.

The linking in of the public liability function was in recognition of the benefits that are gained from well-maintained and hazard-free workplaces for both customers and staff in the retail industry.

The creation of a separate administration stream was in recognition of the importance of efficient data capture and the development of effective reporting mechanisms as a key to achieving ongoing improvements.

SYSTEMS IMPROVEMENT

Safety bonus

In an attempt to achieve a rapid improvement in prevention systems a new bonus system was introduced for the supermarkets. A bonus was paid to stores each six months if four criteria were met:

- Timely meetings of the health and safety team.
- Minutes of meetings being of an adequate standard.
- An incident investigation being conducted for each injury that resulted in a workers' compensation claim.
- Adequate reporting standards for any incident involving a customer.

All of this information is forwarded to the Insurance Department, and is used as part of the ongoing analysis of the occupational health performance and contributes to recommendations for improvements.

This approach was adopted in recognition of the importance of a 'safety diligence' culture in reducing the cost of occupational injury. The research conducted at the Upjohn Institute for Employment Research in Michigan, USA by Hunt and Habeck (1996) is important here.

The research investigated eight variables within organisations and their impact on lost workdays associated with workplace injuries. The eight variables were:

- safety diligence

- return to work programmes
- safety training
- wellness orientation
- people-oriented culture
- active safety leadership
- case monitoring
- ergonomics.

They defined 'safety diligence' as the rigorous behaviours of companies that act on their stated safety goals and put their safety measures into practice. Safety diligence is evident in:

- Excellent housekeeping and continuous equipment maintenance.
- Timely investigation of risks and accidents that uses problem solving for immediate correction and future prevention.
- Constant compliance with company safety measures and the use of disciplinary action for violations.
- Emphasis on safety in all aspects of plant operations.

The study showed that safety diligence had the most powerful effect on lost workday rates, with a 10 per cent higher self-reported level of safety diligence being associated with a nearly 17 per cent lower level of lost workdays per 100 employees.

Woolworths experience has given support to this finding. Analysis was conducted at the end of the first six months following the implementation of the bonus scheme. The total bonus paid to the seven different operational areas was assessed and was compared with total expenditure on workers' compensation during the period.

The analysis indicated that the operational area with the highest workers' compensation expenditure for the period also attracted the worst result in respect to the bonus payable and vice versa.

These results have made it easier to convince management that a safety culture is critical to continue reducing costs associated with occupational injury.

SKILLS DEVELOPMENT

A skills analysis was conducted to determine the strengths and weaknesses in respect to delivery of the new strategies. It is worth noting that in an organisation the size of Woolworths skills development at workplaces was a major task.

Even at the commencement of the improvement programme Woolworths already had invested considerable resources in this area. There were in excess of 130 Workplace Health and Safety Officers who had been accredited by the Division of Workplace Health and Safety in Queensland and approximately 250

Rehabilitation Co-ordinators who had been trained and accredited under the requirements of the WorkCover Queensland Act 1996.

The new training programmes that were given priority included specific focus on incident investigation and running effective health and safety teams. Comprehensive programmes to increase understanding of the aims of and practical issues relating to self-insurance were also conducted, as well as detailed awareness programmes about our current OHS performance.

SERVICE PROVIDER ISSUES

During the author's time with Woolworths, since early 1998, the extent of contact from various service providers has been surprising, as has the low level of understanding some providers appear to have for the time pressures that exist in industry.

Based on this experience, some thoughts on the best approach to take include:

- Make an effort to understand industry, including specific issues – don't just offer a broad-brush approach.
- Examine the workers' compensation scheme in which you operate to understand the major cost drivers and tailor services accordingly.
- Don't expect too much 'air-time' to sell your services; ensure your point of difference is able to be explained in a five to ten minute telephone conversation.
- Don't approach organisations asking for relatively commercially sensitive advice without being prepared to say why you are seeking the information and/or on behalf of which company.
- Basic professional services offered at competitive prices and delivered at geographically spread workplaces will always be in great demand.

CONCLUSIONS

The major changes to Woolworths OHS programmes have not yet had sufficient time to 'bed down' to determine real outcomes. However, some trends, including the overall company cost of workers' compensation, are most encouraging. The support for, ongoing two-way communication regarding, and eagerness to gain more information about the issues which are occurring through all levels of the organisation are also positive indicators of the benefits that should be realised.

References

Hunt, H.A. and Habeck, R.V. (1996). *The Michigan Disability Prevention Study Research Highlights*. Proc. First National Workers' Compensation Conference, Melbourne, March 1996.

WorkCover Queensland Act (1996). Government Printer, Queensland.

Occupational injury: the ergonomist's perspective

David C. Caple

This paper will elaborate on the key issues where ergonomics interface with issues relevant to the prevention of occupational injury. They primarily relate to design: the design of jobs, workplaces, tools, work environments and work organisational systems.

Ergonomists are generally not designers as such. They contribute to the process by identifying and quantifying issues relevant to the process or product undergoing design. They are often seen as the advocate for the user. This is not an industrial relations role, but one fundamental to understanding of the physical, psychological and social needs of user groups. The ergonomist then reflects these needs in a practical series of recommendations for the designer.

Usability studies have been used extensively in validating aspects of the design. This enables potential users to evaluate the key principles to be incorporated in the design brief. This may include suitability for anthropometric or biomechanical needs.

It may also include the behavioural issues such as population stereotype expectation of controls and displays. Perceptual and cognitive issues relating to decision making and information processing requirements are also part of the ergonomic evaluation.

It is interesting to take a consumer product such as a video recorder and quickly appreciate the role ergonomics should play. Why is it that we need a twelve year old to set the correct pre-recording process while adults generally become confused and avoid such devices? Good ergonomics is often synonymous with 'user friendly' designs.

With occupational injury prevention, the ergonomist needs to clearly identify who are those most likely to be injured, and understand the multifactorial causal factors. Sprain and strain remain two of industry's major injuries. Ergonomists take a holistic perspective with questions such as 'Why now has this workplace been associated with such injuries?'.

It is clear that biomechanical and anthropometric factors are important elements to be evaluated. Often issues relating to static strain are precursors to many of these injuries through poor postures and sustained static forces such as in gripping hand-tools.

However, it is also clear that work organisational factors relating to job design, performance expectations, product quality, team cohesiveness and social harmony in the workplace are often more relevant to the 'why now' answers.

Ergonomists often use the term 'discomfort threshold' to reflect that many people regularly experience discomfort at work and home, but that they accept this as part of their job, getting old, sports injuries playing up etc.

However, when their discomfort increases beyond their subjective threshold, they will often report this as an injury and seek treatment. An ergonomist will tend to assess what factors in their work, or in life generally, may explain the extension of discomfort and pain.

This process is often included in the risk assessment process as outlined in various state occupational health and safety legislation in Australia. Although the Manual Handling Regulations of this legislation are biased towards the biomechanical factors rather than the psychological/social factors, they do encourage a broad-based investigation of occupational injury.

A broader uptake of the ergonomics systems analysis process in investigating occupational injury will form a broad-based approach to identifying and controlling causal factors.

Occupational injury: the insurer's perspective

Ruth Mitchell

BACKGROUND

Definition

The definition of insurance as used here is 'coverage by contract whereby one party agrees to indemnify or guarantee another against loss by a specified contingent event or peril' (Oxford English Dictionary).

What does this mean? Basically an insurance company will set a price for a customer to cover the customer's potential loss, whilst attempting to make a profit for their own shareholders. Workers' compensation in Australia, however, falls into the two categories of underwritten and managed funds. Within these categories there are further variations. Currently in Australia, New South Wales (NSW), Victoria (Vic) and South Australia (SA) are considered managed fund states, whilst Western Australia (WA), Tasmania (Tas), Australian Capital Territory (ACT) and Northern Territory (NT) remain underwritten states/territories. In a managed fund environment, insurers do not set the price but are funded by various arrangements with government authorities to manage several aspects of the business. In underwritten environments the insurers set the price – in some cases with government restrictions. There are many aspects considered when setting the price, and one of the biggest variables that an insurer needs to consider is their ability to manage the resultant claims and therefore the claims costs, which are in fact the largest expenditure of the insurer. A claim results from occupational injury and therefore logic suggests that the successful management of occupational injury will reduce claims cost and therefore affect price and, dare it be suggested, outstanding liability.

If it appears so simple the question begs – why are workers' compensation schemes in Australia in financial trouble?

There are some obvious problems, with national consistency of legislation perhaps remaining the biggest one. Many insurers are national or at least operate in more than one state or territory, and yet the rules under which they operate are inconsistent. This makes it almost impossible to deliver consistent policies and procedures, and more often than not insurers operate to the minimum standards that apply in their specific jurisdiction.

There is, however, a way of addressing this problem – insurers can take the initiative and develop a set of standards within their company and apply them across all of their operations, throughout the states and territories. This requires an assessment of all the rules nationally, then applying the toughest requirements as the minimum standard within the company. Some insurers have already adopted this process. The managed fund environments have done more to address the standards required to achieve reduced claims costs than have the underwritten states.

The area, which has commanded more emphasis than any other in recent times, is the return to work process, which could also be called the management of occupational injury.

OCCUPATIONAL INJURY

In managed fund environments insurers have been rewarded for achieving certain standards in relation to their ability to manage and achieve successful return to work outcomes, whilst in underwritten states/territories licence requirements have ensured that insurers met certain standards. This generally suggests that a return to work is the best way of reducing claims costs. Whilst various attempts have been made to improve return to work rates, there has been a lack of consistency in the application of workable policies and procedures in a national sense. One of the reasons contributing to this may be the insurer's emphasis on maintaining their licences or incomes rather than concentrating efforts on return to work strategies. This can be understood, considering that insurance companies are businesses with shareholders who need to ensure a return on investment annually and are therefore dollar driven. In contrast, return to work strategies are people driven, are not short term and require a cultural change in organisation to be successful; this does not always ensure adequate financial returns in the first year.

Organisations that develop a culture of 'caring for people' will have more success with return to work strategies than those who don't. It is often said that the people are an organisation's best asset. However, one might add that this is true until they have a workers' compensation claim. What is it that happens to change a productive worker (asset) into a non-productive claimant (liability)? Could it be the 'system' or could it possibly be the interpretation and implementation of the system?

The system is the workers' compensation legislation, different in all states/territories. The interpretation of the system is different to all players, depending on vested interests. Somewhere in this maze are a worker and an employer whom the system outcome affects the most. What is each player's interpretation? Does it differ from the other players involved in the system interactively? This particularly involves the worker and the employer. How does it affect the outcome?

Communication is the vital and often neglected element in the management of occupational injury and, within this, consultation between all parties involved in the process is the key. Consultation involves asking questions, finding out expectations, and agreeing on actions and time-frames. Consultation is seeking and understanding the other person's point of view. A successful outcome depends on this.

In understanding workers' compensation the basics are the same whether the participants are employers, workers, insurers, rehabilitation providers or other players. Various assumptions are involved, as described below.

'All injuries are genuine'

This is the first assumption. What does this mean to participants in the system? The answers always reflect the make-up of the participants. This statement at no time mentions a worker's compensation 'claim'. Does this then impact on the treatment of the worker? Inevitably, participants agree that the treatment of the worker in relation to the injury will vary, dependent on whether or not a claim is involved. Whether a claim is compensable should not be the driving factor in the treatment of an injury. In a 'caring culture', compensability does not interfere with the management of the injury.

'All incidents result from a system breakdown'

This is the second assumption. Discussion of this statement leads to the agreement that, when companies focus on the system and not the people, then opportunity always exists to make improvements. This system is an occupational health and safety system of which there are many components and of which injury management is just one. In injury management there are two major components: claim administration and rehabilitation. The claims administration covers aspects such as liability determination, communication with all parties of decisions, payment of wages and accounts etc. The rehabilitation component covers aspects of medical intervention, identification of suitable duties, formulation and monitoring of return to work plans/programme and, of course, communication and consultation with all parties. The initial meeting between both the worker and employer, and in particular the decision as to the preferred outcome at that time in a return to work plan/programme, is the most important component. The hierarchy of outcomes can be summarised as follows:

1. same job/same employer
2. similar job/same employer
3. different job/same employer
4. same job/different employer
5. similar job/different employer
6. different job/different employer.

It is the lack of clarity and agreement of the preferred outcome at this first meeting that leads to confusion and the failure to reach a successful conclusion. The most successful programme starts with the end in mind! Only with an agreement of the outcome by all parties at the start can a step by step plan be formulated that will achieve the end in mind. Too often, the parties to the process have an unspoken outcome, towards which they are working.

Some 90 per cent of problems in return to work and claims management come from the initial communication. It's not what you say or hear is said and heard, but what is not said or heard which blocks successful return to work and claims closure.

An example could be that the employer may not want the worker in the workplace, or the worker does not like the job they were doing and would prefer something else. It is vital to a successful return to work to identify these barriers that might be present at the initial stage.

Once an outcome has been agreed, the plan/programme can then be formulated. This should be the simple part: identify the worker's capacity and identify suitable duties. A graduated return to work in either or both duties and hours can be very useful if there is some reluctance (or lack of trust) by the employer, worker or treating doctor. A plan/programme could also incorporate a 'fail-safe' component if it appears the return to work could be sabotaged. What is a 'fail-safe' component? Simply put, it is an ability to monitor and act immediately to prevent any potential failure in the return to work, by identifying problems at the time they occur. A 'fail-safe' system actually allows the worker and employer to accept responsibility for the return to work, as in effect they are shown how to identify problems that occur and replace them with solutions.

Return to work co-ordinators who are able to empower the employer and the worker to manage the return to work process will gain the most rewarding results.

One of the reasons that the insurance industry has had varied results with successful return to work outcomes could be how they see themselves in this relationship. Some see themselves as the controller when in fact they are only the co-ordinator or facilitator in the process. The primary relationship can only be between the employer and the worker; all other parties involved are external to this primary relationship.

It is the understanding of the relationships and the commitment to an 'agreed' outcome that leads to success in the management of occupational injury.

Chapter 2

Causes

Factors and mechanisms in occupational injury

Margaret I. Bullock

INTRODUCTION

Accidents and injuries do not usually occur as a matter of chance. Rather, they are the result of a chain of causation involving some maladjustment between the person and their environment and the interaction between a number of contributing factors.

Statistics reveal that the incidence of musculoskeletal injury and disorder in the community is high. For example, the USA's national health interview survey (NHIS) determined that the most common major classifications of disease and disorder contributing to activity limitations included musculoskeletal and connective tissue disorders, accounting for 17.2 per cent of all conditions contributing to limitations (Brandt and Pope, 1997). Low back pain is the reason for 100,000 million days of lost work in the USA and back injuries account for approximately 40 per cent of annual workers' compensation costs.

It has also been reported that the upper extremities are involved in a third of all disabling industrial injuries and, not surprisingly, chronic hand and wrist disorders are a major cause of lost work and workers' compensation claims in hand-intensive industries.

Many factors can contribute to the incidence of musculoskeletal injuries in the workplace and the complexity of the disorders and their causes is well recognised. Injuries may emanate from a variety of sources including the work environment, workplace design and layout, work postures, work methods, work demands, psychological or emotional stress, or the capacity of the worker to cope with the variety of physical and mental stresses imposed. Even those conditions that arise directly from work may be influenced by personal and perhaps social factors which modify symptoms and how they are reported. The development of a musculoskeletal disorder may also be influenced by pre-existing illnesses or injuries, and may be contributed to by individual characteristics, susceptibilities and the person's 'personal capacity'. From a physical point of view, individual capacity may relate to muscular strength and endurance, joint flexibility and cardiovascular endurance. Where any one of these components falls below the required level to fulfil work demands, the risk of musculoskeletal injury is increased.

A range of other factors, including posture, weakness or fatigue, may interact to produce the symptoms of the disorder and it is unlikely that a single risk factor is the cause of a disorder. Non-occupational risk factors must always be considered when considering causation, even if the disorder has been precipitated at the work site.

Faucett and Rempel (1994) showed that the overall effect of combined risk factors was greater than the sum of separate effects. While physical load can depend on task demands, the worker's perception of that load can create a certain psychological response, so that the imposition of a load which is too great can create both physical and psychological stresses. Because of this interaction, if a musculoskeletal disorder develops, the person may have fewer emotional resources with which to cope with the symptoms and signs.

Within the industrial setting, it is the effect of excessive stress which generates the musculoskeletal disorder and, most often, it is within the soft tissues which are unable to combat those stresses that a pathological process develops. Although the pathophysiological mechanism is considered to be acute or chronic strain of muscles or connective tissue, or fatigue, the way in which the strain develops into tissue damage is not well understood.

From the point of view of those concerned with occupational health, it is important to consider the factors which individually or collectively could lead to an occupational injury. It is also necessary to consider the various mechanisms which are involved in tissue damage, because this provides guidance as to appropriate approaches to take in controlling incidence.

FACTORS GENERATING STRESS

Environmental factors

Environmental factors creating stress and contributing to the production of injury can include temperature, noise, light, exposure to the elements, visual problems and exposure to contaminants. It is beyond the scope of this paper to explore in detail the contribution of environmental factors.

Organisational factors

Stress may arise as a result of the organisational climate in the workplace. For example, problems may occur through the style of supervision, work scheduling, the balance between responsibility and accountability, role conflict and role ambiguity, or interaction and communication patterns. Other organisational factors include introduction of an incentive payment approach or a pacing system, or when a worker attempts to maintain the same output as those more experienced around him. Such social stresses can produce a sense of agitation which, in turn, can lead to an increase in muscle tension and increased static muscle work.

Psychosocial factors

McPhee (1990) highlighted the increased risk for injury when new demands are placed on the individual, the individual habitually works beyond his/her capacity, or personal, social or environmental factors reduce the individual's tolerance to physical stress.

Hildbebrandt et al. (1996) suggested that the psychosocial components influencing work capacity include the individual's ability to cope with work pace (for example time pressures), mental loads (for example mentally taxing tasks, the need to remember facts, to concentrate, to listen clearly and to be accurate), the person's control or autonomy over their own work demands, the organisational and social support available, the level of job satisfaction, including the difficulty of work, its interest and variation, job prospects, appreciation of achievements and salary.

As Melin (1990) noted, psychological loads of various types generate muscle tension, particularly in the cervico-brachial region. When this mentally generated muscular stress occurs in conjunction with the muscle loading generated by repetitive, precision-demanding arm movements, the tension can rise to such a level that the muscle overloads.

Muscle activity developed in association with psychological stress hinders the muscle's coming to rest. An increase in muscle tension can lead to abnormal joint biomechanics, so leading to musculoskeletal problems in the long term. According to Panjabi (1992), muscle tension can also place additional demands on other compensatory structures, influencing the physical performance of the task. Thus psychological demands can be a precursor to physical stress and musculoskeletal injury.

Physical factors

Stress may be caused through physical factors, such as the nature of the work carried out, the work content and workload. The design of the workplace is important in this regard, because a poorly designed workplace and clumsy tools can lead to and perpetuate poor work methods and prevent their improvement. On the other hand, properly designed workplaces and tools not only allow the worker the opportunity of applying the principles of good working techniques, but they also prevent that misuse of the body which is a direct result of poor design.

Either extreme of physical load on the musculoskeletal system can result in a soft tissue disorder. For example, the effects on the back of lifting a load which is too heavy or in a way which, biomechanically, increases the stresses on the intervertebral joints, are well known. On the other hand, the effects of tasks requiring a minimum of muscular effort can be considerable if those tasks are repetitive and the conditions under which the musculoskeletal system is called upon to work are not ideal. Further, muscles not working actively to produce movement can suffer strain if subjected to certain undesirable factors. This can occur when sustaining a particular posture, either as a basis for movement taking place elsewhere in the body, or during work requiring monitoring or surveillance.

The physical factors creating risks for injury are varied. For example, Luopajärvi (1990) lists the following risks for musculoskeletal disorders in the low back:

- Lifting heavy objects, especially below the level of the knee or above the level of the shoulder.
- Prolonged sitting, particularly where the chair does not fit the contours of the body and there is inadequate back support.
- Sustained and/or twisted postures.
- Jerky movements which could induce micro-traumas.
- Whole body vibration.
- Mental stress.

She lists the following exposures as being relevant to development of work-related disorders and pain in the neck:

- Static muscle work exceeding 5–6 per cent of maximum voluntary contraction (MVC).
- Sustained positions with a bend or twist greater than 20°.
- Sudden jerky movements which may cause micro-traumas (often initially unnoticeable minor injuries).
- Mental stress.
- Local chilling or draughts.

Risk factors suggested for the lower limbs include:

- Prolonged sitting or standing.
- One-sided loading.
- Deep squatting.

Each principal source of physical load needs special consideration.

Sustained postures and static muscle work

There are many jobs in which people are obliged to remain sitting or standing for long periods. Working postures are limited by the need to keep the feet on pedals or to keep the eyes in positions that enable the task to be seen. However, the ability and willingness of human beings to adapt themselves to difficult situations should not obscure the costs of adaptation. These include:

- injuries and strains from bad working postures;
- a diminished capacity for dealing with emergencies;
- greater probability of accidents;
- greater probability of error.

Workers in many occupations complain of tension in the shoulders and in the upper and lower back, which interferes with their work performance. This tension may develop for many reasons, including faulty equipment design which demands a prolonged head and/or trunk flexion, or because of an improper relationship of the operator to his work surface, requiring excessive arm abduction.

Static work is characterised by slow contractions with heavy loads or by long lasting holding postures. In a strong static contraction, the blood supply is impaired and waste products accumulate in the muscles, causing acute pain in the static pre-loaded muscle. If this is repeated frequently and for long periods of time, chronic pains and troubles may result. These are due to pathological changes not only in the muscles, but also in the connective tissue of tendons, joint capsules and joint ligaments.

The time for which a muscle contraction can be maintained is related to the maximum force required of it. Researchers have shown that for the maintenance of a static contraction, for example where the muscle contraction must last for over one hour, muscles should not be required to contract more than 5–6 per cent of their MVC. Indeed, Harms-Ringdahl and Schüldt (1990) reported that signs of fatigue occurred in the upper trapezius if 2–5 per cent MVC was maintained for an hour. Continuous loading of over 50 per cent MVC, and high peak loading of over 75 per cent of MVC are also hazardous in terms of the production of musculoskeletal disorders, as are the holding of postures at extreme positions and the imposition of sudden loads in such positions.

Upper limb muscles are involved isometrically during work activities requiring stabilisation of the shoulder girdle, arm or forearm in, for example, occupations demanding manipulation of materials or tools, such as welding, assembling and packing. If the load on these muscles continues for a prolonged period, muscle fatigue may develop. Muscle stresses can also be generated through a general lack of body awareness and unconscious associated movements, for example by elevating shoulders and tensing neck muscles during upper arm activity. In some cases, muscle tension may be due to the lack of opportunity to rest.

Rest pauses entailing no muscle activity are important if the muscles are to perform adequately throughout the working day. The duration of rests between activity should be proportional to the length and intensity of exertion in order to allow the muscles and nerves to recover from fatigue.

According to Wood (1987), the blood vessels of the vertebral plexuses have no valves and blood flow is controlled by pressure of movement. When continuous static postures are maintained, stasis can occur, and the metabolism in the vertebral tissues is impaired. This may play a role in the postural backache suffered by workers not able to carry out normal movement during their working day. As in all other structures of the body, the vertebral column functions best when regular joint movements and muscle contractions are carried out within a normal range, without stress.

It is important to remember that the static level of activity and the fatigue in neck and shoulder muscles can be influenced by the load (caused by the arms and their position) transmitted through the shoulder girdle. Muscle work is increased when the arms are held in abduction, and fatigue can occur where work is carried out with arms in an elevated position. The load on the neck and shoulder muscles is increased if the horizontal distance between the work object and the shoulder is increased, the work object is held in a high position, the table surface is high, the tool design is inappropriate or the tool is too high. The endurance of the muscles involved in maintaining a neck flexed or shoulder elevated position influences the production of fatigue, and endurance relates in part to the person's muscular condition.

Other problems which develop through the maintenance of sustained positions include those involving the lower extremities. Workers who must stand for long periods daily are prone to suffer from circulatory problems, such as varicose veins and from aching, painful feet.

The absence of seats at some assembly lines combined with non-adjustable benches (often too low and too wide) create specific stresses of static muscle work on workers, particularly those who may be very tall or very small. In such circumstances, workers often complain of general fatigue, undoubtedly due to the lack of facilities for matching work height to their individual requirements.

Sedentary work also presents hazards leading to stress and injury. For example, desk workers have problems emanating from their lack of physical activity, such as poor posture, poor breathing pattern, sluggish circulation and, not infrequently, generally decreased physical fitness and increased weight. Such workers, coping as they do with increased mental stress, can also exhibit signs of nervous tension.

Lifting and handling

Although in many countries mechanisation has provided an alternative method of performing work to the physical labour once required, in cases where automation has not been introduced completely, or where prolonged heavy manual work is necessary, specific stresses are imposed on the individual.

Risks for musculoskeletal disorder which have been identified as being associated with lifting include load weight, distance of load from body, vertical lift distance and frequency, and duration and speed of lifting.

Several investigations have revealed an increase in the sickness absence and sickness rate due to back pain in jobs traditionally evaluated as heavy and in jobs where lifting is frequent (Andersson, 1979). Back pain often occurs after a lift and the pain is then increased by all mechanical stress on the spine (Andersson, 1979). The relationship between the subjective feeling that the job is physically demanding and high frequency of low back pain is well documented.

Although a great deal of effort has been directed towards teaching the principles of good dynamic posture as applied to manual handling and lifting, the same concern has not been shown in relation to movements related to other activities. Workers operating in cramped positions and unable to develop a rhythmical movement pattern, or without knowledge of correct foot placement and the value of proper use of the legs in movement, can quickly become fatigued.

Infrequent physical demands, for example an occasional lift of a heavy object or rapid stretch, flexion or rotational movements, seem to give low back pain more often than continuous heavy work. One reason for this is probably a poorer work method.

Sudden unexpected loads can lead to back injury through sudden loading of the spine. This could occur if one of a pair of lifters dropped his side of the load, or a worker was supporting a suspended load and the rope broke, or even when a person picked up a load which was lighter than anticipated.

Repetitive activities

Light repetitive tasks consist predominantly of physical work that does not require a great muscular force. Workers involved in these activities are subject to special types of injury, for minor trauma can be caused by many factors, including the following:

- Imposing a too great or prolonged load of work for the muscles involved.
- Repeated attempts to increase the range of movements in a joint.
- Poor muscle tone.
- Lack of co-ordination of group movements.

There are many examples in industry where workers are performing repetitive tasks, using the feet, the hands, or both, according to the demands of the work. For example, both hands and feet are used actively where pedal operation activates machinery after an object has been positioned by the hands. Indeed, pedal operation in industry is a highly repetitive task, the average frequency of pedal depression being about 8000 times per day.

Whether or not a musculoskeletal injury will occur depends on many factors, including the rate, frequency, magnitude, direction, duration and point of application of forces applied, and the acceleration of repetitive movements. If musculoskeletal injuries have a biomechanical basis affected by the variables of force, duration and frequency of exertion and the magnitude and range of joint motion, it is important that these variables be considered jointly when evaluating risks for injury and margins for safety in any particular task.

Luopajärvi (1990) suggested that disorders in the shoulder are often associated with repeated arm elevation to greater than 30° from the body and forceful, jerky movements. For elbows and hands, she listed risks for disorders as including unaccustomed movements, forceful, jerky movements, repetitive movements at high speed, extreme positions of wrists and figures, direct local trauma and cold environments.

A high level of musculoskeletal complaints is found in workers involved in use of the visual display unit (VDU). While many aspects of computer use have been suggested as offering risks for injury, possible factors associated with the keyboard itself could include layout and slope of keys, frequency, shocks of keystrokes, lack of appropriate tactile and proprioceptive feedback from key stroking, excessive height of the keyboard and lack of a palm rest. Other contributing factors which could be considered in relation to use of the VDU include awkward wrist position, a habit of extending the thumb and not using it when typing; pre-existing joint hypermobility; leaning too far forward, a tendency to use certain fingers excessively, too vigorous hitting of the keys and gripping the mouse too tightly. Karlqvist et al.'s (1996) investigation of self-reported neck and upper limb symptoms and physical exposure factors at VDU workstations showed that working for long durations with the mouse, as well as working with the mouse in a non-optimal position on the table, created risk factors for upper limb symptoms.

Of particular concern in relation to repetitive work is the incidence of cumulative trauma disorder. In discussing risk factors associated with occupational cumulative trauma disorders, Joseph (1989) cited repetition, force requirements, postural requirements, mechanical stress, temperature extremes, glove use and the use of vibrating and non-vibrating tools. Repetitive activities demanding precision on the part of the worker create further risk. The person may be required to position a tool precisely or to apply a precise amount of force on the hand tool to gain the required effect. In either case, it is likely that tension in the shoulder muscles will increase.

Four wrist movements are possible: ulnar and radial deviation and flexion and extension. Where these occur rapidly or in combination, hazards can occur. Where many tendons cross a joint or series of joints, as they do in the case of the wrist, intercarpal and digital joints, then the synovial sheaths and their contained lubricant are candidates for injury as a result of torsion and extreme excursion of these joints. Teno-synovitis may occur as a result of excessive use of the tendons without any torsion, but when the latter is added to normal excursions of the tendon within its sheath, then teno-synovitis is a common result.

On the extensor surface of the wrist, the extensor tendons are kept in place by the transverse ligament, while on the flexor surface the flexor tendons pass through the narrow carpal tunnel, which also contains the median nerve. Movement of the wrist creates a tension in the tendons and mechanical stress may traumatise the tendon and some ligaments. As Tichauer (1978) explained, ulnar deviation combined with supination of the forearm favours the development of teno-synovitis. Radial deviation combined with pronation can increase the pressure between the head of the radius and the capitulum of the humerus, leading to epicondylitis or epicondylar bursitis.

The high forces associated with some repetitive work of the upper limb can exceed the strength of the collagen fibres at the attachment of the tendon and lead to micro-ruptures. This may be the case in lateral epicondylitis, particularly at the site of insertion of the tendon to the bone. Leach and Miller (1987) proposed that these micro-ruptures, which frequently occur in the origin of the extensor carpi radialis brevis muscle, lead to the formation of fibrosis and granulation tissue.

Vibrational conditions

Hand–arm vibration

Studies have shown that prolonged and intensive exposure to mechanical vibration can produce serious health problems and it has been estimated that between 5 and 10 per cent of workers in industrialised countries are exposed to daily vibration at potentially harmful levels.

Vibration occurs in many hand held tools and has long been considered a risk factor for upper extremity musculoskeletal disorders. Use of such implements requires particular skill in maintaining grasp and control over tool positioning and this may be impaired through activation of the tonic vibration reflex or by interruption of sensory feedback. It is also possible that vibration-related anatomical changes reduce the rate of nutrient supply and micro-vascular blood flow, resulting in abnormal tissue metabolism.

Whole body vibration

The effects of whole body vibration (WBV) are compounded by other job-related features such as poor body posture, lack of adequate back support, and long hours of work with accompanying fatigue. Because of human body composition, small external vibrations are amplified and result in relatively large displacements and accelerations of internal organs, in a process termed resonance.

The high frequency of radiographic changes in the thoracic and lumbar spine and particularly the high frequency of low back complaints among truck drivers and drivers of work machines have focused interest on a possible relationship between low back pain and vibration. It is thought that the continuous compression and stretching of spinal structures caused by vibration may result in structural fatigue and repeated micro-trauma.

The greatest dynamic load on the trunk and probably on the spine occurs when it is vibrated at its natural frequency. Thus stress is likely to be greatest when the seated body is vibrated vertically in the range of 4–8 Hz. In a truck, vertical vibration is the dominant vibratory mode and occurs in the range of 2–15 Hz. The seat cushion itself, when sat upon, has a natural frequency similar to that of the body; thus resonance is likely.

MUSCLES AND MUSCLE INJURY

Many musculoskeletal injuries relate to the effect of some aspect of work on muscle tissue. An appreciation of the way in which muscles respond to load, positioning and pain assists in the planning of control measures.

Load on muscle tissue

Unfortunately, the mechanism by which strain occurs is still unclear. However, in considering the influence of load on production of injury, it must be remembered that each particular task is individual and combines a different set of dynamic and static contractions of the muscles of elbow, forearm, wrist and fingers.

Some suggestions have been made as to the effect of loading on muscles. For example, Kuorinka and Forcier (1995) described the effect of mechanical loading on the tissues as including muscle tension, pressure (for example intramuscular pressure or pressure in the carpal tunnel), friction (as occurs with friction of a tendon in its sheath) and irritation (as illustrated by irritation of a nerve).

Authors such as Schiund, Ventura and Pasteels (1992) suggested that muscle and tendon tissues respond to the stresses imposed by prolonged or too great a load with hypertrophic, contractile, fibre content or metabolic changes. Lindman, Eriksson and Thornell (1991) considered that changes in myogenic enzymes and histologic fibre types in shoulder muscles explain the reduction in activity in fast acting and fatigue resistant muscle fibres.

It is possible that when muscles contract near to their maximum force over prolonged periods, the effect is to interfere with their circulation and therefore their nutrition and evacuation of metabolites. This tends to produce excessive fatigue and may lead eventually to an increase in fibrous tissue or permanent shortening of the contracting muscles and over-stretching of the relaxing muscle. This in turn interferes with muscle efficiency and may finally lead to cumulative strain.

Where no muscle activity occurs but extreme joint position is maintained, the load moment is counteracted by passive structures and this can generate pain within 15 minutes, even in healthy subjects (Harms-Ringdahl and Ekholm, 1986).

Intramuscular pressure

Intramuscular pressure (IMP) may be associated with the development of musculoskeletal disorders (Jarävholm et al., 1988).

Valencia (1986) inferred from various research studies that during muscular contraction there is an initial increase in blood flow to the active muscle and that the IMP may increase to levels as high as 20–40 kPa. At this magnitude, the increasing tension within the muscle progressively occludes the intramuscular circulation of blood, with the level of contraction where this occurs varying among muscles and between individuals. For example, blood flow in the supraspinatus muscle decreases markedly at even low contraction levels, while in the trapezius, it is impeded only at higher contraction levels.

Muscle imbalance

Janda and Schmidt (1980) have asserted that changes in muscle function play an important role in the pathogenesis of many painful conditions of the motor system, such as low back pain syndromes. They argue that the activity of individual muscles is not of such great importance as their co-ordinated activity within different movement patterns. Janda and Schmidt (1980) point out that certain muscles respond to pain by tightness and shortening, while others react by inhibition, atrophy and weakness. Those which tend to become tight or short and hypertonic are readily activated in most movement patterns, are less liable to atrophy and have a more pronounced postural function. These authors warn, however, that the postural function must not be identified exclusively with erect standing. Rather, in their terminology, 'postural muscles' are those which maintain posture during the most common activity, 'gait'. Because the postural is favoured and the phasic is neglected during modern life, an imbalance in favour of the tonic, postural system develops. New movement patterns tend to be uneconomic and the redistribution of pressure on joints may produce strain.

When muscle imbalances exist within an individual, changes in the biomechanics of movement occur and poor movement patterns may develop which exacerbate previous muscle imbalances and inefficient movement. When a risk for musculoskeletal injury is introduced (for example prolonged isometric muscle contractions associated with fixed postures or repetitive movements), the deficits in the muscle system may lead to musculoskeletal dysfunction and pain, so leading eventually to a decrease in the person's capacity to carry out further work. The vicious cycle of muscle imbalance, inefficient movement patterns and pain would continue with personal capacity being reduced and injury a likely outcome.

Fatigue

To produce movement, muscles must perform work and this may lead eventually to fatigue if the movement is performed many times and particularly if it is in an antigravity direction. Through its negative influence on motor performance, fatigue places an individual in a situation for potential injury.

The study of work physiology has addressed two aspects of fatigue: local muscular fatigue and longer term systemic fatigue or whole body fatigue (WBF). With strenuous or prolonged voluntary effort, localised muscle fatigue may occur and this must be considered in relation to the effect of the change in local muscle activation on the physiological system as a whole.

Muscle fatigue is considered to be a function of static and dynamic loading on the muscle in relation to the maximum capacity of the muscle for contraction. Muscle fatigue is characterised both by a decrease in the force of muscle contraction and by the increasing time needed for the muscular movement. Due to the build up of lactic acid in the muscle, fatigue is experienced as pain in severe cases. As a result, efficiency of muscle action is decreased and the functional ability to carry out precision work is reduced. It is likely that the person has less ability to cope safely with demands when fatigue exists. The relative stiffness and the slowed reaction time of muscles in these circumstances are considered by Jesse (1977) to be the starting point for most sprains and strains. The loss of co-ordination associated with fatigue is also seen as a precursor for injury: the decrease in co-ordination can be reflected in improper timing and miscalculation of movements, so contributing to injury production.

Sparto et al. (1997) analysed the results of a repetitive lifting test and showed that, with fatigue, there was a change in co-ordination of movements involved in the lift. They noted a decreased range of motion in the knee and hip joints and this, together with an increase in peak lumbar flexion, indicated a change from a squat lift to a stoop lift approach. These researchers hypothesised that adaptation in the motor control and co-ordination which occur due to neuromuscular fatigue could increase the risk of injury for low back pain. In addition to the change of co-ordination of lifting, there was an increase in excursion of the centre of pressure in the antero-posterior direction, so decreasing stability and increasing the chance of balance loss under fatigue conditions.

The level of muscle endurance has a direct effect on the time of onset of fatigue. As a result of muscle fatigue, muscle insufficiency and decreased speed of contraction occur (Sparto et al., 1997). These fatigue effects increase the strain on passive joint structures, so increasing the risk for injury. Further, following injury, the surrounding muscles are often weakened and probably easily fatigued. With inadequate rehabilitation, the loss of endurance may lead to an inability for muscles to perform for prolonged periods, with re-injury being a serious implication.

Kilbom (1997) suggested that the pathophysiological mechanisms of muscle disorders appear to be linked to muscle fatigue and lack of recovery, implying that short contraction periods followed by sufficient periods for recovery would be important in controlling this risk. Researchers are attempting to determine the optimal pattern of work/rest to avoid fatigue.

CONCLUSIONS

The wide range of factors influencing the production of occupational musculoskeletal injury highlights the importance of careful analysis of the workplace to identify risks.

While possible mechanisms for injuries and their manifestations have been proposed, further research is needed to determine the specific pathophysiological processes involved in the development of work-related musculoskeletal disorders. Only in this way can control methods focus on the cause rather than the effect.

References

Andersson, G. (1979). Low back pain in industry – Epidemiological aspects. *Scandinavian Journal of Rehabilitation Medicine*, **11**, 163–168.

Brandt, E.N. and Pope, A.M. (eds) (1997). *Enabling America*. National Academy Press.

Faucett, J. and Rempel, D. (1994). VDT-related musculoskeletal symptoms; interactions between work posture and psychosocial work factors. *American Journal of Industrial Medicine*, **26**, 597–612.

Harms-Ringdahl, K. and Ekholm, J. (1986). Intensity and character of pain and muscular activity levels elicited by maintained extreme flexion position of the lower cervical upper thoracic spine. *Scandinavian Journal of Rehabilitation Medicine*, **18**, 117–126.

Harms-Ringdahl, K. and Schüldt, K. (1990). Neck and shoulder load and load-elicited pain in sitting work postures. In *Ergonomics: The Physiotherapist in the Workplace* (M. I. Bullock, ed.). Churchill Livingstone.

Hildbebrandt, V.H., Bongers, P.M., Dul, J. et al. (1996). Identification of high risk groups among maintenance workers in a steel company with respect to musculoskeletal symptoms and work load. *Ergonomics*, **2**, 232–242.

Janda, V. and Schmidt, H.J.A. (1980). Muscles as a pathogenic factor in back pain. *Proceedings of the IFOMT Conference*, Auckland.

Jarävholm, U., Styf, J., Suurkula, M. et al. (1988). Intra-muscular pressure and muscle blood flow in supraspinatus. *European Journal of Applied Physiology*, **58**, 219–224.

Jesse, J. (1977). *Hidden Causes of Injury: Prevention and Correction for Running Athletes and Joggers*, pp. 45–47. The Athletic Press.

Joseph, B.S. (1989). Ergonomic considerations and job design in upper extremity disorders. *Occupational Medicine: State of the Art Reviews*, **4**, 547–557.

Karlqvist, L., Hagberg, M.M.K., Wenemark, M. et al. (1996). Musculoskeletal symptoms among computer-assisted design (CAD) operators and evaluation of a self-assessment questionnaire. *International Journal of Occupational and Environmental Health*, **2**, 185–194.

Kilbom, Å. (1997). Repetitive work of the upper extremity: Guidelines for the practitioner. *IEA '97 International Ergonomics Association 13th Triennial Congress*, Tampere.

Kuorinka, I. and Forcier, L. (1995). *Work Related Musculoskeletal Disorders (WMSDs): A Reference Book for Prevention*. Taylor and Francis.

Leach, R.E. and Miller, J.K. (1987). Lateral and medial epicondylitis of the elbow. *Clinical Sports Medicine*, **6**, 259–272.

Lindman, R., Eriksson, A. and Thornell, L.E. (1991). Fibre type composition of the human female trapezius muscle. *American Journal of Anatomy*, **190**, 385–392.

Luopajärvi, I. (1990). Ergonomic analysis of workplace and postural load. In *Ergonomics: The Physiotherapist in the Workplace* (M. I. Bullock, ed.). Churchill Livingstone.

McPhee, B. (1990). Musculoskeletal complaints in workers engaged in repetitive work in fixed postures. In *Ergonomics: The Physiotherapist in the Workplace* (M. I. Bullock, ed.). Churchill Livingstone.

Melin, E. (1990). Occupational physiotherapy in a large industry. In *Ergonomics: The Physiotherapist in the Workplace* (M. I. Bullock, ed.). Churchill Livingstone.

Panjabi, M.N. (1992). The stabilising system of the spine Part 1. Function, dysfunction, adaptation and enhancement. *Journal of Spinal Disorders*, **5**, 383–386.

Schiund, F., Garcia-Elias, N., Cooney, W.P. et al. (1992). Flexor tendon forces; in vivo measurements. *Journal of Hand Surgery*, **17A**, 291–298.

Sparto, P., Parnianpour, M., Reinsel, T. et al. (1997). The effect of fatigue on multi-joint kinematics co-ordination and postural stability during a repetitive lifting test. *Journal of Orthopaedic and Sports Physical Therapy*, **25**, 3–12.

Tichauer, E.R. (1978). *The Biomechanical Basis Of Ergonomics – Anatomy Applied To The Design Of Work Situations*. Wiley.

Valencia, F. (1986). Local muscle fatigue, a precursor to RSI? *Medical Journal of Australia*, **145**, 327–329.

Wood, D. (1987). Design and evaluation of a back injury prevention program within a geriatric hospital. *Spine*, **12**, 77–81.

Chapter 3

Epidemiology

New trends in epidemiological research on occupational musculoskeletal injury

Åsa Kilbom

INTRODUCTION

Over the past ten years the number of epidemiological studies on work-related musculoskeletal disorders has grown exponentially, as judged both from journal publications and from the three PREMUS (PREvention of MUSculoskeletal disorders) conferences held in 1992, 1995 and 1998. In fact, the first PREMUS conference was organised by the newly founded ICOH (International Commission for Occupational Health) Committee for Musculoskeletal Disorders, in recognition of the large impact of musculoskeletal disorders on individuals, organisations and nations. Over the years, epidemiological studies of musculoskeletal disorders have been conducted with increasing levels of scientific rigour and sophistication. This paper will discuss the contributions to our knowledge derived from recent epidemiological studies.

AIMS OF EPIDEMIOLOGICAL RESEARCH

Epidemiological research can confirm the importance of suspected risk factors and under favourable circumstances quantify the relationship between risk factor(s) and musculoskeletal outcomes. It can provide support for causal relationships, at least when the studies are longitudinal. The induction period and the episodic nature of musculoskeletal disorders can be demonstrated. When interventions are undertaken, at work or in private life, their effectiveness can be demonstrated if certain stringent criteria are adhered to.

However, many conclusions based on epidemiological research have been overstated or poorly controlled due to failure to take into account confounders and effect modifiers. The problems related to incorrect definitions of risk factors and outcomes has sometimes been underestimated and led to generalisations that are not justified. Moreover, epidemiological studies must be based on hypotheses about injury causation, and therefore cannot identify risk factors that have not been previously suspected. Therefore epidemiology cannot stand alone in research on musculoskeletal disorders; it requires complementary information from field observations where hypotheses are generated, and from experimental research, where the plausibility of new hypotheses can be supported.

RISK FACTORS

Physical risk factors for musculoskeletal disorders have, with slight variations, been classified generically as manual handling, postures (or static loads), repetitive work and vibrations. Numerous reviews have used these classifications and identified all or some of these risk factors for disorders of the low back, neck, shoulder and hand/wrist (Burdorf and Sorock, 1991; Kilbom, 1994; Kilbom et al., 1996; Riihimaki, 1991 and 1996; Stock, 1991; Winkel and Westgaard, 1992).

It was not until the beginning of the 1990s that psychosocial factors were focused as risk factors for musculoskeletal disorders (Bongers et al., 1993). Usually the Karasek–Theorell demand–control–support model has been used (Karase and Theorell, 1990), but in the last few years Siegrest's effort–reward model (Siegrist et al., 1990), as well as personality-related concepts like 'sense of coherence' (Antonowsky, 1987), have also been favoured, although no consistent conclusions are yet available.

For many years, epidemiological studies focused either physical or psychosocial risk factors. In the last few years, studies have emerged where both types of factors were studied, in an attempt to quantify the relative risk of either. According to a recent review undertaken by NIOSH (NIOSH, 1997), the psychosocial factors should be characterised as general risk factors that modify the risk of a number of work-related conditions (musculoskeletal and others), whereas the physical risk factors are more specific, giving rise to disorders of the tissue under mechanical load. Several recent studies, for example by Toomingas and Stäl (Stäl et al., 1996; Toomings et al., 1997), clearly indicate that psychosocial factors seem to increase the risk of muscular complaints centrally in the body (i.e. close to the spine) whereas peripheral complaints, e.g. in the elbow and hand/wrist, are rarely related to psychosocial conditions.

So far the question of the relative importance of psychosocial and physical risk factors remains unsolved. The scientific support for a strong influence of physical factors is convincing, while the psychosocial factors, especially when subdivided into different dimensions, still need more documentation. Moreover, the injury mechanisms in exposure to psychosocial factors need more scientific support, although some plausible mechanisms have been suggested (Theorell, 1996). It has become increasingly obvious that adverse psychosocial and physical factors very frequently occur in the same jobs and among the same individuals, and that strong interactive effects occur between these two types of risk factors (Bildt Thorbjörnsson, 1999). For example, highly repetitive jobs often have strong elements of low control and high demands. Of course this makes the design of studies to clarify their respective roles very difficult.

In conclusion, the 'traditional' risk factors, including psychosocial factors, have been repeatedly identified in epidemiological studies. At present there is a need to describe the exposure–response relationship and to make policy decisions, based on available research, on levels where the risk of injury increases above acceptable levels. Unfortunately this is a complex task that may never be resolved. Epidemiology, by its nature, requires relatively large samples of individuals, preferably followed for a number of years under similar conditions of exposure. At present, labour market conditions change very rapidly and thereby the exposure conditions (Kuorinka, 1998). Union participation seems to decline, which makes it more difficult to trace exposed groups. Epidemiological studies are expensive, and the longitudinal design necessary for a proper exposure–response evaluation becomes next to impossible. Therefore it will probably become necessary to devise new epidemiological designs (retrospective studies; see below) and/or to rely more on experimental research.

'NEW' RISK FACTORS AND INTERACTIONS

Recent research has identified a few new, previously unrecognised risk factors. Several studies in the last few years have pointed out that self-rated, perceived exertion or fatigue may be an important risk factor (Josephson, 1999; Kerr, Shannon and Frank, 1998). Self-rated levels of exposure can be obtained using, for example, the Borg scale (Borg, 1990), and several different self-rating scales have been used to quantify both physical and psychosocial factors. In fact, one of the problems of comparing the consequences of physical versus psychosocial factors is that physical factors are usually assessed using measured, 'objective' levels of exposure, while information about psychosocial factors is usually obtained by asking the worker for his/her opinion about the workload. Attempts are being made to develop methods for external classification of work organisations and thereby get a better grasp of the objective aspects of psychosocial conditions at work, but so far no results are available. Thus there is at present an ongoing discussion about the relevance of objective, measured magnitude of exposure versus self-rated level, since the two measures do not always agree. The mechanism of self-rated exposures is unclear, but it may be possible to throw more light on them by measuring stress indicators, e.g. stress hormones in saliva.

Another recently identified risk factor is speed of motion, or acceleration. Marras and Schoenmarklin (1993), as well as Hansson et al. (1996), have demonstrated that a high speed of wrist motions seems to increase the risk of forearm and wrist disorders.

Research during the last years has increasingly focused on the complexity of causation in musculoskeletal disorders. Not only do we have to consider interactions between factors at work, but factors in family life and leisure time also need attention. For example, it has been demonstrated that factors off work interact strongly with factors at work, and moreso among women than among men (Bildt Thorbjörnsson, 1999; Fredriksson et al., 1999). Thus the overall risk factor pattern among women differs from that of men in some important respects. Such interactions also seem to exert a long-term effect over many years, whereas it has been previously believed that the induction period for soft tissue musculoskeletal disorders is short – a few months up to one year. Therefore a long-term effect of adverse conditions, accumulated over many years, has to be studied in the future. For the prevention of musculoskeletal disorders among middle-aged and elderly people a long induction period and a cumulative effect of risk factors may have important implications. We should probably advise employees to have a long-term plan of their working life. Risk factor exposure should probably be reduced in middle age before disorders have emerged, rather than trying to rehabilitate musculoskeletal patients, which is often a costly and ineffective activity.

NEW DESIGNS AND NEW EPIDEMIOLOGICAL METHODS

In the past, cross-sectional studies have dominated over other study designs in research on musculoskeletal disorders. The drawbacks are large, however, and above all it is not possible to draw conclusions about causality. Therefore longitudinal studies are favoured by epidemiologists, but these too have large drawbacks such as high costs and high drop-out rates. In musculoskeletal disorders with short induction periods (e.g. so-called 'mouse-arm') it may be possible to overcome some of these problems by frequent follow-ups over a short time period. Such a study is at present underway at the Swedish Institute for Working Life. Case-control studies have so far been used to a limited extent because of the problems of identifying the cases unambiguously. In a recently terminated large case-control study of a regional Swedish population it was possible to identify cases by having all care-givers report musculoskeletal patients and then investigating their exposure (Vingård et al., 1998). Since most previous studies have been on highly exposed occupational groups, it was of particular interest to investigate if the risk factors in the general population were similar to those identified for highly exposed groups. For low back disorders, forward bent postures and vehicle driving were identified among men, while among women a high metabolic rate at work increased the risk of back disorders. A preliminary comparison with high risk populations indicates that no large differences in risk factor patterns exist. It will be interesting to compare these results with those of two ongoing large longitudinal studies on high risk populations, one on automobile workers in Canada (Kerr, Shannon and Frank, 1998) and one on industrial workers in the Netherlands (Bongers and Henderik, 1998). Neither of these studies have been finally reported.

Other approaches in epidemiological studies on musculoskeletal disorders are to use public registers on health care and early retirement, or to use retrospective exposure information, i.e. obtaining information about past circumstances in cross-sectional studies. In a recent study, the reliability and validity of retrospective information about exposure for physical as well as psychosocial conditions were tested and found to be reliable as long as no detailed information is collected (Bildt Thorbjörnsson, 1999; Torgen et al., 1999). Using a time-ruler, and asking the subjects to fill in a questionnaire about previous jobs before coming to the investigation, it was possible to reconstruct their conditions at work in a moderately detailed way.

In the last few years, attempts have been made to study not only the specific risk factors like repetitiveness and manual handling, but also to investigate unspecific factors like socio-economic status and education (Bildt Thorbjörnsson, 1999; Dionne et al., 1998). It has been found that low educational status is a risk factor for long duration and recurrence of low back disorders, but not for its incidence. These findings support the need to do multilevel analyses of risk factor patterns (Duncan, Jones and Moon, 1998). With such methods for epidemiological analysis, differences in community and societal levels, as well as specific risk factor patterns at the workplace, can be analysed. These methods are complex and require sophisticated statistical analysis programs, which are now starting to become available.

INTERVENTION STUDIES

The most difficult challenge in epidemiological studies of musculoskeletal disorders is to design and analyse the effect of interventions. Selecting a control group that differs from the intervention group only with regard to factors being intervened against, maintaining control over the working conditions for a prolonged period of time, selecting subjects who are not 'survivors' with a high tolerance to risk factors, and avoiding high drop-out rates constitute nearly insurmountable obstacles. In fact hardly any intervention studies with rigorous control of all intervening problems have been performed. Although the problems are very large, researchers as well as practitioners should be encouraged to follow-up changes in working conditions and their impact on musculoskeletal disorders. Despite the problems outlined above, some interesting findings from interventions have been obtained. Westgaard and Winkel (1997) reviewed intervention studies in order to investigate the effectiveness of different strategies. Participative approaches, work organisational approaches and technical changes were studied and, despite large design problems, some conclusions could be reached.

References

Antonowsky, A. (1987). *Unraveling the Mystery of Health.* Jossey Hall.

Bildt Thorbjörnsson, C. (1999). *A quarter century perspective on low back pain.* PhD thesis, Karolinska Institute.

Bongers, P. and Henderik, D. (1998). Example of exposure assessment in a large cohort study on musculoskeletal disorders. *Abstracts from the PREMUS-ISEOH '98 conference,* Finnish Institute of Occupational Health, Helsinki, p. 167.

Bongers, P.M., de Winter, C.R., Kompier, M.A.J. and Hildebrandt, V.H. (1993). Psychosocial factors at work and musculoskeletal disease. *Scandinavian Journal of Work and Environmental Health,* **19**, 297–312.

Borg, G. (1990). Psychophysical scaling with applications in physical work and the perception of exertion. *Scandinavian Journal of Work and Environmental Health,* **16**, 55–58.

Burdorf, A. and Sorock, G. (1997). Positive and negative evidence of risk factors for back disorders. *Scandinavian Journal of Work and Environmental Health*, **23**, 243–256.

Dionne, C., Von Korff, M., Koepsell, T. et al. (1998). Back pain and educational status. *Abstracts from the PREMUS-ISEOH '98 conference*, Finnish Institute of Occupational Health, Helsinki, p. 130.

Duncan, C., Jones, K. and Moon, G. (1998). Context, composition and heterogeneity: Using multilevel models in health research. *Social Science and Medicine*, **46**, 97–117.

Fredriksson, K., Alfredsson, L., Köster, M. et al. (1999). Risk factors for neck and upper limb disorders: results from a 24 year follow up. *Occupational and Environmental Medicine*, **56**, 59–66.

Hansson, G., Balogh, I., Ohlsson, K., Rylander, L. and Skerfving, S. (1996). Goniometer measurement and computer analysis of wrist angles and movements applied to occupational repetitive work. *Journal of Electromyography and Kinesiology*, **6**, 23–35.

Josephson, M. (1999). *Work factors and musculoskeletal disorders*. PhD thesis, Karolinska Institute.

Karasek, R. and Theorell, T. (1990). *Healthy Work. Stress, Productivity and the Reconstruction of Working Life*. Basic Books Inc.

Kerr, K., Shannon, H. and Frank, J.: The OARPS group. (1998). A detailed examination of the demand-control model in a study of occupational low-back pain. *Abstracts from the PREMUS–ISEOH '98 conference*, Finnish Institute of Occupational Health, Helsinki, p. 85.

Kilbom, Å. (1994). Repetitive work of the upper extremity. Part II: The scientific basis (knowledge base) for the guide. *International Journal of Industrial Ergonomics*, **14**, 59–86.

Kilbom, Å., Armstrong, T., Buckle, P. et al. (1996). Musculoskeletal disorders: Work-related risk factors and prevention. *International Journal of Occupational and Environmental Health*, **2**, 239–246.

Kuorinka, I. (1998). The influence of industrial trends on work-related musculoskeletal disorders in the workplace. *International Journal of Industrial Ergonomics*, **21**, 5–9.

Marras, W. and Schoenmarklin, R. (1993). Wrist motions in industry. *Ergonomics*, **36**, 341–351.

NIOSH (1997). *Musculoskeletal Disorders and Workplace Factors*. National Institute for Occupational Safety and Health, Center for Disease Control, USA.

Riihimäki, H. (1991). Low-back pain, its origin and risk indicators. *Scandinavian Journal of Work and Environmental Health*, **17**, 81–90.

Riihimäki, H. (1996). Hands up or back to work – future challenges in epidemiologic research on musculoskeletal diseases. *Scandinavian Journal of Work and Environmental Health*, **21**, 401–403.

Siegrist, J., Peter, R., Junge, A., Cremer, P. and Seidel, D. (1990). Low status control, high effort at work and ischemic heart disease: prospective evidence from blue-collar men. *Social Science and Medicine*, **31**, 1127–1134.

Stäl, M., Moritz, U., Gustafsson, B. and Johnsson, B. (1996). Milking is a high-risk job for young females. *Scandinavian Journal of Rehabilitation Medicine*, **28**, 95–104.

Stock, S.R. (1991). Workplace ergonomic factors and the development of musculoskeletal disorders of the neck and upper limbs: A meta-analysis. *American Journal of Industrial Medicine*, **19**, 87–107.

Theorell, T. (1996). Possible mechanisms behind the relationship between the demand-control-support model and disorders of the locomotor system. In *Beyond Biomechanics* (S. Moon and S. Sauter, eds), pp. 55–65. Taylor and Francis.

Toomings, A., Theorell, T., Michélsen, H. and Nordemar, R.: Stockholm MUSIC 1 Study Group. (1997). Associations between self-rated psychosocial work conditions and musculoskeletal symptoms and signs. *Scandinavian Journal of Work and Environmental Health*, **23**, 30–139.

Torgén, M., Winkel, J., Alfredsson, M. and Kilbom, Å.: Stockholm MUSIC 1 Study Group. (1999). Evaluation of questionnaire-based information on previous physical workloads. *Scandinavian Journal of Work and Environmental Health* (in press).

Vingärd, E., Alfredsson, L., Hagberg, M. et al. (1998). How much can occupational physical and psychosocial factors explain of low back pain in a working population? *Abstracts from the PREMUS-ISEOH '98 conference*: Institute of Occupational Health, Helsinki, p. 84.

Westgaard, R.H. and Winkel, J. (1997). Ergonomic intervention research for improved musculoskeletal health: A critical reviw. *International Journal of Industrial Ergonomics*, **20**, 463–500.

Winkel, J. and Westgaard, R.H. (1992). Occupational and individual risk factors for shoulder-neck complaints: Part ll: The scientific basis (literature review) for the guide. *International Journal of Industrial Ergonomics*, **10**, 85–104.

The prevalence and morbidity of low back pain in Adelaide metropolitan taxi drivers

Scott Sypek, Marie Williams and Maureen McEvoy

INTRODUCTION

The link between low back pain (LBP) and driving is well established (Burdorf et al., 1993; Damkot et al., 1984; Krause et al., 1997). Driving as an occupation involves the physical stressors of sedentary working postures and whole body vibration (WBV), which have been linked to LBP both epidemiologically (Bovenzi and Zadini, 1992; Magnusson et al., 1996) and experimentally (Hannson and Holm, 1991; Zimmerman et al., 1993). More recently it has been shown that psychosocial factors influence both the presence and the effects of LBP (Dempsey et al., 1997; Papageorgiou et al., 1997).

Taxi driving is an occupation that includes many of the known risk factors for developing spinal disorders. Radbone et al. (1997) report in an independent survey of the taxi industry in South Australia that drivers' shifts average 10 hours in duration, with the majority of the time spent sitting in their car on taxi ranks or driving passengers. This exposes drivers to prolonged sitting and WBV for long periods. It is also possible that psychosocial stresses may be present in taxi drivers who work alone, doing repetitive work for a small financial reward. Despite this there has been little research concerning the musculoskeletal health of taxi drivers. Studies tend to focus on other driving professions such as bus and truck drivers, with LBP prevalences of approximately 40–80 per cent being reported (Bovenzi and Zadini, 1992; Burdorf et al., 1993).

The aims of this study were to investigate the prevalence of LBP in Adelaide metropolitan taxi drivers and, secondly, to identify contributing factors to LBP in taxi drivers.

METHOD

Subjects

A sample of Adelaide's metropolitan taxi drivers was interviewed while waiting at a variety of taxi ranks across Adelaide. A three part survey was used and the angle of their seat inclination was measured. Subjects were included if they were experienced full-time drivers. The criteria for this were that they drove four or more shifts per week and had been working as a taxi driver for the past five years or more. Subjects were excluded if they had experienced significant LBP prior to commencing work as a taxi driver. The definition of significant LBP was LBP that required the subject to seek medical attention in the twelve month period prior to beginning work as a taxi driver or if LBP ever prevented the subject from attending their previous job.

Ethical approval for this study was obtained from the University of South Australia. Between December 1998 and March 1999, taxi drivers were approached while waiting at twenty-two taxi ranks including airports, hospitals and shopping centres. To encourage participation of all drivers and not just those with back trouble, the subjects were told that the study was assessing the health of taxi drivers. The process was explained and written consent obtained before proceeding.

The survey

The study required a survey that recorded data on the prevalence of LBP and the effect of low back symptoms on work and leisure. The survey had to be suitable for use in an interview format and be of appropriate length to administer in the few minutes a taxi driver waits at a taxi rank. A review of the literature identified several possible questionnaires. Two previously validated questionnaires, the Nordic general questionnaire and the Nordic low back questionnaire (Kuorinka et al., 1987), were chosen through consultation with qualitative research experts and an in-depth interview with a small group of taxi drivers. In addition, a series of questions relating to occupational patterns was designed by the authors and modified through the in-depth interview process. The final survey therefore consisted of three parts: the Nordic general questionnaire, the Nordic low back questionnaire and the series of questions on occupational patterns.

The Nordic general questionnaire collects information concerning the subject's height, weight, age, years driving a taxi and handedness. For each of the major joints, subjects were asked to indicate whether they had experienced 'trouble' (ache, pain or discomfort) during the last twelve months. If the response was positive the subject was then asked if this 'trouble' had prevented them from doing their normal work in the last twelve months and if they had experienced any 'trouble' in the last seven days.

The Nordic low back questionnaire asks for more detailed information about low back symptoms. Subjects are asked if they have ever experienced low back trouble (LBT) in their lifetime (lifetime prevalence) and are also asked about LBT in the previous twelve months (twelve month prevalence) and in the last seven days (seven day prevalence). Further questions concern duration of LBT, sick leave due to LBT and any medical attention required for low back complaints. Low back trouble was defined in the survey as 'ache, pain or discomfort in the lower part of the back, whether or not it extends to one or both legs (sciatica)'. For consistency all results and discussion relating to the Nordic low back questionnaire will use the term LBT rather than LBP.

The third part of the survey was a series of questions recording data on taxi vehicles, subject working patterns (time out of vehicle, day/night shifts), psychosocial status (job satisfaction, stress) and presence of other risk factors for developing spinal disorders (smoking, motor vehicle accidents). Questions concerning job satisfaction and stress were modified from those in Bigos et al. (1991).

Seat angle measurement

The angle of the driver's seat was measured using a Smart Level Angle Finder (SLAF) (Macklanburg-Duncan, Oklahoma City, 1995). The measurement involved calibrating the device to the level of the car door-frame. The angle of the seat measured was the inclination of the back of the seat compared with the door-frame. This measurement process was tested for reliability with excellent results (Pearson coefficient, $r = 0.98$).

Data analysis

Data analysis was performed using Epi Info Version 5.01 software (World Health Organization, Centers for Disease Control, Epidemiology Program Office, Atlanta, Georgia). Continuous data were summarised (mean and standard deviation) and significant differences between subjects who had LBT and no LBT were calculated using Student's *t*-test ($p < 0.05$). Univariate odd ratios were used to calculate the risk of LBT for exposure to several known and potential risk factors for LBT. Stratum specific odds ratios were calculated to investigate the risk of LBT when exposed to combinations of risk factors.

RESULTS

There were 4419 accredited taxi drivers in South Australia (Radbone, 1997). The aim was to invite 10 per cent of the population to participate in this study. Four hundred and fifty-five taxi drivers were approached to participate in the study. A total of 256 drivers were excluded from the study (Table 3.1). Forty-six drivers declined to participate and three surveys were incomplete. The resulting final sample was 150 subjects (145 males and five females; response rate 90 per cent). The low number of female subjects in this sample is representative of the taxi driving population, and therefore the prevalence of LBT is reported for the entire sample ($n = 150$). Due to biological differences between males and females with respect to LBT and the inability to create balanced groups for comparison between genders, female subjects were excluded from analysis of contributing factors to LBT ($n = 145$).

Table 3.1 Reasons for exclusion

Less than 4 shifts per week	49
Less than 5 years driving	154
Medical attention for LBP	36
LBP prevented previous work	17
Total	256

Table 3.2 Nordic general questionnaire results ($n = 150$)

Trouble area*	%	No. of subjects
Neck	54.7	82
Shoulders	38.7	58
Elbow	16.0	24
Wrist/hands	30.7	46
Upper back	20.7	31
Lower back	52.0	78
Hips/thighs	24.7	37
Knees	26.0	39
Ankles/feet	22.7	34

* Trouble is defined as ache, pain or discomfort in the last twelve months

Nordic general questionnaire

LBT was experienced by 52% of the sample (50.3% of males, 100% of females) in the twelve-month period prior to the survey. The seven day prevalence of LBT was 27.3% (26.9% males, 40% females), and LBT prevented 11.3% of the sample from doing their normal work in last twelve months (11.7% of males, 0.0% females) (Table 3.2).

Nordic low back questionnaire

Lifetime prevalence for LBT was reported at 69.3% for the entire sample (68.3% males, 100% females). There was a twelve month prevalence of LBT of 50.3% and a seven day prevalence of 30% (Table 3.3).

Contributing factors to twelve month prevalence of low back trouble

No significant differences were detected between the male LBT and no LBT groups for the variables of age, height, weight, driving years, hours per week or the number of times the driver gets out of their taxi per shift (Table 3.4).

The series of questions on occupational patterns provided data on known and potential risk factors for developing LBP. Table 3.5 shows the odds ratios (OR) and 95% confidence intervals (CI) for these risk factors. The risk is considered significant when the lower 95% confidence limit is greater than 1.00. Significant risk associations are indicated by an asterisk (*). The OR is a measure of the risk associated with a particular risk factor. For example, when exposed to stress, the risk of developing LBT is 3.15 times that of subjects not exposed to stress.

Table 3.3 Results of the Nordic low back questionnaire ($n = 150$)

	%	No. of subjects
Lifetime prevalence of LBT	69.3	104
Hospitalised for LBT	5.3	8
Change jobs or duties due to LBT	15.3	23
In the past 12 months, days felt LBT:		
0 days	18.0	27
1–7 days	12.0	18
8–30 days	8.7	13
30+ days	17.3	26
Every day	13.3	20
LBT reduces work activity	18.0	27
LBT reduces leisure activity	20.0	30
Days of reduced activity in last 12 months:		
0 days	47.3	71
1–7 days	8.7	13
8–30 days	6.7	10
30+ days	6.7	10
Required medical attention	17.3	26
LBT in past 7 days	30.0	45

Seat angles measured using the SLAF were divided into two groups: those seats in a more reclined position ($< 108.5°$) and those seats in a more upright position ($> 108.5°$). Drivers with more upright seat angles had an increased risk of suffering LBT (OR = 2.53), 95% CI 1.08–5.98). The angle of 108.5° was chosen as the division point of the two groups as it is approximately the median for the range of seat angles measured.

Table 3.4 Comparison of LBT and no LBT groups with respect to contributing factors

Variable	LBT $n = 73$		No LBT $n = 72$		
	Mean	SD	Mean	SD	p value
Age	46.34	11.18	46.08	11.17	0.88
Height (cm)	175.90	8.46	175.1	6.12	0.52
Weight (kg)	85.78	17.46	85.91	18.22	0.96
Driving years	13.80	7.64	13.09	8.26	0.60
Hours per week	61.07	12.68	58.63	15.37	0.30
No. of times out of taxi	23.74	20.25	20.66	17.87	0.64

Table 3.5 Crude odds ratios for LBT

	OR	CI
Previous LBT	1.96	(0.74, 5.31)
Owning taxi	1.4	(0.67, 2.95)
Night driving	1.22	(0.53, 2.79)
Stressed	3.15*	(1.38, 7.23)
Do not enjoy job	2.27*	(1.06, 4.86)
Previous MVA	2.36*	(1.0, 5.68)
Smoker	0.52	(0.24, 1.11)
> 50 hours/week	3.63*	(1.31, 10.39)

Significant combinations of risk factors for LBT

Each of the exposure variables which demonstrated a significant risk increase for LBT was identified. These were stress, low job satisfaction, previous MVA, working for more than fifty hours per week and an upright seat angle. Each of the significant exposures which was likely to increase the risk of LBT was univariately stratified with each of the other exposure variables that was thought to have a plausible biological relationship. This provided stratum specific odds ratios to determine significant combinations of risk factors for LBT. An increased risk of reporting LBT was found for drivers who had had an MVA and worked more than fifty hours per week (OR = 2.71) compared to drivers who had experienced an MVA and worked less than fifty hours per week (OR = 1.15). Drivers who had had an MVA and were stressed (OR = 4.07) had an increased risk of LBT compared with drivers who had had an MVA and were not stressed (OR = 1.84). Drivers with a more upright seat angle and who had had a previous MVA (OR = 4.41) had increased risk of LBT compared with drivers with an upright seat angle who had not had an MVA (OR = 0.67).

Further attempts to deconfound exposure/disease relationships were not pursued because the confounding or modifying effect per se of proposed exposures was not being sought, but rather an indication of stronger associations within a particular stratum which supported the occupational health and safety focus of this study.

DISCUSSION

Prevalence

Given the enormity of the taxi driving population world-wide and the well-established link between driving and LBP, insufficient information exists regarding the prevalence of LBP in taxi drivers. Table 3.6 summarises the results of the most relevant studies into LBP in driving and manufacturing populations that used versions of the Nordic questionnaires for the analysis of musculoskeletal

Table 3.6 Comparison of other LBP studies

Authors	**12 month prevalence of LBT (%)**	**Lifetime prevalence of LBT (%)**	**LBT prevented work or leisure (%)**
Sypek et al. (1999): Taxi drivers	52 (male 50.3, female 100)	69.3 (male 68.3, female 100)	Work 11.3 Work or leisure 22
Magnusson et al. (1996):		Not reported	Reported in days not %
Bus drivers (USA, Sweden)	81, 49		
Truck drivers (USA, Sweden)	50, 59		
Sedentary workers (USA, Sweden)	42, 42		
Burdorf et al. (1993):		Not reported	Not reported
Crane operators	50		
Straddle-carrier drivers	44		
Office workers	34		
Bovenzi and Zadini (1992):			
Bus drivers	82.9	83.7	36.3
Office workers	65.6	66.4	33.6
Holmstrom et al. (1992):		Not reported	Not reported
Construction workers	54		

symptoms. The figures from the current study (Sypek et al., 1999) have been included for ease of comparison. It should be noted that the figure for the twelve month prevalence of LBT of 52 % in the Nordic general questionnaire compares favourably with the 50.3 % reported in the Nordic low back questionnaire. Similarly there was consistency in the seven day prevalence reported in both questionnaires.

Prevalence reported for LBT in taxi drivers falls within the ranges reported for comparable occupations. There are several aspects of the method used in these other studies which may account for disparity between results. The exclusion criteria, sampling method and recruitment in this study were likely to underestimate the prevalence when compared to other studies. With 256 exclusions it is acknowledged that many subjects with LBT may have been excluded due to the presence of significant LBP prior to commencing driving or having less than five years' driving experience. However, the strict inclusion criteria do mean that the associations made between the taxi driver occupation and LBT are strong and the influence of confounding variables is reduced.

Of the 455 taxi drivers approached in this study, only forty-six did not choose to participate, giving a very high response rate of 90%. Studies which used postal surveys generally reported lower response rates and may have led to over-reporting of LBP prevalence because respondents may be biased with respect to those who have an interest (i.e. those with back pain). Bovenzi and Zadini (1992) reported a response rate of 71.5% for bus drivers and 70.4% for controls, and Holmstrom et al. (1992) reported a response rate of 76% for construction workers. Additionally in this study, the purpose was explained as relating to the health rather than the back pain of taxi drivers in order to limit a bias towards those with LBP.

The prevalence of LBP gives an indication of how many people in the population experience ache, pain or discomfort in their lower back but not of how LBP affects their lives. Low back trouble prevented 11.3% of taxi drivers from doing their normal work and 22% had to reduce their work or leisure in the last twelve months because of low back pain. The effect of LBP on work or leisure is not mentioned in other studies (see Table 3.6) except for the study by Bovenzi and Zadini (1992) which reports higher proportions of the samples whose work was affected by LBP (36.3% and 33.6%). The lower rates of time off work for taxi drivers may be a reflection of self-employment versus company employment, rather than severity of impairment. Many taxi drivers are owner operators so the time they spend away from work means a loss of income. The bus drivers and office workers in the study by Bovenzi and Zadini (1992) were company employees and it is likely that such workers received sick pay benefits.

Stress, low job satisfaction, driving more than fifty hours per week, previous MVA and a more upright seat angle were found to increase the risk of LBT. Previous investigations have demonstrated associations between LBP and psychosocial factors such as stress, inadequacy of income, job dissatisfaction, repetitive work, lack of control and social class (Dempsey et al., 1997; Papageorgiou et al., 1997; Ratti and Pilling, 1997). In this study stress and low job satisfaction were linked to an increased risk of suffering LBP in taxi drivers.

Several aspects of taxi driving as an occupation differentiate it from other driving occupations and may contribute to a stressful work environment. Increased stress and low job satisfaction may result from comparatively low income, competition from other transport services such as 'blue plate' chauffeur-driven vehicles and working on their own for long hours leaving little time for other social activities outside working hours. Conversely, the training course for taxi driver accreditation in South Australia involves only one session on stress management and this makes broad recommendations, such as planning work and 'taking a positive outlook on life'. More occupational-specific stress management education may need to be included in this programme.

The increased risk of LBP for drivers with greater number of hours worked per week could be related to increased exposure time to LBP risk factors. The more hours spent in the taxi, the longer the driver is exposed to WBV and a sedentary working posture. Also, longer hours of repetitive work and low social interaction can lead to further psychosocial stress. These drivers may be more likely to have an MVA due to fatigue and being on the road for greater periods. The issue of long working hours is difficult to rectify in taxi drivers because their only chance of getting paid is when their taxi is on the road, and anecdotally owners like their taxi to be on the road twenty-four hours a day! Many other studies investigate large companies where regulations govern the number of hours worked per week, whereas some taxi drivers are working in excess of 100 hours per week.

The measurement of seat inclination provided information on the relationship between seat ergonomics and LBT. This gross measure indicates that there is a range of seat inclinations within the population and that a more upright seat angle was associated with an increased risk of LBT. The seat angle measurement in this study was unlikely to be a valid indicator of spinal posture. Poor seating postures may be linked to increased intradiscal pressure (Nachemson, 1975) and increased strain on neural structures (Shacklock, 1995). It is tempting to speculate on the links between seat angle and LBT in this population, but without a more detailed analysis of the sitting posture, speculations are just that.

CONCLUSIONS

This is one of the first studies specifically focused on musculoskeletal disorders in taxi drivers. It has shown a 52 per cent prevalence of LBT and that this prevalence is significantly associated with increased stress levels, increasing working hours, job dissatisfaction, a previous MVA and a more upright seat angle.

Intervention strategies for occupationally related LBP aim to either change the worker by making them more resistant to injury or change the working conditions (Frank et al., 1996). Results of this study suggest that changes to taxi drivers as workers would need to address stress management strategies, further defensive driving instruction to avoid MVAs, and education about appropriate postures while driving. Changing the working conditions is often more difficult due to the unique nature of the taxi driver's occupation (taxi drivers being, in effect, a large group of mobile small businesses). Further studies should consider which aspects of the taxi driving occupation cause stress and low job satisfaction, the relationship between time, type and severity of MVAs and the onset of LBP, and drivers' knowledge and expectations of back care and injury prevention.

ACKNOWLEDGEMENTS

The author would like to thank Dr Karen Grimmer (Director, Centre for Allied Health Research, University of South Australia) for invaluable assistance with the analysis of results and Ms Tara Adams for valued assistance with data collection.

References

Bigos, S., Battie, M. and Spengler, D. (1991). A prospective study of work perceptions and psychosocial factors affecting the report of back injury. *Spine*, **16**, 1–6.

Bovenzi, M. and Zadini, A. (1992). Self-reported low back symptoms in urban bus drivers exposed to whole-body vibration. *Spine*, **17**, 1048–1059.

Burdorf, A., Naaktgeboren, B. and de Groot, H. (1993). Occupational risk factors for low back pain among sedentary workers. *Journal of Occupational Medicine*, **35**, 1213–1220.

Damkot, D., Pope, M., Lord, J. et al. (1984). The relationship between work history, work environment and low-back pain in men. *Spine*, **9**, 395–399.

Dempsey, P., Burdorf, A. and Webster, B. (1997). The influence of personal variables on work-related low-back disorders and implications for future research. *Journal of Environmental Medicine*, **39**, 748–759.

Frank, J., Kerr, M., Brooker, A. et al. (1996). Disability resulting from occupational low back pain. Part I: What do we know about primary prevention? A review of the scientific evidence on prevention before disability begins. *Spine*, **21**, 2908–2917.

Hannson, T. and Holm, S. (1991). Clinical implications of vibration induced changes in the lumbar spine. *Orthopaedic Clinics of North America*, **22**, 247–253.

Holmstrom, E., Lindell, J. and Moritz, U. (1992). Low back and neck/shoulder pain in construction workers: occupational workload and psychosocial risk factors. Part 1: relationship to low back pain. *Spine*, **17**, 663–671.

Krause, N., Ragland, D., Greiner, B. et al. (1997). Physical workload and ergonomic factors associated with prevalence of back and neck pain in urban transit operators. *Spine*, **22**, 2117–2127.

Kuorinka, I., Jonsson, B., Kilbom, A. et al. (1987). Standardised Nordic questionnaires for the analysis of musculoskeletal symptoms. *Applied Ergonomics*, **18**, 233–237.

Magnusson, M., Pope, M., Wilder, D. et al. (1996). Are occupational drivers at an increased risk for developing musculoskeletal disorders? *Spine*, **21**, 710–717.

Nachemson, A. (1975). Towards a better understanding of low-back pain: a review of the mechanics of the lumbar disc. *Rheumatology and Rehabilitation*, **14**, 129–141.

Papageoriou, A., Macfarlane, G., Thomas, E. et al. (1997). Psychosocial factors in the workplace – do they predict new episodes of low back pain? Evidence from the South Manchester back pain study. *Spine*, **22**, 1137–1142.

Radbone, I. (1997). *Adelaide taxi industry baseline study, final report*. Transport Systems Centre, University of South Australia.

Ratti, N. and Pilling, K. (1997). Back pain in the workplace. *British Journal of Rheumatology*, **36**, 260–264.

Shacklock, M. (1995). Neurodynamics. *Physiotherapy*, **81**, 9–14.

Zimmerman, C., Cook, T. and Goel, V. (1993). Effects of seated posture on erector spinae EMG activity during whole body vibration. *Ergonomics*, **36**, 667–675.

Chapter 4

Prevention cost effectiveness

The costs and benefits of occupational injury prevention

Maurice Oxenburgh

INTRODUCTION

'Why are occupational health practitioners not effective in the prevention of injuries in the workplace?' After all, there are more occupational health practitioners then ever before but there is no corresponding reduction in injuries. This is, perhaps, the most serious question facing occupational health practitioners; we cannot blithely go on talking to thin air, which seems to be the effect of our efforts so far.

There are lots of excuses such as: the compensation system works against prevention, or there is no political will, or capitalist/rational economics is the antithesis of prevention. These all have elements of truth about them but before occupational health practitioners blame everybody else they must address the question: why are we not effective? Or, if we believe that occupational health practitioners do have some effect, why are they not more effective?

Here, after looking at why they are not effective, the question 'how can occupational health practitioners be effective in the prevention of injuries in the workplace?' will be addressed – and this will be the main theme of the paper.

WHY ARE OCCUPATIONAL HEALTH PRACTITIONERS INEFFECTIVE IN PREVENTING WORKPLACE INJURIES?

To address this question, one needs to look at the employer/enterprise perspective as well as that of the occupational health practitioner.

From the employer/enterprise perspective:

1. Usually occupational health practitioners are outsiders who are only called in when there has been an injury: 'another expense when we could least do with it'.
2. As employees, occupational health practitioners are usually considered to be junior and not part of the production/service (profit generating) team.

3. Occupational health practitioners are regarded as part of industrial relations, used in order to 'keep the troops happy'.

Putting the matter bluntly, occupational health practitioners are seen to be 'humanistic' and not seen to be part of the profit generating side of the enterprise: they are solely a cost. From the occupational health practitioner's perspective:

1. The basic training (for the health sciences, physiotherapy, medicine etc.) is usually for treating an individual and does not look at treating the system (the epidemiological approach).

2. Either as an employee or an outsider, the occupational health practitioner feels that he or she has a lack of status within the enterprise.

3. Often the occupational health practitioner has a lack of knowledge of how a particular enterprise works or 'thinks' or of the power structures within the enterprise.

These perceptions, whether valid or not, have the effect of diminishing credibility within the enterprise. Although the perspectives of the employers and occupational health practitioners may complement each other, it is up to the occupational health practitioners to change the perception – there is no reason to expect the employer to change.

If these are some of the weaknesses that work against occupational health practitioners, what are their strengths?

Some of the occupational health practitioner's strengths are as follows:

1. Occupational health practitioners are highly trained, intelligent, interesting and presentable people.

2. The occupational health practitioner is called in when there has been an incident that reduces profit. Credibility for the occupational health practitioner is gained by realising that the employer may be concerned at the event of an injury but is also very concerned at the effects on cost and profitability.

3. Occupational health practitioners usually deal with middle management, which is the profit generating level.

Occupational health practitioners have to realise where their strengths lie and capitalise on them. Some extra skills are needed but their established position must be used as a starting block.

With these strengths, what extra skills are needed?

1. The occupational health practitioner needs to be able to talk to management on the same footing by speaking the same language. This will put the occupational health practitioner on the same ranking as the profit generating team rather than being seen to be an unwelcome 'add-on'. The importance of a common language directed towards profit cannot be overestimated. Talking the same language will overcome the lack of status of being 'different' and not understanding the enterprise.

2. The occupational health practitioner needs to understand the management perspectives and objectives, which are to do with productivity and quality of the produce/service and ultimately with profit. This can be done by showing that the perspectives/actions of an occupational health practitioner are not at variance with the enterprise's objectives and actually assist in the achievement of those aims.

3. Of course, the pursuit of profit should not be seen to leave the humanistic concerns behind and the real skill is in being seen to be humanistic (by reducing injury; employee and union concerns) as well as directed towards the enterprise objectives (profit).

AN EXAMPLE OF COST-EFFECTIVE INJURY PREVENTION

The following example will illustrate the company point of view. The gain made by the workers was a reduction in back injuries; however, here we need to jump from being health practitioners looking at individuals with bad backs to managers needing to make a profit (profit is not an optional extra – it is a necessity).

Employees are often regarded as expendable; there are always others wanting a job, so if a few are off sick or injured it is no 'big deal' – we can always get more! This attitude of people being expendable (not quite the same as disposable, but one wonders at times) is nowhere more apparent than in the health care industry.

This nursing home decided that it could increase the productivity of the nursing staff by reducing the degree of manual handling. Reducing manual handling is a productivity gain made by manufacturing and other industries over the past forty or so years. In the nursing home the 'materials' lifted were disabled (non-ambulatory) and elderly patients.

The enterprise implemented some of the methods used in the manufacturing industry to reduce the degree of manual lifting. They implemented low cost capital expenditure (putting chairs and commodes on wheels, introducing sufficient patient lifting hoists and electric beds) and administrative controls (training in lifting and the use of people handling equipment and lifting information when and where needed).

The costs to the company (in one year) were as shown in Table 4.1 and the benefits to the company (in one year) were as shown in Table 4.2.

The pay-back period is the cost of the changes divided by the benefits produced by those changes. As a time factor the pay-back is the period in which the investment is repaid: in this example about five months.

There were other benefits besides a reduced insurance premium. The productivity gains included more time spent by the nurses with the patients and thus increased quality of care. In a market-driven economy, to improve services at no additional cost gives a market lead.

The above example illustrates the point that expenditure in injury prevention has a benefit to both the employee (reduced injury rate) and the employer (increased profit) – one does not exclude the other.

Table 4.1 Costs to the company

	Description	Cost ($)
New equipment	40 slings for lifters ($250 each)	10,000
	3 extra lifters ($2500 each)	7500
	20 electric beds ($1600 each)	32,000
Modifying existing equipment	20 lounge chairs on wheels ($500 each)	10,000
	16 commodes on wheels ($50 each)	800
	Toilet/shower conversions	4050
Cost of the changes		64,350

Table 4.2 Benefits to the company

Details	Old system ($)	New system ($)	Difference between new and old ($)
Workers' compensation premium	324,000	168,000	156,000
Benefit due to the changes			156,000
Pay-back period			5 months

The company took an overall approach; they did not analyse each injury or each injured person, but looked at the reasons for their high costs in workers' compensation insurance. Too often the occupational health practitioner is asked to look at a single injury at a single workstation rather than taking the enterprise approach and investigating the reasons more fully.

HOW DO OCCUPATIONAL HEALTH PRACTITIONERS BECOME EFFECTIVE IN INJURY PREVENTION?

So how do we go about showing that occupational health practitioners can give profits, not just costs, to an enterprise? Of course, there are many ways to do this but here the aim is shown to be achieved with the aid of a cost–benefit analysis computer model, the Productivity Model.

The model was originally programmed for computer use about four years ago as a by-product from the book 'Increasing Productivity and Profit Through Health and Safety'. The model has just recently been redeveloped for use as an insurance model and a workplace (ergonomics) model. It is the Workplace Model that will be described in this paper.

Models need data and there is a frequent cry that people do not know where to find data. This can be because people are often not aware of the data they seek; they do not know what they are seeking. In research, it is not usually finding the answers that is the difficulty, but framing the correct questions. Thus, the Productivity Model directs you to the pertinent questions.

Another advantage of a computer-generated model is that it handles the data and mathematics and determines the benefits.

Very briefly, a cost–benefit analysis takes the workplace situation at a particular point in time. It assumes that productivity is not optimal and improvements (changes or an intervention) may be made to increase productivity. Assumptions are made regarding the costs for implementation and the improvements to productivity. This is little different from the assumptions made when an engineer wants to introduce new machinery, the accountant wants extra computers or the restaurateur buys extra plates. The assumption, even if unwritten, is that the expenditure will result in maintained or extra profit.

What occupational health practitioners may forget is that their prediction for the future may be as valid as that of the engineer, accountant or restaurateur. In any event the prediction is not made in a vacuum; it is made in co-operation with the management, with specialist knowledge coming from the occupational health practitioner.

This concept of cost–benefit analysis is valid for all sizes of workplaces and for all types of industry – production, mining, farming, services such as hotels, laundries, shops and office (clerical) work in private enterprise or government.

The concepts behind the model, and some of the questions asked by the model, are not all that much different from what you do already. For example, as a physiotherapist you gather information by interviewing the patient and by physical examination. You make a hypothesis of the cause of the problem and choose a course of action – the treatment – which will determine the future outcome.

In a workplace injury prevention programme one follows a similar course, although the patient becomes a specific workplace and gathering information follows a slightly different route. The eventual aim is to treat the system, rather than an individual, by predicting that a certain course will lead to a certain outcome.

Features of the Productivity Model

What then are the salient features of a cost–benefit model and the Productivity Model in particular?

Firstly, a specific workplace is defined regarding the number of workers, tasks, wages or salaries. One can add extra costs for workers' compensation, taxes, superannuation and supervision to increase the model's accuracy, but principally one is looking at where improvements in work conditions will lead to increased productivity and profit. Thus, one examines the work tasks rather than the people per se. In a large workplace there may be a systematic injury sequence to guide you, but in a small workplace, which encompasses the vast majority of workers, there will be no such help. This is where your professional expertise comes in – look and find where the work tasks do not match the employees' capabilities. Assume the changes (intervention) and, in co-operation with management, determine the probable effects on productivity; add this to the model and the programme calculates the benefit.

From experience, most ergonomics interventions have a pay-back period of less than six months.

That a cost–benefit analysis is effective in altering management perception to injury prevention, as a means to increase profits, was shown by Professor Guy Ahonen of the Economics Research Institute in Helsinki. He obtained preliminary information from 340 small and medium sized companies in Finland and, using the Productivity Model, showed each enterprise individually how much they were potentially losing through poor occupational health and safety practices. Half of them took the hint and started to seriously address their problems. Profit is a strong motivating force.

ACKNOWLEDGEMENTS

The author is grateful for the help and advice of Dr Paula Liukkonen of Stockholm University and Fenestra Software for the computer program development.

References

Oxenburgh, M.S. (1991). *Increasing Productivity and Profit through Health and Safety.* CCH International.

Oxenburgh, M.S. (1994, 1999). The Productivity Model (computer software). Fenestra Software.

Oxenburgh, M.S. (1997). Cost–benefit analysis of ergonomics programs. *American Industrial Hygiene Association Journal*, **58**, 150–156.

Chapter 5

Risk management

Workers' compensation: costs and control

Ann Grant

THE COST

Workplace injury and disease affects us all as it imposes significant costs on individuals, organisations and the community. The Industry Commission estimates the overall cost at around $20 billion per year (Work, Health and Safety, 1995).

Costs include reduced business productivity, overtime payments, loss of income and future earnings, welfare payments and medical costs.

Distribution of the costs shows employers bearing about 40 per cent in workers' compensation, overtime and lost productivity. Injured workers sustain 30 per cent in loss of income now and in the future, pain and suffering, and medical and travel costs. The community also bears about 30 per cent of costs through welfare payments, medical and health costs and loss of human potential.

Every year, over 500 workers suffer a traumatic death from work and up to 2200 die of occupational disease. Given that there are about 2000 road deaths, work safety may be more important than road safety (Work, Health and Safety, 1995).

THE IMPACT

Despite the fact that workplace injury and disease has a far greater impact than many appreciate, there is still a widespread lack of knowledge and understanding of what contributes to the costs and the benefits to be gained by managing workplace risks.

Employers often do not understand their legal obligations in relation to health and safety and in many cases both they and their workers see health and safety as just common sense and accidents and injuries part and parcel of daily work. Many people believe that accidents are caused by careless workers, rather than seeing them as failures of systems of work (Hopkins, 1995).

The burden of the subsequent personal, business and workers' compensation costs is high, and it is estimated that if Australia could reduce its injury and disease by 10 per cent, the gross domestic product would rise by around $400 million (Work, Health and Safety, 1995).

A comprehensive comparison of Australia's ten workers' compensation and occupational health and safety schemes was released by the Labour Ministers' Council in 1998. It shows that the national average cost of workers' compensation per employee rose by almost $80.00 from $641 to $719 between 1993/94 and 1996/97, although changes to workers' compensation legislation have been made in most states in order to control costs (Labour Ministers' Council, 1998).

During that same period, workers' compensation costs rose from 1.8 per cent to an average of 2 per cent of total labour costs – less than superannuation or payroll, but larger than fringe benefits. Victoria, however, recorded a decrease in both measures (Labour Ministers' Council, 1998).

WORKERS' COMPENSATION KEY COST DRIVERS

The key cost drivers for workers compensation include the duration of weekly payments, i.e. time off work, the medical and like injury management and treatment costs and lump sum payments (Victorian WorkCover Authority, 1997).

The Victorian figures for 1996/97 show that gross claim payments totalled $900.3 million, a 23.5 per cent increase from the previous year, despite fewer claims entering the system. A total of $305 million was paid out in weekly benefits and $154 million in medical and similar services (Victorian WorkCover Authority, 1997).

The half-yearly report to 31 December 1998 issued by the Victorian Work-cover Authority shows gross claim payments for the six months to 31 December 1998 were $545 million, an increase of $67.6 million (or 14.2 per cent) on the six months to 30 June 1998. Common law payments for those workers classified as 'seriously injured' was the major cause for this increase (Victorian WorkCover Authority, 1997).

The growth in claims costs and strategies to reduce these costs are clearly issues to be tackled by regulatory authorities, insurers and employers.

In Victoria, the main strategy thrusts are through legislative amendment, regulation and prosecution, financial incentives in premium setting and stake-holder education (Victorian WorkCover Authority, 1997).

The effect or force of these strategies on stakeholders will vary in different contexts, and therefore methods to enhance the effectiveness of these strategies are likely to be constantly under review.

In Victoria, the workers' compensation insurance premium paid by the employer is largely based on the past claims experience of that employer, and their success or otherwise in reducing claims frequency and duration.

This can provide a direct and significant financial incentive for employers, especially large employers, to reduce costs. As their claims costs reduce, so too will their premium. Many organisations have responded enthusiastically to this challenge and from the insured portfolio at Royal and SunAlliance, there are a number of examples of significant achievements in reducing the incidence and cost of injuries.

However, we need to be aware that some employers may be finding less desirable ways of reducing the number of claims by, for example, discouraging workers from claiming, suppressing or hoarding claims and contesting claims unnecessarily (Hopkins, 1995).

With experience-rated premiums, many insurers have taken the opportunity to assist employers to develop structured risk management programmes, with insurers often contributing to the cost.

Compensation costs are affected not only by the number of claims but also by their duration, i.e. the time off work. For savings to be made, it is often easier for an employer to contain the costs of an injury rather than reduce the actual number of injuries. Consequently, a proactive effective claims management programme implemented by an employer is likely to reduce claims costs and therefore the insurance premium.

Early intervention and early return to work programmes are important components of any effective claims management system. A claim that can be turned into a no lost time claim by early intervention at the workplace is a cost saver for the employer. The ability or willingness of the employer to provide suitable alternative or transitional work for injured employees can be instrumental in lowering overall claims costs and subsequent premiums.

The Victorian legislation puts the onus squarely on employers to take responsibility for their employees' rehabilitation and return to work, and provides penalties for failure to comply. Insurers have an important educational role with employers in advising of rehabilitation and return to work requirements and assisting the employer to comply with the injury management and early intervention culture.

Targeted referral to approved occupational rehabilitation providers may be necessary to assist the employer and worker in the return to work process.

The single biggest factor in claims cost growth in Victoria has been the number of long term claimants able to achieve 'serious injury' classification. This threshold was required to initiate common law proceedings and achieve higher weekly benefits. The government moved to correct this trend by excluding secondary psychological factors, but the numbers of long term claims continue to disproportionally add to the overall cost.

This group of claimants has been difficult for insurers to manage, owing to the complex issues surrounding the claim and the claimant, and limited support from the medical field. However, the new insurer remuneration scheme in Victoria will shift the focus of claims handling from administrative and processing accuracy to claims management for outcomes, and insurers will be required to target and review programmes for long term claimants for quality service and cost containment.

As a tactic we might assume that, if we can focus on early return to work and recovery, then claims will be largely resolved before any thought of lump sum payment arises.

Medical and similar costs is another key cost driver. This includes costs such as hospitalisation, physiotherapy, chiropractic, aids and appliances, rehabilitation, medical visits and investigations. Insurers in Victoria are required to pay for reasonable services as stated in the Accident Compensation Act. This is not always easy to determine and many insurers have employed medical and allied health staff to advise claims officers and assist in return to work case management activities.

The Victorian WorkCover Authority has continued to monitor service providers and a peer review process has been in place for physiotherapy, chiropractic, osteopathy and psychology services. Providers with service patterns outside the average have been counselled and advised on treatment regimes and patient self-management techniques. Providers' awareness has been raised to the issues of duration and frequency of treatment and the need for some evidence of continuing treatment benefit in the return to work process. Insurers have been part of that process in co-operation with the Victorian WorkCover Authority.

It is worth noting here that despite reductions in claims costs through tighter management, better health and safety may not necessarily result, i.e. the number of claims may remain the same.

The experience at Royal and SunAlliance is that managers usually respond to increasing claims costs first and then, as cost reductions occur and level out, their attention may turn to occupational health and safety initiatives to prevent claims in the first place and to make further savings.

THE FUTURE

From July 1999, insurers' remuneration in Victoria changed from a premium-based system to an outcome-based structure. The new model will align insurer objectives with the Victorian WorkCover Authority's goals of prevention, return to work and service quality (Victorian WorkCover Authority, 1997).

Insurers will be rewarded for improved employer performance in risk management, return to work, claims cost containment and quality service. Clearly this will be a powerful tool in efforts to address the key cost drivers.

Insurers, employers and service providers will need to continue to work more closely in implementing their own strategies, and those initiated and promoted by the Victorian WorkCover Authority.

In 1997 the legislation was amended to incorporate co-ordinated care plans for long term claimants with acquired brain injury and those with pain and medication problems. The Victorian WorkCover Authority funds two pain centres which provide a much needed avenue of referral for insurers in developing and implementing these plans for better claimant management.

The prevention of back injuries, the most frequent source of claims (Victorian WorkCover Authority, 1997), has been targeted by the Victorian WorkCover Authority, and according to the 1998 half-yearly report, back injuries in 1998 have reduced by around 10 per cent in relation to 1997. At Royal and SunAlliance, one of the responses to the campaign was to target back injury cases who had not returned to work at twelve weeks and, in conjunction with a service provider, to invite them to participate in a self-managed physiotherapy-based programme, rather than continue with passive treatment. The interim results of this pilot programme have been encouraging in relation to increased return to work and reduced claims and treatment costs. The final report and outcomes are expected in the near future.

It is likely that we will see a greater pooling of resources, with preferred service providers being used to tackle some of the harder claims management issues. However, as with insurers, their outcomes for return to work will be increasingly monitored for cost effectiveness.

References

Hopkins, A. (1995). *Making Safety Work.* Allen and Unwin.

Industry Commission (1995). *Work, health and safety – Inquiry into occupational health and safety.*

Labour Ministers' Council (1998). *Comparative performance monitoring: Occupational health and safety and workers' compensation.*

Victorian WorkCover Authority (1997). *1996/97 Annual Report.*

Victorian WorkCover Authority (1999). *Half-yearly Report to 31 December 1998.*

Risk management: some factors that influence this approach

Rhonda Pashen

INTRODUCTION

Risk management is one component of business which employers in general have given more attention to in recent years. However, there is still considerable variation in the effectiveness of risk management strategies in respect to occupational health and safety programmes. This discussion will briefly look at one risk management model and examine some of the issues which influence large employers to devote resources to risk assessment and minimisation strategies.

A RISK MANAGEMENT MODEL

A brief presentation from the Gartner Group (1999) outlined their approach to risk management. They indicated that they use a 'seven A's model' which involves:

- Acknowledge new or existing risks.
- Assess probability, consequences, impact and priority.
- Actions to minimise developed.
- Accountabilities defined.
- Actively manage risk minimisation.
- Advise senior management of risk status.
- Audit processes and management assessment of risks.

It was suggested that many large employers complete the first two stages of this process, namely acknowledgement and assessment of risks, fairly well. However, the number of companies that carry this work through to implementation of effective actions for minimisation of risk is not high.

Why is this so? The answer could well be a fairly basic one – namely, money.

The first two steps can be achieved relatively easily using either internal or external resources. However the actions step, when we are considering occupational health risks, often requires significant redesign of equipment and/or work practices, comprehensive training programmes, and the need to change attitudes of people at workplaces. These are complex tasks and are usually associated with considerable expenditure.

So how can we convince employers that these costs are worthwhile?

One starting point is clearly demonstrating to employers the actual cost of workplace injury. The immediate cost that employers see is the workers' compensation premium that they pay. The design of workers' compensation premium systems can therefore be a critical issue in encouraging employers to adopt a risk management approach to occupational injury.

THE IMPACT OF WORKERS' COMPENSATION PREMIUM CALCULATION METHODOLOGY

Over the last few years workers' compensation schemes in Australia have moved away from basing premium calculation on industry rates (plus or minus some incentives/penalties) to experience-based premium calculation. For large employers this means that the amount they pay is directly impacted by their own claims experience. Previously, under the industry rating methodology, some poor performers were continually cross-subsidised by better performers in the industry.

It is worth noting here that even under an experience-based scheme, smaller employers will not have their claims experience truly reflected in the premium they pay. The premium they pay must be smoothed out – as this is what insurance is all about. It is therefore not possible to design a system which, in the short term, charges premium on the basis of individual claims performance to employers at the smaller end of the scale.

This is one reason why it is so hard to convince smaller employers of the need to have a risk management approach to occupational health and safety (OHS) and one reason why, in general, OHS standards in this part of industry are so poor.

The experience in Queensland in respect to larger employers since experience-based rating was first introduced in July 1997 has been quite dramatic. The number of enquiries for assistance to improve occupational health standards at that time increased significantly. However, the first premium notices where the experience-based premium formula was applied were only released after July 1998, and it was not until some employers received increases in their actual assessment amount that the interest was turned into actions.

Evidence of this is apparent in the following data released by WorkCover. WorkCover completes an annual survey with employers to assess satisfaction with and knowledge of the system. In early 1998 only 10 per cent of employers indicated that they knew the cost of claims was the main driver in the setting of premium rates.

This was despite a massive information campaign during which every policy holder in the state received written information about the experience-based rating system; more than fifty seminars were held state-wide; and a concentrated media campaign was mounted.

This year, just twelve months later, 58 per cent of employers displayed this knowledge. A massive increase in awareness, which was surely based on the fact that the first premium under the new system had then been paid. Employers had either felt premium increases first-hand or heard their colleagues bemoaning their fate.

On the other side, an equal number of employers received significant decreases due to their good past performance, and this message also had impact.

This emphasises the importance of the premium system in prompting employers to adopt the first two steps of the seven A's model – Acknowledgement and Assessment.

Also, once the true direct costs of occupational injury are known, then more accurate cost–benefit analyses can be performed to determine if actions are worthwhile. This is the process which is going on in many organisations now – the author's own included.

One other important point to note is that the internal charging mechanism that organisations utilise for workers' compensation expenditure is also an important consideration when examining how to have risk minimisation strategies accepted throughout the organisation. Just as at the macro level, the need to accurately reflect the true cost of claims internally is critical to promote understanding of the need for risk management systems, so it is essential that this issue is managed well in each unit throughout the organisation.

OTHER ISSUES WHICH IMPACT ON DEVELOPING A RISK MANAGEMENT APPROACH TO OHS

Penalties applying under OHS legislation also have some impact. From experience it is not necessarily the fines that may be applied for breaches under OHS legislation, as significant financial penalties are not applied readily. However, the potential ability to impact businesses by the issuing of Prohibition Notices and the like, can be key factors in driving a risk management approach to OHS. The threat of closing down a section of the business or being unable to use a piece of essential equipment is something that employers will see as a great risk, as it may totally inhibit the organisation's operations.

Likewise, the power to hold individual executives of companies responsible for breaches and the potential imposition of jail sentences on these individuals is another factor which is driving change. The recent cases where this has occurred have promoted a much greater sense of personal accountability amongst senior executives. This in turn has encouraged a true risk management approach to the OHS agenda.

CONCLUSIONS

Convincing companies to spend money to develop a true risk management approach to OHS issues can be a difficult task. It is therefore most important to analyse what factors motivate employers to take this action, in order that services to assist employers in this regard can be developed and presented in an appropriate and timely manner.

Reference

Gartner Group (1999). Gartner Group and risk management: A presentation to the WorkCover Queensland Board IT Committee Meeting.

A portfolio approach to cost containment in injury management

Pamela Veal

INTRODUCTION

There is an old saying that the way to make the gods laugh is to tell them your plans for the future.

This paper will tempt fate and try to address some of the issues and trends which are beginning to impact on the cost-effective management of personal injury, and how Mercantile Mutual is attempting to respond to these changing circumstances.

THE SITUATION

Because personal injury insurance is spread across various business portfolios, it can be costly for the insurer as well as for other key parties. In June 1998, the overall cost for the state of New South Wales (NSW) in workers' compensation was estimated to be $1.5 billion, with an estimated daily increase of one million dollars.

There is an urgent need to find immediate and innovative solutions to this cost over-run if the integrity of the system is to be maintained.

To address this situation the NSW government introduced new workers' compensation legislation, which commenced operation in August 1998.

As a result, insurers were required to develop and implement their own injury management programmes.

At Mercantile Mutual a working party of managers from various areas within workers' compensation developed an injury management programme. The analysis of the occupational health and safety (OHS) and injury management issues, along with the problem solving involved in formulating an injury management programme, resulted in a cross-fertilisation of injury management to and from other lines of insurance.

Mercantile Mutual in NSW has now established a fully operational team of health professionals to provide a comprehensive injury management service to target three insurance products:

- life insurance
- compulsory third party (CTP) insurance
- workers' compensation insurance.

This service provides benefits to all parties: 'best practice' service provision to injured claimants, efficient working relationships with service providers and cost containment for the insurer.

Employment culture also plays a large part in outcomes of disability claims. The key factor bringing benefits to these parties is the case management and injury planning provided by Mercantile Mutual's injury management service.

The injury management service in NSW comprises a team of six rehabilitation professionals who provide a comprehensive injury management service to the team of claims staff who, in turn, provide a claims service in line with the legislation listed below.

Compulsory third party

Motor Accidents Act 1998 (as amended).

Workers' compensation

- Workers' Compensation Act 1987 No. 70
- Workers' Compensation (Workplace Injury Management) Regulation 1995
- Workplace Injury Management and Workers' Compensation Act 1998 No. 86.

Life and income protection

- Life Insurance Act 1995
- Life Insurance Act 1945
- Insurance Contracts Act 1984.

Within the scope of the legislation, for each product, the primary functions of the injury management model are designed to:

- Assess the risk exposure of each claim.
- Mitigate loss on the claim by assisting claimants to receive necessary treatment and rehabilitation services.
- Promote the philosophy of 'wellness' for each claimant.
- Reduce costs to the claim.
- Develop an injury management plan.
- Monitor progress.
- Achieve a cost-effective outcome.

The decision to fund services is linked to the injury management objectives and the anticipated and desired outcomes in each claim.

The outcomes achieved rely upon a well-structured claims management policy, trained staff and a belief in claims 'management' – not just processing of claims.

This is particularly poignant in life insurance claims where there are no specific statutory requirements for injury management mechanisms to be enacted.

Where no *structured* claims management policy exists, i.e. where the claims administrators are not provided with adequate support and training, and where the delivery of a high quality treatment and rehabilitation service fails to occur, a culture can be developed which is counter-productive to cost-effective injury management.

In these situations an alienating culture of passivity and illness behaviour is reinforced, rather than a culture which responds to a partnership relationship between the claimant, other parties and insurer.

Although this is a negative depiction of what can happen when someone has a compensable injury, it reinforces the impact of positive synergy that occurs when a proactive injury management service is delivered – and is delivered in tandem with timely management decisions by all stakeholders in the process.

Within disability insurance, there is an important trend towards utilising case management strategies to reduce cost and duration of the injury and claims. With the advent of case management, the management of costs is tighter. Earlier reporting of the injury and intervention that is driven by the nature of injury, employment of health professionals within claims departments, and a general expectation for safer work practices to be initiated are all helping to improve the system and contain costs.

Even in life insurance policies where no particular injury management mechanism may be mandatory, it is exciting to see the trend towards an integration of injury management and claims management practices – and to see these services dovetail and act in a complementary arrangement, rather than be in conflict. With conflict an adversarial attitude is frequently generated, with everyone losing as a result.

In this paper the injury management service within workers' compensation insurance in NSW is referred to. Within this scheme there are indications that Mercantile Mutual's injury management programme and risk management programme are impacting positively on the culture. There are now clearer expectations and responsibilities required of employers, workers and their treating doctors. Some of these are outlined below.

Employer culture

- Early notification of injury.
- Maximise control for the injured worker via relationship.
- Greater accountability of employer to manage return to work plan – discouraging abdication of responsibility to others encourages accountability by worker and doctor.

- Positive relationship between worker and employer within the organisational culture, and with individual injured worker.
- Communication is early and responsive.
- Liaison with treating doctor.
- Clear expectation of early return to work.
- Co-operation with injury management plan.
- Provide suitable duties.
- Initiate appropriate referrals.
- Involve insurer early in problem solving.
- Key co-ordinator identified and responsibility given.
- Undertake training opportunities.

Insurer culture

Here we need to remember that the business need is to minimise the impact of negative drivers and promote opportunities for positive drivers.

- Responsive to early injury notification.
- Develops an injury management plan for each worker.
- Assesses risk exposure of each claim – identifies elements of worker's situation.
- Case management model prompts:

  proactive decisions by parties involved;

  early assessment of needs;

  set objectives and goals;

  specified treatment and rehabilitation plan with realistic time frame and cost;

  reinforces commitment to the return to work plan.
- Strong consultation and communication to:

  negotiate simple return to work plans in consultation with employer;

  ensure complex return to work plans engage rehabilitation service provider;

  obtain quick opinions from external providers;

  involve the claims administrator in all injury management decisions.
- Monitor injury management plans to follow up progress – keep momentum going and manage the case for the duration of established time frame.
- Injury management plans integrated with claim payments/other actions.

- Set an expectation of accountability for timely outcomes.
- Utilise a network of effective service providers.

With their range of professional qualifications and injury management experience, the team of Injury Management Advisers brings a wealth of knowledge to involve a partnership approach with the key players. Their understanding of the essence of injury management serves to coach partners who have little experience in this relatively new field.

Frequently the employer has very little training or exposure to this area and responds to guidance. This applies especially to the necessity of locating suitable duties for partially incapacitated workers.

Woven into the injury management culture are the worker's attitudes and expectations following an injury. The type of insurance coverage may influence their attitude towards their recovery and independence from receiving ongoing claim benefits.

A case management approach by the Injury Management Adviser begins to address any issues that arise, and appropriate referrals to rehabilitation or treatment providers are made. Whilst the referral body may deal with the obstacle as part of their injury management plan, the Injury Management Adviser also supports a commitment by the worker. Where this does not occur, financial penalties may apply and the workers' compensation legislation has provision for penalties to be applied in these circumstances.

REHABILITATION SERVICE PROVIDERS

Rehabilitation service providers are mainly involved in complex return to work/ rehabilitation plans.

The expectations for proactive cost-effective case management are as follows:

- Promote a philosophy of wellness – to empower workers to take control of their injury.
- Reinforce claimants' responsibility for their own rehabilitation and the fact that this brings obligations and responsibilities.
- Solid co-ordination, liaison and negotiation with the treating doctor and other key parties.
- Establish *early* return to work (RTW) plan.
- Identify risk – identify strategies and realistic solutions.
- Refer to other appropriate service providers for specific issues.
- Performance and reports to have objective foundations – recommendations are to rely on evidence-based practice.
- Use of substantial and reliable labour market data to support redeployment goal.

- Accountability for cost-effective outcomes.
- Drive the injury management programme – it is to be time driven.
- Impact on treatment (e.g. effective utilisation of physiotherapy) based on increase in ability/decrease in disability.
- Business relationship with insurer – report performance results against costs.

An example of outstandingly effective injury management involves a company managing four country nursing homes, which has a reasonably large number of injuries, especially back injuries.

The approach at Mercantile Mutual under the new workers' compensation legislation has seen a collaborative partnership with local rehabilitation providers to ensure early intervention. So early that, even as our Injury Management Adviser called in relation to a new injury, a return to work plan had already commenced. This employer had also established a risk minimisation programme.

The effects of such innovative and proactive actions are:

1. Reduced lost time.
2. Increased awareness of availability of suitable duties.
3. Focus on early intervention.

The characteristics of the rehabilitation provider which impact upon their performance are:

1. Open communication which occurs regularly but not so regularly that it becomes too time consuming.
2. Good telephone and communication skills between the rehabilitation provider, worker, insurer and treating providers.
3. Cost-effective interventions.

Whilst there are signs that employers are beginning to initiate early return to work activity, there is still a long way to go. Statistics for 1999 show that 80 per cent of employers still report their injuries too late, that is, outside the forty-eight hour time frame required by WorkCover NSW for notification of significant injuries.

Delayed reporting means delayed action which incurs increased costs and decreased control to the worker.

Under the new workers' compensation legislation, the participation of the treating doctor is becoming stronger. As a result of the new WorkCover requirements, the claimants' nominated treating doctors are now much more responsive and co-operative with return to work plans. Increasing numbers of doctors are now organising return to work plans very early – even before the Insurer makes contact!

There is a definite change in the claims culture to one where doctors and employers are initiating early action. They are also clearer about the rights and responsibilities of each stakeholder. Whilst we all have a way to go, all indications are that a partnership approach is becoming a stronger part of the claims culture.

THE FUTURE: INJURY MANAGEMENT INITIATIVES

As the practice of injury management within compensable claims matures, there is a growing need for the development of 'best practice' protocols. Such protocols meet the needs of the various stakeholders, but particularly provide high quality and cost-effective service to injured claimants.

An example under compulsory third party (CTP) insurance was the development of neuropsychological guidelines to manage the process of psychometric testing. Although this protocol relies upon the co-operation of the various stakeholders, including solicitors acting for the plaintiff, it has met with reasonable success. It has prevented duplication of neuropsychological testing and provided for a more equitable service to the injured parties.

Also within the CTP legislation are the Section 37 guidelines which encourage 'best practice' in rehabilitation management. This emphasises the importance of determining the needs of the claimant as early as possible, and the need for rehabilitation advisers, within insurers, to ensure that rehabilitation takes place in a timely and appropriate fashion.

Mercantile Mutual is currently developing other protocols to provide for 'best practice' case management and cost-effective outcomes in areas such as:

- management of trauma/assault
- stress management
- back injuries.

There is also an urgent need for the development of 'best practice' guidelines between rehabilitation providers and the insurer. This will provide for accountable performance evaluation and develop targets that will bring mutual benefits to the organisations involved.

A protocol that is established in co-operation with other parties will consider issues such as:

- evidence-based practice
- partnership responsibilities
- case management tracking
- cost-effective outcomes.

An example of outstanding performance by an employer, where their activity made a highly substantial difference in the return to work outcomes, is outlined below.

As a result of high injury costs, a national manufacturing company actively fostered the following processes in their employment culture:

1. Risk minimisation: They created a culture of safety and care and safe work

practices, and invested substantial sums of money in new equipment to minimise injury.

2. Wellness model: Employee/management relationships were personable and the work environment made to feel like home, with attitudes of care, responsibility and accountability.
3. Communication: The Rehabilitation Coordinator provided a strong presence, enabling an immediate response to all injury notifications.
4. Support: The local doctor and/or physiotherapist were involved, with a strong emphasis on providing suitable duties.

This employer utilised many of the effective Return to Work Drivers that were identified in a WorkCover required literature review conducted in 1998. This company clearly demonstrated that their proactive management does reduce the frequency and duration of claims.

Although it is too early for Mercantile Mutual to provide statistics to demonstrate the benefit of the Injury Management Service to Life, CTP and Workers' Compensation products, each day there are instances of short duration programmes which return injured people back to their place of work, safely and quickly.

It is pleasing to see the advent of insurer support to deliver injury management services to Life, CTP and Workers' Compensation. It clearly demonstrates that a high quality and cost effective service can influence the culture, and get injured workers back to work quicker, and make a difference to the cost of personal injuries to employers and the taxpayers.

Good occupational health and safety is good business

Libby MacWhirter

It is difficult to convince employers that excellence in occupational health and safety (OHS) initiatives will be profitable. It is simple to convince employers that such programmes save money.

Proof positive exists in:

1. Decrease in days lost, i.e. absenteeism, for all reasons – personal and compensable illness and injury.
2. Decrease in days lost following workplace injury due to effective return to work initiatives.
3. Decrease in workers' compensation premiums.
4. Decrease in overtime worked to cover absence.

Effective initiatives, usually introduced by specific departments, need to be embraced by the managers at all levels, and in some businesses by the enterprise union. Departments, such as claims management, health management and safety, should act as internal consultants to the core business.

This means that line managers need to understand the intent of the programme, the benefit to the business and the role expected of them. In unionised businesses, a similar approach might need to be taken with the appropriate representatives.

It is disastrous for a good idea to flounder because care was not taken with introduction and communication, in other words, poor marketing.

In the past, some employers did not see good OHS practices as crucial to their business; however, the following factors have ensured that OHS is now undertaken seriously be the majority of employers:

- public odium for unsafe work practices
- strong OHS laws
- an ageing workforce
- an increased emphasis on global competitiveness
- rising workers' compensation costs.

South Pacific Tyres has introduced several initiatives to assist employees to work in a safe and productive manner to the maximum of their ability.

The 'Welcome Back' programme was designed for injured employees unable to fulfil their normal contract of employment in the short term. The programme consists of seven hours attendance per week, made up of two sessions of hydrotherapy, one session of gym and two sessions of learning and development. In order to commence, the injured person must gain a clearance for selected duties.

Each day an employee who would otherwise be at home has to get up, get dressed and attend a place at a specified time. It is much harder to enter the sick mode or remain in the sick mode with a schedule like this.

All sessions are tailored to the individual's needs. Learning and development sessions are co-ordinated on-site so that a link with the workplace is maintained. As recovery occurs, other sessions are added, or perhaps a return to the workplace on selected duties for limited hours will be deemed appropriate.

The success of the programme has been based on the emphasis of using the time of rehabilitation to enable the employee to regain fitness, learn new skills, maintain the discipline of attending the workplace, meet with others dealing with like issues, and improve self-esteem and confidence. Some people have chosen to continue to attend in their own time, following a return to full-time work.

Wherever possible health professionals have been allocated who will provide individual injury management – not injury treatment. Hydrotherapy and gym are conducted at three sites in the Melbourne suburbs, close to the three manufacturing sites. Learning and development is conducted at the company training centre. A room containing seven state of the art computers and ergonomic furniture, easily accessed from the car park, is used.

A tutor from Kangan Batman TAFE attends all sessions. Participants enter and leave the programme based on their recovery.

Basic computer skills are taught in a supportive environment. Introduction to computers is considered to be a lifestyle skill which will be needed by everyone. Due to the composition of the South Pacific Tyres workforce (at the last count, forty-four countries of origin), English is also taught under the guise of keyboard skills. Interestingly, for many people who attended school in Australia, English is still a second language!

The second programme, South Pacific Tyres 'Newskills', was introduced to broaden the work options of injured employees unable to perform their normal contractual work medium to long term.

This programme is still in the pilot stage; evaluation will take place in the near future. Injured employees entering this programme work closely with all parties normally involved in rehabilitation, plus training and career path experts from Kangan Batman TAFE. The programme works as follows. When advice is received from a treating health professional that the injured employee will be unable to return to any meaningful work in the medium term, a referral is made to a dedicated person at TAFE. Following assessment, discussion and interview, a course is chosen based on the individual's life experience, interests, abilities and aptitudes. Ultimate employment is the aim.

For both programmes, senior management support has been critical. The effectiveness has been established by such intangibles as employees' reaction to the programme, union and insurer support, and by tangibles such as return to productive work and decrease in days lost.

This paper has been an attempt to demonstrate one company's approach to one aspect of OHS. The important points are translatable to all aspects of OHS:

- Understand that, for all people, in all businesses, safe and productive work is a must.
- Recruit management, employee and union support for all OHS issues.
- Innovation pays.
- Define benefits of OHS to all parties.
- Never allow an adversarial approach to develop.
- Safety teams can form the basis of a focus group to deal with a range of issues.
- Constantly educate management so that they can assume their leadership role in OHS with confidence.

Change the way you view a situation: South Pacific Tyres views rehabilitation as an opportunity for someone released from their normal work commitments to learn new skills and gain new competencies.

This paper has purposely given examples of what works in practice rather than looking at OHS legislation, which is hopefully well understood by everyone. Legislative guidelines are firm; it is up to employers and health professionals to use them as a basis for producing a safe, healthy and productive workplace.

So be innovative, creative and educate others.

Good health and safety is good business.

Chapter 6

Prevention

Prevention programmes: the imperatives and systems

David C. Caple

METHODOLOGY

This paper is based on a review of five studoies which have been undertaken by David Caple & Associates Pty Ltd between 1990 and 1999. These studies include:

1. A review of occupational health and safety (OHS) management systems used within the Australian meat processing industry.
2. An evaluation of injury prevention models within a large government department with multiple locations across regional areas.
3. The development of a strategic plan for injury prevention within a large government department involved in the running of prisons.
4. The approach towards injury prevention within a large public hospital.
5. A manufacturing company involved with the making and distribution of polymer compounds.

Each of these case studies involved an objective of assessing the effectiveness of the OHS systems for developing an injury prevention model suitable for the culture and hazards associated with the respective workplaces. Each project primarily involved the following methodology:

1. A review of the workplace's injury history for the previous three to six years and identification of the primary types of injuries as well as their location and causal agents.
2. A review of incident reports and safety committee minutes, as well as consultation with key stakeholders in identifying the variety of hazards that are evident within the workplace.
3. A series of walk-through inspections and audits of targeted areas within the workplaces.

4. Technical assessments based on a risk management approach for identifying hazards, with assessing based on legislative and best practice models, and development of appropriate risk controls.
5. Maintaining consultation with the stakeholders throughout the risk assessment approach and monitoring the adoption and evaluation of recommendations.
6. Integrating the results of the risk assessments into a range of appropriate business plans relevant for the size and scope of issues managed in the business.
7. Debriefing the senior management of the organisation on the major findings and recommendations.
8. Developing key performance indicators, in consultation with the stakeholder groups, to ensure an approach of ongoing implementation and continuous improvement with respect to addressing injury prevention in the workplace.

RESULTS

On the basis of the research conducted in these workplaces, a range of business imperatives was clearly identified within those companies which were successful in addressing OHS risks. The key imperatives were as follows:

1. Management commitment and active participation.
2. Participation of the employees.
3. Setting of goals and measuring performances.
4. Integration of OHS strategies into business plan.
5. Positive feedback and recognition of achievements.

The commitment of senior management and their participation in the prevention systems was vital. The direct involvement and commitment of the senior management was the major determinant within specific workplaces as to the level of improvement and sustained performance in injury management. Without their commitment and participation, the prevention appeared to achieve a 'glass ceiling' above which the performance appeared not to improve. This was particularly evident where responsibility for OHS management was delegated to a 'middle level' manager, in particular those with non-operational responsibilities, such as human resource managers or OHS officers.

The successful integration of OHS with other management systems will ensure that the long term objectives of the organisation incorporate a desire to develop OHS initiatives through each stage of the design and development process.

CONCLUSIONS

It is evident from these case studies that the five basic imperatives outlined should be key components of a system which will produce a sustained focus on injury prevention. Many of the OHS management systems available on the market were found to be too complex and too time consuming and costly to implement and maintain for the majority of the businesses assessed. However, the requirement of at least a simple system which contains these key imperatives would seem a sensible starting place for organisations contemplating a programme focusing on injury prevention at the workplace level. The gradual adoption of other elements, with an ultimate goal of measuring the system up against one of the available OHS management systems, could be a subsequent stage to the programme.

References

Caple, D.C. (1991). *OHS Management System for the Australian Meat Processing Industry.* Meat Research Corporation.

Caple, D.C. et al. (1997). *Evaluation of the National Standard for Manual Handling.* Worksafe Australia.

Kinhill Economics (1996). *Cost–Benefit Study of the SABS and SABS Exempt System.* Kinhill.

Primary prevention at work

Barbara McPhee

Preventive health care (the prevention of accidents and illness and the care of health which may be threatened) for workers' musculoskeletal fitness has proven difficult to implement.

The benefits of prevention are so obvious that it is hard to understand why it is not pursued more vigorously. The reasons are complex and involve organisations and people and how they work together and make decisions. Reaction to solve an existing problem is far easier to understand and justify; the parameters are there and success is measured by whether the problem is solved or not.

PRIMARY VERSUS SECONDARY PREVENTION

Primary prevention may be extremely difficult to justify where no obvious problems have arisen, as it requires a thorough understanding of the nature and causes of problems. The philosophy in the workplace is often 'it has not happened, therefore it cannot happen'. How do we prove that something might have happened when it did not?

Primary prevention requires insight into a set of circumstances (risks) that may lead to a problem and knowledge of how these risks may be eliminated or minimised. It means that people must work systematically and proactively. It also requires confidence, commitment and courage. These are personal qualities that rarely can be attributed to an organisation as a whole. Prevention necessitates that people make the decisions and take risks – this is not easy at the best of times as most people and organisations are conservative by nature. Where preventive action is undertaken it is often a single person or, less commonly, a group of key people who are responsible and who have exceptional skills, motivation and dedication. How do we find, nurture and support these people within organisations?

Secondary prevention is usually much easier because we have the benefit of hindsight and there is a need to fix an obvious problem. The person who finds and implements the solution is considered to be a problem solver. The difficulty is that the problem as it manifests itself may be only part of a larger issue that needs to be addressed in the long term. Ad hoc, reactive problem solving is usually expensive in terms of costs and human resources and is likely to be less effective.

RESOURCES AVAILABLE TO HELP IN PREVENTION

There is now a range of products that can assist organisations to develop integrated occupational health and safety management systems. However, most of them appear to be directed at the control of catastrophic risks and are unlikely to be used as a resource for the many more subtle risks, for example those associated with areas such as ergonomics and with the development of musculoskeletal disorders. Nevertheless, the process can and should be applied to the controls of these risks too.

Health and safety management plans have a number of elements. The first is commitment from all levels of the organisation and, most importantly, from senior management. Then there is a need for human and financial resources. These need not be large but it is necessary that key people are equipped with appropriate skills and knowledge. From this point plans and procedures can be put in place. The most important aspects for any plan are the involvement of people at all levels of the organisation, and the development of systems to review, document, manage, monitor and evaluate.

PRACTICAL STEPS IN PRIMARY PREVENTION

One very effective method for the promotion of primary prevention is incorporating occupational health and safety requirements into the process of purchasing goods and services through specifications, design briefs and tender documents. This includes furniture, machinery, tools and equipment as well the services of professionals such as architects and designers. Many of the problems commonly encountered by ergonomists and other health and safety personnel could be eliminated if the correct processes were undertaken for the design of the workplace and the selection of furniture and equipment. In addition, injuries suffered by maintenance personnel when trying to gain access to equipment of all kinds can be addressed in this way. This must be followed through, as designers, engineers, the purchasing department and the health and safety personnel may not communicate frequently.

The most important element for workspaces, furniture, tools, machinery and other equipment is that they are 'fit-for-purpose' and are appropriately designed for the range of people who may use them. This means that users should be properly consulted before a specification or tender is prepared. If the range of options commercially available does not include the appropriate item it may need to be designed especially for the job.

Therefore, when the design is being formulated or furniture, tools or other pieces of equipment are being purchased, it/they must:

- Be appropriate for the job.
- Meet operator needs.
- Meet ergonomics requirements.
- Be easy to maintain.
- Have readily available spares and service.
- Meet cost requirements.

The process of selection and purchase should include:

- Consultation with users.
- Supply of catalogues and other product information including tests.
- Demonstrations on-site of how equipment should be used.
- Trial of options.
- Feedback to designers and manufacturers on design improvements.

EVALUATION

Evaluation of the way a system, furniture or equipment works in practice is one aspect which is often overlooked. Everybody involved needs active support and encouragement to undertake this. It is often difficult for people to revisit a solution and evaluate it objectively. Sometimes people responsible 'fall in love' with their solutions, or they move on to the next problem without truly analysing whether the last problem has been properly solved. In addition, it is likely that not all problems are identified in the initial stages. Informal feedback and consultation with employees and managers can be very effective in determining if and where residual problems exist.

The development of a model for the prevention of musculoskeletal injuries in the workplace: a case study

Christine Aickin

INTRODUCTION

In the developed world work-related musculoskeletal disorders are the commonest causes of workers' compensation claims, sick leave and early retirement (McPhee and Aickin, 1996). Work-related musculoskeletal injuries result in losses for individuals and organisations. The most obvious loss, and the most important one, is the suffering and damage to quality of life for individuals who sustain an injury. However, injuries also have a financial impact on both employee and employer, and the costs of these injuries are not usually fully calculated. For the employee there is the loss of earning capacity and the associated ramifications. For the employer there are not only the costs related to the injured employee, but also the roll-on effects in the organisation. Usually the workers' compensation and medical costs are calculated but this is often only a fraction of the total costs (McPhee and Aickin, 1996). Consideration should also be given to costs associated with production delays and interruptions, legal expenses, investigation time, equipment/tools/materials damage, and wages paid for time lost, replacement staff, overtime, clerical time etc. (Bird and Germain, 1982). In effect, there can be considerable loss to productivity, efficiency and quality as a result of a work-related musculoskeletal injury (McPhee and Aickin, 1996).

In the past attempts to prevent or reduce musculoskeletal injuries at work have been largely unsuccessful. The approaches which have failed include:

- Legislating the maximum weight to be lifted.
- Selecting strong people to do manual materials handling work.
- Training people to lift correctly.

They have been unsuccessful because they do not address the multifactorial nature of musculoskeletal disorders systematically.

In Australia, the Worksafe Australia National Standard for Manual Handling, its supporting Code of Practice (1990) and the National Code of Practice for the Prevention of Occupational Overuse Syndrome (1994) have attempted to redress the imbalance. Both codes have similar objectives including (McPhee and Aickin, 1996):

- Putting a focus on work, workplace and equipment design to control injury.

- Putting a focus on practicability by considering the feasibility of technical and cost options.
- Ensuring that multifactorial risk assessment is undertaken.
- Defining employer and employee duties.
- Determining solutions by effective consultation in the workplace.

This encourages the development of a systematic approach to the prevention of injuries.

This paper describes a model for a musculoskeletal injury prevention programme and describes the process of implementing the model, which is in line with the National Codes of Practice for Manual Handling and the Prevention of Occupational Overuse Syndrome at BOC Gases Australia Limited.

BACKGROUND

BOC Gases Australia Limited (BOC) is a company which employs approximately 2000 people in a number of operational and retail sites across Australia. It is primarily involved in the production, compression and distribution of industrial gases. The gas is stored in cylinders which are designed to withstand the high pressure of the gas they contain. Production processes involve a high degree of manual handling of cylinders including:

- Moving and storing cylinders.
- Connecting and disconnecting cylinder filling leads.
- Opening and closing cylinder valve handwheels.
- Stamping, painting and labelling cylinders.

Although handling techniques at BOC have improved significantly over the years with the introduction of palletisation, forklift trucks, adjustable height truck platforms, pneumatic torque wrenches, improved cylinder stamping techniques, ergonomically designed cylinder trolleys, drum handling equipment etc., there remain a number of manual handling issues to be addressed and resolved. Some issues cannot be addressed in the short term because the technology does not exist to do so, but others certainly can (Aickin and Morris, 1993).

BOC decided to address musculoskeletal injury prevention for three reasons. First, the company acknowledged that it is in a business that requires extensive manual handling of gas cylinders. A preliminary review of the injury and illness statistics revealed that a significant proportion of incidents were related to manual handling, and the company wanted to improve its occupational health and safety performance. Second, the introduction of manual handling regulations and codes of practice in Australia provided further impetus. Finally, although many advances in handling had been made within the company, it was acknowledged that a more systematic approach was required (Aickin and Morris, 1993).

Any approach, if it was to be implemented successfully, had to be integrated with the existing company initiatives. BOC was introducing the philosophy of the International Safety Rating System (Bird and Germain, 1992), total quality management and ISO 9001 at the time this programme was developed (Aickin and Morris, 1993).

METHOD

The model for the programme was developed first (Figure 6.1). It was designed to fit with the philosophy and requirements of the Worksafe Australia National Standard for Manual Handling, its Code of Practice and the Worksafe Australia National Code of Practice for the Prevention of Occupational Overuse Syndrome and to integrate with the existing organisational initiatives. It includes policy, standards, procedures and training material which define the responsibilities of, and provide the implementation tools for, employees in operational areas, employees with responsibility for work and workplace design, and those involved in materials management. It is an iterative model.

Programme development and implementation occurred next. Change management principles were followed to ensure that the development and implementation process was as successful as possible (Kuorinka and Forcier, 1995). The change management process was divided into six phases including:

- Management commitment.
- Development of the components of the programme.

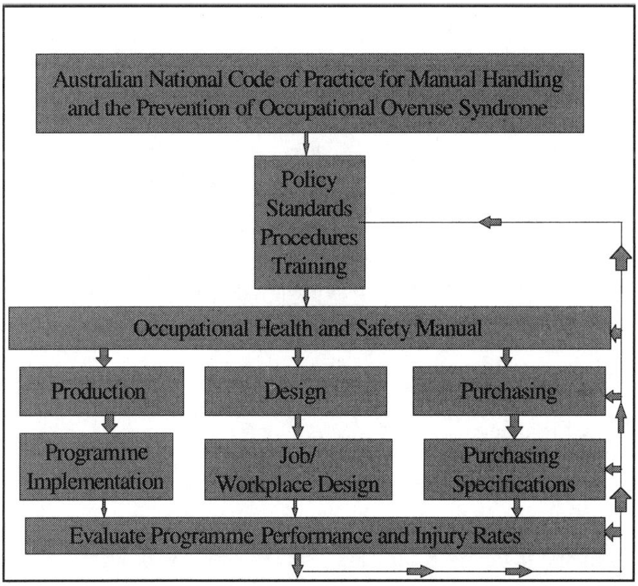

Figure 6.1 Model of the musculoskeletal injury prevention programme

- Allocation of responsibility for the programme.
- Planning programme implementation.
- Implementation.
- Evaluation and review.

What follows is a description of the activities involved in the six phases of the change management process.

Management commitment

It is important to ensure that the process is supported by top management and that management is fully aware of the resources involved in implementing the musculoskeletal injury prevention programme. There was already awareness at BOC that musculoskeletal injuries accounted for a high proportion of the company's injuries. There was also a culture of excellence and continuous improvement.

Top management support is achieved through a musculoskeletal injury prevention steering committee which is chaired by a director of the company, with technical support from the company ergonomist and senior engineering managers. The steering committee developed and works to the following terms of reference (Aickin and Morris, 1993):

- Overview and support the implementation of the BOC musculoskeletal injury prevention programme.
- Approve the initiation of new manual materials design projects.
- Allocate resources and accountability for the implementation of the BOC musculoskeletal injury prevention programme.

The steering committee set up a manual handling project team as a subcommittee. The role of the team is to complete engineering design projects which would reduce musculoskeletal injury risk at the major operational and retail sites. The team consisted of the following staff (Aickin and Morris, 1993):

- Manager of Occupational Health and Safety (ergonomist).
- Manager of New Technology (engineer).
- Project Engineer.
- Production Engineer.
- Appropriate employee representatives.

This team completed a number of design projects in the early stages of the development of the BOC musculoskeletal injury prevention programme. It was later disbanded when ergonomic design procedures were developed and implemented.

Development of the components of the programme

It is important to develop the musculoskeletal injury prevention programme components in line with existing company initiatives. Here these included quality, health and safety, human resources, finance and environmental programmes. The programme components include policy, standards, procedures, training materials and methods of programme evaluation and review. At BOC, there was already a comprehensive occupational health and safety programme. The programme requirements were defined within the occupational health and safety manual, which was part of the company quality programme. A description of the components of the programme follows.

Policy

The musculoskeletal injury prevention policy statement is integrated into the general occupational health and safety policy. It defines management commitment to consult with employees to identify, assess and control workplace hazards and to design plant, equipment, systems of work and the work environment with employees and end users in mind.

Performance standards

Musculoskeletal injury prevention performance standards provide guidance on what is to be done, how often it should be done, by whom and to what quality within the programme (Bird and Germain, 1992). They are included in the occupational health and safety manual and cover the requirements of all personnel including managers, designers, OHS staff, materials management staff, supervisors, team leaders, team members/employees and occupational health and safety committees/representatives.

The work required to implement the programme and continuously improve it is contained within the performance standards. They are graded from basic entry level to advanced level through ten grades. Employees involved in programme implementation are encouraged to begin at the basic entry grades, which provide the building blocks for the programme, and over time work through the programme requirements, until predetermined acceptable programme performance is reached. The speed at which a work site works through the programme is determined by the priorities of the business, the musculoskeletal injury risk and the musculoskeletal injury prevention knowledge within the personnel at the work site (Aickin and Morris, 1993). The standards also contain information which is useful in programme planning, measurement, training competency statements and employee performance review.

Procedures and training material

At BOC initially there was little knowledge of musculoskeletal injury prevention methods. To improve knowledge levels, implementation tools including procedures and training materials were developed, and appropriate personnel were trained in their use. The tools address identification of risks, assessment and control of risks, handling skills, ergonomic design procedures and purchasing procedures.

A 'train-the-trainer' training programme was developed. This is used to introduce the programme to different parts of the company and is run as a two-day course. The target audience is managers, engineers, OHS staff, team leaders/supervisors, employees/team members and union representatives. There is a requirement for all attendees to gain course accreditation. Accreditation involves showing proof of the ability to perform a musculoskeletal risk assessment of an identified hazard.

The train-the-trainer programme contains three separate modules:

1. Introduction to the musculoskeletal injury prevention programme and risk identification. This module covers an introduction to the legislative requirements and a practical risk identification workshop.
2. Risk assessment and risk control. This module covers risk assessment using a checklist and a team approach. This approach is defined in the National Codes of Practice for Manual Handling and Prevention of Occupational Overuse Syndrome (1990, 1994).
3. Skills training which is tailored to the specific requirements of BOC. This covers back care, lifting, handling, team lifting, specific handling skills and office ergonomics.

Employees who successfully complete the train-the-trainer programme can identify risks, run risk assessment sessions, develop ideas for controlling risk and provide skills training to assist their work site in implementing the programme.

Ergonomic design procedures have also been developed and designers are trained in their use. This ensures that workplace and job design occurring within the organisation takes into account human capability as well as production requirements. The contents of the ergonomic design procedures require specialist ergonomic skills for development and implementation, and include (Sullivan, 1992; Aickin et al., 1994; McPhee and Aickin, 1996):

- Gathering information which details risks in similar designs.
- Performing a functional analysis on the proposed process. This involves developing the flow of events and activities involved in the system performance.
- Developing alternative concepts for design. This involves lateral thinking to determining alternative designs. A mock-up (life-size or to scale) or a model may be developed to visualise the alternative concepts.
- Performing specific task analysis or task synthesis on the best design options.
- Performing detailed ergonomic assessment on the preferred design and improving the design using an iterative process.

Regard for human capability in the design of work and the workplace is also achieved through the purchasing function. Specifications are developed for materials and equipment purchased. These specifications take account of musculoskeletal injury prevention requirements, as well as production requirements (McPhee and Aickin, 1996).

Allocation of responsibilities for the programme

At BOC allocation of responsibility for implementing the programme is achieved through individual employees' position descriptions and setting specific, measurable objectives for employees (performance review requirements), as well as through action planning. Position description statements make general reference to responsibility for the occupational health and safety programme (Figure 6.2). More specific musculoskeletal injury prevention responsibilities are included in the performance review requirements (Figure 6.3). The performance standards provide suitable statements for this (McPhee and Aickin, 1996). Typical position description and performance review statements are prepared for business units to assist implementation.

Planning programme implementation

It is necessary to plan the implementation phase. At BOC this is done in line with organisational planning and includes both strategic and operational planning. Strategic planning required the definition of a vision, objectives, critical success factors and key performance indicators (McPhee and Aickin, 1996). Table 6.1 is a generic example of a strategic plan for musculoskeletal injury prevention.

Operational planning is more action oriented and is facilitated by the development of action plans for sites, areas and departments (Table 6.2) (McPhee and Aickin, 1996). It is important to monitor action plans continuously by upgrading them as progress is made.

Position:	Site Manager
Accountability:	Occupational Health and Safety
Definition:	Ensure effective implementation of Profit Centre Occupational Health and Safety Programme Measurement - Occupational Health and Safety operating plan, personal and site compliance with plan and statistical performance.

Figure 6.2 Position description example

Position:	Supervisor/Team Leader
Performance Objective:	Ensure that all musculoskeletal injuries in your area are investigated using the risk assessment method.

Figure 6.3 Performance review example

Table 6.1 Example of musculoskeletal injury prevention (MIP) programme strategic plan

Business objectives	Critical success factors	Key performance indicators	Milestones 1993	1994	1995	Action plans	Responsibility: Head office	Business unit	Vision achieved
1. To implement a MIP programme including work, workplace, equipment and product design and risk management	MIP programme implemented in all sites	Action plans developed on all sites	Approved	Continue as per plan	Implement (review)	Develop site action plans	HO	Co-ordinator	MIP implementation is 'part of the job'
						Develop department action plan		Co-ordinator/ department manager	Company leads in user-centred design of the work, workplace, equipment and products
	Incidence of injuries reduced in all locations	Total incident case rate (MI)	Determine baseline rate	Reduction 20%	Reduction 20%	Improvement of injury rate	HO	Co-ordinator	Total incident case rate (MI) is reduced by 50% cf. 1993
2. To integrate ergonomic design principles into design work and product and equipment design	Ergonomic principles integrated in new workplace designs, equipment and products as appropriate	Issue of ergonomic design manual	Timetable approved; draft manual issued; training tools prepared; designers use ergonomic tools	Continue as per timetable and use manual	Development of tools continued	Develop guidelines/ tools	HO	Project and OHS Dept	Company uses the concept of user-centred design
		Audit versus project plans				Develop training to assist implementation	HO	Engineering Services Manager/ OHS Dept	Leading company with regard to user-centred design of workplaces, equipment and products
						Pilot guidelines; refine guidelines	HO	Projects and OHS Dept	

Table 6.2 Example of a musculoskeletal injury prevention programme action plan

Action	Date and person involved
Nominate programme co-ordinator	January General manager
Run train-the-trainer course	March Human resources
Set timetable for train-the-trainer participants to obtain accreditation	March Programme co-ordinator
Perform risk assessment on all injuries as they occur	March Accredited train-the-trainers
Perform risk identification on previous injuries and identify and prioritise tasks for assessment	August Programme co-ordinator
Consult with all employees to identify and prioritise risks and add to task list for assessment	August Programme co-ordinator
Commence retrospective risk assessment	August and on-going Programme co-ordinator

Implementation

Once it is decided who is responsible for implementing the programme, it is important to assist these people in carrying out their duties. At BOC this is achieved through employee training and the support of the company ergonomist. Implementation is based on the materials contained in the standard procedures and training, which are available to each site.

At each major BOC site, a team approach is used to implement the programme as this is how the rest of the occupational health and safety programme is managed.

The team members are chosen because of their area of influence and their skills. In general, team members are supervisors or team leaders of areas with a high manual handling requirement, or employees with training expertise and occupational health and safety expertise. The majority of members of the team attend the 'train-the-trainer' course.

The aims of the team are to reduce the number of musculoskeletal injuries in the workplace by training, consultation and risk management. This is achieved by (Aickin and Morris, 1993):

- Development of an action plan for the implementation of the programme.
- Promotion of the identification of all musculoskeletal hazards.
- Management of the assessment of all musculoskeletal risk.
- Development of recommendations for the management of control measures.

- Provision of assistance to risk assessment teams.

The action plans become part of management, supervisory and team meeting agendas and this helps to achieve accountability and action.

Evaluation and review

Evaluation of the musculoskeletal injury prevention programme is difficult because the majority of musculoskeletal injuries develop slowly. In some cases harm may not be apparent for up to twenty years following the initial damage. Simply measuring outcomes such as injury and illness rates or severity rates does not give a true indication of the work being done to control musculoskeletal injury risks. These measures only show improvement in the longer term. It is important to measure programme implementation as it progresses.

At BOC methods of evaluating programme implementation, such as programme auditing, are used. The audit protocol reviews the programme using set questions, document review, interview and observation, and a level of programme implementation is determined. The audit is repeated at set time intervals. Other positive evaluation methods include the identification of factors which are critical for the success of the programme and a method of measuring these factors. The benefit of measuring indicators of work being done is the ability to identify areas of the programme which require improvement and then to measure these improvements over time (McPhee and Aickin, 1996).

At predetermined intervals evaluation of programme progress is undertaken. This evaluation information is used to review the strategic and operational planning process and to refine the components of the programme. The evaluation provides information which ensures that the programme is targeted at identified areas of high risk and that trends are identified over time. This encourages continuous improvement of both the musculoskeletal injury prevention programme and the performance of the organisation with regard to musculoskeletal injuries over time (McPhee and Aickin, 1996).

CONCLUSIONS

This programme has now been in place at BOC with a continuous improvement approach since 1990. During that time there have been a number of successful design projects to reduce or eliminate manual materials handling. Work also continues to assess and control manual handling risk following identification of manual materials handling hazards. Training employees in risk identification and handling skills occurs at commencement of employment and intervals during service. During this time, anecdotal evidence indicates that knowledge of musculoskeletal risk management is improving within the company at all levels. Programme evaluation has led to improvements in standards, procedures and training. After four years of programme implementation a decline in musculoskeletal injuries began to occur.

ACKNOWLEDGEMENTS

The author would like to thank Shelton Smith, Robert Clarke, Mike Rollings, Richard Rawling, Russel Skilleter, Andy Hoh, Professor John Wilson, Aileen Sullivan, Phil Morris, Rod Kitchen, Sue Rowe, Shirley Wong and Judy Hollier for their input to and support of the development of the programme, and Marion McLean and Dr Maurice Oxenburgh for their critical review of this manuscript and their constructive comments.

References

Aickin, C. and Morris, P. (1993). Development and implementation of the CIG manual handling programme – head office and branch perspective. In *Proceedings of 29th Ergonomics Society of Australia Conference*, Perth, pp.160–165.

Aickin, C., Rollings, M. and Wilson, J. (1994). Providing a foundation for ergonomics: systematic ergonomics in engineering design (SEED). In *Proceedings of International Ergonomics Association Conference*, Toronto.

Bird, F.E. and Germain, G.L. (1992). *Loss Control Management: Practical Loss Control Leadership*. International Loss Control Institute.

Kuorinka, I. and Forcier, L. (1995). Managing change. In *Work Related Musculoskeletal Disorders (WMSDs): A Reference Book for Prevention*, pp. 271–297. Taylor and Francis.

McPhee, B. and Aickin, C. (1996). Manual handling. In *Workplace Health and Safety Manual*, pp. 31-000–31-085. CCH.

Sullivan, A.M. (1992). Part 1. Human factors in the engineering design process. In *Proceedings of 25th Annual Conference of the Human Factors Association of Canada*, pp. 239–245.

Worksafe Australia (1994). *National Code of Practice for the Prevention of Occupational Overuse Syndrome.*

Worksafe Australia (1990). *National Standard for Manual Handling and National Code of Practice for Manual Handling.*

Sprains and strains reduction programme

Heather Dale

INTRODUCTION

There is a need to focus on the prevention of workplace injuries in order to reduce pain and suffering as well as the financial burden that accompanies these injuries. Australia has up to 100,000 cases of occupational back injuries a year. Forty-five per cent of these cases involve five or more days off work and 10 per cent result in periods of up to six months lost time from work.

Compensation costs alone are $22 million and total costs to industry and the community are several times greater. Most back injuries are due to poor workplace design and work practices, and inadequate training, which means they can be avoided (Workplace Health and Safety, 1996).

In 1997, there were 17,624 WorkCover Queensland claims for back injuries. These resulted in claims costs, including damages claims, of over $26 million. Sprains and strains of the back accounted for over $24 million (statistics received from the Management Information Branch, WorkCover Queensland, 1998).

The most successful approach to reduce these statistics is that of risk management. This systematically aims to design out the range of possible causes of sprains and strains and involves all of the workforce. This system complies with Section 22 of the Workplace Health and Safety Act, 1995.

STATISTICAL ANALYSIS

As part of a large metal refinery's safety improvement plan for 1997/98, an analysis of incident and injury statistics for 1997 was conducted. Figures 6.4–6.6 and Tables 6.3 and 6.4 show some of the relevant data. It was considered unlikely that the rate of injury would be reduced by traditional approaches which concentrated on correct lifting techniques and saw the weight of the load as the only source of danger.

While back sprains and strains were not the most common injury for this company, they are the most costly in terms of WorkCover Queensland Australia claims costs and lost time. Therefore the sprains and strains reduction programme focused on the prevention of back injuries while not excluding sprains and strains of other parts of the body. Details of the results of the analysis of the 1997 incident statistics are contained in this paper. The most frequently injured body parts were the hands and fingers. The highest number of incidents occurred in the tankhouse. The most frequent mechanism of injury was being hit by moving objects. The mechanisms of trips and slips, repetitive movements and other

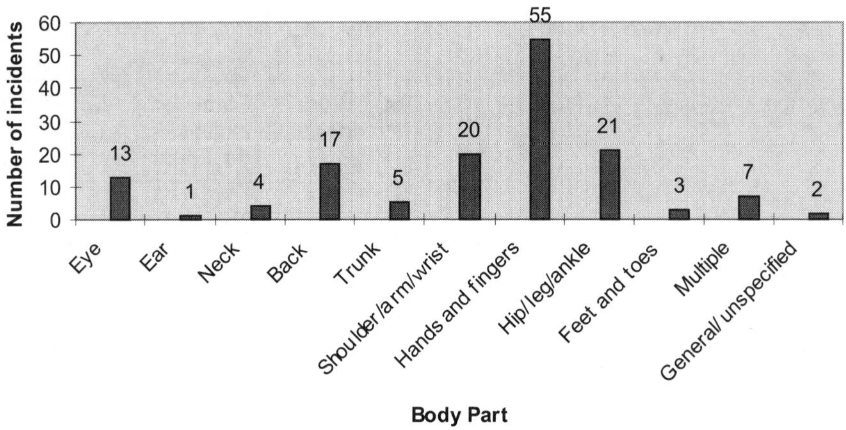

Figure 6.4 Number of incidents by body part

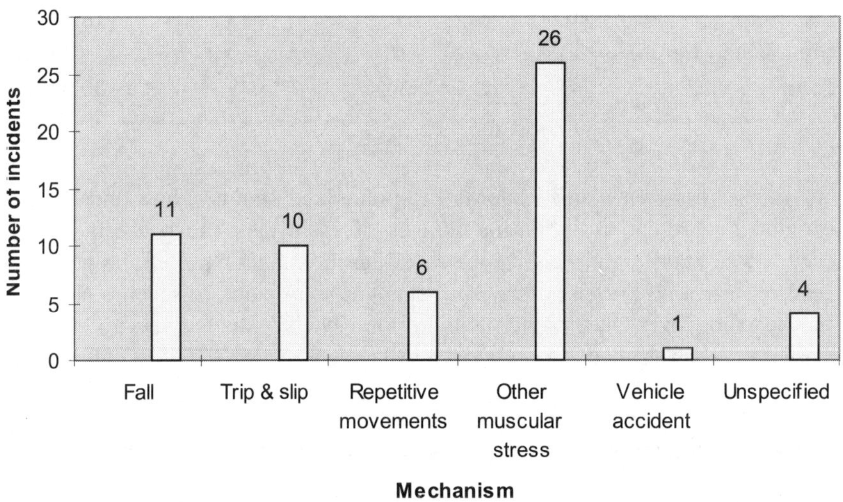

Figure 6.5 Number of incidents by various mechanisms

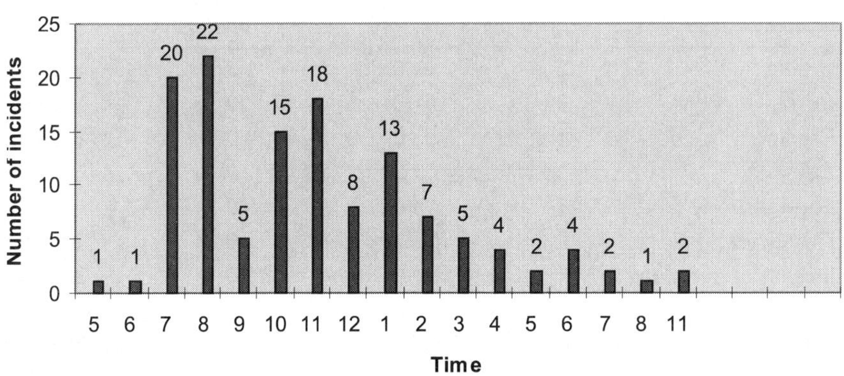

Figure 6.6 Number of incidents by time of day

Table 6.3 WorkCover Queensland statutory claims for the 1997 calendar year

Nature of injury	Number of claims	Total work days lost	Total excess days lost	Total cost ($)
Bruise	3	0	2	651.62
Burns	3	0	0	202.08
Concussion	1	0	0	0
Crush	1	0	0	0
Cut	6	0	2	302.94
Foreign body	2	0	2	115.02
Fracture	1	0	0	670.75
Industrial deafness	11	0	0	9597.48
Laceration	2	0	0	160.14
Strain/sprain	16	67	13	18,863.78
Unspecified nature	1	0	0	115.37
Total	47	67	19	30,679.18

muscular stress created the majority of sprains and strains. These mechanisms combined represent a significant number of incidents. The peak in incident occurrences at seven and eight o'clock in the morning supported the perceived need for warm-up exercises. Day shift starts at six o'clock or seven o'clock.

The WorkCover Queensland premium for 1996/97 was $204,922.52. One of these claims has resulted in a common law (damages) action. The cost of this action

Table 6.4 WorkCover Queensland statutory claims for the 1998 calendar year

Nature of injury	Number of claims	Total work days lost	Total excess days lost	Total cost ($)
Bruise	2	0	2	94.79
Burns	2	0	0	31.94
Crush	1	0	0	99.40
Cut	1	0	0	31.49
Foreign body	1	0	0	131.70
Fracture	2	2	6	1557.02
Industrial deafness	4	0	0	3311.49
Laceration	1	2	4	366.69
Strain/sprain	16	13	18	7614.99
Total	30	17	30	13,239.31

will be reflected in future premiums. WorkCover Queensland claims costs are now reflected in the employer's premium for the three subsequent years. Damages claims costs are then reflected in the employer's premium for the next two years. This company returns workers to work as early as is safely possible. It is therefore vital to reduce the occurrence of injuries in order to reduce the premium.

AIMS AND OBJECTIVES OF THE PROGRAMME

The aim of the programme was to identify the high risk tasks with regard to musculoskeletal sprains and strains and then to assess these tasks and recommend control measures. By doing this, it was expected that the incidence and severity of musculoskeletal sprains and strains at the workplace would be reduced. The workforce was provided with the theoretical knowledge and practical skills necessary for the prevention of strains and sprains. Workers were given the opportunity to reduce their own risk of back injury.

On successful completion of this programme the workforce would be able to assess the risk of a task and identify and implement methods of risk control. They would understand and be able to utilise basic back care and manual handling techniques.

DURATION OF THE PROGRAMME

The programme was expected to take twelve months to implement, with an evaluation at the end of each month and on completion of the programme. Expansion in the tankhouse has meant that there was further work to be done in that area. This related largely to the new machines.

PARTICIPANTS AND FACILITATION

The total workforce was involved in the programme. The programme had a theory component and practical application. Learning was facilitated through group presentation, discussion, practical demonstration, active participation and involvement.

CONTENT OF THE SPRAINS AND STRAINS REDUCTION PROGRAMME

Group training of supervisors in risk assessment

This consisted of a two hour session to enable supervisors to facilitate discussion with their workers. High risk routine tasks with regard to sprains and strains could then be determined. They were provided with the knowledge to determine the risk of sprains and strains in routine and non-routine tasks. National, state and company injury statistics, including the incidence and cost of back injuries, were also included to emphasise the need for the sprains and strains reduction programme.

The structure and function of the discs, joints, muscles, ligaments and vertebrae were included. This provided the foundation on which to build the relationship between the various structures, posture, fitness and manual handling principles. The nature and early detection of back pain and injury were discussed. Correct posture was defined and demonstrated. The importance of maintaining correct posture and the relationship between correct posture and manual handling were included. Strategies for maintaining correct posture were outlined. Spinal stability and muscular control, plus the importance of exercise and fitness were covered.

The definition and principles of manual handling were discussed. Risk assessment in accordance with the Code of Practice on Manual Handling was given. The assessment and control of identified risks were outlined and the supervisors were trained in the use of the risk assessment checklist and instructed in ergonomic and environmental considerations. An attendance record was signed by each participant and maintained as a future record of attendance.

Risk identification

Supervisors then facilitated their work group's participation in the determination of high risk routine tasks. This took the form of safety meetings and assistance was provided on request. High risk tasks were also determined from previous assessments, the experience of the workplace health and safety officer and by observing work practices. Completion of a checklist for each high risk task was done by the supervisors in consultation with the workers. A total of sixty-five high risk tasks were identified.

Risk assessment including work analysis

Each of these high risk tasks was assessed in consultation with supervisors and workers. Quantitative assessment using ergonomic assessment tools, such as the Ovako Working Posture Analyzing System (OWAS) (Karhu, Kansi and Kuorinka, 1977) and the Rapid Upper Limb Assessment (RULA) (McAtamney and Corlett, 1993), as well as observation, discussion and photography were used. The frequency and repetitions were also noted.

OWAS determines the risk of a working posture on a scale of one to four. The range is from 'no action required' to 'immediate action required'. It is particularly useful in assessing the risk of back and leg injuries. The score is calculated from the analysis of the position of the back, arms and legs, as well as the force required. RULA likewise determines the risk on a similar scale from one to four. Its application is in the assessment of the risk of neck and arm injuries. This score is calculated from an analysis of the position of the shoulders, lower arms, wrist, neck and trunk, plus muscle action and the force required. Of the sixty-five identified high risk tasks, twenty-seven were assessed as having a score of four according to OWAS. Twelve had a score of three according to OWAS. Seven had a score of four on the RULA scale and thirteen scored three on RULA. Hence, over 50 per cent of the identified high risk tasks had a score of three or four on OWAS, while almost 33 per cent had a score of three or four on RULA. This represents a high level of risk with respect to sprains and strains at this workplace.

Implementation of control measures

This was determined by the risk assessment process and in accordance with the hierarchy of control and so included elimination, substitution, engineering and administration measures. This commenced with a feedback session, with each supervisor and the Manager of Safety, Health and Environment, to outline the recommended risk control options for each of the identified high risk tasks. Following this discussion, a copy of the work analysis and risk control options was provided for the supervisor and the Manager of Safety, Health and Environment. The supervisor was then responsible for implementing control measures. An update on the progress of implementation of risk control measures was requested for six weeks after the feedback session.

Elimination of high risk tasks was achieved by changing work practices so that the task was no longer performed. In some cases, new machinery resulted in the elimination of high risk tasks. Substitution was also utilised to reduce the risk of a task. Examples include the purchase of trolleys and replacement of rollers to facilitate the transport of manufactured items. Engineering controls consisted of the supply of equipment such as drum tippers. This reduced the risk of sprains and strains as the task was then performed at a more suitable height and with easier access to the substance in the drum. Administrative controls have included the rotation of workers performing high risk tasks. Also, the frequency of the task was sometimes increased in order to reduce the load. For example, the weight of bucket loads was reduced by increasing the frequency with which the bucket was emptied.

Manual handling training was included as one method of controlling the risk of sprains and strains. A risk management and competency based approach was used during training. Strategies used included the video recording of workers performing high risk routine tasks. This was then replayed to reinforce suitable techniques and to correct unsuitable techniques. This feedback process was well received by workers and a significant number stated that they altered their work practices following the training sessions.

Back care bulletins were issued periodically to maintain awareness of back care amongst workers. A ‘Safety at Home’ pamphlet was used to facilitate a flow on from back care at work to back care at home. This was in line with the cumulative trauma process of back injury and its prevention.

ADDITIONAL OPTIONAL COMPONENTS OF THE PROGRAMME

Warm-up exercise programmes

These were introduced in one work area with limited success. Subsequently, in manual handling training sessions, each worker was given a handout on warm-up exercises.

'Reduce the risk' back assessment

This was developed in conjunction with the treating physiotherapists at North Queensland Physiotherapy Centre as a result of the limited success of the warm-up exercise programme. It was made available to workers on a voluntary basis and consisted of an initial assessment with reviews.

EVALUATION OF THE PROGRAMME

The purpose of ongoing evaluation was to ensure that the programme was progressing through the various stages and to identify and overcome barriers that may have hindered the process. A review and brief report was completed each month. This took the form of a summary of the month's activities of the programme, the outcomes and any programme modifications that were required. This report was presented to management.

Formal evaluation took place at the completion of the programme. This included a summary of the sprains and strains programme, its outcomes in terms of risk control measures, statistics for each department, obstacles to the programme and recommendations. This report was also presented to management.

Of the total of sixty-five identified high risk tasks, eighteen have been, or are being, eliminated. Of these, ten had an OWAS score of four and one had an OWAS score of three. One had a RULA score of four and one had a RULA score of three. Thirteen tasks with an OWAS score of four have had the risk of the task reduced while nine with an OWAS score of three have had the risk reduced. Five tasks with a RULA score of four have had the risk reduced and ten tasks with a RULA score of three have had the risk reduced. This represents a significant reduction in the risk of sprains and strains at this workplace.

There was a 33 per cent decrease in the total incidents for 1998 compared with 1997. Of these, there was a 25 per cent decrease in the incidence of sprains and strains at this workplace. The details of the WorkCover Queensland claims during 1998 are discussed below. A decrease in the WorkCover Queensland premium resulted.

CONCLUSIONS AND RECOMMENDATIONS

The sprains and strains reduction programme represents comprehensive management of the risk of injury at the workplace. The focus of the programme has been the involvement of all at the workplace. Sixty-five high risk tasks were analysed and risk control options were recommended. These were outlined according to the recognised hierarchy of control. Many of the risk control measures have been implemented and there is further work planned to reduce the risk of sprains and strains. There has been a significant reduction in sprains and strains incidents and a marked decrease in the number and duration of WorkCover Queensland claims for the 1998 calendar year. The challenge now is to maintain or further reduce these statistics. With an ageing workforce, this challenge is considerable. Most of the back injury claims resulted from routine manual handling tasks. Some follow-up work remains to be done, particularly in the tankhouse. It is recommended that ongoing work be done as risks are identified. This is in line with the philosophy of continuous improvement. Further manual handling training is planned with an increased emphasis on practical application and achievement of desirable competency levels. Practical sessions will again focus on regular tasks in that particular section.

The programme has enjoyed co-operation throughout the plant. Workers have readily discussed their tasks and possible control measures. Due to their knowledge of the principles of workplace health and safety, supervisors have been in tune with the process followed. The superintendents and managers have given their support. This co-operation, participation and support from across the plant was essential for the successful reduction in the risk of sprains and strains at this workplace.

OTHER APPLICATIONS

This programme has been, or is being, implemented at four other workplaces. It has been successful in each case with regards to reducing the incidence of sprains and strains at the workplace.

The process followed in this programme could be utilised to reduce other workplace injuries, for example injuries to hands or eyes. The process of analysing statistics, identifying risks, assessing those risks and implementing risk control measures, and then evaluating the control measures, can be implemented to reduce a range of injuries at a workplace.

ACKNOWLEDGEMENT

The author wishes to acknowledge the direction given by Joe Millard in the formulation and supervision of this programme.

References

Division of Workplace Health and Safety (1996). *Back Care at Work*. Government Printer, Brisbane.

Karhu, O., Kansi, P. and Kuorinka, I. (1977). Correcting working postures in industry: A practical method of analysis. *Applied Ergonomics*, **8** (4), 199–201.

McAtamney, L. and Corlett, E.N. (1993). RULA: a survey method for the investigation of work-related upper limb disorders. *Applied Ergonomics*, **24** (2), 91–99.

WorkCover Queensland (1997). Back injury statistics: Management Information Branch, Brisbane.

Preventing work-related back pain

Leon M. Straker

INTRODUCTION

Work-related back pain is the single largest occupational health issue in most jurisdictions, probably accounting for around one quarter of all occupational health costs (see Chapter 11, pp. 255–260).

Governments, private organisations and individuals have invested considerable resources implementing interventions aimed at the primary prevention of work-related back pain. Given this expenditure of resources over a number of decades it would be reasonable to expect that there now exists a reasonable body of evidence on the efficacy of these interventions.

The magnitude of the problem, in terms of the personal, organisational and community costs associated with work-related back pain, also suggests the need for evidence on the efficacy of preventive interventions. Further, the relatively poor efficacy of treatment of work-related back pain similarly argues the importance of knowing and implementing effective preventive interventions.

This raises the question: 'Does adequate evidence exist to judge the efficacy of common interventions used to prevent work-related back pain?' If adequate evidence does exist then a supplementary question is: 'Which interventions have evidence of efficacy sufficient to warrant implementation?'.

The internationally favoured approach to preventing work-related back pain involves the four steps of hazard identification, risk assessment, risk control and follow-up evaluation (Straker, 1997). However, the research literature on interventions rarely uses this language and is more likely to talk about an intervention such as an education programme.The question therefore arises: 'How do the interventions discussed in research literature relate to the favoured approach for preventing work-related back pain?'.

The aim of this paper is therefore to provide some insight into how common interventions relate to the favoured approach and what level of evidence exists for common interventions.

APPROACH

There appears to be widespread acceptance that the hazard identification, risk assessment, risk control and follow-up evaluation approach is appropriate for preventing work-related back pain. After a decade of literature searching and reading by the author, no thorough critique of this approach has been found.

The approach is copied from general risk assessment work which has been well used in other occupational health areas such as chemical exposure. However, possible problems with this approach are identifiable and relate to approach assumptions.

The approach assumes hazards can be identified. Superficially this may appear fairly easy for work-related back pain. Hazards commonly reported include work factors such as manual handling, sitting and whole body vibration. However, should hazards also include worker factors such as height, weight, age, fitness, personality, musculoskeletal degeneration and injury history? Further, should hazards include work–worker interaction factors such as postures assumed and movement strategies selected?

Ignoring the issue of whether worker and work–worker interaction factors should be considered as hazards, the list of work factors includes just about every activity performed in occupational contexts. Therefore, rather than having a few chemicals identified as hazards, the whole job (and non-occupational activities for that matter) is a hazard. This tends to make a mockery of this stage of the process, as so much of a job has to be included as a possible hazard. In reality the stage usually involves the identification of those hazards thought to be most significant, i.e. prioritisation of hazards. However, our understanding of how important various hazards are is based mainly on epidemiological evidence, which is very limited in its precision and its account of interaction between possible hazards.

A further major assumption of this approach is that permissible levels can be determined. The risk assessment stage involves collection of information and comparison of this information with some threshold deemed to be acceptable (Straker, 1997).

Our current understanding of thresholds is very crude and very tentative. For example, perhaps the most widely used threshold is lumbar spine compression force of around 3000–3500 N. This figure is related to the end-plate compression strength of a fairly small number of cadaveric spinal segments exposed to mainly a single, slow velocity force. The validity of this threshold is highly questionable (Straker, 1997). Single, peak force application may not be the important aetiological mechanism. We may need a broader assessment of biomechanical loading that includes not only the peak force but also the average, the integral and the variance – given what we know about how tissues respond to force. More recent research has tried to address some of these issues by looking at cumulative loading and loading on individual spinal structures.

Our current thresholds for permissible risk are therefore imprecise and tentative. Thus, although this approach is widely used, it should be questioned.

INTERVENTIONS

Three interventions are commonly used to try to prevent work-related back pain:

- Selecting workers unlikely to report work-related back pain.
- Training workers to reduce their report of work-related back pain.
- Redesigning workplaces to reduce the reports of work-related back pain.

Table 6.5 Relationship of interventions and risk assessment process

	Hazard identification	**Risk assessment**	**Risk control**	**Follow-up**
Selection	Worker weakness, fitness, history, attitude ...	Measure strength, fitness, history, attitude ...	Employ only strong, fit, uninjured, positive affect ...	Remeasure strength etc. post employment
Training	Worker weakness, fitness, attitude, skill ...	? Measure (or assume) strength, fitness, attitude skill ...	Train to increase worker strength, fitness, attitude skill ...	Remeasure strength etc. post training
Design	Task load, postural constraints	Measure lumbar stresses, duration in certain postures, whole body physiological costs, ratings of exertion ...	Reduce (?) task load, change postural constraints ...	Remeasure lumbar stresses etc. post work changes

(The ambiguity as to whether workers actually get less pain or just report less pain is intentional to highlight the ambiguity with respect to reasons for interventions and outcome measures.)

How these interventions relate to the risk assessment process is suggested in Table 6.5. Whilst this relationship is rarely discussed, it is important to understand how implementation of interventions can fit within the risk assessment process. From the suggested relationship shown in Table 6.5, it can be seen that selection and training options tend to focus on changing the worker, whilst design tends to focus on changing the work. It can also be seen that each intervention has the option of using short term changes in risk measures as well as longer term outcome measures such as work-related injuries (Straker, in press b) (Figure 6.7). However, follow-up evaluation of these interventions has rarely been reported in peer-reviewed literature.

Although these three headings are commonly used to describe intervention options, the range of interventions are a little more complex than the headings suggest.

Whilst the Selection option is a single option (although various characteristics have been used to select workers), within the Training and Design options there are several interventions. Training programmes have been reported which:

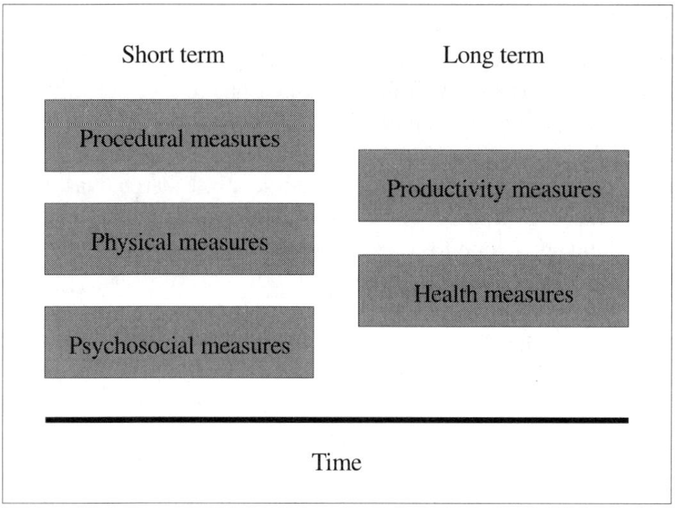

Figure 6.7 Factors involved in preventing work-related back pain

1. Address manual handling skill or some other postural habit such as how to sit.
2. Address healthy/unhealthy lifestyle factors such as stress management and smoking.
3. Address physical fitness specifically through exercise.
4. Address worker skills in making changes to their own workplace.

Two Design intervention options are reported:

- Design changes based on expert advice.
- Design changes based on a participative group approach.

There is also some overlap between interventions; for example, design changes based on a participative group approach require training of workers in the skills involved in making changes in their own workplace. Other interventions do not sit neatly within these headings; for example, should protective equipment such as back belts be considered a design intervention or a worker intervention? Further confusing the evidence, many reports of interventions include several interventions made simultaneously on the same group of workers, making the effect of single interventions unable to be detected.

This paper has so far tried to provide some insight into how common interventions relate to the favoured approach. The remainder of the paper will provide some insight into what level of evidence exists for the efficacy of common interventions.

INTERVENTION EFFICACY

Literature was searched using electronic abstracting systems (Medline, OSHROM and Ergonomics Abstracts) with the keywords back pain, prevention, selection, training, ergonomics and manual handling. The focus for selection of papers was recent papers describing original research evaluating the efficacy of interventions on primary prevention of back pain. Additional research was located using ancestry (references within papers).

Some evidence was found for six interventions: selection, education, exercise training, work design by experts, participative work design and back belts.

Back belts have been the focus of considerable research in the last decade, perhaps because of the ease of implementation. The studies on back belts have also tended to be of better design (perhaps due to recent increased awareness of the importance of randomised controlled trials, and again the ease of implementation). These studies have been reviewed on several occasions (for example McGill, 1999) and will not be further considered here.

A number of reviews on the other interventions have also been completed recently. Some of these are quite useful, although they have usually focused on treatment or mixed treatment and primary prevention intervention (Frank et al., 1996; Karas and Conrad, 1996; Kaplansky et al., 1998; Lahad et al., 1994; van Poppel et al., 1997).

This paper will not provide a review of all the evidence of intervention efficacy for the primary prevention of back pain. Rather, by describing some key papers for each intervention, it attempts to provide an understanding of the evidence and some of the difficulties in establishing appropriate evidence.

SUMMARY OF KEY PAPERS

To illustrate the state of knowledge on the prevention of work-related back pain several key papers reporting original research on common interventions are reviewed. Two papers were selected for each intervention: the one providing the best recent evidence (in the opinion of the author) and a further significant paper. The design, intervention and outcomes of each paper are summarised and some comments provided. Comments have concentrated on the broader issues rather than a detailed critique of the particular study, as the aim is to provide insight into the nature of the evidence available. A couple of reports on multiple facet interventions are worth noting (Marks, 1997; Shi, 1993).

Selection

The search was unable to locate a report on a randomised controlled trial evaluating use of the selection intervention to reduce work-related back pain. The majority of studies have used weaker cross-sectional designs and few have actually set out to evaluate the effectiveness of selection. However, the study by Reimer et al. (1994) used a stronger, longitudinal, though retrospective and uncontrolled, design to assess the effect of selection. The study by Smedley et al.

(1997), whilst not actually evaluating the effect of selection, is representative of most of the research used to support this intervention.

Paper: Reimer, S., Halbrook, B., Dreyfuss, P. and Tibiletti, C. (1994). A novel approach to pre-employment workbee fitness evaluations in a material-handling industry.

Design

A longitudinal study of warehouse workers in a grocery distribution centre in the USA is reported in this paper. The warehouse employed around 150 people to collect grocery orders from shelves on to pallets. Retrospective data on low back injuries was collected for one year prior to intervention and then two years with intervention.

Intervention

All prospective employees were measured on fifteen isokinetic trunk function measures and on two dynamic lifting tasks. Some attempt was made to relate these to specific job requirements. Performance thresholds were set, based on a sample of current, uninjured workers with at least three months experience (using the sixteenth percentile). For employment, fifteen of the seventeen thresholds needed to be exceeded. Evidently there was quite high worker turnover as they tested an average of 300 per year for a workforce of less than 150.

Outcomes

A decrease in reported low back injuries of 32 per cent was claimed in the first year, with a further 9 per cent reduction in the second year of intervention.

Comments

Whilst hardly novel, this study is a good attempt at trying to provide evidence for the effectiveness of selection in primary prevention of back pain. The study context was very suitable, with a reasonable number of workers doing a fairly constrained number of tasks (nearly continual manual handling of groceries). The duration of the study was only just adequate, and the lack of earlier data is disappointing, as year to year fluctuations in injury reports is common (although the company is reported as saying the data used were representative).

Some important aspects affecting the validity of the study include the high worker turnover, the move by the organisation to self-insure in the second year of intervention and the use of isokinetic trunk function tests (perhaps better than isometric but still not real-world motion). (A minor annoyance with this paper is that SI units were not used – but this should have been dealt with by the journal.)

Perhaps the most significant limitation is the lack of a control group. The paper reports on a 'control group' but it was actually just a sample of workers used to establish a threshold for test performance and not really an outcome comparison group.

Therefore, whilst a very significant effect was recorded, without a control group it is unclear what caused the effect. The paper thus provides some hope, but not sufficient evidence.

Paper: Smedley, J., Egger, P., Coope, C. and Coggon, D. (1997). Prospective cohort study of predictors of incident low back pain in nurses.

Design

This paper reports on a prospective study on 961 nurses in the National Health Service in the UK. The nurses were a sub-sample from a baseline questionnaire and selected on the basis of willingness to participate and no back pain for the last month. Nurses were sent questionnaires every quarter for two years.

Intervention

The researchers did not implement any interventions; rather they tried to identify personal (age, weight, height, mood, history of back problems) and occupational factors (patient handling tasks) related to higher risk of back pain and absence from work related to back pain.

Outcomes

No significant relationship was found between age or weight and back pain. Taller nurses had a slightly higher odds ratio (1.7). History of back pain was strongly related with the odds ratio, increasing from around 2 for short duration pain more than one year ago to around 6 for pain lasting more than one month in the last year. Odds ratios for frequent patient handling for various tasks were typically around 1.5.

Comments

This study is indicative of a number of well-constructed studies which have used epidemiological methods to identify factors which could be used for selection. The design was strong, in being prospective and just nurses without back pain in the month prior to the study starting. Weaknesses in the study included only 30 per cent of the nurses remaining in the study the full two years, only females being included and, more importantly, weak exposure measures being used. Work hazard exposure was quantified by nurse self-report in a questionnaire. Patient handling hazards were only identified at a task level rather than a technique level, yet risk measures are known to vary widely depending on technique. No non-patient handling work hazards are reported.

Selection summary

There is insufficient evidence available to determine whether selection can be effective in primary prevention of work-related low back pain. A level of hope is supported by some factors being identified in many studies (for example prior history of back pain), but use of these factors is likely to have the potential to eliminate only a small proportion of cases (Smedley et al., 1997).

Education

In contrast to selection, the education intervention for primary prevention has been evaluated in several randomised and non-randomised controlled trials. In addition, education is a large component of the back school intervention widely used for treatment. Reddell et al. (1992) and Walsh and Schwartz (1990) conducted randomised controlled trials but only used a single one hour intervention. The lack of demonstrated effect could therefore be due to inadequate intervention. In contrast, the intervention used by Daltroy et al.'s (1993, 1997) randomised controlled trial appears to have given this intervention a reasonable chance of effect. Whilst Daltroy and colleagues' study is arguably the best evaluation, it provides little positive evidence for the use of education. Versloot et al.'s (1992) study provides some hope of usefulness. Three studies on patient handlers are also of note: Feldstein et al. (1993); Lagerstrom and Hagberg (1997); Videman et al. (1989).

Paper: Versloot, J.M., Rozeman, A., van Son, A.M. and van Akkerveeken, P.F. (1992). The cost effectiveness of a back school programme in industry.

Design

This study was a case control longitudinal study using two convenience groups within a Dutch bus company. The intervention group was 200 randomly selected bus drivers from the south region, whilst the control group was 300 randomly selected bus drivers from the north region. Baseline data was collected on the two years before intervention, with the same data collected during the two years of intervention and for a further two years post intervention.

Intervention

The intervention consisted of education only, with three sessions provided at six-monthly intervals. Groups of twelve to fourteen drivers attended the sessions. Only 108 of the 200 drivers attended all three sessions. Session 1 lasted three hours and covered general responsibility for health, stress and coping, body mechanics, sports, working posture, seat adjustment, and advice to walk between drives. Sessions 2 and 3 lasted one and a half hours and were a revision of session 1.

Outcomes

Comparison groups were not equal on some significant factors such as years of employment and perception of strenuousness of work. Covariance analysis was used to allow for these differences.

The main outcome measure used was absenteeism from all reasons. There was no change in absenteeism incidence. There was a decrease in the duration of absenteeism in the intervention group of around six days per person per year.

The authors also attempted simple cost–benefit modelling using the change in absenteeism duration (benefit of $800 per person per year) and the programme costs and lost work time ($230 per person per year), to show a benefit of around $600 per person per year.

Comments

The study used reasonable numbers for a sensible duration, a reasonable intervention and a good idea to provide a comparison group. The decrease in absenteeism may well have been due to the intervention, providing some hope for education to be an effective intervention.

The main weakness in the study is the weak outcome measure used. No rationale is provided for why a measure more specifically related to back pain was not used. Further, the paper gives the impression that the authors hunted for a positive effect, re-analysing the information until a significant effect was found.

Paper: Daltroy, L.H., Iversen, M.D., Larso, M.G. et al. (1997). A controlled trial of an educational programme to prevent low back injuries.

Design

This study was a large randomised and controlled trial involving some 4000 postal workers at two mail processing facilities in the USA for five and a half years. Thirty-four work units (supervisor and a shift of workers) were arranged into seventeen pairs matched for worker category and type of work. One unit from each pair was randomly allocated to the intervention.

Intervention

The intervention work units received two one and a half hour classroom sessions one week apart on biomechanics of the back, causes of back pain, proper lifting techniques, exercises for relaxation and fitness, and brief general healthy lifestyle instruction. Supervisors also received additional training in supervisor-only sessions on how to recognise unsafe lifting and reinforce safe lifting. Physiotherapists also visited each work unit to observe lifting practices and unsafe practices were addressed at work unit safety meetings. Additional reinforcement training was provided after six months and then annually. Suggestions were also made for physical and procedural changes such as adjustment of shelf heights, use of lumbar supports on chairs, installation of rollers on chairs and changes to machine pacing.

All workers received a standard back injury prevention film on starting, as well as periodic safety talks at the supervisor's discretion.

Outcomes

An interim sub-sample study found increased knowledge scores in the intervention group but also found decreased scores on ratings of supervisor and worker help and reinforcement and no effect on reported back tiredness.

No differences were found with intervention for rate of primary back injury, time off work per injury and cost of injury.

Comments

This is a very impressive study in terms of having good design, good subject numbers, good study duration and good education intervention. It is therefore quite sobering to see that the results provide little evidence for the effectiveness of education as an intervention for primary prevention of back pain.

There are some weakness in the study which may account for the lack of effect (other than that education had no effect). Cross-contamination of work changes and knowledge presumably occurred during the study, as some 20 per cent of the control group were trained by the end of the study (due to worker transfers between units). The authors also acknowledge that social support expectations and expectations of reasonable working conditions may have negatively influenced the intervention group results.

Education summary

Whilst there is more evidence available for education than for selection, the available evidence is still insufficient to judge the efficacy of education. A best guess is that the effect of education in the primary prevention of work-related back pain is likely to be quite small. Further, its mechanisms of effect are quite complex, making it difficult to judge whether it will be useful in a particular situation.

Exercise

Perhaps the most famous intervention study is that by Cady et al. (1985); however, as the study design was weak, it provides a low level of evidence. Gundewall et al.'s (1993) study probably provides the best available evidence of the effect of exercise. Another notable controlled study on exercise by Kellet et al. (1991) was limited to workers with moderately chronic back pain.

Paper: Gundewall, B., Liljeqvis, M. and Hansson, T. (1993). Primary prevention of back symptoms and absence from work: A prospective randomized study among hospital employees.

Design

This study was a normalised, randomised prospective study of sixty nurses and nurse aids in Sweden. Two groups of workers (exercise and control) were randomly selected and balanced for age, history of back pain and job position. It was not stated how many workers had a history of back pain.

Intervention

Workers in the exercise group were given individual exercise instruction and had their exercise plans reviewed five times over the approximately one year intervention period. Exercise group workers were to exercise for twenty minutes at the ward during working hours. Actual exercise frequency was 1.5 times per week. Exercise group workers also had access to a physiotherapist for advice on dealing with low back pain.

Control group workers were not supposed to do exercise; however, they came from the same work units. Exercise by these participants is not reported.

Outcomes

Workers in the exercise group increased isometric back strength by 20 per cent, whilst workers in the control group increased back strength by only 10 per cent.

One person from the exercise group was absent due to low back pain during the intervention period, whilst twelve from the control group were absent. Lost work days, days with symptoms and intensity of back pain were all less with the exercise group.

Comments

Whilst this appears to be a reasonable study, and possibly the best evidence there is that exercise is useful in primary prevention, it provides only limited evidence.

Important limitations include:

- The study only reports on about one year of intervention, and uses data from that year, where strength and endurance changes may well have taken a quarter of that period to develop (longer term effects are thus unknown).
- Differences in back pain outcomes may have been due to better management of pain following access to physiotherapy advice rather than strength change.

The authors are appropriately cautious in their conclusions, suggesting the back pain outcomes may have been the result of one or both of: (1) increase in back strength; and (2) psychosocial factors, including having someone interested in the workers.

Finally, as this type of study is relatively easy to do, it is perhaps surprising that more are not reported. It may be that other studies have been performed but not reported as they found either no effect or a negative effect.

Paper: Cady, L., Thomas, P. and Karwasky, R. (1985). Programme for increasing health and physical fitness of fire fighters.

Design

This paper reports on what is really a series of longitudinal and cross-sectional studies on fire fighters in the USA. Whilst there was no control group, the intervention group was quite large (over 1600) and outcomes were followed for quite a long time (ten years).

Intervention

The study intervention involved physical examination and fitness testing of fire fighters followed by twenty minutes of individual exercise prescription and counselling. The physical examination and fitness testing was repeated every three years on average. To encourage workers to exercise, exercise bikes were provided at each fire station. Nutritional counselling was also provided.

Outcomes

Longitudinal and cross-sectional comparisons showed that physical work capacity, cardiovascular fitness, strength and flexibility either improved or at least decreased with age less than expected.

When 1652 workers were grouped into three levels of fitness, 7 per cent of the least fit workers experienced low back injury during the observation period, compared to 3 per cent of middle fitness workers and less than 1 per cent of the fittest workers.

In another analysis of a sub-sample of 320 fire fighters, the most flexible, strongest and highest physical work capacity workers had less associated back injury costs than the least flexible, weakest and lowest capacity workers.

Comments

The authors acknowledge that societal changes in attitudes to fitness during the intervention period may have accounted for the improved fitness score. This provides an example of the weakness of studies lacking control groups. In providing information about causal relationships, associations such as those reported in this study are indicative at most. For example, the increase in fitness may not have been preventive at all; rather it may be that there is an underlying factor which causes both fitness and back injury outcomes (such as personal attitudes to health and safety).

Exercise summary

There is not sufficient evidence to judge the effectiveness of exercise on primary prevention of back pain. The little available evidence follows the pattern of evidence from treatment studies. Exercise probably therefore has a mild positive effect.

Work design by experts

Despite several decades of literature stating that work design offers the most potential for effective primary prevention of work-related back pain, very few reports on original research evaluating this contention exist. The series of papers by Garg and Owen (1994, 1992) describing work at a nursing home provide perhaps the best evidence for effectiveness. Few other reports exist, though some weaker design studies do provide some support (Burdorf and van Duuren, 1993).

Paper: Garg, A. and Owen, B. (1992). Reducing stress to nursing personnel: An ergonomic intervention in a nursing home.

Design

This paper reports on a prospective study with staggered intervention using two groups of convenience (wards) in a nursing home in the USA. Fifty-seven nursing assistants participated in the study. Modifications were made in one ward, and five months later in a second ward. Retrospective injury measures over four years prior to intervention were compared with four to eight months of post intervention data.

Intervention

Intervention was aimed at reducing the physical load of patient handling for nursing assistants. Intervention was based on an ergonomic evaluation which included questioning and observing staff and a series of laboratory studies. Intervention included modification of the work environment (for example toilet and shower room modification to allow easier use of the shower chair), provision of new equipment (hoist, walking belt) and training in the use of equipment.

Outcomes

Based on observation of staff post intervention, there were high levels of acceptability of the redesigned tasks (80 per cent). Staff also reported that ratings of perceived exertion for patient handling tasks were changed from about 13 before intervention to about 9 post intervention. Laboratory simulations of tasks showed biomechanical risk indicators improved post intervention (hand force from 312 to 122 N; per cent population strength capable from 41 to 83 per cent; L5S1 compression force from 4800 to 2000 N).

Injury incidence and lost and restricted days were reduced post intervention (injury rate 83–47/200,000 work hours; lost and restricted days 634–0/200,000 work hours).

Comments

This study has a number of very good features including the use of multiple outcome measures and staggered intervention. However, the intervention in the second group probably occurred too early (for research purposes), highlighting the need for a control group. Also, the reduction in lost and restricted days is nearly too good to be true.

Paper: Burdorf, A. and van Duuren, L. (1993). An evaluation of ergonomic improvements in the woodworking industry.

Design

This study was a cross-sectional survey of twenty-eight wood machining operators using eleven machines spread across five small businesses in the Netherlands.

Intervention

As a cross-sectional study, the researchers made no changes to the environment themselves; rather they used the naturally occurring variation in machine process design to evaluate different work designs. The wood-cutting machines varied in the provision of supplementary devices to improve working postures (rollers, raised platforms, stacking tables, lifting devices).

Outcomes

Risk estimates only were used in this survey, with no documentation of back pain/injury outcomes. The risk estimate used was posture, captured using the OWAS system. The presence of a roller, raised platform and stacking table all reduced the time spent in non-neutral postures by about 5–19 per cent each.

Comments

The authors acknowledge the limitations of this study, including the multiple sites of testing which may have confounded the differences in supplementary devices. Cross-sectional studies thus provide only tentative support for causal relationships.

The other major limitation acknowledged is in the crude outcome measure used. Risk estimates such as posture have a questionable link to pain and injury.

The study demonstrates the difficulty in measuring all physical load aspects in real work situations.

Work design by experts summary

There is strangely little evidence available upon which to judge the efficacy of this intervention for primary prevention of work-related back pain. However, what little evidence is available suggests a significant potential.

Participative work design

Like work design by experts, participative work design is an intervention which has been promoted in the literature for several decades. Also like work design by experts, very little evidence exists to evaluate its potential for preventing work-related back pain. Perhaps the best available evidence is a study by Wickstrom et al. (1993). The author struggled to find other evidence, and has included the Koda et al. (1997) study despite its design weaknesses.

Paper: Wickstrom, G., Hyytiainen, K., Laine, M., Pentti, J. and Reijo, S. (1993). A five-year intervention study to reduce low back disorders in the metal industry.

Design

This study was a case-control prospective study using two convenience groups in the metal fabrication industry in Finland. The intervention group consisted of two work units [88 planners (white collar workers) and 125 sheet metal workers (blue collar workers)] in a large (800 workers) metal fabrication plant. The control group consisted of a metal fabrication plant 100 km away and of similar size. The study lasted six years, with two years for baseline data collection, two years for intervention and two years follow-up.

Intervention

The main intervention in this study was the use of participative groups to 'profit from the knowledge and experience of the company staff and to achieve durable results from the intervention measures' (pp. 27 and 28). A work group was established in each unit and consisted of an engineer, supervisor, workers and physiotherapist/occupational health nurse. The groups met monthly for one to two hours for one year, determining the main causes of back pain and developing solutions. They were given details of the baseline surveys and were also given specific aims to reduce lumbar muscle and ligament fatigue, reduce sudden unexpected lumbar loads, and provide suitable diversified loading of lumbar tissues. The details of how working conditions were changed by these groups are not provided.

There were two other aspects to the intervention: education and exercise. A single presentation was given to supervisors and safety representatives on lumbar biomechanics, and basic principles dealing with the use of the back at work were presented on staff notice-boards and in a staff magazine. Middle-aged workers were also invited (a third came) to two sessions on back fitness. Additionally, workers with recent back pain were invited to participate in a two-month home exercise programme (half came).

Outcomes

This study used intermediate outcome variables of estimates of biomechanical work load, ergonomic ways of working and fitness of back tissues, in addition to occurrence of back pain and sick leave due to low back disorders.

Biomechanical (two-dimensional static) estimates of risk remained at the same low level for planners, but decreased for sheet metal workers. Self-reports of adherence to ergonomic ways of working principles increased, as did the use of equipment for sheet metal workers. Participation in physical exercise possibly increased slightly. There was no change in lumbar mobility or abdominal muscle performance, though there was an increase in extensor muscle performance in sheet metal workers.

There was a trend for a reduction in back pain in both the case and control groups of white collar workers, but only in the intervention group of blue collar workers. There was no reduction in sick leave due to back disorder for white collar workers. However, sick leave due to back disorders did decrease from three to two days per person per year for the intervention group of sheet metal workers.

Comments

This study used reasonable worker numbers for a good duration using a reasonable comparison group. It therefore provides reasonably good evidence that this intervention can be effective in primary prevention of work-related back pain. The authors were also very aware of the study limitations and provide a very good discussion on trials of intervention studies. The results also provide a good example of the normal fluctuation in measures like sick leave due to back pain – which creates the need for such long duration studies. It also shows how similar levels of pain can result in different levels of sick leave (compare white and blue collar workers), perhaps due to occupational stresses.

Paper: Koda, S., Nakagiri, S., Yasuda, N., Toyota, M. and Ohara, H. (1997). A follow-up study of preventative effects on low back pain at worksites by providing a participatory occupational safety and health programme.

Design

The paper reports on a prospective study on a single intervention group of around 10,000 workers at Tokyo Metropolitan Bureau of Waste Management. Whilst there was no control group, the study uses data from all Japanese industry for comparison. The study collected two years of baseline data followed by eight years of data during various interventions and follow-up.

Intervention

The main intervention was the use of a participative approach to improving work conditions. All employees participated in small groups (less than ten people) with 'employers' to propose improvements to working conditions while considering effectiveness, feasibility, priority and cost of improvements. A walk-through survey was conducted by each group every one to two weeks and there were monthly occupational safety and health committee meetings. The participative programme resulted in staff discussion of accident causes, collaborative revision of safety manuals, improvements in garbage carts, trucks and containers and improvements in protective equipment.

Additionally, all workers received annual training in safe work procedures (developed by a participative process) and there were five days of training each year for safety and health representatives. Workers performed morning calisthenics.

Outcomes

Intermediate outcomes were reported as changes in equipment and procedures for waste collection.

Low back pain compensation cases decreased by 73 per cent from the start of the intervention (1986) to 1994, compared with national all-industry figures for the same period decreasing by only 34 per cent.

Comments

The paper describes a study on a very good number of workers over a very good duration. It also provides suggestions for how a participative intervention can be used and shows that physical and psychosocial aspects of risk can be dealt with using this intervention. However, the lack of detail in terms of the changes made limit the utility of the evidence, although the most important weakness is the comparison data used. It would have been preferable to have a more comparable group rather than total Japanese industry.

Participative work design summary

Insufficient evidence exists to judge the efficacy of this intervention. The available evidence suggests a significant positive effect on primary prevention of work-related back pain may be possible.

REASONS FOR LACK OF CONVINCING EVIDENCE

Despite around 1000 scientific publications on work-related back pain prevention, there are but a handful of good quality studies which have actually evaluated the efficacy of an intervention. This could be seen as a serious omission by the professions involved in prevention of back pain. However, this is not the only professional area where little evidence exists for current practice.

The lack of evidence can be explained to some extent by the following issues:

- Back pain is not a simple phenomenon.
- Limitations in the risk assessment model (we don't know what hazards are, nor what thresholds are, nor how best to measure them).
- Large budgets are required (e.g. the Wickstrom et al. study cost $250,000).

- Interventions used may have been incorrect (e.g. in teaching lifting techniques, inappropriate movements may have been taught).
- Intervention effects may be small and may interact in complex ways, which means we are unable to successfully measure them.
- The site of research is the real world and outside researcher control.

To improve the pitiful state of knowledge, perhaps we need to focus our intellectual resources more on intervention studies than on laboratory studies. However, this may be a misguided plea.

Laboratory studies are attractive for researchers as they can be controlled, in the broader sense. They are attractive to funders of research as they cost less, take less time and are more likely to be completed. They are also potentially useful in helping our understanding of the aetiology of back pain, and thus for developing suitable measures to use in intervention studies.

Furthermore, intervention studies require adequate short term outcome measures, and these have yet to be developed (see Chapter 11, pp. 255–260).

CONCLUSIONS

We have very little evidence upon which to justify any preventive intervention for work-related back pain.

Available evidence provides some support for using history of back pain to select workers, little support for education of workers, moderate support for training workers to maintain fitness, and some support for work design changes by experts and by a participative approach.

Professionals involved in prevention of work-related back pain have a responsibility to contribute to the knowledge base.

References

Burdorf, A. and van Duuren, L. (1993). An evaluation of ergonomic improvements in the woodworking industry. *Annuls of Occupational Hygiene*, **37**, 615–622.

Cady, L., Thomas, P. and Karwasky, R. (1985). Programme for increasing health and physical fitness of fire fighters. *Journal of Occupational Medicine*, **27**, 110–114.

Daltroy, L.H., Iversen, M.D., Larson, M.G. et al. (1997). A controlled trial of an educational programme to prevent low back injuries. *The New England Journal of Medicine*, **337**, 322–328.

Daltroy, L.H., Iversen, M.D., Larson, M.G. et al. (1993). Teaching and social support: Effects on knowledge, attitudes and behaviours to prevent low back injuries in industry. *Health Education Quarterly*, **20**, 43–62.

Feldstein, A., Valanis, B., Vollmer, W. et al. (1993). The back injury prevention project pilot study: Assessing the effectiveness of Back Attack, an injury prevention programme among nurses, aides and orderlies. *Journal of Occupational Medicine*, **35**, 114–119.

Frank, J., Kerr, M., Brooker, A. et al. (1996). Disability resulting from occupational low back pain: Part 1. What do we know about primary prevention? A review of the scientific evidence on prevention before disability begins. *Spine*, **24**, 2908–2917.

Garg, A. and Owen, B. (1992). Reducing stress to nursing personnel: an ergonomic intervention in a nursing home. *Ergonomics*, **35**, 1353–1375.

Garg, A. and Owen, B. (1994). Prevention of back injuries in healthcare workers. *International Journal of Industrial Ergonomics*, **14**, 315–331.

Gundewall, B., Liljeqvist, M. and Hansson, T. (1993). Primary prevention of back symptoms and absence from work: A prospective randomized study among hospital employees. *Spine*, **18**, 587–594.

Kaplansky, B., Wei, F. and Reecer, M. (1998). Prevention strategies for occupational low back pain. *Occupational Medicine: State of the Art Reviews*, **13**, 33–45.

Karas, B. and Conrad, K. (1996). Back injury prevention interventions in the workplace. *American Association of Occupational Health Nurses Journal*, **44**, 189–196.

Kellet, K., Kellet, D. and Nordholm, L. (1991). Effects of an exercise programme on sick leave due to back pain. *Physical Therapy*, **71**, 283–293.

Koda, S., Nakagiri, S., Yasuda, N. et al. (1997). A follow-up study of preventative effects on low back pain at worksites by providing a participatory occupational safety and health program. *Industrial Health*, **35**, 243–248.

Lagerstrom, M. and Hagberg, M. (1997). Evaluation of a 3 year education and training programme for nursing personnel at a Swedish hospital. *American Association of Occupational Health Nurses Journal*, **45**, 83–92.

Lahad, A., Malter, A., Berg, A. et al. (1994). The effectiveness of four interventions for the prevention of low back pain. *Journal of the American Medical Association*, **272**, 1286–1291.

Marks, N. (1997). An evaluation of a multifaceted back care programme for the construction industry. *Applied Occupational Environmental Hygiene*, **12**, 642–647.

McGill, S. (1999). Update on the use of back belts in industry: more data – same conclusion. In *The Occupational Ergonomics Handbook* (W. Karwowski and W. Marras, eds), pp. 1353–1358. CRC Press.

Reddell, C., Congleton, J., Hutchingson, R. et al. (1992). An evaluation of a weightlifting belt and back injury prevention training class for airline baggage handlers. *Applied Ergonomics*, **23**, 319–329.

Reimer, D., Halbrook, B., Dreyfuss, P. et al. (1994). A novel approach to pre-employment worker fitness evaluations in a material handling industry. *Spine*, **19**, 2026–2032.

Shi, L. (1993). A cost–benefit analysis of a California county's back injury prevention program. *Public Health Reports*, **108**, 204–211.

Smedley, J., Egger, P., Cooper, C. et al. (1997). Prospective cohort study of predictors of incident low back pain in nurses. *British Medical Journal*, **314**, 1225–1228.

Straker, L.M. (1997). *A Critical Appraisal of Manual Handling Risk Assessment Literature*. International Ergonomics Association Press.

Straker, L.M. (in press b). An overview of manual handling injury statistics in Western Australia. *International Journal of Industrial Ergonomics*.

van Poppel, M., Koes, B., Smid, T. et al. (1997). A systematic review of controlled clinical trials on the prevention of back pain in industry. *Occupational and Environmental Medicine*, **54**, 841–847.

Versloot, J.M., Rozeman, A. and van Son, A.M. (1992). The cost effectiveness of a back school programme in industry. *Spine*, **17**, 22–27.

Videman, T., Rauhala, H., Lindstrom, K. et al. (1989). Patient handling skill, back injuries and back pain: An intervention study in nursing. *Spine*, **14**, 148–156.

Walsh, N. and Schwartz, R. (1990). The influence of prophylactic orthoses on abdominal strength and low back injury in the workplace. *American Journal of Physical Medicine and Rehabilitation*, **69**, 245–250.

Wickstrom, G., Hyytiainen, K., Laine, M. et al. (1993). A five-year intervention study to reduce low back disorders in the metal industry. *International Journal of Industrial Ergonomics*, **12**, 25–33.

Chapter 7

Ergonomics

Ergonomic tools to objectively assess workplace risks

David C. Caple

INTRODUCTION

Ergonomics was originally derived through a military research environment where the design of man/machine systems was requiring the multidisciplinary expertise of key professionals such as engineers, physiologists and psychologists. The adapting of design issues to reflect the capabilities and needs of the full range of the population is the primary focus for ergonomists. The following tools are utilised by ergonomists to objectively assess workplace design risks.

Systems analysis

The initial tool involves the ergonomist in understanding the overall work system objectives and the key performance indicators relevant to each of the main stakeholders. This is based on the systems model (Figure 7.1).

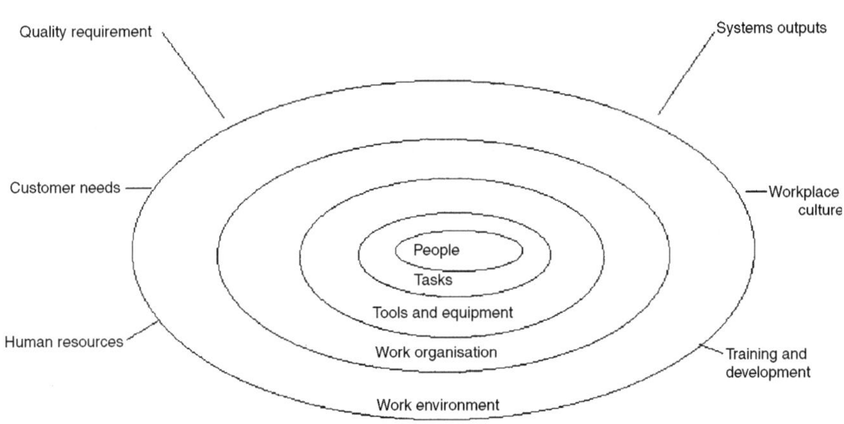

Figure 7.1 Systems model used in systems analysis

It is important that the ergonomist is provided with the opportunity to obtain a systems analysis to enable quantification and documentation of key performance elements.

People involved

The primary focus to the ergonomic analysis relates to definition of the people, or stakeholders, in the systems under analysis.

In manufacturing industry, the key focus is normally on the operator who performs the tasks within the work system. However, other stakeholders such as maintenance staff and cleaners, as well as contractors, must also be considered in the analysis process. It is often found that the workplaces may be well designed from the operator's perspective but quite hazardous for maintenance access.

It should also be noted that the contingent or contract workers are now the fastest growing sector of employment in Australia (Caple, 1998). This results in a range of new challenges in defining who the people or 'users' of designs will be. The sharing of workplaces due to shift work rosters and 'hot-desking' further diffuses the process of defining user needs.

Performance measures

The quantified data relating to the tasks need to be defined. This may be productivity related such as 'units per hour', or quality related such as 'zero defects'.

Where multi-skilling or task rotation occurs, the data may be team based, or individual operator based.

Task analysis

This is an essential element of ergonomic appraisal and is generally a chronological description of the activities performed by the relevant user group. The analysis should identify not only the normal tasks undertaken but also those irregular tasks where ergonomic concerns may be identified.

This analysis should be documented after consultation with and observation of the people who do this work. If necessary, consultation with various shifts is required to ensure any differences in work systems are identified in the task analysis.

Quantitative assessments

People issues

A range of tools are used by ergonomists in evaluating the needs of each user group. These tools include:

- focus group discussions
- health surveillance surveys

- individual consultations
- work diaries
- 'step dot' surveys
- injury and incident data
- safety committee minutes
- toolbox meeting minutes.

Workload demands

A range of objective measures is available to assess the workload and enable comparison with research data. These measures include:

- NIOSH
- RULA
- OWAS
- electromyography
- heart rate
- thermography
- nerve conduction
- video analysis
- vibration assessments.

Tools and workstation assessments

Objective data can be taken of the tools and workstations used. These include:

- working heights
- reaches
- grips
- postures
- materials handled
- forces exerted
- storage of materials
- hand/eye co-ordination needs
- leg space
- movement patterns.

Work organisation assessment

This assessment covers such areas as:

- work rosters
- task variation
- staff rotation
- multi-skilling
- team-based work systems
- overtime
- staff turnover
- training and skill development
- opportunity for performance feedback.

Work environment

Assessment of the overall work environment includes consideration of issues such as:

- heating/cooling
- noise
- vibration
- dust
- chemicals
- light.

In addition, work environment issues relating to social interactions and opportunities for users to experience identity with their work group are important elements of the ergonomics analysis.

Cost–benefit analysis

To help justify the degree of change to be recommended, the principles of cost–benefit analysis will regularly be required. It is generally found that most ergonomic changes that require large capital investment can best be justified if there are quality and/or productivity benefits as well as efficiency and safety improvements.

Ergonomics research was founded on a philosophy of efficiency in the design to maximise the contribution of the human/machine interface. As we move into the twenty-first century, this philosophy is as valid today.

References

Caple, D.C. (1998). Contingent workers. *Proceedings of the Ergonomics Society of Australia 45th Annual Conference*, ESA, Canberra.

Work design, organisation and environment

Barbara McPhee

INTRODUCTION

Today, even when we know so much about how to design work, so few jobs are actually designed. It seems that good job design is often achieved by accident. If good job design has been achieved by intention, often the people concerned do not know why the design has been successful.

DESIGN OF WORK

In order to design good jobs we need to know about the work and how it will be done. We also need to know about the people who will do the work and their capabilities and limitations in order to achieve a suitable match. As work changes over time, reviews and modifications are constantly required if systems and people are to work harmoniously and efficiently.

An ergonomics assessment should be conducted to review jobs, the way they are organised, and any associated requirements for workplace design in terms of the worker(s), their efficiency and productivity, and their health. After this any mismatches between the job demands and the workers' capabilities and limitations can be identified and corrected.

Therefore, when designing work, there are four major areas to consider:

1. Task design: determining what people will do (job content), including task variation, work demands (including responsibilities) of the task(s), restrictions and time requirements (deadlines etc.).

2. Workplace design: the physical design and layout of the work areas, including work spaces, furniture, equipment, tools, illumination and lighting, noise and vibration.

3. Work organisation: patterns of work and task sequencing; how the work is organised and why; shift work; workload including peaks and troughs in demands; rest and work breaks; supervision and support at work; team work; inefficiencies or organisational difficulties; the nature of the organisation, its clients and its problems; and economic and social influences.

4. The worker: experience and skill development; education and training; personality; health and other problems; the match of skills to the demands of the job; the need to adjust to the work conditions; the use of personal protective equipment.

Nevertheless, no matter how well designed the workplace is, it can be undermined by poor work design and organisation.

THE IMPACT OF NEW TECHNOLOGY ON WORK

Products of modern technology such as computers are excellent job aids but should not be used as a total job. One problem today is that decisions are made on technology, workplaces and work design for 'rational' or 'financial' reasons, disregarding the negative impact on people – particularly their ability to be productive. These decisions may be made without any analysis of the work, who does it and how, and without the participation of, or consultation with, the people directly affected. This can have the reverse effect to the one desired. Productivity can drop, inefficiencies develop and errors and sick leave increase.

Consultation is the sharing of information and exchange of views between employers, employees and/or employee representatives, including the opportunity to contribute to decision making in the resolving of problems. It is required for the development of safe systems of work by occupational health and safety legislation in Australia. However, although it sounds logical and reasonable, too often it does not happen. Participation in decision making and consultation takes time and skill, and often the planning process does not allow for it. Planning may start early enough, but usually at this stage it is in areas quite divorced from the people who ultimately have to make the system work. Nevertheless, it has not been demonstrated that allowing employee participation in the planning or redesign of their work and/or workplaces is more costly than getting it wrong because these procedures were not followed.

Workers are flawed, imperfect and subject to personal and emotional responses rather than rational, logical ones. No matter how good the technology, how wide the debate and how cogent the arguments, individuals will not always agree with the 'experts' about the benefits of change – whatever form they take. Responses will vary depending on the age, sex and education level of the person, plus a range of other personal and social factors. What works well in one location for one group may not work in another – and yet designers and decision makers appear to be eager to transpose technology and systems from one workplace to another with the minimum of analysis.

Most people like to believe that the work they do is of value and that when they work they can be productive, efficient and can produce high quality work (quality, quantity and time). Very few of us achieve this consistently because we work in human (and therefore imperfect) systems. The most the majority of us can hope to achieve is to do a satisfying job, under reasonable conditions, for reasonable remuneration or some other reward.

It is unreasonable and counter-productive to become too prescriptive when developing solutions for recognised and predicted problems. This approach may have been appropriate in the past but it tends to stultify imagination and discourage local solutions. However, if general principles of good work and workplace design are understood and applied, and people's needs are given adequate consideration within the system, the basic mismatches and obvious problems can be avoided. Input from specialists becomes necessary as the complexities of the systems increase and as the need to contain costs and to reduce errors and wastage becomes more critical.

PARTICIPATORY ERGONOMICS

The aim of all task and workplace design is to provide a new way of doing things and to improve on current designs. Unfortunately, designers often ignore the users' opinions and feedback, and this often leads to perpetuating problems or even introducing new ones.

Some of the most successful ergonomics applications in the workplace have involved the people who do the work in an active way. This is referred to as participatory ergonomics. In this approach, information generated by employees is harnessed by managers and designers to achieve more workable solutions for identified problems and, more importantly, to prevent problems occurring with new products and in new systems of work.

Successful participation and consultation takes time and skill, and often the planning process does not allow for it. Participatory ergonomics does not cost more and it is likely to save money when applied at the right time. When workers implement new systems and technology, they are more able to modify them to solve future problems due to their practical experience. In addition, as many people have found, the ownership of ideas enhances the likelihood of implementing change successfully.

JUST FOR NEW TECHNOLOGY

The following is an outline of the areas to be addressed when introducing new computer technology to a workplace.

Job design

Be aware of the impact on worker satisfaction and health of:

- work organisation
- job content
- responsibilities
- demands versus control.

No matter how well designed the workplace, it can be undermined by poor work design and organisation.

Understand

Understand the strengths and limitations of different types of technology and workplace design. Understand how the limitations of some systems may lead to problems for users. This requires true consultation with the people who will be doing the work from the start of the design phase.

Beware of two types of decision makers – the misinformed optimist and the technology junkie. Both will be tempted to select and purchase equipment and systems which do not deliver their much-touted benefits to the majority of users.

Understand exactly how much can be delivered under normal conditions. Do not put people under unnecessary pressure when it is not called for. Save up the goodwill and ask for superior efforts when you really need it. Allow people to ease off occasionally and appreciate that everybody has 'off' days.

Support

People need to be supported consistently and fully throughout the design and implementation phases. Encourage their full participation and input. Provide real 'help-line' services for new technology. Allow time for people to 'learn by doing' and to gain confidence with new systems. Keep a user focus and continually reappraise and fine tune.

Keep the support going when the system is up and running, especially for the crisis times – either at work or in individuals' personal lives.

Train

The introduction of new technology and changes in systems will mean a lot of training. It must be tailored to the needs of the individuals and groups and therefore must be:

- appropriatc
- timely
- high quality
- on-going if necessary.

There is a huge range of computer hardware and software technologies available and there are many different skills which users may bring to a job. No two users of the same equipment will operate it in the same way. If it is important that the system is used in a systematic and standardised way, then much more training (relearning) will be required.

Where complex and highly specific products are used, much time and money may be needed to train, evaluate the work system and retrain. Airline pilots are a good example of how training can help people to use complex systems competently. However, pilots are also very carefully selected, and well paid. Asking for the same amount of effort and accuracy from workers paid a quarter of the salary may mean that employers' or managers' expectations are too high.

Effects of work design and environment in parcel sorting

Kerry L. Butler

INTRODUCTION

In this new millennium we are seeing a multitude of different people getting involved in ergonomics in the workplace. This includes occupational health and safety (OHS) representatives, safety officers, occupational health nurses, occupational therapists and physiotherapists. Workstation set-up, which involves basic ergonomic factors, is now more commonly assessed, and training conducted by internally appointed individuals who themselves have received no expert training. As a consequence, all too often the basis of assessment and training is the relevant standards and codes of practice. In addition, training content in particular has often not been accurately tested for effectiveness.

In those cases in which workplaces are assessed by people with only basic training and expertise, there is a danger of potential risk factors being overlooked. For example, the particular work techniques or habits of the individual using the workstation being assessed may either be overlooked or not taken into adequate consideration. That is, the specific musculoskeletal factors involved in performing the work are often not taken into account although these form a significant part of injury risk. Thus, an employee using a computer workstation may have had his work area checked by the relevant company representative for correct furniture and equipment set-up and pronounced ergonomically correct, but still be at significant risk of injury.

Different types of work require particular postures in performing the work. Posture in this sense is defined as the positioning of all joints of the body. If the posture adopted is repetitive or of long duration, and the work is performed over a period of years, then it is possible for changes to occur in agonist/antagonist muscle balance.

Described here are the preliminary results of an ongoing study carried out in a parcel sorting work area. It serves to assess a range of musculoskeletal factors potentially involved in performance of the common tasks or affected by the work environment, and includes a wider range of musculoskeletal factors than has previously been the case in typical assessments of work environment. The results suggest that workplace risk assessment would benefit from a more detailed analysis by specialist practitioners.

METHODOLOGY

Volunteers from the workplace were invited to participate in the study. The total workforce was eighty to one hundred employees. Twenty people volunteered and were then assessed both for subjective symptoms of pain or discomfort that had occurred in the previous twelve months or were still occurring, and for objective signs at the time of assessment. Subjective information was sought by way of a questionnaire on symptoms related to the back/neck, arms and legs. Information was also collected on gender, age, hand dominance, recreational pursuits, treatment for symptoms, the perceived relationship of work tasks, and current symptom status.

Each person was then assessed objectively using a number of protocols. A standard postural assessment was conducted, and the range of movement of the cervical and thoracic spines and the gleno-humeral complex, and the muscle strengths of the middle and lower trapezius, rhomboids, serratus anterior and latissimus dorsi were tested. In addition, the cervical and thoracic segments were palpated for signs of pain or discomfort.

RESULTS

Of the twenty people in the survey, eleven people (55 per cent) reported persisting subjective symptoms. This included seven with persisting back symptoms, eight with persisting arm symptoms and four with persisting leg symptoms. Five people (25 per cent) complained of one symptom area, four (20 per cent) complained of two symptom areas, and two (10 per cent) complained of three symptom areas. Eleven people (55 per cent) stated that work caused some pain.

Objective assessment of symptoms revealed an even larger proportion of people with tenderness on palpation than those reporting subjective symptoms. Subjects were palpated at all cervical and thoracic levels. Of the twenty assessed, eighteen (90 per cent) had tenderness on palpation of the spine–thirteen (65 per cent) had both cervical and thoracic tenderness, another four (20 per cent) had only cervical tenderness and one (5 per cent) had only thoracic tenderness.

Of those experiencing cervical tenderness, 75 per cent exhibited common points of tenderness. Of those experiencing thoracic tenderness, 55 per cent exhibited common points of tenderness. Fourteen people had cervical trigger point tenderness, and a further six had thoracic trigger point tenderness. A total of six had combined thoracic and cervical trigger point tenderness.

On muscle testing, three people (15 per cent; all males) had below average rhomboid strength, seven people (35 per cent; four males and three females) had below average lower trapezius strength, five people (25 per cent; all males) had below average middle trapezius strength, and eleven people (55 per cent; ten males and one female) had below average latissimus dorsi strength.

CONCLUSIONS

Based on decreased muscle strength, nine persons (45 per cent) were found to be at an increased risk of injury. Based on complaints of symptoms, eleven people (55 per cent) were found to be at possible increased risk of injury. Based on symptoms on palpation, twelve people (60 per cent) were found to be at possible increased risk of injury. For each of these categories, five people (three men and two women) were found to be in all of the risk groups, i.e. decreased muscle strength, complaints of symptoms and symptoms on palpation. Two were in the risk groups for decreased muscle strength and symptoms on palpation. This study was undertaken as the preliminary part of an ongoing investigation to assess the effectiveness of instigation of a work-based simple exercise programme. It is due to be repeated after the exercise programme has been going for three months.

The results in terms of both numbers of people exhibiting signs and symptoms and the overall outcomes from muscle testing and symptom distribution are quite alarming. Examination revealed a number of common areas of pain or tenderness in the cervical and thoracic spines, and the trigger points at C7, upper trapezius and middle trapezius. A proportion of individuals demonstrated below average muscle strength in the rhomboids and lower trapezius and, to a lesser extent, middle trapezius. Anecdotally, there appears to have been little attention paid to thoracic signs at a clinical level in the past, so these symptomatic areas are commonly not assessed or treated. Furthermore, strengthening exercises are often given for the upper trapezius which may well increase trigger point problems and not address the signs found during this survey, i.e. decreased muscle strength in specific muscles and active trigger points.

There is the possibility of bias in this study due to participants being volunteers. However, even if those who volunteered were all the people experiencing symptoms, it still demonstrates a concerning number of workers in a specific workplace who are having symptoms at a particular point in time.

The results presented here demonstrate the importance of further investigation. It suggests in particular that musculoskeletal factors require greater consideration in the workplace, and that providing correct furniture and equipment is only one aspect of reducing risk factors associated with the work area. It also points to the need for more in-depth expertise in the workplace in order to identify musculoskeletal risk factors and thereby develop appropriate strategies to reduce these factors.

The biomechanical effect of posterior load carrying systems

Steven Milanese

INTRODUCTION

Many occupations utilise a posterior load carrying system (PLCS), where loads are suspended at the back of the wearer, for the movement of loads. The load in a PLCS is usually suspended from straps that encircle the shoulders, and may include waist and chest straps to stabilise the load. The most popular version of the PLCS seen in the community is the backpack. Benefits of this load carrying approach include the freeing up of the wearer's hands and arms for other functions, and the greater mobility this load carriage system allows in the movement and use of equipment. Occupations that utilise this system include the military services, industrial cleaners, firemen, farmers and park rangers.

Musculoskeletal symptoms, including knee pain and low back pain, and local discomfort have been reported in the literature with the use of posterior load carrying systems (Knapik et al., 1996). Concerns have also been raised about the potential for heavy backpack wearing to be a source of stress on the adolescent spine – a particular concern in the school environment (Balague et al., 1988).

This paper results from work carried out at the Centre for Allied Health Research, University of South Australia, into the effects of backpack wearing on adolescent school students. This subject sample was selected as an ideal group to assess the effects of a PLCS as they were a readily available sample group utilising a posterior load carrying system on a daily basis. The high incidence of musculoskeletal symptoms reported amongst adolescents, and the concerns regarding the potential for the PLCS to be a factor in the aetiology of these symptoms, encouraged further investigation.

This paper considers the potential biomechanical influence of PLCS variables on the wearer. In the study of traditional manual lifting systems (e.g. anterior load carrying) three approaches have been used. The 'biomechanical approach' utilises the laws of physics to study the effects of externally applied loads on the body. Other approaches used are the 'physiological approach', where the effects of manual handling on the physiological parameters are investigated, and the 'psycho-physical approach', where subjects determine the relationships between 'work factors and the perceptions of physical stress, exertion, fatigue and discomfort on the body' to determine safe exposure to these work factors (Krawczyk, 1996). Whilst this paper will concentrate on a biomechanical approach to investigating the effect of a PLCS on the wearer, it is prudent to also review findings from the other approaches.

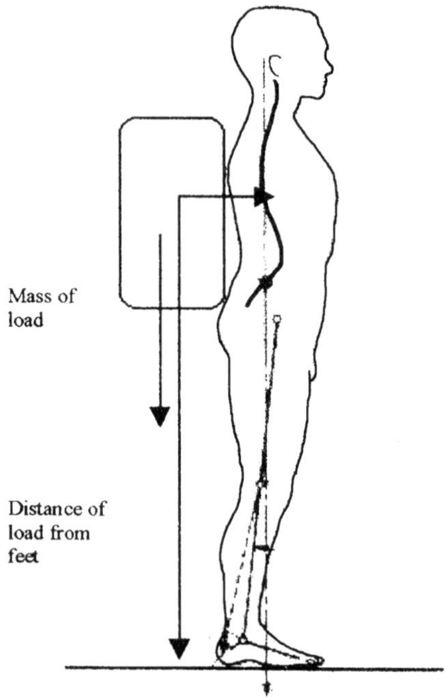

Figure 7.2 PLCS variables that may affect biomechanical, physiological and psycho-physical parameters

PLCS variables of interest include the weight of the load transported by the PLCS and the position of the PLCS in relation to the wearer. For ease of discussion we will concern ourselves with the position of the PLCS in the sagittal plane only. We therefore assume that the PLCS is centred at the back in the frontal plane, and suspended evenly between both shoulders. The dimensions that determine the position of the PLCS relative to the wearer are the distance of the PLCS from the feet and the distance of the PLCS from the body (Figure 7.2).

PHYSIOLOGICAL STUDIES

Studies to date have concerned themselves primarily with the physiological costs of different PLCS systems and carriage weights whilst walking or hiking in military or civilian adult populations (Pascoe et al., 1997).

Physiological costs of load carrying increase with increased loads in the PLCS (Epstein et al., 1988; Knapik et al., 1996), as would be expected. Increasing weight has also been reported to have effects on maximum effort times (Knapik et al., 1997) and heart rates (Holewijn, 1990).

The influence of the position of the load relative to the centre of gravity of the body on physiological parameters appears to be less consistent. A number of studies have reported a significant decrease in energy expenditure when the load is carried close to the centre of gravity of the body (Malhotra and Gupta, 1965; Winsmann and Goldman, 1976).

Other authors have reported no alteration in physiological parameters between different posterior load carrying systems. Legg and Mahanty (1985) found no difference in mean cardiorespiratory and metabolic costs during treadmill walking when comparing five modes of PLCS ranging from a backpack with a frame, with the load posterior to the trunk, to a trunk jacket where weight was distributed evenly around the trunk.

PSYCHO-PHYSICAL STUDIES

Knapik et al. (1997) reported an increase in the ratings of perceived exertion with increases in weight with PLCSs. This trend reflects the findings of psycho-physical studies into the traditional anterior load carrying systems.

Roberts et al. (1996), in their study of the influence of backpack design on a group of physically fit marines whilst performing treadmill walking, found that the backpacks that the subjects rated the most comfortable after four hours of walking were those that appeared to place more pressure on the legs than the back. This was monitored by the degree of fatigue in the lower limb muscles, as measured by EMG, following exercise with each of the backpacks. The authors recommended that the most suitable backpacks placed the load close to the centre of mass of the wearer. This was reinforced by the findings of Legg and Mahanty's (1985) study in which the five adult male subjects rated the PLCS that resulted in a more even distribution of weight as the most comfortable. The more even distribution of weight occurred through the use of a trunk jacket that allowed the weight to be carried evenly around the trunk.

BIOMECHANICAL

The function of the musculoskeletal system is to:

1. Maintain an upright posture, through ensuring that the body's line of gravity passes through its base of support.
2. Allow mobility of the system, facilitating locomotion and function.

A number of factors will influence the biomechanical effect of a PLCS on the musculoskeletal system. These include the mass of the load carried by the PLCS, the point of application of the load on the body, and the position of the PLCS load relative to the wearer. When describing the position of the load relative to the wearer in biomechanical terms, we need to consider the position both relative to the centre of gravity of the wearer and the axis of rotation of each body segment.

The line of gravity of the body in the 'relaxed standing posture' passes through the centre of gravity of the body, behind the hip joint and in front of the knee and the ankle joint (Figure 7.3). The maintenance of an upright balanced posture involves the maintenance of this line of gravity within the base of support. The positioning of a load posterior to the body, as occurs in a PLCS, will have the effect of displacing the line of gravity of the body posteriorly (Figure 7.4). If this

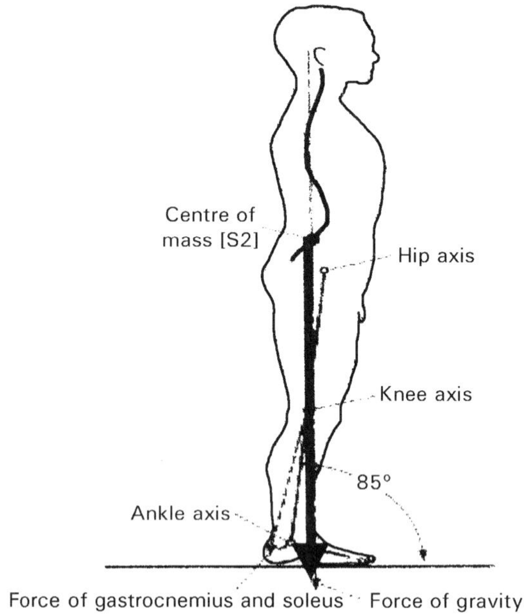

Figure 7.3 Line of gravity in relaxed standing posture (adapted from Adrian and Cooper, 1989)

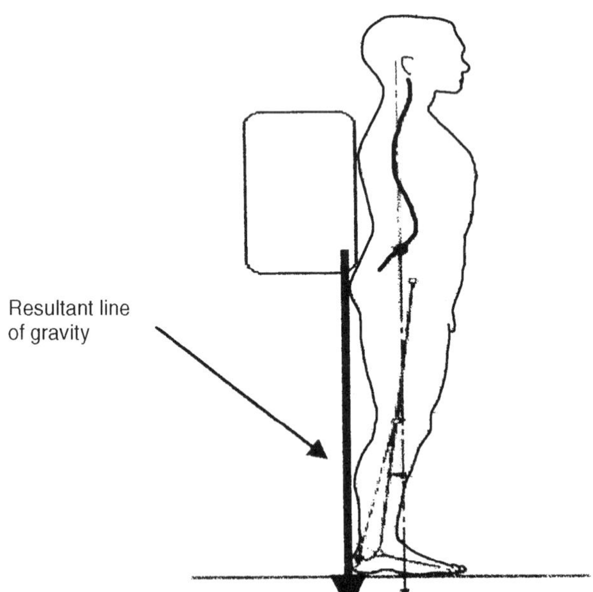

Figure 7.4 Resultant line of gravity with backpack (adapted from Adrian and Cooper, 1989)

displacement is significant enough, the line of gravity will fall outside the base of support and the wearer would be at risk of falling over. To maintain an upright posture the musculoskeletal system will be required to make adaptations to compensate for these alterations. These adaptations may involve the ankles, the hips, the lumbar spine, cervical spine and shoulder girdle.

It has been noted that no general balance pattern exists when the body is seeking to maintain balance (Adrian and Cooper, 1989); however, when a PLCS is applied to the body, there are potentially two mechanisms for the movement of the body's new line of gravity back over the base of support. These are the movement of sufficient body segments forward to counterbalance the load, keeping the resultant line of gravity of the body over its base of support, or movement of the load itself over the base of support. Which mechanism is chosen to overcome the backward movement of the line of gravity remains unclear but may theoretically be related to the position of the backpack relative to the centre of gravity of the body.

The line of gravity, by definition, passes through the centre of gravity of the person. The centre of gravity is a point at which all the body parts exactly balance each other, and will be affected by the person's anatomical build and the influence of external forces applied to the body (Luttgens and Hamilton, 1997). The centre of gravity of the human body is located at the approximate level of the L2 vertebrae and maintains a fairly constant ratio to body height throughout life, being found approximately 56 per cent of body height from the feet (Luttgens and Hamilton, 1997).

Positioning a load above the body's centre of gravity will lead to an elevation of the body's centre of gravity. This new centre of gravity is the result of an effective increase in body mass of the upper trunk. Raising the body's effective centre of gravity whilst maintaining a similar sized base of support will make the body less stable (Luttgens and Hamilton, 1997). This is reflected in the findings of Hellebrandt et al. (1944), who found increased body postural sway in standing amongst military personnel wearing army packs with high load placement. The higher position of the load relative to the wearer's centre of gravity means that less body segments are required to rotate forward to locate the body's resultant centre of gravity over the base of support.

With a lower placed load there is greater stability in the system, as the body's resultant centre of gravity moves downwards. This is reflected in reductions in the amount of postural sway seen with low backpack wearing compared to unloaded stance (Knapik et al., 1996). Low backpack wearing also results in greater body lean forwards, as the body tries to move the resultant centre of mass of the body over the base of support, compensating for the disturbance.

The influence of the PLCS on individual body segments will depend on the postural adaptations that result and the resultant position of the PLCS centre of mass on the axis of rotation of the segment.

At the level of the lumbosacral spine, the increase in load posterior to the axis of rotation of the lumbar motion segment will result in the development of an extensor torque. The musculoskeletal system will recruit appropriate muscle activity to resist this externally applied torque. At the level of the lumbar spine, the extensor torque will be resisted by the trunk flexors, e.g. the abdominals. This is a mirror image of the situation with anterior load carrying systems, where the flexor torque, generated by the application of an anterior load, is resisted by activity in the trunk extensor muscles.

Posterior load carrying systems are somewhat more advantageous than the anterior load carrying systems for a number of reasons:

1. The moment arm of the abdominals is significantly greater than that of the erector spinae (Figure 7.5).
2. The load is able to be placed closer to the axis of rotation of the motion segments. In contrast with anterior load carrying systems, the abdominal cavity is not between the load and the axis of rotation in PLCSs. This results in the load generating a smaller moment arm, effectively reducing the torque generated by the load.

The resultant effect is that less torque is required to be overcome at the level of the motion segment, and the muscles responsible are at a greater mechanical advantage to overcome this extensor torque. This should result in less stresses across the lumbar spine in the carrying of a load in a PLCS compared with an anterior load carrying system.

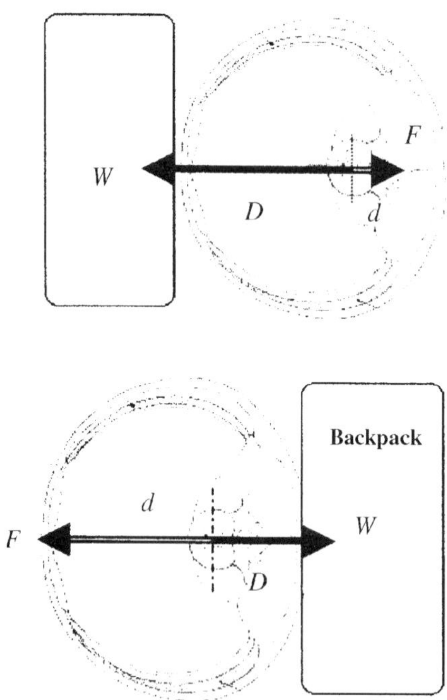

Anterior load carrying system

To maintain equilibrium:

$W \times D = F \times d$

W = mass of load
D = moment arm of weight
F = force required from erector spinae
d = moment arm of erect or spinae

Posterior load carrying system

To maintain equilibrium:

$W \times D = F \times d$

W = mass of load
D = moment arm of weight
F = force required from
d = moment arm of abdominals

Figure 7.5 Difference in muscle moment arms between anterior and posterior load carrying systems

At the point of application of the PLCS to the body (e.g. the shoulder girdle) the posteriorly and inferiorly directed force will result in a tendency towards shoulder girdle retraction and depression. The actual angle of retraction and depression that the PLCS generates will depend on the position of the backpack relative to the shoulder point of application. A low backpack will generate a greater depression effect than a higher backpack, which will generate a relatively greater retraction effect. This has been demonstrated in findings in adolescent students, where a low backpack has been shown to correlate with a greater degree of shoulder sag (depression).

At the level of the shoulder girdle, the muscles providing a protraction and elevation influence are as described in Table 7.1. As discussed, the actual muscles required to overcome the effect of the backpack will be influenced by the direction of the force vector created by the load. A more depressing load will be overcome more by the shoulder girdle elevators, whilst an applied load with a greater retracting influence will recruit more of the shoulder girdle protractors.

Increases in the mass of the load will magnify the biomechanical effect of the application of a posterior load on the line of gravity of the wearer. The greater the value of the mass, the greater the influence it will have on the resultant centre of mass of the body plus pack. There is insufficient justification to determine a critical value of load mass in the adult population, as the effects of other PLCS parameters appear to have an important influence on the effect of mass. This reflects the trends with anterior load carrying recommendations where we have moved away from prescriptive load limits. It is more useful to consider the design of the PLCS to reduce the potential biomechanical influence of load mass.

A number of studies have sought to identify weight limits for the adolescent student population. Voll and Klimt (1977), as cited by Pascoe et al. (1997), recommended weight limits of 10 per cent of body weight, after which they visually observed postural changes. Malhotra and Sen Gupta (1965) reported no visually observed postural changes with weights of 10–12 per cent of body weight. As discussed, differences in the potential for the load to result in observed postural changes may have been due to differences in the biomechanical design of the backpacks.

On an individual body segment level, the greater the mass of the load, the greater the magnitude of the force that the musculoskeletal system must overcome. This results in greater muscle activity and recruitment, and hence energy usage.

Table 7.1 Muscles of the scapulothoracic articulation involved in protraction and elevation (from Smith et al., 1996

Protractors	**Elevators**
Serratus anterior	Upper trapezius
Pectoralis major	Levator scapulae
Pectoralis minor	Rhomboids

CONCLUSIONS

Aspects of posterior load carrying systems that may biomechanically influence the wearer include:

1. Position of the backpack relative to the line of gravity of the wearer. This will be influenced by the position of the centre of mass of the backpack relative to the spine in the antero-posterior sagittal plane.
2. Position of the backpack relative to the centre of mass of the body. This will be influenced by the position of the centre of mass of the backpack relative to the spine in a cephalo-caudal plane.
3. Mass of the load.

References

Adrian, M.J. and Cooper, J.M. (1989). *Biomechanics of Human Movement*. Benchmark Press.

Balague, F., Dutoit, G. and Waldburger, M. (1988). Low back pain in schoolchildren. *Scandinavian Journal of Rehabilitation Medicine*, **20**, 175–179.

Epstein, Y., Rosenblum, J., Burstein, R. et al. (1988). External load can alter the energy cost of prolonged exercise. *European Journal of Applied Physiology*, **57**, 243–247.

Hellebrandt, F.A., Fries, E.C., Larsen, E.M. et al. (1944). The influence of the Army pack on postural stability and stance mechanisms. *American Journal of Physiology*, **140**, 645–655.

Holewijn, M. (1990). Physiological strain due to load carrying. *European Journal of Applied Physiology*, **61**, 237–245.

Knapik, J., Harman, E. and Reynolds, K. (1996). Load carriage using packs. A review of physiological, biomechanical and medical aspects. *Applied Ergonomics*, **27** (3), 207–216.

Krawczyk, S. (1996). Psychophysical methodology and the evaluation of manual materials handling and upper extremity intensive work. In *Occupational Ergonomics* (A. Bhattacharya and J.D. McGlothlin, eds), pp. 137–145. Marcel Dekker.

Legg, S.J. and Mahanty, A. (1985). Comparison of five modes of carrying load close to the trunk. *Ergonomics*, **28**, 1653–1660.

Luttgens, K. and Hamilton, N. (1997). *Kinesiology – Scientific Basis of Human Motion*. Brown and Benchmark Publishers.

Malhotra, M.S. and Gupta, S. (1965). Carrying of school bags by children. *Ergonomics*, **8**, 55–60.

Pascoe, D., Pascoe, D., Yong Tai W. et al. (1997). Influence of carrying book bags on gait cycle and posture of youths. *Ergonomics*, **40** (6), 631–641.

Roberts, D.E., Reading, J.E., Daley, J.L. et al. (1996). *A physiological and biomechanical evaluation of commercial load-bearing ensembles for the US Marine Corps*. Naval Health Research Centre Report No. 96–7.

Smith, L.K., Weiss, E.L. and Lehmkuhl, L.D. (1996). *Brunnstrom's Clinical Kinesiology*, 5th edn. F.A. Davis Company.

Voll, H.J. and Klimt, F. (1977). Strain in children caused by schoolbags. *Offentliche Gesundheitswesen*, **39**, 369–378.

Winsmann, F.R. and Goldman, R.F. (1976). Methods for evaluation of load-carriage systems. *Perceptual and Motor Skills*, **43**, 1211–1218.

Evaluating neck and shoulder posture in keyboard operators

Grace Szeto, Chris Kirtley, Sally Raine and Leon M. Straker

INTRODUCTION

The increased incidence of work-related neck and upper limb disorders (WRNULD) in the last two decades has occurred despite the introduction of ergonomic modifications and guidelines intended to reduce occupational health problems (Grandjean, 1988; Putz-Anderson, 1988; Winkel and Westgaard, 1992a and b). Among the many contributing factors, postural alignment of the upper body is thought to be one important consideration (Colombini, 1998). The posture of the head, neck and shoulders has been the subject of a number of research studies, which have investigated muscular loading in the neck and upper limb region (Aaras et al., 1988; Enwemeka et al., 1986; Hagberg, 1981; Hanten et al., 1991; Schuldt et al., 1986).

The ideal sitting posture frequently recommended by clinicians involves a retracted head position with an erect cervical spine and retracted shoulders and with the spine fully supported on the backrest of the chair (McKenzie, 1983). Grandjean et al. (1983) observed from a large number of VDU workers that, given adjustable workstation settings, they preferred to adopt a backward-leaning posture rather than maintain an upright position. However, the backward-leaning posture may inevitably lead to a more forward head position and periods of sustained neck flexion when the worker focuses on the computer screen. In a cross-sectional survey study of 420 medical secretaries, a significantly increased risk of neck and shoulder pain was reported when five or more hours were spent working with office machines (Kamwendo et al., 1991).

One of the consequences of sustained neck flexion in sitting is the increased compressive loading in the cervical spine and the creep response in the tissues (Gooch, 1993; Harms-Ringdahl et al., 1986; Twomey and Taylor, 1982). Creep has been defined as 'the progressive deformation of tissue in response to a constant load that is below the fatigue or fracture point for that tissue' (Twomey and Taylor, 1982, p. 116). Gooch (1993) reported significant creep occurring during a period of sustained end-range neck flexion for ten minutes, and a significant increase in pain intensity and distribution in subjects with a current or past history of neck pain. Harms-Ringdahl et al. (1986) calculated the compressive load at the C7-T1 junction and found it to be 3.6 times higher in the fully flexed posture than in the erect posture of the cervical spine. These phenomena may occur concurrently with increased EMG activity in the cervical musculature, as demonstrated by Schuldt et al. (1986). Together these factors may have important implications for people who suffer from WRNULD.

There have been a number of studies that have examined the 'natural' head and shoulder posture in relaxed standing and sitting (Braun and Amundson, 1989; Raine and Twomey, 1994 and 1997; Refshauge et al., 1994). These authors have conducted quantitative studies of posture in the sagittal plane through still photography and/or goniometric measurements of joint angles from skin markers. Raine and Twomey (1997) measured the sagittal head tilt and the C7-tragus angle in a large sample of 160 asymptomatic individuals, providing a useful reference for comparison with the working posture. Refshauge et al. (1994) reported a high consistency and reliability in measuring angles of cervical inclination, comparing within-trial, within-day and between-day measurements. Their study was performed on seventeen 'normal' subjects who were photographed in the sagittal profile and the angles were measured from markers attached along the spine. While their study reported a high consistency of relaxed standing posture over a period of time, there is a lack of information on how posture may change over time in a work situation.

Clinically, rounded shoulders implying scapular protraction have been speculatively associated with forward head posture, although this association has not been fully substantiated in the literature (Greenfield et al., 1995; Janda, 1988; Raine and Twomey, 1994). During keyboard operation, both the position of the head and the shoulder joint may be directly affected by the position of the scapula. Scapular protraction and elevation have seldom been measured in postural analysis studies. Previous studies have mainly examined neck flexion angles and shoulder flexion angles, and there has been strong evidence of increased trapezius muscle activity with sustained postures of the neck and shoulder (Hagberg 1981; Schuldt et al., 1986).

In the ergonomic literature, studies on work posture have mostly included the head and neck angles as part of a composite score for whole body posture, rather than detailed regional analysis (Bendix, 1984; Corlett and Manenica, 1980; Grandjean et al., 1983; Persson and Kilbom, 1983). Neck posture was often measured as a straight line approximating the angle of inclination of the cervical spine by connecting the upper cervical (C2) and lower cervical (C7) spinous processes. More recent studies have turned to computer-aided methods including electronic devices and digitising systems for measuring joint angles (Aaras et al., 1988; Colombini, 1998; Wiktorin et al., 1995). Generally, these studies have attempted to monitor joint movements with different work tasks in order to identify occupational risk factors. The approach used has tended to categorise joint motions in 'zones' of 10–20°, rather than examining precise joint angles. The nature of VDU work tends to involve rather static postures and movements in small ranges in the neck and shoulder region. Thus, more precise analysis is required to understand the changes or patterns of movements in different workers.

Wrigley et al. (1991) reported one of the few studies that recorded body posture during a keyboard operation task on videotapes, where the neck, shoulder, elbow and wrist angles were computed and compared with joint angles measured through goniometry. Kietrys et al. (1998) reported on the relationship between head and neck posture and VDT screen heights. Subjects were photographed while using a computer, and a goniometer was used to measure the visual images of the subject projected on to a wall. The use of manual goniometry to measure joint angles may be susceptible to a certain degree of error in measurement. The use of computer-aided video analysis of movements provides much more precise and detailed kinematic data (Stillman, 1991). The idea of recording neck and shoulder movements in office workers at their actual workstations has important implications in understanding the development of WRNULD. Understanding the postural patterns of individual workers may contribute towards our understanding of why they develop symptoms. The present study aimed to evaluate the neck and shoulder posture and movements in the course of a typical working day. It is postulated that as workers perform VDU work continuously for hours, their neck and shoulder posture would deteriorate with time. A two-dimensional (2-D) motion analysis system was used to examine the head, neck and scapular movements in the sagittal plane of office workers by periodic sampling in the course of a typical working day.

METHODS

Subjects

Eleven female subjects were recruited for this on-site investigation (age range = 22–40, mean age = 30.2). The subjects' job titles ranged from personal secretaries and administrative officers to clerical officers. They were recruited from the clerical staff at a local university. The tasks they routinely performed using the computer included word-processing, data entry, and text editing. Besides computer tasks, they also performed other clerical duties such as filing, photocopying, making journal entries and other typical clerical tasks. The inclusion criteria were that the subjects had to perform a minimum of 2–4 hours of computer work daily. Prior to participating, the subjects were asked a series of questions to gather information about their history of computer work as well as any previous history of, or current complaints of, neck and upper limb discomfort.

Research procedures

The subject's posture was videotaped using a digital video camcorder (Panasonic NV-DX100EN). Ten minutes of videotape was recorded for each subject while performing VDU work and this process was repeated five times throughout a typical working day. The exact timing of the trials had to be flexible to fit in with the work routine of the subjects, but all subjects were able to complete two trials in the morning and three trials in the afternoon (with a gap of approximately one hour in between two consecutive trials). Segments of the videotapes were selected for digitisation using the Peak 5 motion analysis system (Peak Performance Technologies Inc., 1992). The digitisation process produced raw data in terms of pixel co-ordinates that could be used to compute the head tilt and neck flexion angles, and the displacements of the acromion process along the *x*- and *y*-axis.

The video camera was set up at a suitable distance of approximately 1–1.5 m away from and perpendicular to the subject's sagittal profile. A wooden board covered with black cardboard was placed behind the subject to provide the necessary contrast to the anatomical markers. Skin markers consisting of white foam balls (2.5 cm in diameter) glued on to strips of black Velcro tapes were attached to the subject's skin with adhesive tape. The markers were placed on the four named anatomical landmarks, and this procedure was always carried out by the same investigator to reduce the variability in marker placement. The four anatomical 'landmarks' used were: (1) midpoint of forehead, (2) tragus of ear, (3) C7 spinous process and (4) acromion process (see Figure 7.6).

At the start of each videotaping trial, an aluminium rod of a known length (30 cm) was placed in the sagittal plane of the subject for approximately thirty seconds. The calibration procedure was performed in accordance with the requirements of the Peak system. The images with the aluminium rod were captured and digitised in order to compute the 'scaling factor' for the videotape. The scaling factors were used by the Peak program to convert the pixel co-ordinates obtained from digitising into real units of measurements (e.g. centimetres). This procedure had to be performed each time the camera was adjusted or turned off.

Prior to the main study, a pilot study was conducted to establish the intra-rater reliability for placing the markers consistently in the correct and same positions. The intra-class correlation coefficients were high (ICC 3,3 = 0.62–0.81) for the intra-rater reliability. In the pilot study, comparison was also made between positioning the video camera on the left versus the right side of the subject. The

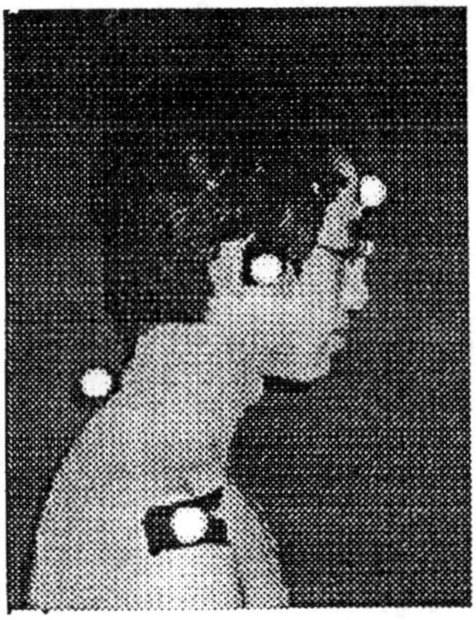

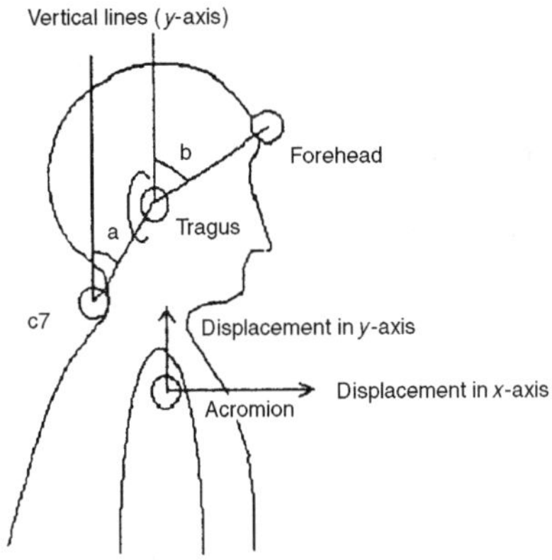

Figure 7.6 Left-hand side: Photograph showing positions of the four markers in the sagittal plane. Right-hand side: Diagram showing the defining lines of the joint angles of head tilt (a) and neck flexion (b). Acromion displacements in the *x*-axis and *y*-axis define the movements of protraction and elevation respectively

results suggested that there was no significant difference in the head tilt and neck flexion angles when approaching from the left or right. This is an important consideration, as the actual office settings often involved limited space for positioning the camera.

Subjects were asked to carry on with their normal clerical duties and the video camera would only capture certain periods when they were using the computer. They were instructed to be as natural as possible, and assume their normal posture. The only restriction was that they were advised not to swivel on the chair if possible, to reduce out-of-plane artefacts.

In the first and the last period of recording, i.e. during the morning and again in the late afternoon, two minutes of 'static sitting posture' was recorded as a baseline measurement to reflect the subject's normal relaxed sitting posture when not working. For this part, the instructions to the subjects were to look straight ahead in front of them, with the arms resting on their laps and the back resting on the backrest of the chair. After each video-recording period, the markers were removed and subjects continued with their work.

Data management and analysis

All the digital videotapes recorded were duplicated to super VHS tapes which were encoded and digitised using the Peak system. For each segment of videotape recorded, two sections of ten seconds each were analysed by the Peak (= 500 frames each lot). For each trial, the two sections of videotape were selected with the first one in the first three to five minutes of the film and the second segment in the eight to ten minute period. The images selected for analysis were based on the criteria that they represented the typical posture of that particular subject, with minimal body movements or out-of-plane artefacts. The digitisation process produced raw data in terms of x,y pixel co-ordinates for each of the four markers, with reference to a fixed point of origin (0,0) on the lower left-hand corner of the screen. The raw data were put through the data-conditioning process using the Butterworth filter with a cut-off frequency of 4 Hz.

The conditioned data of markers 1, 2 and 3 were used to compute the angles of head tilt and neck flexion (see Figure 7.6). The x and y co-ordinates of the acromion marker were used to compute the displacement of the scapula in terms of protraction and elevation. The displacement of the acromion marker along the x-axis indicated protraction of the scapula, while movements along the y-axis indicated elevation. The root mean squares (RMS) of the x and y co-ordinates were computed to reflect the magnitudes of the displacements in the two directions.

In summary, the kinematic parameters computed by the Peak system and analysed statistically were:

1. Head tilt: the angle between the line joining the forehead and tragus, and the y-axis.
2. Neck flexion: the angle between the line of the tragus and C7, and the y-axis.

3. Scapular elevation: the RMS of the upward displacement of the acromion along the y-axis.
4. Scapular protraction: the RMS of the forward displacement of the acromion along the x-axis.

The conditioned data were transformed into Excel spreadsheets and the SPSS package was used for statistical analysis. In the statistical analysis, paired t-tests were used to compare the means of the 'a' and 'b' segments of each trial, as well as to the means of the first and second static sitting trials. Repeated measure ANOVA was performed to compare the means of the four types of kinematic parameters in the five trials, and those in the static sitting trials (S1 and S2). Within-subject contrasts were used to compare each trial individually against static sitting, which was defined as trial 6.

RESULTS

The means and standard deviations of the head tilt and neck flexion angles are presented in Table 7.2. The measurements within each trial were generally consistent, as the coefficients of variation were within the range 0.1–0.15.

For both the head tilt and neck flexion angles, paired t-tests revealed no significant difference between the two trials of static sitting, recorded in the morning and late afternoon ($p > 0.05$). There was also no significant difference between the means of the 'a' segment and the means of the 'b' segment ($p > 0.05$). Thus, for subsequent analysis, the mean values of the 'a' and 'b' segments of each trial were computed and used for the between-trial comparison.

The data were compared at different time periods of the day (trials 1–5), as well as compared to the 'static sitting posture' of each subject. For the head tilt data, the repeated measure ANOVA reported an overall statistically significant difference comparing all six trials ($p = 0.02$). The within-subject contrasts also showed significant differences between trials 1–5 when each trial was compared to static sitting or trial 6 (p values = 0.003–0.039). However, there were no significant differences comparing each of the five trials individually among themselves ($p > 0.05$). For the neck flexion data, the repeated measure ANOVA produced an overall p value of 0.000. Statistically significant differences were reported in trials 1–5 when contrasted against the static sitting (trial 6) (p values = 0.002–0.044). Again no significant difference was found when the five trials were contrasted against each other ($p > 0.05$).

The same statistical tests were performed on the means of the RMS data of the x and y co-ordinates of the acromion data (see Table 7.3). Generally the displacements were of very small magnitudes (0.1–1.5 cm). Comparing the RMS data of the five trials against those of static sitting revealed mostly non-significant results, except for trial 3 (x-axis) and trial 5 (y-axis). Generally it can be considered that there was no significant change in the acromion position among the various trials.

Table 7.2 Summary of head tilt and neck flexion angles comparing trials 1–5 against static sitting ($n = 11$)

	Trial 1 Mean ±SD	**Trial 2 Mean ±SD**	**Trial 3 Mean ±SD**	**Trial 4 Mean ±SD**	**Trial 5 Mean ±SD**	**Static sitting Mean ±SD**	**Overall *p* value RMANOVA**
Head tilt (°)	60.35 ± 6.56*	60.27 ± 7.32*	59.85 ± 6.88*	60.75 ± 5.42*	60.02 ± 7.14*	55.61 ± 4.60	0.020 (power = 0.631)
Neck flexion (°)	56.50 ± 7.31*	55.71 ± 6.98*	54.43 ± 7.47*	53.30 ± 8.14*	57.22 ± 8.49*	48.92 ± 5.45	0.000 (power = 0.998)

* $p < 0.05$ indicates statistical significance, trial versus static sitting (repeated measure ANOVA followed by contrasts).

Table 7.3 Summary of RMS of acromion *x,y* co-ordinates comparing trials 1–5 against static sitting ($n = 11$)

Acromion	**Trial 1 Mean ± SD**	**Trial 2 Mean ± SD**	**Trial 3 Mean ± SD**	**Trial 4 Mean ± SD**	**Trial 5 Mean ± SD**	**Static sitting Mean ± SD**
RMS of *x* co-ordinates	0.37 ± 0.37	0.29 ± 0.26	0.33 ± 0.39*	0.48 ± 0.66	0.34 ± 0.31	0.04 ± 0.04
RMS of *y* co-ordinates	0.22 ± 0.21	0.21 ± 0.17	0.18 ± 0.11	0.25 ± 0.23	0.21 ± 0.19*	0.04 ± 0.02

* $p < 0.05$ indicates statistical significance, trial versus static sitting (repeated measure ANOVA followed by contrasts).

DISCUSSION

Comparing head tilt, neck flexion and acromion movements in keyboard operators

The present results suggested that the head tilt and neck flexion angle measurements showed rather similar patterns among all the subjects. Both the head tilt and neck flexion angles were significantly different from the static 'relaxed' sitting posture of the subjects ($p > 0.05$). This finding may possibly suggest that the subjects tended to increase the flexion in their cervical spine as well as the head tilt when they focused on the VDU. This finding is consistent with previous reports (Grandjean et al., 1983) that workers tend to adopt a more forward head posture when they perform VDU work in comparison to their sitting postures.

However, examining the joint angle data in the different trials, there was no obvious pattern of change from morning to afternoon. This finding is in contrast to the initial hypothesis that the forward head posture would continue to increase with prolonged VDU work. The present finding may be partly contributed to by the varied nature of the subjects' work tasks. The workers recruited in the present study were not 'typists' as such, but were mainly office workers who performed a variety of office duties. Even their work with the computer consisted of a number of tasks and the length of time they spent at each VDU task varied greatly. This may have accounted for the subjects' ability to maintain their postures within a consistent range throughout the day. It is still possible that if the computer work was sustained for a prolonged period (more than an hour for example), the posture recorded would show a more detectable pattern of change. In future, the investigation may be extended to include workers who perform keyboard work for longer periods of up to six to eight hours per day. The sample size in the present study is relatively small (average power = 0.702), and further investigations need to be conducted on larger sample sizes in order to provide more conclusive evidence in this area.

The study by Raine and Twomey (1997) reported the means of the sagittal C7-tragus angles to be 128.1–133.2° (measured from the horizontal), with the standard deviations ranging from 4.4 to 6.2°. These data were recorded in asymptomatic females covering a wide age range and they were measured in relaxed standing. When the present head tilt and neck flexion angles were converted to similar measurements (with reference to the horizontal) as used in the work of Raine and Twomey (1997), the results were within similar ranges in terms of the mean angles and standard deviations (mean neck flexion in static sitting was 138.92 ± 5.45, and ranged from 143.30 to 147.22 in the five working trials). Some of the differences in the measurements between the two studies may be related to the difference in sitting versus standing postures. The head tilt angle in the present study was measured from the mid-forehead to the tragus, and therefore is not directly comparable to that in other studies which have examined the eye–ear line. The angle offset would have to be measured on the subjects before the present data could be directly compared to those in other studies.

The acromion data showed relatively little change in terms of movements in the *x*- and *y*-axes. This finding may suggest that there was no significant increase in the amount of protraction and elevation of the scapula during the course of a working day. However, the subjects may have subconsciously restricted their own movements as they were instructed to refrain from moving excessively in the chairs. Further investigation is required to confirm the present finding. The use of EMG to study muscle activity concurrently with kinematic assessment may provide more useful information in this respect.

Factors affecting subjects' movements and postures

In the present study, it has been observed that the nature of the work task, the furniture and the equipment have considerable effects on the subjects' movements. The tasks performed by the subjects were varied and included word-processing, text editing, data entry and reading/answering e-mail messages on-screen. It was noted that if the subjects were typing from a document placed to one side, there were considerable head movements towards that side. Most of the subjects did not have to look at the keyboard frequently. Most of the time they would be looking at the monitor screen or the documents placed on either side. This factor appeared to have more effect on the subjects' head movements rather than their intrinsic postural habits. Karlqvist et al. (1998) also reported similar problems in isolating the 2-D movements of the markers in their study of varying the mouse positions. The authors commented that their results were specific to the nature of the work performed (text editing), and that the results could not be generalised to other work tasks.

On-site kinematic studies versus laboratory investigations

The present study describes a method to evaluate posture within a worker's actual work environment. The advantages of the system lie in the use of a single video camera and the fact that the procedure is relatively non-intrusive. The worker only needs to stop work when the markers have to be placed. The markers themselves do not interfere with the worker's movements or vision, and it has been observed that the workers can proceed quite naturally with their work. However, it is still difficult to tell whether the subjects were psychologically conscious of their posture. This problem would always exist in any postural analysis study, unless a hidden camera is used and the subject is totally unaware of the process.

The present study is a 2-D analysis of posture and movements. As VDU work is a relatively sedentary job, this system is adequate to provide kinematic information in the sagittal plane. However, if the subjects had the tendency to rotate their heads frequently, there may be a considerable margin of error in computing the joint angles in the sagittal plane. In selecting the appropriate frames for digitisation, the investigator had to visually inspect the images and look for ones that represented the typical posture of the subject and check that there were minimal out-of-plane movements.

A more precise approach would be to perform 3-D kinematic analysis, where a system of four to six video cameras is required. Karlqvist et al. (1998) used a 3-D system to study the upper body posture with varying positions of the mouse. Three-dimensional studies are usually conducted in a laboratory situation, where the cameras are strategically positioned to capture the images in all three planes. It would be difficult to study postural changes for long periods with laboratory investigations and the workstation would have to be simulated, which may not give an environment completely similar to the actual work situation.

CONCLUSIONS

The present study describes a method for evaluating neck and shoulder posture in the sagittal plane which was conducted at the workers' actual workplaces. The results showed that there was a significant increase in the head tilt and neck flexion angles when the workers performed VDU work, as compared to their relaxed static sitting posture. The acromion showed relatively very little movement in terms of protraction and elevation during VDU work or in static sitting.

Contrary to the initial hypothesis, the present results revealed no significant difference in the neck and shoulder posture at different times of the day. This would suggest that there was no increasing forward head posture and no increasing forward scapular movements with prolonged seated VDU work. However, the results were greatly influenced by the tasks performed by the workers and the workstation characteristics. The present results may suggest that the working posture adopted by VDU workers may be more a function of personal or pre-existing postural habits, which do not show great changes in the course of a working day. Further investigations are required to substantiate these claims using larger sample sizes.

References

Aaras, A., Westgaard, R.H. and Stranden, E. (1988). Postural angles as an indicator of postural load and muscular injury in occupational work situations. *Ergonomics*, **31** (6), 915–933.

Bendix, T. (1984). Seated trunk posture at various seat inclinations, seat heights and table heights. *Human Factors*, **26** (6), 695–703.

Braun, B.L. and Amundson, L.R. (1989). Quantitative assessment of head and shoulder posture. *Archives of Physical and Medical Rehabilitation*, **70**, 322–329.

Colombini, D. (1998). An observational method for classifying exposure to repetitive movements of the upper limbs. *Ergonomics*, **41** (9), 1261–1289.

Corlett, E.N. and Manenica, I. (1980). The effects and measurement of working postures. *Applied Ergonomics*, **11** (1), 7–16.

Enwemeka, C.S., Bonet, I.M., Ingle, J.A. et al. (1986). Postural correction in persons with neck pain. II: Integrated electromyography of the upper trapezius in three simulated neck positions. *Journal of Orthopedics and Sports Physiotherapy*, **8**, 240–242.

Gooch, L. (1993). A controlled study of sustained cervical spine flexion. *Masters Thesis*, Curtin University of Technology, Western Australia.

Grandjean, E., Hunting, W. and Pidermann, M. (1983). VDT workstation design: preferred settings and their effects, *Human Factors*, **25** (2), 161–175.

Grandjean, E. (1988). *Fitting the Task to the Man*, 4th edn. Taylor and Francis.

Green, R. and Briggs, C. (1990). Prevalence of overuse injury among keyboard operators: characteristics of the job, the operator and the work environment, *Journal of Occupational Health and Safety – Australia and New Zealand*, **6** (2), 109–118.

Greenfield, B., Catlin, P.A., Coats, P.W. et al. (1995). Posture in patients with shoulder overuse injuries and healthy individuals. *Journal of Orthopedics and Sports Physiotherapy*, **21** (5), 287–295.

Hagberg, M. (1981). Electromyographic signs of shoulder muscular fatigue in two elevated arm positions. *American Journal of Physical and Medicine*, **60**, 111–121.

Hanten, W.P., Lucio, R.M., Russell, J.L. et al. (1991). Assessment of total head excursion and resting head posture. *Archives of Physical and Medical Rehabilitation*, **72**, 877–880.

Harms-Ringdahl, K., Ekholm, J., Schuldt, K. et al. (1986). Load moments and myoelectric activity when the cervical spine is held in full flexion and extension. *Ergonomics*, **29** (12), 1539–1552.

Janda, V. (1988). Muscles and cervicogenic pain syndromes. In *Physical Therapy of the Cervical and Thoracic Spine* (R. Grant, ed.), pp. 271–289. Churchill Livingstone.

Kamwendo, K., Linton, S.J. and Moritz, U. (1991). Neck and shoulder disorders in medical secretaries. Part II: Ergonomic work environment and symptom profile. *Scandinavian Journal of Surgery*, **23**, 135–142.

Karlqvist, L.K., Bernmark, E., Ekenvall, L. et al. (1998). Computer mouse position as a determinant of posture, muscular load and perceived exertion. *Scandinavian Journal of Work and Environmental Health*, **24** (1), 62–73.

Kietrys, D.M., McClure, P.W. and Fitzgerald, G.K. (1998). The relationship between head and neck posture and VDT screen height in keyboard operators. *Physical Therapy*, **78** (4), 395–403.

McKenzie, R.A. (1983). *Treat Your Own Neck*. Spinal Publications.

Peak Performance Technologies Inc. (1992). *Peak 5 User's Reference Manual*. Englewood, Colorado.

Persson, J. and Kilbom, A. (1983). VIRA – a simple video film technique for registering and analysis of work positions/places and movements. *Investigative Report*, NIOH, Sweden, p. 10.

Putz-Anderson, V. (1988). *Cumulative Trauma Disorders*. Taylor and Francis.

Raine, S. and Twomey, L. (1994). Posture of the head, shoulders and thoracic spine in comfortable erect standing. *Australian Journal of Physiotherapy*, **40** (1), 25–32.

Raine, S. and Twomey, L.T. (1997). Head and shoulder posture variations in 160 asymptomatic women and men. *Archives of Physical and Medical Rehabilitation*, **78**, 1215–1223.

Refshauge, K., Goodsell, M. and Lee, M. (1994). Consistency of cervical and cervicothoracic posture in standing. *Australian Journal of Physiotherapy*, **40** (4), 235–240.

Schuldt, K., Ekholm, J., Harms-Ringdahl, K. et al. (1986). Effects of changes in sitting work posture on static neck and shoulder muscle activity. *Ergonomics*, **29** (12), 1525–1537.

Stillman, B. (1991). Computer-based video analysis of movement. *Australian Journal of Physiotherapy*, **37** (4), 219–228.

Twomey, L. and Taylor, J. (1982). Flexion creep deformation and hysteresis in the lumbar vertebral column. *Spine*, **7**, 116–122.

Wiktorin, C., Mortimer, M., Ekenvall, L. et al. (1995). HARBO, a simple computer-aided observation method for recording work postures. *Scandinavian Journal of Work and Environmental Health*, **21**, 440–449.

Winkel, J. and Westgaard, R. (1992a). Occupational and individual risk factors for shoulder-neck complaints: Part I: Guidelines for the practitioner. *International Journal of Industrial Ergonomics*, **10**, 79–83.

Winkel, J. and Westgaard, R. (1992b). Occupational and individual risk factors for shoulder-neck complaints: Part II: The scientific basis (literature review) for the guide. *International Journal of Industrial Ergonomics*, **10**, 85–104.

Wrigley, T.V., Green, R.A. and Briggs, C.A. (1991). Microcomputer video image processing technology in working posture analysis. *Applied Ergonomics*, **22** (1), 2–8.

Chapter 8

Functional capacity assessment

Commercially available work-related assessments: are they reliable and valid?

Ev Innes and Leon Straker

INTRODUCTION

The move from clinic-based to workplace-based interventions in occupational rehabilitation services has resulted in a subsequent change in the use of various assessments to determine an injured worker's functional abilities and the suitable duties that can be performed. The work-related assessments used commonly assess tasks and skills, and extrapolate this information to the ability to perform a specific job (Innes and Straker, in press b). Most commercial work samples and evaluation devices, however, have limited research-based literature on which to support their use.

The ongoing concern for clinicians is the usefulness of assessment results in guiding the safe and swift return to work of injured workers. To be useful to clinicians the results must provide valid and reliable information to enable appropriate clinical decisions to be made. Concerns over the usefulness of current work-related assessments have fuelled the call for these assessments to demonstrate valid and reliable results (Abdel-Moty et al., 1996; Gibson and Strong, 1997; Innes, 1997a; Innes and Straker, 1998b; King et al., 1998; Krefting and Bremner, 1985; Lechner et al., 1991). Ensuring an appropriate match between the injured worker's abilities and work requirements is also an important purpose of work-related assessments (Innes, 1997a and b).

This indicates that the assessment should be appropriate to the functional level of the individual and the job requirements (Innes and Straker, 1998a).

The purpose of this study was to: (1) identify the functional level of commercially available work-related assessments, and (2) conduct a survey of current research and documentation regarding the reliability and validity of these assessments. The objective was to determine the extent and quality of the research conducted on a wide range of work-related assessments that are currently in use, or available to therapists in occupational rehabilitation in Australia.

Level of assessment

There has been criticism that many functional assessments, particularly work-related assessments, have an over-emphasis on the assessment of the individual separate from the situational context, as opposed to the interaction of the individual with the environment (Velozo, 1993). This highlights the need for the assessment to have high face validity in relation to actual job requirements and worker performance.

An individual's function can be considered at the role, activity, task, skill or body system level (Packer, 1995). Jobs can be considered in relation to the position, duties, tasks, task elements or elemental motions involved (U.S. Department of Labor Employment and Training, 1991). For example, a person may have a role as a worker, or more specifically a cabinet-maker (job position). The activities or duties that are required to perform this role/job position include making and installing custom-made furniture and fittings. The tasks that make up the activities/duties include lifting and carrying wood and equipment, measuring a length of wood, sawing, hammering nails, and sanding. In order to complete these tasks it is necessary to have appropriate skills or consider the task elements that make up the tasks. These may include manual dexterity to manipulate tools and equipment, and sufficient strength to lift 25 kg from the ground to waist level. At the body system level or considering the elemental motions required aspects such as range of motion and muscle strength are considered.

When these aspects are combined to determine the ability of an individual to perform a job, it is possible to consider the most appropriate type of work-related assessment that will assess an individual at an appropriate level in relation to the job. Figure 8.1 (Innes and Straker, 1998a) demonstrates how the type of work-related assessment is related to the individual functional level and the job requirements level. It can be seen that some forms of assessment may be used for more than one functional level or job requirement level (e.g., work samples may be used to assess activities, tasks or skills in the individual, or duties, tasks or task elements of a job). The reason for this is related to the specific details of individual assessments. For example, there may be sub-components or sub-tests within an assessment that address different levels of individual function or job requirement level.

Reliability and validity of work-related assessments

Selecting an instrument on the basis of assessment at an appropriate functional level is important, but so too is selecting a tool with acceptable reliability and validity. It is widely recognised that one of the major problems associated with the administration of work-related assessments is that of insufficient evidence for

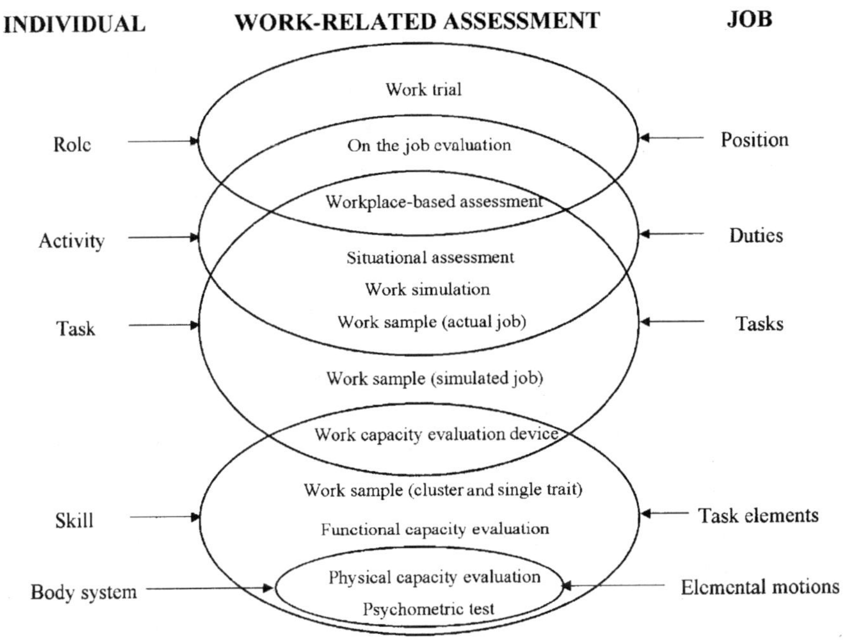

Figure 8.1 Comparison of work-related assessments to individual functional level and job requirements level

reliability and validity (e.g. Gibson and Strong, 1997; Innes and Straker, 1998b; King et al., 1998; Lechner et al., 1991).

There have been two major reviews of commercial work-related assessments (King et al., 1998; Lechner et al., 1991). Lechner et al. (1991) reviewed ten assessment systems used in the United States of America (USA) for evidence of validity and reliability (Blankenship FCE, BTE Work Simulator, Isernhagen FCE, Key FCA, Matheson, Physio-Tek, Polinsky FCA, Smith PCE, Sweat Valpar CWS). The results from that review were of major concern. Of the assessments examined, it was reported that none had inter-rater reliability studies, and only one or two had intra-rater reliability, content, criterion-related or construct validity studies (Lechner et al., 1991). Unfortunately, the sources of information on which some of the results were based were not reported, and so it is not possible to review the original studies. There were also a number of published studies not considered.

Since the review by Lechner et al. (1991) further assessments have been developed, and existing systems revised, modified and updated. Some assessments are no longer commercially available although they may remain in use. King et al. (1998) conducted a more recent review, also of ten commercial work-related assessments, only three of which were included in the Lechner et al. (1991) study (Blankenship FCE, Isernhagen FCE, Key FCA). The remaining seven assessments (ARCON, AssessAbility, ERGOS work simulator, ErgoScience Physical Work Performance Evaluation (PWPE), WEST-EPIC, WorkAbility Mk III, WorkHab) had either been developed since 1991 or were not included by Lechner et al. King et al. reported that only two assessments had inter-rater and intra-rater reliability studies published, and only one had a published validity study. There was, however, no discussion or critique of either these studies.

Both Lechner et al. (1991) and King et al. (1998) reviewed a wide range of aspects associated with a limited range of work-related assessments, including evidence of reliability and validity. Neither of these reviews, however, focused exclusively on these issues and so was unable to explore reliability or validity in depth. For this reason, the current study has examined the existing available literature in detail in order to review the extent to which reliability and validity have been established for a range of work-related assessments (Innes and Straker, in press a and b).

The most common types of reliability studies that have been conducted on work-related assessments are test–retest or intra-rater reliability studies. Inter-rater reliability has also been examined for some assessments. Some forms of reliability, such as alternate forms, split-half or internal consistency, are usually impractical to determine in functional assessments. There is usually no equivalent form of the work-related assessment with which it can be compared. Split-half reliability may be determined on some work samples where multiple identical test items are produced, but this does not apply to many current work-related assessments.

The validity of work-related assessments has not been examined to the same degree as reliability. The main areas of study have been various aspects of criterion validity, both concurrent and predictive validity, and more rarely, construct and content validity. There are studies, however, which may be considered to contribute to the construct validity of assessments, particularly in demonstrating a measurable change following intervention (e.g. Moran and Strong, 1995).

METHODOLOGY

This study surveyed an extensive range of information sources to the end of 1997 to determine (1) the level of the assessment; and (2) the extent of evidence of reliability and validity of all forms for work-related assessments. Methods used to access these sources were:

- CD-ROM searches of the CINAHL (1980–Dec 1997), Medline (1970–Dec 1997), Psychinfo (1984–Dec 1997) and ACEL Occupational Health and Safety databases, using the key words 'functional capacity evaluation', 'vocational assessment', 'work assessment', 'work evaluation', 'work sample', and the specific names of the various assessments (e.g. Valpar);
- Using secondary sources (i.e. reference lists from published articles) to locate further literature;

- Examining administration and procedure manuals for specific assessments when these were available;
- Contacting distributors of specific assessments;
- Accessing proceedings of conferences where it was known papers had been presented on specific work-related assessments; and
- Accessing theses, or abstracts of theses, where it was known that research had been conducted on specific work-related assessments.

Twenty-eight work-related assessments were included in the study from a total of 55 that were identified (Innes and Straker, in press a and b). Of these 28, eleven are presented here. The selection criteria for inclusion in the study were work-related assessments that are: (1) currently in use in occupational rehabilitation in Australia, (2) currently commercially available or still in use, (3) referred to in publications, and (4) predominantly focused on physical factors associated with work.

The 11 assessments included in this paper are: Blankenship FCE, BTE Work Simulator, EPIC Lift Capacity Test, ERGOS Work Simulator, ErgoScience PWPE, Isernhagen FCE, Key Method FCA, Valpar Component Work Samples, WEST Standard Evaluation, WorkAbility Mark III, and WorkHab Australia.

These assessments cover a wide range of work demands and include instruments that are based on the observation skills of the clinician (e.g. Isernhagen FCE, PWPE). Some instruments are computerised (BTE Work Simulator, ERGOS Work Simulator), while others have specific equipment that is used (e.g. Blankenship FCE, Valpar CWS, WorkAbility Mk III, WorkHab Australia). A number focus specifically on lifting (EPIC Lift Capacity Test, WEST Standard Evaluation), while others cover the wide gamut of physical demands (e.g. Blankenship FCE, Isernhagen FCE, Key FCA).

Determination of level of assessment

Each assessment was examined to determine how it related to the individual functional level and job requirements as indicated in Figure 8.1. Assessments may be at more than one level if the sub-components of sub-tests address different levels of individual function or job requirement (e.g. assess tasks and skills).

Categorisation of evidence for reliability and validity

Each work-related assessment was examined for evidence of reliability, instrument precision and validity, as well as any contributory evidence. The evidence was categorised according to the quality of the information provided. Each piece of evidence was also critiqued in terms of the study design, subjects, analyses and interpretation of results to enable a judgement to be made on the acceptability of the reliability or validity of the assessment studied.

The levels of evidence for the reliability of work-related assessments included in this review were categorised into six broad categories (Table 8.1). Some assessments in this study had evidence of reliability and/or validity from a number of these levels. It should be noted, however, that although the reliability or validity of an assessment has been examined and reported in adequate detail in a peer-reviewed forum (i.e. Level 5), this does not indicate that the reliability or validity is acceptable for clinical purposes.

For each work-related assessment all available evidence of reliability and validity was located and examined. Following a thorough analysis of the information for the detail necessary to determine the quality and usefulness of the evidence presented, the level of evidence was determined and summarised. For those assessments with acceptable levels of evidence (Levels 4 and 5) the level of reliability or validity was then determined based on the interpretation of measures of reliability or level of validity described in Tables 8.2 and 8.3.

RESULTS

Functional level

The functional levels of the work-related assessments included in this study are presented in Table 8.4. It can be seen that all the instruments assess function at either the skill or task level, usually both. Very few assess at the activity or body

Table 8.1 Levels of evidence for reliability and validity (from Innes and Straker, in press a and b)

Level	Description
0	No reliability/validity demonstrated or reported.
1	Reliability/validity is assumed from previous studies conducted on aspects now incorporated into the current assessment. Previous studies may be in either a non-peer-reviewed or peer-reviewed forum.
2	Reliability/validity is reported, but there is no detail provided to enable examination of the results. Maybe in either a non-peer-reviewed or peer-reviewed forum.
3	Reliability/validity is reported with some detail to enable a cursory examination of the results, but more detail is required. Maybe in either a non-peer-reviewed or peer-reviewed forum. Often, but not always, an abstract of a conference presentation.
4	Reliability/validity is reported with sufficient detail to enable examination of the results. Results and detail are provided in a non-peer-reviewed forum (i.e. conference presentation, administration manual, book, Honours, Masters or Doctoral thesis).
5	Reliability/validity, with sufficient detail to enable examination of the results, is reported and published in a peer-reviewed forum (i.e. peer-reviewed journal).

Table 8.2 Interpretation of measures of reliability (from Innes and Straker, in press a)

Measure of reliability	Range of values	Interpretation of values
Correlation coefficients (*r*)	0.00–0.25	Little or no relationship
	0.26–0.50	Poor to fair
	0.51–0.75	Moderate to good
	> 0.75	Good to excellent
	$\geqslant 0.90$	Required for clinical application to ensure valid interpretation of findings
Intra-class correlation coefficient (ICC)	$\leqslant 0.75$	Poor to moderate
	> 0.75	Good reliability
	$\geqslant 0.90$	Required for clinical application to ensure valid interpretation of findings
Kappa (κ) value	0.00	Chance agreement
	0.01–0.40	Poor to fair agreement
	0.41–0.60	Moderate agreement
	0.61–0.80	Substantial agreement
	0.81–1.00	Excellent to perfect agreement

system levels, and none at the role level. This is a reflection of the nature of the work-related assessments included, with all described as work samples (Valpar Component Work Samples), work capacity evaluation devices (BTE Work Simulator, ERGOS Work Simulator) or functional capacity evaluations (Blankenship FCE, EPIC Lift Capacity, Isernhagen FCE, Key Method FCA, PWPE, WEST Standard Evaluation, WorkAbility Mk III, WorkHab).

Reliability

A summary of the level of evidence for reliability and precision that could be located for the 11 work-related assessments is presented in Table 8.5. For assessments with acceptable levels of evidences (Levels 4 and 5) the level of reliability is reported in Table 8.6.

Validity

The level of evidence for validity that could be located is summarised in Table 8.7. Table 8.8 presents the level of validity for those assessments with acceptable levels of evidence (Levels 4 and 5).

Table 8.3 Levels of validity (from Innes and Straker, in press b)

Type of validity	Level of validity	Interpretation of level
Face validity	Unknown	Insufficient evidence upon which to base a sound judgement.
	Poor	Most experts, clients and/or test users consider there is little relation between the test and what it intended to measure.
	Moderate	Most experts, clients and/or test users consider there is some relationship between the test and what it intended to measure; however, some relevant components are not included.
	Good	Most experts, clients and/or test users agree that the test measures what is intended, and all relevant components are included.
Content validity	Unknown	Insufficient evidence upon which to base a sound judgement.
	Poor	Most experts consider there is little relation between the test and what it intended to measure.
	Moderate	Most experts consider there is some relationship between the test and what it intended to measure; however, some relevant components are not included.
	Good	Most experts agree that the test measures what is intended, and all relevant components are included.
Criterion validity	Unknown	Insufficient evidence upon which to base a sound judgement.
	Poor	Statistical evidence suggests there is little similarity between the test and criterion measure (e.g. percentage agreement $<70\%$, $\kappa \leqslant 0.40$, $r > 0.50$).
	Moderate	Statistical evidence suggests there is some similarity between the test and criterion measure (e.g. percentage agreement $\geqslant 70\%$, $\kappa > 0.40$, $r > 0.50$).

Table 8.3 *(continued)*

Type of validity	Level of validity	Interpretation of level
	Good	Statistical evidence suggests there is substantial similarity between the test and criterion measure (e.g. percentage agreement $>90\%$, $\kappa > 0.60$, $r > 0.75$).
Construct validity	Unknown	Insufficient evidence upon which to base a sound judgement.
	Poor	Statistical evidence suggests a poor ability to differentiate between groups or interventions (small effect size), or poor convergence between similar tests (e.g. $r < 0.30$), or poor divergence between similar tests.
	Moderate	Statistical evidence suggests a moderate ability to differentiate between groups or interventions (medium effect size), or moderate convergence between similar tests (e.g. $r < 0.60$), or good divergence between similar tests.
	Good	Statistical evidence suggests a good ability to differentiate between groups or interventions (large effect size), or good convergence between similar tests (e.g. $r \geqslant 0.60$), or good divergence between similar tests.

DISCUSSION

Evidence of reliability

The results of this study indicate that the evidence for reliability of a wide range of work-related assessments ranges from non-existent to being investigated and reported in sufficient detail to enable decisions to be made regarding their clinical utility. There does not appear to be a single assessment that has been thoroughly and comprehensively investigated for all relevant aspects of reliability. Some systems, however, appear to have a promising basis on which to build further studies to provide sufficient evidence of reliability.

It is recognised that a limitation of this study is the limited evidence of reliability at Level 4. Studies may not have been located, as reference to them is very limited and obtaining them is equally difficult. It is possible that there are many more studies at this level, but they were not located for this study. This limitation highlights the importance of researchers at all levels to publish their findings in public forums that are accessible around the world rather than in a limited geographical region.

A positive outcome of this study is the number of work-related assessments found to have evidence of reliability reported in sufficient detail to enable evaluation and presented in a peer-reviewed forum (Level 5). The BTE Work Simulator, EPIC Lift Capacity, ERGOS Work Simulator, Isernhagen FCE (Lifting), PWPE and WEST Standard Evaluation all have reliability studies published in peer-reviewed journals. It should be noted, however, that while it is commendable that these studies are published, it does not indicate that these assessments have acceptable reliability for clinical purposes. Also, many have only investigated some portions of the overall assessment for reliability, or only have some forms of reliability investigated.

Level of reliability

For assessments with an adequate level of evidence (i.e. Level 4 or 5), it is possible to also comment on the acceptability of the reliability for clinical purposes using the guidelines previously described (Table 8.2). It is not possible to comment on the reported reliability for those assessments with evidence at

Table 8.4 Functional level of work-related assessments

	Functional level				
Assessment	**Role/ positions**	**Activity/ duties**	**Tasks**	**Skill/ task elements**	**Body systems/ elemental motions**
Blankenship FCE	No	No	Yes	Yes	Yes
BTE Work Simulator	No	No	No	Yes	No
EPIC (PLC II was precursor of EPIC)	No	No	Yes	No	No
ERGOS Work Simulator	No	Yes	Yes	Yes	No
Isernhagen FCE	No	No	Yes	Yes	Yes
Key FCA	No	No	Yes	Yes	No
PWPE	No	No	Yes	Yes	No
Valpar CWS	No	Yes	Yes	No	No
WEST Standard Evaluation	No	No	Yes	Yes	No
WorkAbility Mk III	No	No	Yes	Yes	No
WorkHab	No	No	Yes	Yes	Yes

lower levels (0–3) due the lack of necessary information to enable an adequate critique of the results presented.

The assessment with a consistently good level of instrument precision, test–retest and intra-test reliability across a number of attachments is the BTE Work Simulator. This is only true, however, when it is used in the static mode.

Those assessments that focus on a single or limited number of aspects of work-related function, such as the EPIC Lift Capacity and Valpar Component Work Samples (4 and 19), also demonstrate good levels of reliability. The EPIC in particular has consistently demonstrated good to excellent reliability over a number of studies, therefore increasing confidence in this assessment.

Work-related assessments consisting of multiple sub-tests or components range from having no evidence of reliability at all (Key FCA), through those that assume reliability from previously developed sub-tests (Blankenship FCE, WorkHab), to those that have examined at least some components for reliability (Isernhagen FCE, PWPE, WorkAbility Mk III). It is not possible to comment on the level of reliability for the first two groups. Of the latter group, the lifting components of the Isernhagen and PWPE have acceptable test–retest reliability. The PWPE, however, has also demonstrated acceptable inter-rater reliability for the entire assessment, while the Isernhagen FCE has only focused on the lifting component. WorkAbility Mk III has some promising results for its manual dexterity sub-tests; however, further detail in a peer-reviewed forum is required before more confidence can be placed in this assessment. All require further and ongoing studies to cover all aspects of the assessments.

Level of validity

Face and content validity appear to be rarely formally established for the majority of work-related assessments. It would seem that most consider a work-related assessment to demonstrate adequate content validity when it is possible to identify most, if not all, physical demands as described in the Dictionary of Occupational Titles within the instrument (King et al., 1998; Lechner et al. 1991). This determination is usually made at a cursory level without support or justification for the acceptance of these criteria. It also assumes that inclusion of job task elements at the skill level, such as lifting, standing and climbing, will be adequate for determining an individual's ability to perform the duties and tasks associated with a specific job (Innes and Straker, 1998a).

Only the WorkAbility Mk III demonstrates moderate to good content validity. The VCWS 19 and WEST Standard Evaluation have also had content validity established through expert panels; however, it was found to be poor for both assessments. This is in contrast to both King et al. (1998) and Lechner et al. (1991) who report 'good' content validity for the ERGOS, Isernhagen FCE, Key FCA, PWPE, Valpar CWS and WorkAbility Mk III, but without justification for these decisions, other than comparison with the Dictionary of Occupational Titles physical demands.

Table 8.5 Summary of level for reliability of work-related assessments (from Innes and Straker, in press a)

Assessment	Type of reliability: Test–retest/ intra-rate	Inter-rater	Intra-test	Instrument precision	Other: alt. forms, int. consistency (split half and test item)
Blankenship FCE	1 (some sub-tests)	0	1 (some sub-tests)	0	0
BTE Work Simulator	5 (unknown) 5 (162) 5 (161, 170) 5 (181, 701, 901)	0	2 (302, 502, 503, 701) 4, 5 (302, 802) 5 (302, 502, 503, 601, 701) 5 (162)	4 (static and dynamic) 4, 5, 5 (dynamic) 5 (static)	
EPIC (PLC II was precursor of EPIC)	2, 5, 2 5 (PLC II)	5	0	0	0
ERGOS Work Simulator	5 (comp. and human instructions)	0	5 (comp. and human instructions)	0	0
Isernhagen FCE	3 (LMH lifts) 5 (floor-waist lift)	3 (LMH lifts) 4 (lifts) 5 (floor-waist lift)	0	0	0

Key FCA	0	0	0	0	0
PWPE	5 (lifts)	3, 5 (all) 5 (lifts)	0	0	0
Valpar CWS	4 (19) 4 (4)	4 (19)	0	0	0
WEST Standard Evaluation	4 5 (shoulder-eye lift)	4, 4 (MHRWS)	0	4 (weights)	0
WorkAbility Mk III	2 (manual dexterity tests)	0	0	0	0
WorkHab	1 (grip strength)	0	0	0	0

NB Unless otherwise indicated, the entire assessment was studied. For all other assessments the sub-test or portion of the assessment studied is in parentheses. The items for the BTE Work Simulator and the Valpar Component Work Samples indicate the number of the specific attachment or work sample studied.

Table 8.6 Summary of level of reliability of work-related assessments (from Innes and Straker, in press a)

Assessment	**Type of reliability**				
	Test–retest/ intra-rater	**Inter-rater**	**Intra-test**	**Instrument precision**	**Other: alt. forms, int. consistency (split half and test item)**
Blankenship FCE	Unknown	Unknown	Unknown	Unknown	Unknown
BTE Work Simulator	Good–Excellent, with clinical utility (161, 162, 181, 302, 701, 802, 901)	Unknown	Excellent with clinical utility (162, 302, 802); unable to determine acceptability of CV (302, 502, 503, 601, 701)	*Static*: Excellent, with clinical utility *Dynamic*: Poor	Unknown
EPIC (PLC II was precursor of EPIC)	Good–Excellent, with clinical utility	Good–Excellent, with clinical utility	Unknown	Unknown	Unknown
ERGOS Work Simulator	Good–Excellent, with clinical utility (comp. and human instructions)	Unknown	Unable to determine acceptability of CV (comp. and human instructions)	Unknown	Unknown

Isernhagen FCE	Substantial (floor-waist lift)	Substantial (floor-waist lift); unable to determine (lifts)	Unknown	Unknown	Unknown
Key FCA	Unknown	Unknown	Unknown	Unknown	Unknown
PWPE	Excellent, with clinical utility (lifts)	Moderate–Excellent	Unknown	Unknown	Unknown
Valpar CWS	Moderate–Excellent (19) Moderate–Good (4)	Substantial–Excellent, with clinical utility (19)	Unknown	Unknown	Unknown
WEST Standard Evaluation	Unable to determine acceptability	Poor-Excellent (MHRWS)	Unknown	Unacceptable (weights)	Unknown
WorkAbility Mk III	Unknown	Unknown	Unknown	Unknown	Unknown
WorkHab	Unknown	Unknown	Unknown	Unknown	Unknown

NB The assessments in **bold** are those with evidence at Level 4 or 5. The sub-test or portion of the assessment studied is in parentheses. The items for the BTE Work Simulator and the Valpar Component Work Samples indicate the number of the specific attachment or work sample studied.

Table 8.7 Summary of level of evidence for validity of work-related assessments (from Innes and Straker, in press b)

	Type of validity			
Assessment	**Face/content**	**Criterion-related**	**Construct**	**Screening**
Blankenship FCE	**3** (DOT physical demands) *2 (DOT physical demands)*	**0**	**0** *3 (behavioural profile)* *5 (compared LBP subjects with max. and sub-max. performance)*	**0**
BTE Work Simulator	**0** *2 (DOT physical demands)*	**5** (181, 701, 901 – compared VO_2 and HR in simulated and actual light, medium and heavy tasks) **5** (122, 141, 171, 181, 191, 502, 701, 802, 901 – compared VO_2, HR and BP in simulated and actual tasks) **5** (131, 171, 181 and arm cranking – VO_2 and HR) **5** (162 and Jamar – different elbow positions) *3 (162 and Jamar – ♂ and ♀* *5 (pron./sup. – attachment no. not specified and WEST 4)* *5 (162 and Jamar – injured and uninjured hands)* *5 (attachment no. not specified – impairment rating as predictor of functional loss)*	**0** *5 (162, 801 – compared exercise methods for UE injury)* *5 (attachment nos. not specified – compared subjects with fibromyalgia, RA and no disorder)* *5 (131, 162, 302, 502 – compared replantation and revision of thumb amp.)* *5 (131, 171, 181 – compared ♂ and ♀ for VO_2 and HR)* 5 (802 and pron./sup. – attachment no. not specified – compared 2 types of surgery for brachial plexus lesions) *5 (171, 181, 191B, 802 – compared control and shoulder surgery groups)*	**0** *5 (302, 502, 503, 601, 701 – CV cut-offs)* *5 (162, 302, 502 – level of effort)*

EPIC (PLC II was precursor of EPIC LC)	**0**	**5** (PLC II and Lido Lift) **5** (PLC and Lido Passive Back Machine) **5** (EPIC and ERGOS – human vs. computer instructions)	**5** (pre/post treatment change – LBP, 3 age groups) *5 (effect of using lumbar belt on lifting)* *5 (effect of age, resting, HR, weight)*	**3** (indicators of sincere effort)
ERGOS Work Simulator	**2** (DOT physical demands) *2 (DOT physical demands, NIOSH guidelines)*	**5** (EPIC and ERGOS – human vs. computer instructions) **5** (ERGOS and therapist evaluation, workshop tasks, VCWS)	**0** *5 (compared subjects with LBP and LL injuries)* *5 (compared CVs for different groups)*	**0**
Isernhagen FCE	**2, 2** (DOT physical demands) *2 (DOT physical demands)*	**0**	**0** *3 (RTW outcome)* *4 (compared physico-physical and kinesio-physical lifts; injured and uninjured groups)*	**0**
Key FCA	**2** (DOT physical demands) *2 (DOT physical demands)*	**0**	**0** *2 ('Validity' profiles from database)* *3 (RTW re-injury rate)*	**0**
PWPE	**2** (DOT physical demands)	**3, 5** (PWPE and RTW level) **3** (PWPE and RTW level)	**0** 3 (floor-waist lift and anthropometrics to predict safe lifting max.) *3 (co-ordination component; compared ♂/♀, 4 age groups)* *3, 5 (differences in lifting and use of LS belt)*	**0**

Table 8.7 *(Continued)*

	Type of validity			
Assessment	**Face/content**	**Criterion-related**	**Construct**	**Screening**
Valpar CWS	**2** (all VCWS–DOT aptitudes, physical demands, temperaments) **4** (19) *2 (DOT physical demands)* *3 (8–physical demands)*	**5** (VCWS 4, 5, 8, 9 and 11, therapist evaluation, workshop tasks and ERGOS)	**5** (convergent–4, 6, 7, 8, 9, 10, 11 and GATB aptitude) *2 (all VCWS–correlations with numerous other tests)* *3 (7, 9, 11–compared workers and non-workers)* *3 (2, 3, 5, 6, 7, 9, 11–correlations with GATB)* *3 (6, 7, 8, 11–compared hearing impaired and other groups)* *5 (6–correlations with neuropyschological tests; compared workers and subjects with mental illness)* *5 (4–compared hand injured and healthy groups)* *5 (8, 9–neck pain; sick/not sick listed)* *5 (5–change in earning capacity with RA)* *5 (1–functional loss attributable to hand impairment)*	**5** (6–compared subjects with physical impairment, psychiatric disability and brain damage) *3 (6–neurological impairment)*

WEST Standard Evaluation	**4** *2 (DOT physical demands)* *3 (physical demands)*	**4** *(MHRWS and 3-D motion analysis)* 5 (prediction for RTW) *5 (WEST and Lido trunk dynamometer and future work injury)*	**0** *4 (norms for different occupational groups, injury types, ♂/♀,* *4 (compared US and Aust. 'norms' – considered to be concurrent V)* *5 (pre/post treatment change – LBP)* *5 (pre/post treatment change – body mechanics instruction)* *5 (pre/post treatment change – LBP)*	**0**
WorkAbility MK III	**2** (DOT physical demands) **3, 4** (MODAPTS activity groups)	**0**	**0**	**0**
WorkHab	**0**	**0**	**0**	**0**

NB Numbers (**0–5**) in **bold** type indicate level of evidence, while numbers (*0–5*) in *italic* type indicate a contribution to validity. Unless otherwise indicated, the entire assessment was studied. For all other assessments the sub-test or portion of the assessment studied is in parentheses. The items for the BTE Work Simulator and the Valpar Component Work Samples indicate the number of the specific attachment or work sample studied.

Table 8.8 Summary of level of validity of work-related assessments (from Innes and Straker, in press b)

	Type of validity			
Assessment	**Face/content**	**Criterion-related**	**Construct**	**Screening**
Blankenship FCE	Unknown	Unknown	*Unknown* (compared LBP subjects with max and sub-max performance)	Unknown
BTE Work Simulator	Unknown	**Moderate–good** (181, 701, 901 – compared VO_2 and HR in simulated and actual light, med. and heavy tasks) **Moderate** (122, 141, 171, 181, 191, 502, 701, 802, 901 – compared VO_2, HR and BP in simulated and actual tasks) **Fair** (171); **Poor** (131, 181) – compared with arm cranking – VO_2 and HR **Good** (162 and Jamar) *Poor* (pron./sup. – attachment no. not specified and WEST 4) *Good* (162 and Jamar); *Good* (injured hands); *Moderate* (uninjured hands) *Poor* (impairment rating as predictor of functional loss)	Moderate (*162*); Poor (*801*) – *compared exercise methods for UE injury* *Moderate* (differentiate between patient (fibromyalgia and RA) and healthy groups); *Poor* (differentiate between fibromyalgia and RA groups) *Unknown* (131, 162, 302, 502 – compared replantation and revision of thumb amp.) *Poor (NS difference)* (131, 171, 181) – compared ♂ and ♀ (weight adjusted) for VO_2 and HR Poor (NS difference) (*802 and pron./sup. – attachment no. not specified – compared 2 types of surgery for brachial plexus lesions)* *Unknown* (171, 181, 191B, 802 – compared control and shoulder surgery groups)	*Unable to determine* (302, 502, 503, 601, 701– CV cut-offs) *Unknown* (162, 302, 502–level of effort)

EPIC (PLC II was precursor of EPIC LC)	Unknown	**Unknown** (PLC II and Lido Lift) **Unknown** (PLC and Lido Passive back machine) **Unknown** (EPIC and ERGOS – human vs. computer instructions)	**Good** (pre/post treatment change) *Poor (NS difference)* (effect of using lumbar belt on lifting) *Good* (effect of age, resting HR, weight)	Unknown
ERGOS Work Simulator	Unknown	**Moderate–good** (EPIC and ERGOS – human vs. computer instructions) **Moderate** (ERGOS and overall physical activity determination); **Poor–good** (ERGOS and therapist evaluation, workshop tasks, VCWS)	*Moderate* (differentiation between subjects with LBP and LL injuries) *Poor (NS difference)* (differentiation between client groups on basis of CV)	Unknown
Isernhagen FCE	Unknown	Unknown	*Moderate* (compared psycho-physical and kinesio-physical lifts) *Poor* (compared injured and uninjured groups)	Unknown
Key FCA	Unknown	Unknown	Unknown	Unknown
PWPE	Unknown	**Fair–moderate** (PWPE and RTW level)	*Moderate* (differences in lifting and use of LS belt)	Unknown

Table 8.8 *(Continued)*

	Type of validity			
Assessment	**Face/content**	**Criterion-related**	**Construct**	**Screening**
Valpar CWS	**Poor** (19)	**Poor** (VCWS 4, 5, 8, 9 and 11, and ERGOS); **Moderate** (VCWS and therapist evaluation); **Moderate** (VCWS and workshop tasks) *Poor* (impairment rating as predictor of functional loss, using 1)	**Moderate** (4); **Poor–moderate** (8, 9); **Poor** (6, 7, 10, 11) – convergent validity with GATB aptitude) Moderate (*6*) – *correlations with neuropsychological tests*; Poor (NS difference) – *comparison of workers and subjects with mental illness)* *Moderate* (4 – compared hand injured and healthy groups) *Good* (8 – differentiate between sick/not sick listed); *Unknown* (9) *Moderate* (5 – compared in earning capacity with RA)	**Moderate** (6 – compared subjects with physical impairment, psychiatric disability and brain damage)

WEST Standard Evaluation	**Poor**	**Poor–fair** (*MHRWS and 3-D motion analysis*) Poor (NS difference) (*prediction for RTW*) *Unknown* (WEST criterion measure and Lido trunk dynamometer and future work injury)	*Unknown* (norms for different occupational groups, injury types, ♂/♀) *Unknown* (compared US and Aust. 'norms' – considered to be concurrent V) *Moderate* (pre/post treatment change – LBP) *Poor – moderate* (pre/post treatment change – body mechanics instruction) *Good* (pre/post treatment change – LBP)	
WorkAbility Mk III	**Moderate–good** (MODAPTS activity groups)	Unknown	Unknown	Unknown
WorkHab	Unknown	Unknown	Unknown	Unknown

NB The assessments in **bold** are those with evidence of validity at Level 4 or 5, while those in *italic* type indicate a contribution to validity at level 4 or 5. The sub-test or portion of the assessment studied is in parentheses. The items for the BTE Work Simulator and the Valpar Component Work Samples indicate the number of the specific attachment or work sample studied.

Criterion-related validity was the most common formally evaluated type of validity examined in work-related assessments. There was moderate validity demonstrated for the ErgoScience PWPE when compared with the ability to return to work (i.e. sedentary, light, medium, heavy, very heavy). When compared with work simulation or workshop tasks the BTE and ERGOS Work Simulators and the Valpar Component Work Samples demonstrated moderate concurrent validity.

The WEST Standard Evaluation has poor criterion-related validity when compared with a three-dimensional motion analysis system. The poor outcome may be the result of either an incompatible criterion being selected for comparison, or the criterion being too sensitive. Good criterion-related validity was only demonstrated when a work-related assessment was compared with a similar instrument (e.g. BTE 162 compared with the Jamar dynamometer – Beaton, et al., 1995). This highlights the difficulty of attempting to establish the validity of work-related assessments. It also indicates the need to carefully select an appropriate and acceptable criterion standard.

Construct validity was rarely formally evaluated. However, approximately half of the work-related assessments included in this study had some contributory evidence of construct validity. This was most commonly in the form of demonstrating a treatment effect or differentiating between different groups.

Convergent and divergent aspects of construct validity were only addressed for Valpar Component Work Samples. VCWS are based on the same system used to analyse jobs in the Dictionary of Occupational Titles (U.S. Department of Labor Employment and Training, 1991), and can therefore be compared with other instruments using the same constructs. Given that many work-related assessments are reportedly based on the physical demands of the Dictionary of Occupational Titles (DOT), it would seem reasonable that these constructs could be examined.

Whilst a number of work-related assessments purport to identify subjects producing maximal or sub-maximal performance, no Level 4 or 5 studies examining this feature were located for any work-related assessment. There is some promising research, however, which begins to address this concern (Jay et al., 1998).

SUMMARY

This paper has provided an overview of research (to the end of 1997) that examined the reliability and validity of commercially available work-related assessment systems. These systems are: the Blankenship FCE, BTE Work Simulator, EPIC Lift Capacity, ERGOS Work Simulator, Isernhagen FCE, Key Method FCA, Physical Work Performance Evaluation, Valpar Component Work Samples, WEST Standard Evaluation, WorkAbility Mk III and WorkHab. Based on this review clinicians are provided with information regarding the presence or lack of evidence for reliability and validity that may influence their selection of assessment instruments.

All work-related assessments in this study provide information at the task and skill levels of individual performance. When using these assessments, clinicians should be aware of this and consider whether interpretation of the results is appropriate when determining function at a role or activity level.

Many work-related assessments have limited evidence of reliability or validity. A number had insufficient evidence on which to base an assessment of the level of reliability or validity. For the limited number of work-related assessments with an adequate level of evidence on which to judge their reliability, most demonstrate a moderate to good level. Few work-related assessments, however, have demonstrated levels of reliability sufficient for clinical purposes. Fewer still have this demonstrated over a number of studies, in varying contexts: and with different populations.

Of those work-related assessments that had adequate evidence, validity ranged from poor to good. Assessments with adequate evidence of moderate to good validity included some attachments of the BTE Work Simulator, EPIC Lift Capacity, ERGOS Work Simulator, PWPE, Valpar CWS and WorkAbility Mk III. Other instruments had contributory evidence that began to establish moderate to good validity. These included Isernhagen FCE and the WEST Standard Evaluation.

There was, however, no instrument that demonstrated moderate to good validity in all areas. Very few work-related assessments were able to demonstrate adequate validity in more than one area, or with more than one study, even when contributory evidence was included. This highlights the need for further research to be conducted in this area. Test developers, clinicians and academics are strongly encouraged to continue investigating the validity of work-related assessments.

The acceptance of work-related assessments on the basis of their longevity in the marketplace and clinic should not be assumed to equate with adequate reliability or validity. With this review clinicians are now able to examine their options with regard to the reliability and validity of the work-related assessments they choose to use.

References

Abdel-Moty, E., Compton, R., Steele-Rosomoff, R., Rosomoff, H. and Khalil, T.M. (1996). Process analysis of functional capacity assessment. *Journal of Back and Musculoskeletal Rehabilitation*, **6**, 223–236.

Beaton, D.E., O'Driscoll, S.W. and Richards, R. (1995). Grip strength testing using the BTE Work simulator and the Jamar dynamometer. A comparative study. *Journal of Hand Surgery*, **20A** (2), 293–298.

Gibson, L. and Strong, J. (1997). A review of functional capacity evaluation practice. *Work*, **9** (1), 3–11.

Innes, E. (1997a). Work assessment options and the selection of suitable duties: An Australian perspective. *New Zealand Journal of Occupational Therapy*, **48** (1), 14–20.

Innes, E. (1997b). Work programmes to enhance motor and neuromusculoskeletal performance components. In J. Pratt and K. Jacobs (eds), *Work practice: International perspectives* (pp. 224–244). Oxford, UK: Butterworth-Heinemann.

Innes, E. and Straker, L. (1998a). A clinician's guide to work-related assessments: 2 – Design problems. *Work*, **11** (2), 191–206.

Innes, E. and Straker, L (1998b). A clinician's guide to work-related assessments: 3 – Administration and interpretation problems. *Work*, **11** (2), 207–219.

Innes, E. and Straker, L. (in press a). Reliability of work-related assessments. *Work*.

Innes, E. and Straker, L. (in press b). Validity of work-related assessments. *Work*.

Jay, M.A., Lamb, J.M., Watson, R.L., and Young, I.A. (1998). Sensitivity and specificity of the indicators of sincere effort of the EPIC Lift Capacity test on a previously injured population [Abstract]. *Physical Therapy*, **78** (5), S84.

King, P.M., Tuckwell, N. and Barrett, T.E. (1998). A critical review of functional capacity evaluations. *Physical Therapy*, **78** (8), 852–866.

Krefting, L.M. and Bremner, A. (1985). Work evaluation: Choosing a commercial system. *Canadian Journal of Occupational Therapy*, **52** (1), 20–24.

Lechner, D., Roth, D. and Straaton, K. (1991). Functional capacity evaluation in work disability. *Work*, **1** (3), 37–47.

Moran, M. and Strong, J. (1995). Outcomes of a rehabilitation programme for patients with chronic back pain. *British Journal of Occupational Therapy*, **58** (10), 435–438.

Packer, T.L. (1995). A rationale for choosing technology versus clinical technique in assessing functional disability. *Proceedings of the 'Quest for Quality', 12th World Congress of the International Federation of Physical Medicine and Rehabilitation* (on disc). Sydney, Australia: IFPMR.

U.S. Department of Labor Employment and Training. (1991). *The revised handbook for analyzing jobs*. Indianapolis, IN: JIST Works.

Velozo, C.A. (1993). Work evaluations: Critique of the state of the art of functional assessment of work. *American Journal of Occupational Therapy*, **47** (3), 203–209.

Functional capacity assessment: what do you want and what do you get?

Robyn Rankin

The purpose of a functional capacity assessment (FCA) is to provide measured information regarding a person's ability to undertake functional types of tasks safely. This information is generally focused on work tasks. Therefore the report should be written using a format and terminology that enables a comparison of a person's capability and the measured physical demands of a job, i.e. results of an FCA need to be in a form relevant to the setting in which they will be used. The type or brand of assessment chosen is only relevant to the appropriateness for the task. This means the results should be in a format relevant to the setting in which the resultant information is to be used. Caveat emptor, let the buyer beware.

It is appropriate to use a functional capacity assessment when trying to determine whether a person has the physical ability to safely undertake a specific job whether it is pre placement or post injury. Where the result is negative in the post injury situation, it is then frequently necessary in a rehabilitation milieu to determine what jobs the person could physically do safely either with the same employer or, if that is not possible, elsewhere in the workforce. Hence it is often important to have data about the person's physical capacities that can be compared to the measured physical demands of any job. The language used in the results of both the assessment of the person and the assessment of jobs must be comparable.

FCA reports often contain descriptions of the activities undertaken and the specific outcomes of those. Some include measures of muscle group strength and individual joint ranges of movement. The bottom line is: this mass of information must be presented in some form of summary of what the person can do safely.

It is important to know, reliably, if the person can lift from point A to point B, using a method safe for them, how much they can lift and how often.

Actual grip strength and whether it falls within the norms for the tool being used is usually irrelevant. However, the length of time and frequency of a person's functional upper limb activities is often relevant and whether any constraints apply such as shoulder girdle support. One usually doesn't need to know how much the person can bench press or quads lift, but it is important to know how much a person can lift functionally, how often and what method or body mechanics they have a tendency to adopt. We usually don't need to know the precise joint range of any joint; however, we do need to know the intensity, duration, frequency and endurance or tolerance to specific activities.

In situations where a person is unlikely to return to a previous job or has had re-aggravations in spite of having had a functional capacity assessment, some relevant information may be missing such as reliable measures of sitting, standing, walking and workday tolerances rather than estimates based on clinical experience.

FCA results and reports should provide the referrer with information that can readily be interpreted to determine whether the person's capacities are equal to or greater than the physical demands of the job. Often there needs to be education for the employer, the insurer, the rehabilitation counsellor and the treating therapist so that the focus will be on strategic planning when looking at (i) whether the person will be able to do their previous job (a) with or without modifications to process or method and/or (b) with or without further interventions such as further physical or medical management or specific training or skills development; (ii) the goals of specific interventions that will enable the eventual return to work at the previous or another job; (iii) safe alternative jobs by providing the maximal safe capacities of the person taking into account the whole person, not only one specific injury. Therefore high quality relevant job analyses are essential.

In order to provide such information, there are some significant criteria to be considered. Functional capacity assessments are contraindicated when the physical condition is unstable.

The person may not be at their ultimate maximal recovery from an injury but they should have plateaued, unless the assessment is being used as a baseline measure to evaluate a specific intervention.

The assessment must be as objective as possible and safe. This means the person must not be urged to do more, equally they should not be encouraged to fall short of demonstrating their ability. It is important to remember that exercise heart rates may be elevated to 75–85 per cent of an individual's Age Adjusted Heart Rate in training programmes. However, workers cannot sustain that level of activity. Therefore recommending work capacities that require that level of exertion is not likely to assist in moving in on occupational injury for injury management or injury prevention.

Manual functional capacity evaluation versus computerised functional capacity evaluation

Jane Bell

INTRODUCTION

The Ergos system is a fully computerised physical/functional capacity evaluation and work simulation system. The system was developed in the late 1980s, with the objective of producing an integrated medical/vocational process for providing services to industrially injured workers, employers and insurers.

Ergos uses fully computerised components to measure physical functional capacities as they relate to work performance. This is driven by and controlled by a computerised local area network featuring five online computers linked to a separate master computer station. The participant and the evaluator receive immediate visual performance feedback through the colour video monitor at each station. Standardised instructions are provided through visual graphic displays, written instructions and audio prompting.

The system features in its software the ability to compute the Coefficient of Variation as described by Dr. Leonard Mathesson, to establish consistency of performance. The Ergos system also features in its software complete listing of all Department of Labor (USA) DOT jobs. In Australia some Ergos systems also featured Australian standard classification of occupations (ASCO). Thus, an individual's post injury performance can be compared to an individual standard.

The methods time measurement (MTM) is a procedure used to analyse any manual operation or method, into the basic movements required to perform it, and assigns to each movement a pre-determined time standard which is determined by the nature of the movement and the conditions under which it is made. The MTM standards featured in the Ergos system allow the individual performance to be measured against a work standard. These standards have been internationally accepted and court tested.

MEASUREMENT FACTORS

The five component units featured in the Ergos system are designed to measure the following physical activities.

1. Unit 1 Static Strength. A height adjustable device set to the participant's body dimensions is used to measure static lift push and pull strength.
2. Dynamic Strength is measured using progressive free lifting activities. Weight,

velocity and quality of movement are monitored. The data are integrated and analysed for consistency and accuracy.

3. Unit 2 Whole Body Range of Movement. Whole body work range is evaluated in bending, squatting, kneeling and forward and overhead reaching positions, using job simulation tasks. These activities are evaluated against competitive work (MTM) standards.
4. Unit 3 Work Endurance. A process which integrates repetitive sorting, lifting, carrying, walking and stair climbing activities.
5. Unit 4 Standing Work Tolerance. The participant sorts a series of items onto a vibrating conveyor belt which fills a storage tray. Each storage tray is off-loaded onto a shelf at a standard distance. The participant then returns to the unit with an empty tray and repeats the process until all the empty trays have been filled or to tolerance. Performance is measured against MTM standards.
6. Unit 5 Seated Work Tolerance. Seated body position and work speeds are electronically monitored over a significant time span using work simulation tasks. Seated body position and work speed are electronically monitored. Handling, fingering and feeling activities are monitored using electronic measurement technology.

USES FOR A COMPUTERISED SYSTEM FOR FUNCTIONAL CAPACITY EVALUATION

A computerised system should be used as a tool, to provide objective reproducible data about an individual's capacity to work against established job requirement criteria. The system can also be used to provide a standardised work conditioning protocol against established job requirement criteria. Used in this way it can be a powerful early intervention tool in occupational rehabilitation.

A computerised system can also be useful in providing an effective standardised format for pre-placement evaluation to compare performance against specific job requirements where the physical demands of the jobs are known and documented.

ADVANTAGES OF A COMPUTERISED SYSTEM

Computerisation provides reliable valid unbiased non-discriminatory objective and reproducible data, standardised procedures and reporting, instant feedback and relates performance to job specific requirements.

In some jurisdictions, certification is sufficient qualification to be an evaluator. It also facilitates:

1. Computer generated reporting.
2. Ease of feedback to the operator.
3. Less physical demand on the operator.

DISADVANTAGES

1. Lack of flexibility in body mechanics and posture.
2. Difficulties associated with proprietary software and help desk services.
3. Year 2000 compliance.
4. High cost of system.

There are very few fully computerised systems in operation, therefore it may be assumed that in the partially computerised systems some of the advantages/disadvantages may apply.

SUMMARY

The concept of physiotherapists using a computerised functional capacity assessment system is a good one as the process is directed toward return to work (function) as opposed to the medical condition (dysfunction). Use of a computerised system provides a controlled environment, for analysis.

Functional capacity assessment is a measurement tool and not a stand alone rehabilitation programme. If it is used as a means to establish treatment goals, the recommendations must be clearly understood and applied.

Measured functional trends in military personnel discharged medically due to low back pain

Torsten M. Becht and David Roberts

INTRODUCTION

The use of functional capacity evaluations (FCEs) is usually confined to either clinical or medico-legal areas to identify and determine the limitations of an individual unable to return to their pre-injury state. These limitations are particularly important in relation to the individual's capacity to work.

The Military Occupational Rehabilitation Programme (MORP) at the 2nd Field Hospital, Gallipoli Barracks, Enoggera, Queensland, Australia, has been developed to assist injured and ill members of the Australian Defence Force (ADF), being discharged medically, make a smooth transition to civilian life.

A significant component of the MORP is to objectively establish the functional status of the ADF member to assist vocational rehabilitation providers identify suitable civilian occupations, in order to maximise employability and minimise risk of further injury. This, in turn, reduces defence compensation liability.

The purpose of this study is to collate the results of FCEs performed over the last eighteen months in an attempt to establish any trends, significant findings or other relevant information. The information obtained may indicate that a well-performed, standardised FCE could be used as a prime resource to determine physical criteria for medical discharge. The information may also be used to assess incapacity in relation to compensation and superannuation benefits, assessments that are currently based largely on subjective examinations.

Finally, the findings of this study may assist in developing successful injury prevention and early intervention treatment programmes by examining trends in relation to age, fitness, activities, perceptions and manual handling skills.

SUBJECTS

A total of sixty-five FCEs were available for the study. Thirty-six of these were individuals medically unfit primarily due to low back pain. Two of the subjects were female and subsequently excluded to leave a specific population of thirty-four male soldiers with low back pain.

Age of the subjects ranged from twenty to forty-seven years (mean 30.5 years). Age of injury was calculated from the time of diagnosis to presentation for the MORP, i.e. the FCE. Length of injury ranged from six months to twenty years, with a mean of 5.8 years.

Diagnoses were divided into four groups relating to the complexity of the injury. Twelve of the subjects had low back pain only, twelve had low back and neck pain, eight had low back and lower limb problems and two had low back pain in combination with other orthopaedic or medical conditions.

The FCEs on these individuals were conducted at 2nd Field Hospital between July 1997 and January 1999, using the WorkHab Australia FCE System.

METHODOLOGY

The WorkHab FCE was chosen for the MORP for its availability, affordable training, registration and equipment. In addition, the WorkHab FCE can be performed with equipment readily accessible in a rehabilitation unit, in a relatively short period of time (one to two hours) and provides practical, objective functional information without the need to relate findings to a standard population.

Each subject underwent a WorkHab FCE, which tested all components of a basic FCE. There were some differences related to a subject's specific condition. However, each subject performed the following tasks: Lifestyle treadmill; three static postural activities (reaching forward, reaching overhead and squatting); and three dynamic activities (safe maximal lift, safe maximal carry and endurance lift). These particular tests were chosen for the study for their diversity and standardised testing across the thirty-four subjects.

TASK DESCRIPTION

The Lifestyle treadmill test was used for its accessibility and ease of application. It provides a standardised general fitness rating, based on research conducted by the American College of Sports Medicine and Life Fitness.

Each subject performed a five-minute test at 5 km/hr with a 5 per cent gradient. The test consists of a one-minute warm-up and a four-minute test. The treadmill monitors the subject's heart rate and provides a fitness rating at the end of the test, in relation to males of the same age group as the subject.

The other tests were performed in accordance with the WorkHab Australia protocol (WorkHab, 1988).

Reaching forward was a set task carried out at an 800 mm high bench with a manual dexterity task placed at arm's length, between 500 and 650 mm from the edge of the bench. This required a full forward arm reach combined with some trunk flexion. Both arms were unsupported and the task was performed for three minutes. Demonstration of the task suggested means to alleviate undue stress on the low back but most clients chose a personal posture for the duration of the task.

Reaching overhead was tested with the subject standing and performing a manual dexterity task at eye level. Both arms were set to work at that level and had to be maintained, unsupported, for the duration of the task, being three minutes.

Squatting was defined as a position close to the floor where neither knee nor hands were resting on the floor. The posture may be symmetrical (both knees flexed equally) or asymmetrical (one knee flexed more than the other). The subject's specific posture was not recorded. The subject performed a manual dexterity task on the floor for three minutes.

The safe maximal lift was defined as a lift from bench (600–800 mm) to shoulder (1200–1600 mm) level. The bench and shoulder heights were anthropometrical measures for each individual subject. The subject was given a brief instruction on lifting technique and asked to lift a square Umber box (with cutout handles) from bench to shoulder level. The subject performed a continued lift, with the evaluator adding 1.25 kg each time, secured over a central spike inside the box, until the evaluator ceased the test. The total weight of the box and the weights was recorded as the safe maximal lift. Parameters for cessation of the test were:

- behaviour of heart rate, using the BABI (beats above baseline index) heart rate index (Pine, 1992);
- value and position of pain using the visual analogue scale (0–10);
- value of perceived exertion using a modified Borg scale (0.5–10) (Dunbar et al., 1996);
- biomechanical observations based on the changes of the body's movement patterns due to mechanical and other stressful forces;
- other observations of the subject's behaviour, which relate to signs of increased load on the body and adaptation to this load.

Manual handling principles were observed and graded throughout the test as part of the biomechanical observation and based on the principles and ideas from the consensus meetings on safe and effective lifting, held throughout Australia between 1992 and 1994 (Cumberland College of Health Services, 1993).

The safe maximal carry was similarly performed with the subject carrying the timber box over a distance of 17 m. Load was increased by 1.25 kg after each 17 m lap and the test continued until ceased based on the parameters stated above. The total weight of the box and weights was recorded as the safe maximal carry.

The endurance lift is based on the strength-endurance continuum described mathematically by Berger (1969). Doolittle and Kaiyala (1988) tested the concept in a series of articles using firefighters performing repetitive lifts at various percentages of maximal load. For the endurance lift, a load equalling approximately 50 per cent of the safe maximal load was used. The endurance lift allows the evaluator to compare safe maximal lift with a sub-maximal load repeated many times by use of a mathematical formula. The formula provides a predicted safe maximal lift, which is expected to be close to the actual safe maximal lift; this comparison was made during this study to help profile the lifting behaviour of the subjects, as well as establish a level of consistency of performance by the subjects.

RESULTS

Several sets of data were collected and displayed in table form. The data demonstrated a number of trends and common findings, in addition to confirming expectations of the evaluator, based on the clinical picture.

General fitness ratings of the subjects were higher than might be expected. Worthy of note is the fact that most subjects maintained good general fitness despite their back (and other) complaints. This is likely to be due to the high fitness demands, and levels of physical training, required of military personnel.

Fitness ratings from the treadmill (below average, fair, average, above average, good, very good and excellent) were graded from one to seven respectively. The range was one to seven for the subjects with a mean score of 4.1, indicating above average fitness for the population.

The three static postures were graded as unlimited tolerance (able to sustain posture over eight-hour day), reduced tolerance (able to sustain posture over eight-hour day with frequent postural changes), limited tolerance (able to attain posture only infrequently and sustain for less than three minutes), not recommended (due to clinical presentation) and not tested. Gradings were scored from four (unlimited tolerance) to zero (not tested) respectively.

The data showed that subjects found reaching forward most difficult. None of the subjects were graded at unlimited tolerance and the 50 per cent of the subjects recorded their highest pain score for reaching forward. Table 8.9 shows the gradings for the three static postures.

Most subjects also recorded their highest perceived exertion scores for reaching forward, despite other tasks being aerobically more demanding. The significance of this, together with the high pain scores and poor tolerance gradings, is that these static postures have often been overlooked in favour of manual/loaded activities when returning people to work. Vocational counsellors, as well as medical professionals, commonly suggest sedentary work for the back-injured individual, yet these findings demonstrate that the back-injured individual may in fact have more difficulty with the static postures than the loaded activities, particularly if the person is fit and has been taught good manual handling skills.

Reaching overhead was the activity, out of the three, which resulted in the least pain and perceived exertion scores. Squatting was found limiting by most subjects and was not recommended more frequently than both reaching activities. Tables

Table 8.9 Tolerance gradings for static posture

Static posture	Unlimited tolerance	Reduced tolerance	Limited tolerance	Not recom'd	Not tested	Average grading
Reaching overhead	9	15	9	0	1	3.0
Reaching forward	0	6	26	0	2	2.2
Squatting	2	16	11	4	1	2.4

8.10 to 8.13 show the detailed data for pain and perceived exertion, in relation to the various activities. Noteworthy is that most clients recorded their lowest pain and perceived exertion scores for the treadmill, supporting the relatively high general fitness findings.

Table 8.14 details the findings for both the safe maximal lift and carry. The findings show that the average values for both the lift and the carry are very similar. These findings suggest that the load is the limiting factor in relation to back pain, more so than the means by which the load is handled. An interesting comparison might be assessing the same tests for an uninjured population.

Table 8.10 Pain and perceived exertion data summary

	Range	Average
Highest pain	4–9	6.8
Lowest pain	0–7	2.5
Highest perceived exertion	4–10	6.9
Lowest perceived exertion	0.5–5	1.4

Table 8.11 Postures which resulted in the subjects' highest reported pains scores in relation to their condition (note that some subjects had multiple complaints and reported the score for more than one posture)

Posture	Number	Back pain	Back and neck	Back and lower limb	Back and other
Reaching forward	17	9	1	7	0
Stooping	7	6	0	1	0
Endurance lift	7	5	2	1	0
Squatting	6	3	0	3	0
Endurance carry	6	4	1	1	0

Table 8.12 Postures which resulted in the subjects' highest reported perceived exertion scores in relation to their condition (note that some subjects had multiple complaints and reported the highest score for more than one posture)

Posture	Number	Back pain	Back and neck	Back and lower limb	Back and other
Reaching forward	14	7	2	4	1
Safe maximal carry	10	7	1	2	1
Safe maximal lift	9	6	1	1	1
Endurance lift	5	2	1	3	0
Squatting	4	3	1	0	0

Table 8.13 Tasks that resulted in the lowest pain and perceived exertion scores (note that some subjects reported their lowest score for more than one task)

Task	Lowest pain	Highest pain
Treadmill	14	13
Sitting	10	11
Reaching overhead	7	13
Floor to bench lift	4	1
Squatting	4	5
Kneeling	4	6

Table 8.14 Values for safe maximal lift and carry and correlation with the predicted safe maximal carry, based on the endurance carry

Task	Range (kg)	Average (kg)	Within 10% (of predicted)	Within 15% (of predicted)
Safe maximal lift	9.75–28.5	16.14	24	33
Safe maximal carry	8.5–34.25	16.01	–	–

A further important finding is that 97 per cent of the subjects recorded a predicted safe, maximal lift (from the endurance lift) within 15 per cent of the actual lift and 70.6 per cent within 10 per cent. This supports the research, indicating that the endurance lift provides a good test of correlation with the safe maximal lift. The data also suggest that the above average general fitness of the subjects had no effect on the endurance activity and that, most likely, the low back pain was the primary limiting factor.

The FCE contains an analysis of the subject's manual handling skills. The subjects are rated in five categories (stance, posture, leverage, torque, and pacing and timing) resulting in a total score out of twenty, a higher score indicating better manual handling skills. Scores for the subjects ranged from thirteen to twenty (mean 17.4), demonstrating very good manual handling skills across the subject population. Despite this, and the above average fitness findings, average lifting and carrying capacities were relatively low, indicating that the nature of the complaints are significant, as well as the indication that the low back pain is the primary limiting factor.

Table 8.15 provides a comparison of fitness levels, lifting and carrying capacities, as well as pain and perceived exertion values. These figures show that, generally, the fitter individuals not only recorded higher lifting and carrying loads, but also relatively lower pain and perceived exertion scores. These trends can be expected from the clinical findings and are supported by the data.

Table 8.15 Comparison of general fitness level, lifting and carrying capacity and pain and perceived exertion scores

Fitness level	Average age of injury (years)	Average SML (kg)	Average SMC (kg)	Highest pain (out of 10)	Highest perceived exertion (out of 10)
Excellent	3	12.25	11.2	8	5
Very good	4	22.3	22.0	5.75	6.7
Good	6	20.5	19.9	6.8	8.1
Above average	6.3	14.3	15.7	6.3	5.6
Average	7.4	14.1	14.4	6.8	6.7
Below average	2	16	11.25	7	9
Fair	4.6	14.1	13.25	7	7.5

CONCLUSION

The study shows that a large number of individuals medically discharged from the ADF suffer with low back pain, be it exclusively or in combination with other complaints. It is also noted that many do not present to a rehabilitation unit until some time after injury, at which point their signs and symptoms are significant and have a profound impact on the individual's functional status; this is despite the person maintaining an above average level of general fitness and having good manual handling skills.

Possibly the most important finding is the relatively substantial problems the subjects encountered with the static postures, specifically reaching forward. This is potentially very significant for vocational rehabilitation providers when attempting to return back-injured individuals to work. Sedentary work may be equally as inappropriate as manual work and this needs to be further researched.

This study is a pilot study and the first of its nature involving both the WorkHab Australia FCE and injured military personnel. It is essential that such data analysis be continued and compared with both an uninjured population and populations with other complaints and from varying backgrounds. Nonetheless, this study has demonstrated some important trends and interesting findings for the authors.

References

Berger, R.A. (1969). Determination of a method to predict 1-RM chin and dip from repetitive chins and dips. *Research Quarterly for Exercise and Sport*, **38** (3), 330–335.

Cumberland College of Health Services, Institute for Fitness Research and Training, Inc. (1993). *Consensus meetings on safe and effective lifting*. Handbook and pre-reading manuals.

Doolittle, T.L. and Kaiyala, K. (1988). Prediction of maximum dynamic strength from multiple repetitions with a submaximal load. *Trends in ergonomics and human factors*. North-Holland.

Dunbar, C.C., Kalisnski, M.I. and Robertson, R.J. (1996). A new method for prescribing exercise: Three-point ratings for perceived exertion. *Perception of Motor Skills*, **82** (1), 139–146.

Pine, Z.M. Colbran, E. and Corpolongo, R. (1992). Reliability and validity of a new measure of task difficulty. *Archives of Physical Medicine and Rehabilitation*, **73**, 987.

Roberts, D.M. and Bradbury, S.F. (1988). *WorkHab Procedure Manual*. WorkHab Australia.

Assessing pain and disability exaggeration with the functional capacity evaluation process

R.G.M. Sellars, M. O'Neill, C. Amber-Scott and G. Hayhow

INTRODUCTION

Chronic pain leading to inability to work is a well-known problem in the industrialised world. Often following seemingly simple or trivial injury, chronic pain is a frustrating problem for the patient, doctor, employer and insurer alike. About 10 per cent of acute LBP patients experience symptoms and inability to work four months after onset. Most of these patients will continue to be disabled after two years (Gatchel, R.J. and Gardea, M.A. (1999).

Despite a huge variety of treatments and rehabilitation protocols, the problem of chronic pain continues. The resultant problems of patient anger, physician frustration and expense to the employer and insurer often leads to expensive legal involvement that rarely leads to resolution satisfactory to all parties.

Part of the difficulty in identifying and treating chronic low back pain (CLBP) is that no single factor in isolation – pathophysiological, psychological or social – will adequately explain chronic pain status (Gatchel, R.J. et al. (1994).

Moreover, Dworkin et al. (1990) showed that CLBP should be conceptualised as an ongoing long-term fluid condition with reciprocal interplay between the patient's biological, psychological and social factors.

The physician is thus faced with a patient with multiple widespread symptoms who fails to respond to treatment interventions, complains of strong pain and blames back pain for changes and breakdowns in every facet of their lives – social, recreational, familial and employment. Inevitably they see themselves as being unable to work.

An important part of the treatment of chronic pain is restoring the individual to normal activity, including employment. Yet many return to work plans are never achieved because of the increase in pain and disability.

In recent years there have been attempts to more objectively quantify the biopsychosocial problems in understanding back pain and work disability (Flores, L. (1997). In an effort to provide a more scientific basis for determining safe work ability a number of developers have assembled batteries of tests, the functional capacity evaluation (FCE) process, to provide a total 'picture' of a patient's abilities. Generally, the tests aim to assess disability perception, movement and strength, safe working ability and provide an accurate baseline for treatment and rehabilitation.

There are a large number of medical, physical and psychological investigations that can be used to assess impairment. However, it has not been until the advent of the FCE process that the association between impairment and function has been able to be measured or understood with any degree of accuracy.

FCEs are done to assess work capacity. For the assessment to be valid it is essential that the patient gives maximum effort and displays appropriate test behaviour. Good test validity gives confidence that the data collected are valid and represent the patient's safe functional ability.

Most FCE systems profess to be able to reliably indicate those patients who do not give full effort during the FCE and are thus not demonstrating their full potential. Consequently, FCEs have been presented as legal evidence to support that work ability is present or that pain and disability is being exaggerated (King et al. (1998).

Maximum effort by the patient gives a good indication of the effect that function has on injury and, conversely, the effect that injury has on function. Thus treatment and rehabilitation recommendations can be made on objective findings of the FCE. To assess if maximum effort has been given and if the degree of disability matches the injury the results, behaviour and manner of testing should be assessed, as well as the correlation between impairment and disability.

The FCE process involves several hours of physical and functional testing, thus allowing the evaluator to observe patterns of movement during deliberate testing and on distraction. The effect of injury on function and of function on injury can be observed in a way that is not possible during a standard medical or psychological assessment.

In order to assess the effect of function on impairment it is vital to:

1. Understand the injury pathogenesis.
2. Assess the patient's perception of pain and disability.
3. Conduct a thorough physical assessment.

When the medical, psychological and physical perspectives of the impairment are known then the results of functional testing can be compared to provide an objective basis for certifying the following:

1. If functional ability correlates with the medical impairment.
2. Safe work ability.
3. Assessing the degree of symptom and disability exaggeration that is present.
4. Providing an objective baseline of physical ability.

PURPOSE OF STUDY

Two concurrent surveys were done to assess the degree of symptom and disability exaggeration present in long-term clients receiving compensation benefits as a result of personal injury. Data analysis was done to investigate the predictive effect of the behavioural questionnaires and tests used in the FCE process.

All the patients in the survey were assessed by the four authors, who are physiotherapists (RGMS, MNO'N, GRH) and one occupational therapist (CA-S) working for FCE Systems (N.Z.) Ltd. Patients were referred for assessment from ACC (the government-run Workers' Compensation Scheme) and private insurance companies.

METHOD

Two concurrent surveys were conducted.

Survey One

Five hundred and sixty-three consecutive FCEs were analysed for demographic data and for broad indications of symptom and disability exaggeration (Tables 8.16 and 8.18).

Table 8.16 Demographic data

Item	Survey One		Survey Two	
Database	563 consecutive FCEs		82 long term patients	
Sex	Male	55%	Male	68%
	Female	45%	Female	32%
Age	Male:	41 (range 21–61)	Male:	48 (range 28–63)
	Female:	40 (range 16–62)	Female:	48 (range 26–62)
Vocational status	Unskilled	61%	Unskilled	62%
	Semi-skilled	18%	Semi-skilled	13%
	Skilled	19%	Skilled	23%
	Professional	2%	Professional	1%
Injury–FCE	4.65 years		8.84 years	

Table 8.17 Injury site

Injury site	Survey One	Survey Two
Lumbar spine	45%	73%
Overuse injuries	21%	4%
Neck	7%	2%
Shoulder	6%	4%
Wrist	4%	2%
All other areas	17%	15%

Survey Two

Eighty-two FCEs of long-term clients were analysed in greater detail to assess what common behavioural factors were present and if any of the behavioural tests were more consistently present than others. These clients were randomly chosen from two country areas of New Zealand, most of them being clients who had been receiving compensation benefits for a number of years.

A database was maintained of all patients assessed and the test results accessed by filtering the required data.

Patients were divided into four groups (Table 8.18), depending on their FCE results. The groups were decided on the following two criteria (Blankenship, (1994).

Table 8.18 Degree of symptom and disability exaggeration

Group	FCE score	Characteristics
No exaggeration (Non-SE)	Good to excellent physical effort	No non-organic signs and consistently good correlation between tests. Good correlation between the patient's perception of disability and the test results.
Minimal exaggeration (Minimal SE)	Fair or equivocal physical effort	Some indications of sub-maximal performance and some non-organic signs. Apprehension or fear of re-injury may be present. A heightened perception of pain and disability is present compared to the test results.
Marked exaggeration (Marked SE)	Poor to very poor test effort	Consistent and significant signs of sub-maximal effort and multiple non-organic signs. A perception of a high degree of pain and disability exists that is not correlated by the FCE performance.
Overt exaggeration (Overt SE)	Very poor test effort with 'crazy' behaviour	Marked sub-maximal effort, often with inability to complete or even attempt tests. Bizarre methods of function with gross emotional reactions (e.g. crying, writhing, hyperventilation, collapsing) that have no connection with the injury.

1. FCE score: Passing 80 per cent or more of the tests in the FCE process indicates good effort; 70–80 per cent indicates fair effort; less than 70 per cent is poor or equivocal effort; less than 60 per cent is very poor effort.
2. Behaviour: Non-organic signs (Waddell, el al., 1980), sub-maximal performance and an abnormally heightened perception of pain and disability when compared to impairment and demonstrated functional ability.

Generally, the greater the number of non-organic signs of disability present, the lower the FCE score. However, there was some variance, thus a patient could score well with good effort and demonstrate normal function yet report elevated levels of pain and disability. This patient would be classified as displaying 'minimal exaggeration' if there was a moderately elevated perception of pain and/or disability or even 'marked exaggeration' if a high perception of pain and disability was present.

Prior to the FCE process, all patients signed a consent form explaining the purpose of the FCE, that good effort was expected and that there were indicators in the FCE process to determine if exaggeration was present.

The purpose of each questionnaire and each test was explained beforehand and 'trial' efforts were allowed prior to each physical test.

Significant differences between Survey One and Survey Two (Table 8.19):

- Survey Two had a higher percentage of males than Survey One
- The time from injury to FCE was significantly greater (90 per cent) in Survey Two.
- More patients in Survey Two showed symptom/disability exaggeration (89 per cent) than in Survey One (77 per cent).

RESULTS: SURVEY TWO

Thirty-five per cent of all patients had had surgery for their injury

A number of self-assessed questionnaires were given to the client to fill out prior to testing commencing.

The scores (Table 8.20) have been averaged to provide an indication of total perception of pain and disability for each group. Numbers in italics indicate a low perception of pain and disability.

Table 8.19 Test validity

Degree of exaggeration	Survey One	Survey Two
No exaggeration	21%	11%
Minimal symptom and disability exaggeration	30%	36%
Marked symptom and disability exaggeration	45%	49%
Overt symptom and disability exaggeration	4%	4%

Although it is not mathematically correct to average dissimilar values the table does provide an indication of the heightened degree of pain and perception.

Questionnaire results

On average, all the questionnaires used reflected the eventual FCE outcome (Table 8.21). The non-SE group scored consistently lower on all questionnaires than the other three groups. On individual analysis the higher the averaged score for all questionnaires the lower the eventual FCE score.

However, there was considerable variation in individual questionnaires. For example the average Oswestry score for marked symptom exaggerators was 54 per cent with a range from 32 per cent to 74 per cent.

Pain perception appeared to have little correlation to perceived disability. Those with a pre-FCE pain level (recorded immediately prior to the FCE commencing) of 3/10+ recorded an Oswestry score of 51 per cent, those with a pre-FCE pain of 5/10+ recorded 49 per cent and those with pre-FCE pain of between 8–10/10+ recorded 61 per cent. Again there was a wide variance in individual answers.

Overall, all four groups had similar degrees of medical impairment – as assessed from medical reports, physical examination and observation of movement on distraction. However, perception of disability varied considerably and this had significant impact on overall FCE performance.

The pain drawing was the exception to the individual variability of questionnaire responses and consistently showed a significantly lower average score than other questionnaires. Generally, clients were quite anatomically accurate about drawing the symptoms asked for (numbness, pins and needles, burning, stabbing) and surprisingly few drew inappropriate diagrams of their symptoms. In contrast, the post-FCE pain drawing, which asked only for 'pain' often reflected a regional or global pattern of pain that did not correlate to the medical impairment. However, like all questionnaires there was a wide range of individual responses.

Medical impairment

A standard clinical examination, appropriate for the injury of each patient, was done. The degree of medical and physical impairment for all four groups was about the same – as assessed by examination and reports from medical examiners.

The pattern of movement changed *during* the course of the FCE only in two patients (3 per cent). Changes in movement were assessed as being due to fatigue and neuromuscular weakness from the original injury. In the two whose movement patterns changed during the FCE the changes correlated with the medical signs of injury – muscle wasting and neurological deficit.

'Pattern of movement' is the manner of how any task or movement is done. The 'normal' manner of movement may vary from person to person, as will the way that movements may alter in the presence of impairment or disability.

Table 8.20 Pain and disability questionnaire results

	Overt SE	Marked SE	Minimal SE	Non-SE	Cut-off
Dallas – physical	85	74	70	59	50
Dallas – psychological	71	53	48	44	50
Pain scale (during FCE)	100	74	*54*	*30*	60
Oswestry	69	54	47	45	40
MSPQ	34	26	19	16	15
Pain Drawing	*13*	*13*	*12*	*3*	30
McGill	52	30	28	*18*	21

Scores are all adjusted to */100°. Italicised numbers are low score.

Altered patterns of movement may indicate compensatory movements due to injury or impairment. Altered patterns of movement may also be demonstrated in a way that does not correlate with the stated injury or in an attempt to demonstrate greater disability than may be present. Thus professional expertise is required to interpret movement patterns and understanding the relevance to injury perception and work ability.

Straight leg raise

Straight leg raise (SLR) is a commonly used test to indicate if compression or irritation of the sciatic nerve is present. If the nerve root is affected there should be a significant difference in the SLR result between the affected leg and unaffected leg.

For those with low back problems (including sciatica, low back pain, discectomy, fusion) there were insignificant changes in the straight leg raise test in all four groups (Tables 8.22 and 8.23).

In 20 per cent of cases the SLR of the affected leg was the same or better than the unaffected leg.

Table 8.22 Average SLR ability

	Affected leg	Unaffected leg
Overt SE	31	38
Marked SE	45	50
Minimal SE	64	66
Non-SE	64	69

Table 8.23 Average SLR differences: affected leg compared to unaffected leg

	Difference
Overt SE	7
Marked SE	6
Minimal SE	2
Non-SE	5

Table 8.21 Self-assessed questionnaires and results

Questionnaire	Description	Scale	FCE result
Dallas Pain Questionnaire	A four-part questionnaire. Two parts reflect perceptions of physical impairment and two parts reflect behavioural perceptions.	$>$ 50% of each part considered significant.	On average the higher the perceived disability, the greater the degree of exaggeration.
Inappropriate Symptoms Questionnaire	A list of low back symptoms considered inappropriate. Helps to identify abnormal illness behaviour.	2 or more positive findings	On average negative for non-SEs, positive for all SEs.
McGill Pain Measurement	A quantitative measure of pain able to be treated statistically.	Pain Rating Index of pain descriptions	Marked SE clients reported 72% more pain symptoms than non-SE patients did.
Modified Somatic Perception Questionnaire	Measures increased bodily awareness associated with psychological distress.	$>$ 5/39 (15% or more) indicates high perception	Marked SE clients reported 60% more distress on average.
Pain Drawing	A screening tool to determine if symptoms are out of proportion to medical impairment.	3 or more indicates poor psychometrics	All groups scored 'low' on average in contrast to the results from all other questionnaires. 15% of individuals scored high.
Numeric Pain Scale	A category scale with ratio properties. Easy to understand and a quick way of self-assessing change in pain during the FCE.	6/10+ represents high impairment or symptom exaggeration	The greater the degree of symptom/disability exaggeration, the higher the level of their 'lowest' pain. The level of the 'highest' pain was about the same for all four groups.
Oswestry Low Back Pain Disability Questionnaire	Measures perceived disability and can be used to assess change as a result of treatment.	$<$ 40% considered 'severe disability'	The overt group perceived they were 'crippled'. All other groups perceived that they were 'severely disabled'.

ALGOMETRY – TENDERNESS PERCEPTION

Algometry (or dolorimetry) is used as an objective indication of tenderness perception (Fischer, 1988). A 1 sq-cm rubber tipped pressure gauge is pressed on areas that are not regarded as 'trigger points'. Based on Fischer's work, a reading of less than 3 kg of pressure was deemed abnormal and more than 5 kg as normal. Results were regarded as an indication of an abnormal perception of tenderness if areas remote from the injured area were recorded as abnormal.

Algometry showed a good correlation to the eventual outcome. The lower the reading that tenderness was reported, the lower the FCE score and the higher the degree of symptom and disability exaggeration (Table 8.24).

Dallas Pain Questionnaire

This questionnaire is partly physical and partly behavioural. There was insignificant difference between the four groups in the scoring proportion between the physical and behavioural aspects (Table 8.25).

The difference in scores between each of the groups was insignificant.

However, the differences in demonstrated physical performance were significantly more. The differences are estimated to be in excess of 50 per cent between each group of clients for each of the material handling tests.

Table 8.24 Perception of tenderness – algometry (%)

	Abnormal tenderness	Low tenderness	Normal tenderness
Overt and marked SE	48	33	20
Minimal SE	20	28	52
No SE	0	14	86

Table 8.25 Dallas Pain Questionnaire results (%)*

Group	Physical impairment		Psychological/behavioural	
Overt SE	80	90	63	78
Marked SE	69	77	51	56
Minimal SE	62	71	*43*	*47*
No SE	49	60	*42*	*41*

*Less than 50% (in italics) is considered 'low' for all of the four Dallas categories.

Self-reported pain levels

Lowest and highest pain levels during the previous thirty days were asked for. The change in self-reported pain level during the FCE was also reported. Figure 8.2 presents the results in graphical form.

On average all groups reported having pain of greater than 8/10++ at some time in the thirty days preceding the FCE. Only four patients (5 per cent) reported having no pain on at least one occasion (including sleeping) and only one patient reported having no pain at the start of the FCE. Thirty per cent of patients reported having pain of 6/10++ or more at the start of the FCE.

The overt and maximum SE groups reported a greater increase in pain during the course of the FCE. On average their pain increased from 'strong+' (5.7/10+) to 'very strong+' (7.6/10+) by the end of the FCE.

In contrast the non-SE group commenced the FCE with 'moderate+' (3.5/10+) pain which actually decreased to 'moderate pain' (3/10+) by the end of the FCE.

Only one patient commenced the FCE with 'no pain' and only four patients reported having 'no pain' at some time in the previous thirty days.

Generally, the overt SE and maximum SE groups reported the highest pain levels. They also reported having the highest intake of analgesic medication.

Waddell's non-organic signs

Waddell identified five criteria of non-organic signs of disability – abnormal tenderness, simulated stress, straight leg raise differences, regional disturbances and overreaction.

Three or more criteria are considered positive and indicate a need for further psychological assessment.

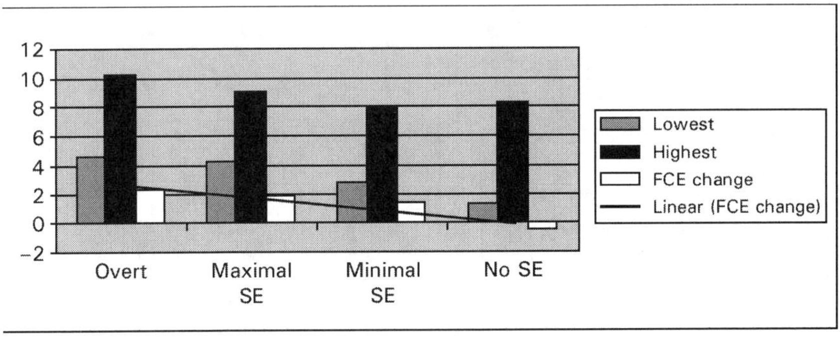

Figure 8.2 Self-reported pain levels and pre-FCE to post-FCE pain change (with pain assessed on a 0–10+ scale: 2 = weak pain, 3 = moderate, 5 = strong, 7 = very strong, 10 = very very strong, 10 + = maximal pain)

Frequency of Waddell's signs

The greater the degree of symptom exaggeration, the greater the number of non-organic signs. The results correlated with the study by Menard (1994) who found that those with a high Waddell's score were more likely to display symptoms of abnormal illness behaviour (Figure 8.3).

The most common positive signs were excessive difference in straight leg raise (67 per cent positive) and simulated trunk rotation (61 per cent). The frequency of other signs varied between 33 and 43 per cent.

Of the 61 patients assessed for Waddell's criteria just five were negative for all five criteria.

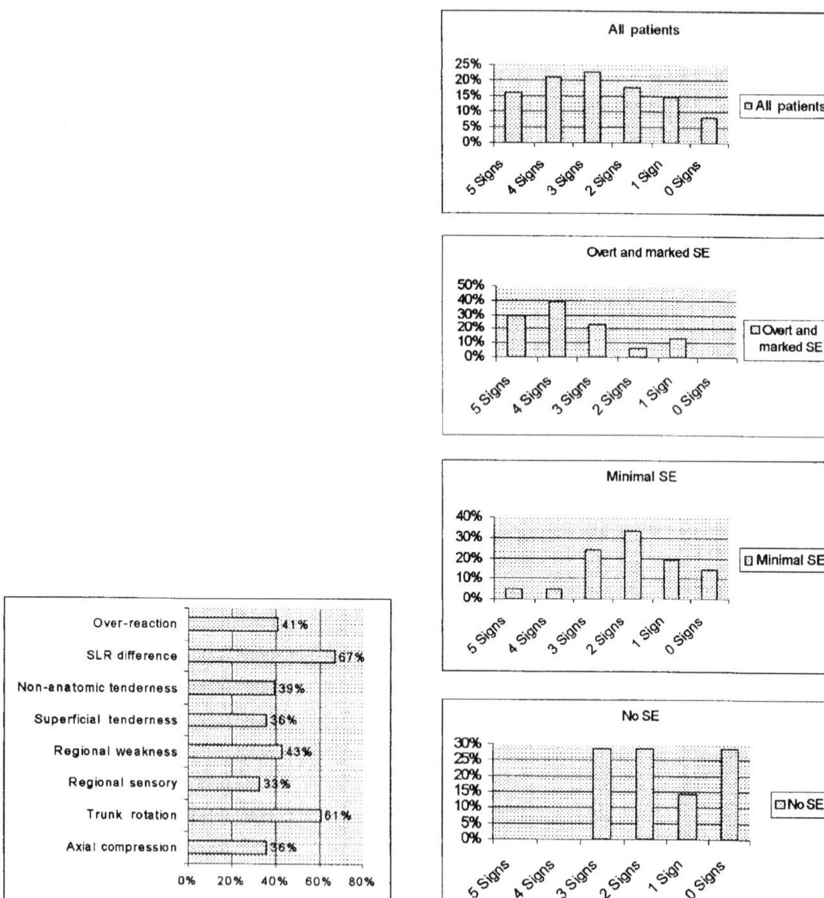

Figure 8.3 Incidence of Waddell's signs in patients displaying symptom exaggeration

Table 8.26 Handgrip test – validity score (%)

	Validity score
Overt SE	35
Marked SE	62
Minimal SE	77
Non-SE	83

Handgrip testing

Matheson et al. (1998) tested the theory that use of the JAMAR Hand Dynamometer may be a useful indication of symptom magnification for low back pain patients. His results showed that this could be used as one of several indicators of whether maximum voluntary effort (MVE) was given by a patient but was not valid enough as the sole indicator of MVE.

As summarised in Table 8.26 testing validity decreased according to the degree of exaggeration.

However, there was a wide variation of performance in all groups apart from the overt SE group and the handgrip test should not be relied on as the sole indicator of the sincerity of a low back problem.

SLEEP DISTURBANCE

Loss of restorative sleep is often quoted as being a significant factor in chronic pain syndrome. Amitriptyline or similar medications may be prescribed to help restore normal sleep patterns.

Self-reported sleep disturbance averaged 6.5 for those taking no sleep medication (91 per cent).

$$(0 = \text{normal sleep},\ 10 = \text{no sleep})$$

For those taking amitriptyline (9 per cent of patients) the self-reported sleep disturbance was 6.7.

Thus there was no improvement in perception of sleep improvement with amitriptyline.

TREATMENT

All patients reported having multiple assessments and treatments. All 82 patients reported having no lasting success from any form of treatment – surgical, medical, physical, psychological, alternative or occupational.

PAIN AND DISABILITY PROFILE versus MOVEMENT PATTERNS

This is assessed by observing the patient's patterns of movement on deliberate testing distraction. If there is significant disparity between the pain/disability rating and movement patterns, then symptom and/or disability exaggeration is present. There are six criteria on which this decision is made:

1. Self-reported high pain levels should result in significant protective movements.
2. Compensatory or protective movement patterns noted during testing should be the same as observed on distraction.
3. There should be close correlation of test results that place similar stresses on the same area.
4. Tests that stress uninjured parts of the body should reflect normal movement patterns and significantly better peak performance than those tests that stress the injured area.
5. Significant changes in pain during the FCE testing should result in concurrent changes in patterns of movement.
6. There should be objective signs of good effort.

Only six patients demonstrated that they had pain and disability that matched their perception and report of pain and disability. On average, all groups perceived that they were 'severely disabled' but this degree of disability was not evident for 76 of the 82 patients assessed (93 per cent) (Figure 8.4).

The most common indications that significantly less disability was present than was claimed were:

- Normal patterns of movement that did not correlate with the claimed disability.
- Poor correlation of results between tests.
- Significantly better patterns and range of movement on distraction.
- Claims of significant increases in pain in the presence of submaximal effort.

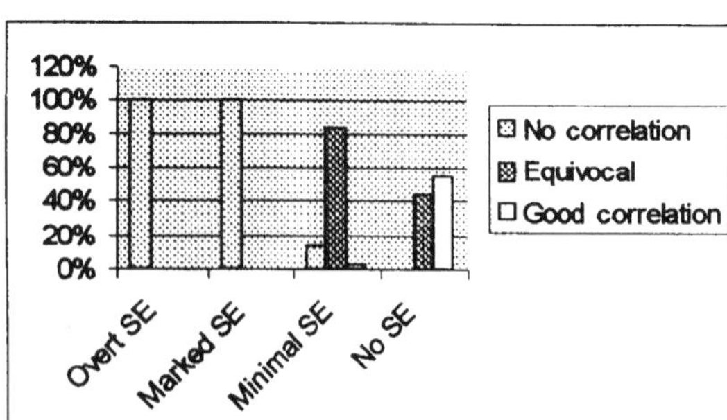

Figure 8.4 Correlation between disability and movement

The patterns of movement for all but two clients were quite normal, with no indication of physical disability. The lower the FCE score, the less mobility was *demonstrated* and the greater the discrepancy between perception and mobility as observed on distraction.

All the overt SE and most of the marked SE patients displayed patterns of movement that were bizarre or blatantly impossible when compared to their documented medical impairment. Some examples of the most common impossible displays of disability:

- Demonstrating in excess of 70 per cent loss of quadriceps muscle strength yet able to complete 105 steps of the step test with no sign of fatigue or compensatory movements.
- Demonstrating gross loss of unilateral leg strength (in excess of 40 per cent) but having no disuse muscle wasting, normal gait and no signs of unilateral fatigue on repetitive stair climbing.
- Bilateral straight leg raise of 30 or less, yet able to sit on the examination couch with legs extended straight ahead thus demonstrating ability for SLR of at least 70.
- Reporting pain on gentle passive trunk rotation (simulated lumbar spine rotation) yet naturally choosing to twist the trunk and spine during material handling activities.
- Inability to squat (less than 45° of knee flexion) because of strong pain, yet able to stair climb normally and able to get up and down to floor level with minimum support.
- Gross overreaction (gasping, groaning, grabbing for support, hyperventilating, excessive slowness, verbalising etc.) when asked to deliberately forward flex yet able to sit, get into a car, dress and undress in a normal manner with a normal pattern and improved range of spinal flexion with no reaction.

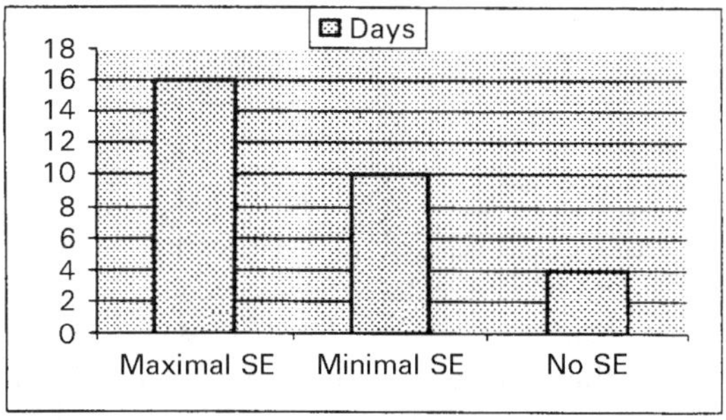

Figure 8.5 Perceived FCE recovery time

POST-FCE REPORTS

The time to recover from exercise and stressing a stable injury was expected to average one to two days. The better the effort, the shorter the perceived time to recover from any post-test soreness.

One client with overt symptom exaggeration perceived that he would take about six months to recover from a single lift of a 3 kg weight from floor level and three forward bends to knee level.

Generally, the more sub-maximal the effort and the greater the number of non-organic signs, the greater the perceived length of time for recovery (Figure 8.5).

Nineteen patients (42 per cent) reported having regional or global pain after the FCE. The pain distribution did not correlate with the injury.

Comments made by patients were very focused on pain and disability. Many took the opportunity to vent their anger and frustration at ACC for perceived failings. Despite an invitation to comment about job ability, very few took the opportunity.

Fifty per cent (11 of 22) overt SE and marked SE patients who returned post-FCE questionnaires thought that the FCE process was ‘hopeless and unfair’, compared to 7 per cent (1 of 15) of the minimal SE or non-SE patients.

All 563 FCE reports were sent to the patients’ GPs with a letter inviting them to ring or write if they had any queries about the FCE. Five doctors rang or wrote, three to request further information and two to disagree with the FCE results. Phone follow-up by the evaluator was made with about twenty doctors, all of whom agreed with the FCE results.

WORK ABILITY

Of the 82 patients assessed in Survey Two, all but two demonstrated that their injury was stable, that three to four hours of physical testing did not result in any change in patterns of movement during testing and no physical or functional barrier to returning to work appeared to exist.

Of the two that were assessed as not having a capacity to safely return to some sort of work, one had an unrelated cardiac condition and the other (a manual labourer) had a very poor level of cardiovascular fitness.

A brief period of rehabilitation was recommended in conjunction with a return to work for eleven patients (13 per cent).

SUMMARY

The results of 563 long-term injury compensation clients were examined; 79 per cent (445) demonstrated exaggeration of their symptoms and/or disability; 49 per cent demonstrated this to a marked extent. Their perception of pain and disability was significantly greater than what was demonstrated and observed in the FCE.

The results of 82 long-term patients from two provincial areas were also examined in greater detail. Questionnaires universally reflected that perceived pain and disability was high in almost all patients. However, functional testing and observation indicated that 95 per cent of patients had stable injuries and a functional ability to safely return to some type of work.

There was a strong correlation between the FCE score and the degree of symptom and disability exaggeration. The lower the score the greater the number of non-organic signs of disability and the greater the degree of discrepancy between movement patterns demonstrated compared to movement patterns observed on distraction.

The medical impairments of all clients were stable and on the basis of the FCE about 80 per cent had an estimated safe ability to immediately return to some sort of work on a full-time basis without any indication for any physical rehabilitation. Only two had an estimated inability to return to more than half-time work safely without aggravating their injury. Further active physical rehabilitation was recommended for 15 patients (15 per cent) in conjunction with a return to work.

The degree of medical impairment was about the same for all clients. Only 11 per cent of patients displayed movement patterns and physical performance that appeared to correlate with medical impairment.

No single clinical test or questionnaire indicated with accuracy if a patient was exaggerating disability. The overall averaged score remains the most accurate and fairest way of assessing perception compared to actual physical performance.

The most consistent test for assessing work ability was observing function during physical testing. Non-symptom exaggerators demonstrated consistent patterns of movement and function that correlated reasonably well with their medical impairment. Those in the marked SE group reported a high perception of pain and disability but had normal patterns of movement and improved function on distraction.

CRITIQUE OF MEDICAL ASSESSMENTS

The referrals for all patients assessed included one or more medical reports, which provided useful background on the medical history of the patient. From a functional point of view medical reports were of little help in assessing functional ability.

- Most specialist medical reports provided an adequate synopsis of the patient's history.
- Most GP reports merely reported the patient's symptoms and the patient's perception of work ability.
- Most medical reports had an excellent recitation of the patient's symptoms.
- Clinical examination of the lumbar spine in most cases was perfunctory. Straight leg raise was the only test done that could be relied on as an objective baseline for future testing.
- Behavioural assessment was rarely mentioned. In most cases where behavioural issues were mentioned it was in the form of the examiner's opinion without any corroborating evidence or notes of any testing criteria.

- Functional testing was never done.
- For some medical assessments, the criteria published in 'Guides to the Evaluation of Permanent Impairment' was used as the sole means of deciding the degree of impairment, with no mention made of disability for the type of work performed by the patient. The 'Guides' itself states that other criteria such as the accuracy and reproducibility of tests, clinical procedures and the observer's interpretation need to be taken into account when deciding on impairment. The presence of a given degree of *impairment* does not necessarily mean that *function* is restricted to the same degree, particularly if the work situation does not involve use of the impaired body area.

Medical examination and function

Medical examiners do not test function. However, medical examiners commonly feel able to state what they believe to be the patient's functional ability. The doctor's certified functional ability is invariably conservative because that ability is only the opinion of the doctor, based on assessment of medical impairment. In some instances the patient's own assessment of work ability is what is certified.

The behavioural aspects of functional testing are rarely done in a medical assessment. Unless the patient demonstrates functional ability then it is impossible to objectively comment on how abnormal illness behaviour or non-organic signs may be affecting function or if the patient's stated work ability is accurate.

Patterns of movement, compared to impairment and the patient's perception of pain and disability, appear to be the most reliable way of assessing if a patient is giving good effort and is truly reflecting their safe work capacity. Medical assessments rarely measure anything other than range of movement. The FCE examines movement patterns that includes range, repetition, material handling ability for four different work frequencies, non-material handling and performance during functional tasks (generic or task specific). Observation of movement ranges, patterns and consistency give significantly greater understanding of the patient's functional abilities and if symptom and/or disability exaggeration is present.

Clinical applications

A suggested application for clinicians when treating long-term clients or those whose recovery time appears excessive:

- Establish a baseline of the patient's perception of pain and disability. The 0–10 pain scale (record current pain, worst/least pain in last month and pain change before and after treatment) and the Oswestry scale are probably the easiest and quickest to complete and understand.

- Measure tenderness perception by algometry on injured *and* non-injured areas as an objective indication of pain tolerance and as an indicator of non-organic problems.
- Observe patterns of movement as an indication of disability and differences in performance as demonstrated and as observed on distraction.
- Record the patient's self-reported 'estimated time to recover' from the effects of assessment exercise or treatment.

The greater the discrepancy between professional expectation and patient perception the greater the likelihood that behavioural problems are interfering with rehabilitation.

CONCLUSIONS

Physical assessments on long-term compensable clients should always include behavioural tests to indicate if the patient's perceived disability correlates with test results. A purely physical assessment without behavioural testing is a waste of time on most long-term compensation patients and merely reflects what the patient chooses to demonstrate, rather than what they are potentially capable of.

Some surgery, particularly spinal surgery, appeared to be done mainly on the basis of the patient's report of pain, rather than the unconvincing clinical indications for surgery. It is recommended that an FCE prior to surgery would help to identify those patients whose disability appeared to be behavioural rather than medical or physical.

Medical assessments do not test function and statements on functional ability are made on the basis of medical impairment. There is no evidence of any clinical test being able to predict work ability. No procedure, including the FCE process, can predict with total certainty what a patient's future work ability is but it is reasonable to expect that several hours of physical and functional testing will provide a better indication of current and future work ability than a short static medical examination.

Most general practitioners see themselves as 'patient advocates' and will present and defend the patient's point of view. It is difficult to prove or disprove disability during a brief medical examination and most doctors were quite grateful that the FCE results did indicate objectively what their patient's behavioural, physical and work status was. The FCE report usually gave the GP an excuse to raise behavioural and psychosocial issues affecting recovery and return to work.

The value of prescribing amitriptyline is questioned in those who have significant behavioural problems preventing return to work. Whilst chronic pain is a complex problem, this FCE survey does indicate that drug therapy does not appear to have significant effect in 'pain' control or perceived sleep deprivation. Medication appeared to have little effect on pain control, indeed those patients taking the strongest medication also reported the highest level of pain. It is recommended that the FCE process is an excellent method of indicating if medication is having any effect on pain control or function. Indeed most patients appeared to be 'suffering' from their injury rather than having any particular physical pain.

RECOMMENDATIONS

The FCE process gives an objective indication of safe work capacity providing good effort is given and motivation to return to work is evident. The results of these two surveys indicate that other uses of the FCE process include:

1. Assessing the validity of injury and understanding if inability to work is due to physical or psychosocial factors.
2. Establishing a baseline of functional performance on which to measure the effect of treatment (medical, surgical or physical).
3. Assessing what degree of symptoms and disability are due to behavioural problems prior to surgery being considered.
4. Understanding the effect that impairment may be having on function and vice versa. Concurrent to this, the effect of behaviour can be factored in.
5. Assessing if any physical or functional sequelae of injury are still present.

These two surveys provide an indication of the problems of the long-term compensable patient. Whilst the numbers of patients assessed in Survey Two was small (82), further analysis of the 1000+ FCEs now completed by the authors will provide a more accurate assessment of a wider spectrum of patients and conditions.

References

American Medical Association (1993). Guides to the Evaluation of Permanent Impairment, Ed 4. AMA.

Blankenship K.L. (1994). *Functional Capacity Evaluation. The Procedure Manual*, 2nd edn. The Blankenship Corporation.

Dworkin, S.F., Von Korff, M.R. and LeResehe, L. (1990). Multiple pains and psychiatric disturbance: An epidemiological investigation. *Arch. Gen. Psychiatry*, **47**, 239–244.

Fischer, A.A. (1988). *Muscle Pain Syndromes and Fibromyalgia. Pressure algometry for quantification of diagnosis and treatment outcome*. Haworth Medical Press.

Flores, L. (1997). Objectification of functional improvement after nonoperative care. *Spine*, **22** (14), 1622–1633.

Gatchel, R.J. and Gardea, M.A. (1999). Psychosocial issues. Their importance in predicting disability, response to treatment, and search for compensation. *Neurologic Clinics*, **17**, 149–166.

Gatchel, R.J., Polatin, P.B., Mayer, T.G. et al. (1994). Psychopathology and the rehabilitation of patients with chronic low back pain disability. *Arch. Phys. Med. Rehab.*, **76**, 666–670.

King, P.M., Tuckwell, N. and Barrett, T.E. (1998). A critical review of Functional Capacity Evaluations. *Physical Therapy*, **78**, 852–865.

Matheson, L.N., Bohr, P.C. and Hart, D.L. (1998). Use of maximum voluntary effort grip strength testing to identify symptom magnification syndrome in persons with low back pain. *J. Back and Musculoskel. Rehab.*, **10**, 125–135.

Menard, M.R. (1994). Pattern of performance in workers with low back pain during a comprehensive motor performance evaluation. *Spine*, **19** (12), 1359–1366.

Waddell, G., McCulloch, J.A., Kummel, E. et al. (1980). Non-organic physical signs in low-back pain. *Spine*, **5**, 117–125.

Rethinking functional capacity evaluation

Eva Schonstein and Dianne Kenny

INTRODUCTION

In an era of accountability, litigation and escalating costs of workers' compensation, functional capacity evaluations (FCEs) have gained currency in the assessment of occupational injury. Because FCEs hold the promise of precise and accurate measurement of function upon which to base decisions related to return to work (RTW) and payments for functional loss, they appear to be an attractive alternative to physicians' judgement and measures of impairment such as CT scans and MRIs, none of which have provided convincing evidence of their prognostic value (Fordyce, 1995).

This paper will argue that:

- Current published literature fails to provide evidence for the reliability and validity of FCEs.
- FCEs do not predict RTW, rather they predict work capacity, with the inference that a match between work capacity and work demands will allow a safe and durable RTW.
- An FCE alone cannot fulfil the role of predictor of RTW, since RTW is determined by a multiplicity of factors some of which are unrelated to the physical functioning of the worker. It is therefore important to consider the whole range of identified predictors and to assess their putative significance on an individual basis for each worker, as he or she moves through the injury management process.

HISTORICAL BACKGROUND

The concept of functional evaluation is not new and several instruments have been developed in the past to determine an individual's ability to perform activities of daily living such as Functional Assessment Inventory, Functional Status Index, Older American Resources and Service Methodology (Tramposh, 1992). From these first attempts followed the development of work-oriented functional evaluations and most of these were developed in the USA.

FCEs were developed in the late 1970s as the American Workers' Compensation Administrations became alarmed at the rising delays in workers returning to work after injury and consequent increased costs (D'Orazio, 1993). A major factor for this was the difficulty physicians had in deciding when an injured worker could return to work or determining the level of work he or she could sustain upon returning to work (D'Orazio, 1993). In response to this situation a 'workers' compensation functional capacity form' was developed which required the physician to provide specific information about actual physical abilities of the worker (D'Orazio, 1993). Allied health professionals, mostly physical therapists, have taken up the challenge in the USA of further developing the concept of FCEs resulting in a variety of commercially available protocols. Many of these have found their way into the Australian workers' compensation system and are currently being marketed to and conducted by physiotherapists and occupational therapists. These FCEs have penetrated the Australian workers' compensation system because it has undergone similar changes to the American system since its inception in NSW ninety years ago. The changes have also been driven by the need to reduce costs. The introduction in 1983 of the NSW Occupational Health and Safety Act legislated employer responsibility for workplace safety, and the 1987 Workers' Compensation Act legislated employer responsibility for the occupational rehabilitation of injured workers. Within the first six months of introduction of the latter, self-insurers reported that the cost of claims had halved. This was attributed to the introduction of compulsory rehabilitation that involved the provision of suitable duties for injured employees as well as a system of early reporting and referral to rehabilitation (Kenny, 1994). This positive situation did not last, and unfavourable trends emerged as early as 1992 when it was noted that permanent impairment payments (section 68 of the Act) had dramatically increased and by 1996 the NSW WorkCover Scheme had an accumulated deficit of $454 million (Grellman, 1997).

Prompted by this situation, the NSW Government commissioned the Grellman Report in 1997. The Grellman report identified 'permanent impairment and pain and suffering awards, claimants' duration on weekly benefits, commutations and disputes as well as litigation' as key cost drivers (Grellman, 1997, p. 3). The report made several important recommendations that resulted in a revised Workplace Injury Management and Workers' Compensation Act introduced in 1998. These changes related to the process of injury management, in which the workplace was specified as the focal point for injury management. Returning the worker to maximum productivity is viewed as a shared responsibility between the treating doctor and the employer, with the insurer as an overseer of the injury management plan. Effectively, this new Act requires doctors to provide appropriate medical certification of incapacity, medical reports relating to the worker's fitness for work and recommendations for suitable duties that the worker is capable of performing (information on changes to the Act provided by the WorkCover Authority, 1998).

However, the basis upon which medical practitioners determine impairment and disability is unreliable and lacks scientific validation. de Kort, Uiterweer and Dijk (1992) showed a lack of consensus among experienced occupational physicians with regard to assessing medical fitness for specific jobs. Medical determination of work incapacity is a difficult process because assessment of pathology does not predict back pain outcomes (Haldeman, 1990; Waddell and Main, 1984). Range of motion is not usually an adequate measure for the functional status of the patient (Clark et al., 1988). Finally, reported pain is not a good indicator of disability (Pettingill, 1979; cited in Abdel-Moty et al., 1993). Estlander, Takala and Viikari-Juntura (1998) state that 'a report of pain is a measure of behaviour, not an objective measure of pain experience' (p. 451). In other words, physicians need more specific and objective information upon which to base their judgement of whether a worker is fit to return to work and the recommendations for suitable duties. FCEs hold the promise of providing this information and that is why they continue to be of great interest to health professionals in the area of management of injured workers.

FUNCTION AND ITS ASSESSMENT

A variety of FCEs are currently available in Australia. Their protocols have some similarities and some major conceptual differences. Uniting all FCEs is their aim to assess injured workers' physical capacities and sincerity of effort during one assessment. On the basis of this information, the health practitioner predicts the timing of RTW and the level of physical work a worker can safely sustain upon his or her return to work. Another common use of FCEs is to ascertain the earning capacity of injured workers in litigation cases.

However, major differences exist between the FCEs. Firstly, some focus on specific tasks such as lifting capacity (e.g. PILE and the EPIC Lift Capacity) or upper limb function only (e.g. BTE Work Simulator), whilst others assess several job factors such as standing, walking, sitting, lifting, carrying, pushing, pulling etc. (e.g. IWS, PWPE, RFCE). These job factors are based on the key elements identified in a US government publication, the Dictionary of Occupational Titles (DOT) as physical demands of a specific job (Fishbain et al., 1994). There are 20 job factors described in the DOT, such as standing, walking, sitting, lifting, carrying, pushing, pulling etc. and these are the ones mostly used by FCEs to determine physical work capacity (Fishbain et al., 1994). Another major difference between FCEs is the criteria used to assess work capacity. These criteria vary from computerised isoinertial or isometric tests to simple observation of performance of work tasks. It is beyond the scope of this paper to describe these criteria in any detail.

One other major difference between FCEs is who determines when the worker has reached his or her maximum level of task performance. On one hand there are those who believe that the worker is able to judge his or her own safe maximum, and on the other those who believe that the professional administering the test can (based on his or her observation) determine the worker's maximum level of performance.

There are two main issues related to the assessment of function. Firstly, FCEs attempt to 'measure' an ill-defined concept, that of function. Traditionally, occupational therapists used the term function and activities of daily living (ADL) interchangeably. That is, function was defined as the physical performance of tasks or activities that were largely dependent on appropriate skills and abilities (Unsworth, 1993). (Abdel-Moty et al., 1996) suggested that abilities are influenced by attitudes as well as by external factors including injury, pain and environmental stressors. In other words, when function is assessed, skills, abilities and motivation are also implicitly evaluated. Assessing function, it appears, is a complex undertaking. It is therefore not surprising that those who attempt this using FCEs may wish to limit the concept of 'function' to what the FCE intends to measure (Unsworth, 1993). In other words, function is a hypothetical construct that is inferred from the observation of selected behaviours that have been determined by the constructors of FCEs to measure function. (Talo et al., 1996) propose that the term functioning should be regarded as an umbrella term that incorporates body, mind and environment. It follows that the concept of function is not a clearly defined term and that most FCEs report on observed physical performance of work tasks and from this they make inferences related to the worker's capacity to perform these in the workplace.

At this point, we should make a distinction between the prediction of work capacity and the prediction of return to work. FCEs are designed to contribute to the RTW process by contrasting work capacity to work demands. This is a valid inference; however, if FCEs attempt to predict a worker's return to work, many other factors need to be considered in addition to an individual's capacity to perform work tasks, including workplace and psychosocial factors.

Secondly, FCEs are assessments that measure performance over one (or two) days. Based on this observation of performance, predictions of the level of physical performance a worker would be able to sustain without risk of re-injury, are made. However, there are major problems with this process. Von Korff and Saunders (1996) suggest that assessing back pain status on a single day can provide an unreliable assessment in the same way as assessing blood pressure with a single reading is an unreliable measure of a patient's blood pressure. This is supported by other researchers such as van den Hoogen et al. (1998) and Croft et al. (1998) who point out that in the normal course of back pain, relapses occur in many cases within a year. Findings such as these indicate that assessing performance at one point in time cannot accurately predict subsequent risk of further episodes of back pain. Inclusion of information regarding the natural history of work-related disorders would need to form part of the FCE process.

RELIABILITY AND VALIDITY OF FCES

A review of the literature relating to FCEs revealed agreement that FCEs:

- are tools used to determine a person's capacity to return to work after injury;
- attempt to predict the maximum safe capacity for work; and/or daily tasks (Abdel-Moty et al., 1996; King, Tuckwell and Barrett, 1998; Lechner, Roth and Straaton, 1991; May et al., 1998);
- can be 'measured in individuals who may or may not have medical impairment' (Abdel-Moty et al., 1993 p. 170);
- need demonstrated reliability and validity, especially predictive validity, for them to be useful tools in the injury management process (Abdel-Moty et al.,

1996; King, Tuckwell and Barrett, 1998; Lechner, Roth and Straaton, 1991; Tramposh, 1992).

Several studies describing a variety of FCEs have been published in peer-reviewed journals and these are summarised Table 8.27.

The authors could locate only five reliability and two validity studies (see Table 8.27). Reliability is a pre-requisite for predictive validity. In other words, an FCE can be reliable but not valid (i.e. it does not predict work capacity and/or RTW), however an FCE cannot be valid without demonstrated test-retest inter- and intra-rater reliability. Even if reliability is demonstrated, different protocols give reliability testing different meanings. As mentioned before, some FCEs allow the worker to determine his or her safe maximum level of task performance. In these tests the reliability of the tool is more a comment on the worker's performance, whereas in the tests where the assessor is in charge of determining the maximum safe limit, reliability of the test is more a comment on the assessor's performance.

Although Dusick et al. (1993) and Lechner, Jackson and Straaton (1994) have concluded that the FCEs they studied (ERGOS and PWPE respectively) are valid, a careful examination of the methodologies and findings of these two studies reveals that these conclusions are difficult to sustain. Dusick et al. (1993) have compared workers' performances on two FCEs, namely the ERGOS Work Simulator and the Rehabilitation Therapy Physical Evaluation (RTPE), which the authors describe as a structured exercise oriented evaluation that assesses physical tolerances consistent with the guidelines established by the Canadian Classification and Dictionary of Occupations. The authors conclude that there is concurrent validity between these two assessments on measures of strength variables such as lifting, carrying, pushing, pulling and grip strength ranging from r value of 0.48–0.87 ($p < 0.001$) (Dusick et al., 1993). The clinical significance of this is questionable given that the RTPE is not regarded as an acceptable 'gold standard' and that correlations of 0.48 are too low to be used for clinical decision making. In fact, except for grip strength, all correlations ranged between 0.45 and 0.71 (lifting bench/hip height), reflecting generally unacceptably low concurrent validity.

Lechner, Jackson and Straaton (1994) have attempted to demonstrate validity of their FCE, the PWPE, by assessing the PWPE's ability to predict the level of work subjects were able to perform compared to actual work the subjects were doing. The levels of work predicted were those described in the US Dictionary of Occupational Titles (ranging from unable to perform sedentary work to able to perform very heavy work). These predictions were made in terms of general categories of work, not in specific terms relating to work tasks. This is a major shortcoming of this protocol. Even if one considers these criteria useful in practice, the generalisability of this study is questionable as the subjects had rheumatoid arthritis, that is, they did not belong to the commonest group usually assessed by FCE, that is, workers with low back pain (LBP).

However, there is a much larger problem than the scant and methodologically flawed reliability and validity studies on FCEs. The problem is conceptual. To evaluate the validity of an FCE one needs either a 'gold standard' against which one can compare the outcome of the FCE, or an independent outcome such as return to work. The problems are: firstly, there is no gold standard; and secondly, work capacity, however well measured, is only part of the factors influencing return to work outcomes. Therefore, we cannot expect to find high validity coefficients between FCEs and RTW outcomes.

In addition to predicting capacity to perform work-related tasks, FCEs are also used to assess sincerity of effort. Since performance is effort-based and influenced by such factors as attitudes, motivation and personality it would be desirable to find a way of taking account of these factors (Fordyce, 1995).

Different FCEs reach conclusions regarding sincerity of effort in different ways. Examples include the coefficient of variation (CV) (e.g. comparison of test dynamometry to normative data) alone, or a combination of CV and professional judgement of consistency of performance throughout the test (Isernhagen, 1992), or in combination with a measure of heart rate (Mayer et al., 1988). Simonsen (1995) suggests that measurement of sincerity of effort is difficult by definition 'because the goal is to establish an objective measurement of something which is by its nature subjective' (p. 519). Hamilton-Fairfax, Balnave and Adams (1995) have questioned the use of measures of strength variability as a means of determining sincerity of effort, and have demonstrated that applying a single CV classification cut-off value appears discriminatory against females, because females seem to have greater strength variability. In FCEs which use isoinertial testing methods, a physiologic index of effort is proposed which is the relationship between peak force generated during a lift and the weight being lifted (Hazard et al., 1991). Baker (1998) reviews a number of methods that health professionals use to demonstrate sub-maximal effort during FCEs. She suggests that workers should be warned that FCEs include tests aimed at identifying sub-maximal effort and individuals should be confronted when inconsistencies are noted and given a chance to improve their efforts. She further suggests, however, that reports should include findings of sub-maximal effort. However she concludes that much more research is needed in this area.

MOVING FORWARD

Most workers, employers and insurers agree that a timely return to work is the desired outcome of injury management. For FCEs to be useful in injury management FCEs should be used as part of an assessment protocol that takes account of the whole range of factors known to influence RTW outcome. These factors have been identified in prognostic studies. Prognostic studies are those that are prospective and where the authors follow-up a cohort of persons for a defined period of time. Some of the most recently published prognostic studies reveal that for low back pain, factors such as age, initial diagnosis, previous history, self report and several psychosocial indicators such as job satisfaction and workers' RTW expectations are associated with delayed recovery and/or delayed return to work. Careful consideration needs to be given to all factors influencing the return to work process of injured workers. That is, in addition to observation

Table 8.27 Published FCE studies

FCE name	Country of origin	Published reliability research	Published validity research	Criteria used to assess work capacity and end point of weighted activities
PILE	USA	Test–retest reliability ($r = 0.87$, $p < 0.001$) (Mayer et al., 1988)	No	Isoinertial frequent (12 lifts/minute) lifting strength testing. End-point of task is determined by client or evaluator if 85% of age determined maximum heart rate achieved, or safety end point when 55–60% of body weight lifted or less than 12 lifts/minute.
RFCE	USA	No	No	Isoinertial strength testing and DOT job factors. Task ended when client feels has achieved maximum with (Fishbain et al., 1994).
ISW	USA	(Smith, 1994) inter-rater kappa = 0.64 intra-rater kappa = 0.73	No	Therapist's judgement of when maximum safe achieved in all weighted activities based on operational definitions.
ERGOS	USA	No	Concurrent validity for lifting $r = 0.71$ and 0.63 ($p < 0.001$) and $r =$ around 0.5 for other tasks (Dusick et al., 1993)	Static strength and endurance during isometric and dynamic tasks. End point determined by the client.

WorkAbility Mark III	Australia	No	No	Predetermined time standards as ways of determining the labour content of tasks such as the time it takes for a finger to shift 25 mm from one side of a large nut to the other (Shervington and Balla, 1996).
BTE Work Simulator	USA	Test–retest reliability $r = 0.74–0.87$ for VO_2 and $r = 0.58–0.78$ for HR	Limited criterion validity demonstrated (for light levels of effort only) (Kennedy and Bhambhani, 1991)	Repetitive upper limb static and dynamic motions against measurable resistances over a measurable period of time.
PWPE	USA	Inter-rater reliability for determining maximum dynamic ability $\kappa = 0.74$ (Lechner et al., 1994)	Spearman correlation between predicted work level by PWPE and work being performed at the time of testing ranged from 0.41 ($p = 0.002$) to 0.55 ($p < 0.001$) (Lechner et al., 1994)	Therapist clinical judgement maximum dynamic ability, quality of movement pattern and subject's co-operation.
EPIC Lift Capacity	USA	For 14 subjects with musculoskeletal impairment test–retest reliability r varies from 0.95 to 0.82 ($p < 0.001$) (Matheson et al., 1995)	No	Isoinertial lifting strength testing. Testing stops if evaluator detects one of the following: presence of 'high risk work style' based on guidelines, or inability to safely complete the task based on changes of posture and muscle recruitment or heart rate limits exceeded. In addition evaluee can stop testing due to self-perception of maximum reached.

of performance during an FCE, the clinician must consider other factors that are likely to influence the return to work of injured workers.

Table 8.28 shows that several studies have demonstrated that the initial diagnosis is a significant factor in the outcome of low back pain. A more specific diagnosis predicts a more protracted and costly outcome.

Abenhaim et al. (1995) propose two interconnected reasons for this association, firstly that certain types of spinal disorders could lead to a natural history of poor prognosis and secondly that making a 'specific' diagnosis, at the beginning of a compensated episode of LBP could, in the mind of the patient and doctor, give the message that the condition is serious. This may have the effect of shifting the goals of the back problem towards investigations and treatment rather than focusing on functional recovery. Furthermore, this encourages the patient to pursue a cure rather than focus on return to function. This view has been supported by Fordyce (1995) who suggested that 'the major problem in non-specific low back pain disability appears to be the medicalization of suffering' (p. 23). The implication of this for FCEs is that health practitioners must understand the judgemental nature of the diagnostic process, and need to incorporate education and explanation of the significance of specific diagnoses to patients.

Table 8.29 shows that increasing age is a predictor of poor outcome. This implies that an FCE report needs to flag the effect that age may have on outcome, and therefore extra care and special attention needs to be given to older injured workers in order to minimise chronicity and associated health care costs.

Table 8.30 provides evidence that previous history of musculoskeletal pain is a predictor of poor outcome. This finding highlights the importance of prevention. It also indicates that the natural history of low back pain may include recurrences. This means that health professionals predicting work capacity on the basis of an FCE need to clearly flag to workers, insurers and employers the fact that RTW should happen as soon as the worker is capable, but that it is likely that some workers will experience further episodes of back pain. This should not deter the worker from returning to work nor the employer from offering suitable duties. In other words recurrent back pain episodes need to be viewed as a normal part of the gradual restoration of function after low back injury.

PSYCHOSOCIAL PREDICTORS

There are a host of psychosocial factors that have been associated with RTW outcomes. We define the term 'psychosocial' in the broadest possible way, as the combination of both the psychological and social factors that influence RTW following work-related injury. Social factors include workplace factors as well as availability of work. A detailed discussion of identified psychosocial predictors can be found in Kenny and Jones (1999). In that paper, it was argued that the search for predictors is only useful if it has some impact on the injury management plan. In this section, we will focus on only those predictors that meet this prerequisite. Chief among these is intended work outcome, which is variously described as an RTW goal (Tan, 1997), RTW intention, RTW expectation (Pfingsten et al., 1997) or job-attached status to the pre-injury employer, where the RTW expectation is implied. Voaklander, Beaulne and Lessard (1995) studied 1527 discharges from a rehabilitation centre over a 22 month period, and found that workers with a job-attached status to their pre-injury employer were three times more likely to gain employment post-discharge than other workers. Those from large employers were twice as likely again to be employed post-discharge. The provision of modified duties if workers are initially unable to return to their pre-injury duties is one way to keep injured workers attached to their pre-injury employers. Provision of modified work has been found to enhance RTW in a cost effective manner (Krause, Dasinger and Neuhauser 1998). Attempts to maintain this employee – employer relationship should therefore be a priority for the injury management programme, and providers and insurance carriers need to work co-operatively to achieve this goal. Further support for the importance of this factor in RTW is provided in a study by Fishbain et al. (1997), who found that explicitly stated intention not to return to their pre-injury job was highly predictive of negative RTW outcome. Similarly, Carosella (1994) found that those workers who expressed low expectations of RTW were least co-operative with the RTW programme after rehabilitation.

Time spent on the examination of the role of personality factors in failure to RTW is not well spent, firstly because the findings to date have been disappointing, and secondly, because, even if personality differences are found, it is very difficult to alter core personality traits. A more useful approach is to examine an individual's pain beliefs and fear avoidance behaviour as predictors of poor RTW outcomes. Pain beliefs are often in error and correcting them through the provision of carefully structured information has been found to decrease fear avoidance behaviours. For example, a simple pamphlet encouraging early activity and early RTW following an episode of LBP, and discouraging inevitability beliefs and fear avoidance behaviours was disseminated at a workplace. This strategy resulted in a 70 per cent reduction in the extended absences due to back pain, and a 60 per cent reduction in the number of days of absence (Symonds, et al., 1995). These findings are particularly interesting in view of the fact that they were not accompanied by significant changes in attitude as measured by standard questionnaires such as the Fear Avoidance Behaviour Questionnaire (FABQ) and Pain Locus of Control Questionnaire (PLCQ) in employees who had experienced a previous episode of low back pain.

In addition to the above mentioned predictors there are several clinical tests and measures which have been found to be predictors of low back pain outcome. These are the Modified-Roland Morris Low Back Questionnaire (RM-18), the Absolute Visual Analogue Scale (AVAS) for measuring pain, the Short-form McGill Pain Questionnaire (SFMPQ) and the Biering-Sorensen test for measuring trunk extensor endurance. All these tests are described in detail by Maher, Latimer and Refshauge (1999).

A generic model of LBP FCE is proposed below. It combines current FCE protocols with known predictors of low back pain outcomes (bold characters). The proposed model is limited to LBP. Further research is needed for an FCE model aimed specifically at cervical spine and upper limb dysfunction. It is a preliminary model that will have to be validated through prospective studies.

Table 8.28 Diagnosis as a predictor of LBP outcome

Item	***n***	**Follow-up days**	**Author/year**	**Outcome of interest**	**OR/RR CI 95%**
Sprain/pain vs. disorder	305	1228	(Infante-Rivard and Lortie, 1996)	Workers with a diagnosis of sprain or pain were twice more likely to return to work than those diagnosed with intervertebral disc disorder.	OR = 2.2 (1.23–3.91)
Specific vs. non-specific	2147	730	(Ehrmann-Feldman et al., 1996)	Workers with a specific diagnosis were more than twice as likely to be absent from work for more than 60 days than those with a non-specific diagnosis.	OR = 2.2 (1.1–4.5)
Disc disorder/sciatica vs. arthritis	986	365	(Engel et al., 1996)	Back pain patients diagnosed with disc disorder/sciatica were more than three times as likely to have high health care costs than those diagnosed as having arthritis.	OR = 3.7 (2.4–5.7)
Specific vs. non-specific	1848	730	(Abenhaim et al., 1995)	Patients with specific diagnosis were almost five times as likely to evolve towards chronicity than those diagnosed with non-specific low back pain	OR = 4.9 (2.8–8.4)

Table 8.29 Age as a predictor of LBP outcome

Age	***n***	**Follow-up days**	**Author/year**	**Outcome of interest**	**OR/RR CI 95%**
Age (45–54)	1848	730	(Abenhaim et al., 1995)	Patients aged between 45 and 54 were almost three times as likely to evolve towards chronicity than younger ones.	OR = 2.7 (1.1–6.5)
Age (55–64)	1848	730	(Abenhaim et al., 1995)	Patients aged between 55 and 64 were almost five times as likely to evolve towards chronicity than younger ones.	OR = 4.7 (1.8–12.3)
Age (between 21 and 30 compared to > 30)	305	1228	(Infante-Rivard and Lortie, 1996)	Workers between 21 and 30 years of age were 1.43 times more likely to return to work than those over 30 years old.	OR = 1.43 (1.04–1.98)

Table 8.30 Previous history of musculoskeletal pain as a predictor of LBP outcome

Item	*n*	Follow-up days	Author/year	Outcome of interest	OR/RR CI 95%
Previous LBP	454	730	(Thorbjornsson et al., 1998)	Women with previous LBP were 1.6 times more likely to develop LBP in subsequent years.	OR = 1.6 (1.0–2.4)
Seeking medical care for lower extremity pain	222	730	(Burdorf et al., 1998)	Workers with pain in the lower extremities who sought medical care for their complaint were eleven times more likely to stay off work longer.	RR = 11.31 (1.08–43.46)
Musculoskeletal pain 12 months before commencement of study	222	730	(Burdorf et al., 1998)	Workers who reported musculoskeletal pain in the 12 months before the study were more than three times likely to be absent from work than those who did not.	RR = 3.35 (1.73–6.47)
History of previous LBP for females	2715	365	(Papageorgiou et al., 1996)	Females who did consult a GP 12 months before study and reported previous LBP were almost three times more likely to report a new episode of LBP in the 12 month follow-up period.	OR = 2.9 (1.7–5.1)
History of back pain	238	365	(Van Poppel et al., 1998)	Workers who had a history of back pain were almost ten times more likely to report an occurrence of a new episode during the follow-up period.	OR = 9.8 (2.8–34.4)

WORK CAPACITY EVALUATION PROTOCOL FOR WORKERS WITH LOW BACK PAIN

1. Explanation to the worker of the elements of the evaluation and enlisting his or her co-operation.
2. History of previous symptoms.
3. Awareness of medical diagnosis and explanation of prognosis.
4. Assessment (via observation and questionnaire) of the workplace in order to ascertain:
   a) availability of suitable duties
   b) attitude of management towards the injured worker and willingness to offer appropriate duties
   c) attitude of co-workers and supervisors
   d) performance of real work tasks.
5. Self-reported disability (RM 18).
6. Subjective assessment of lumbar spine to include:
   a) AVAS (Absolute Visual Analogue Scale)
   b) Short McGill questionnaire.
7. Objective assessment of lumbar spine.
   a) Trunk muscle performance
      (i) Biering-Sorensen test (trunk extensors) described in Maher, Latimer and Refshauge (1999)
      (ii) Ito et al. test (abdominal endurance) described in Maher, Latimer and Refshauge (1999).
8. Observation of work task performance (FCE)
   a) Lifting
   b) Pushing/pulling
   c) Carrying
   d) Crawling
   e) Kneeling
   f) Crouching
   g) Squatting
   h) Sitting
   i) Standing
   j) Walking
   k) Climbing stairs/ladder
   l) Balance
   m) Other work tasks as appropriate.
9. Cardiorespiratory endurance
   a) Cycle ergometry or treadmill, if possible; if not, YMCA 3 minute step test (described in Maher, Latimer and Refshauge, 1999).

10. Assessment of psychosocial factors such as:
    a) RTW goals and expectations
    b) High fear avoidance questionnaire (FABQ)
    c) Depression (Modified Zung questionnaire)
    d) Job satisfaction.
11. Estimate of sincerity of effort
    a) Consistency of performance throughout the assessment
    b) Waddell's signs (Magee, 1997).

CONCLUSION

FCE is a tool currently used in injury management to predict a person's physical abilities in order to assist in his or her timely and safe return to work. At present, there is a lack of reliability and validity studies that demonstrate the usefulness of this tool. In addition, FCEs do not incorporate known predictors of return to work and thus their validity in terms of an RTW outcome is difficult to prove. It is proposed that in order for an FCE to be able to predict workers' timely and durable RTW, it needs to incorporate known predictors of outcome as well as take into consideration the normal course of return to function after an episode of back pain. Such a model is proposed.

References

Abdel-Moty, A.R., Crompton, R., Steele-Rosomoff, R. et al. (1996). Process analysis of functional capacity assessment. *Journal of Back and Musculoskeletal Rehabilitation*, **6**, 223–236.

Abdel-Moty, E., Fishbain, D.A., Khalil, T.M. et al. (1993). Functional capacity and residual functional capacity and their utility in measuring work capacity. *The Clinical Journal of Pain*, **9** (3), 168–173.

Abenhaim, L., Rossignol, M., Gobeille, D. et al. (1995). The prognostic consequences in the making of the initial medical diagnosis of work-related back injuries. *Spine*, **20** (7), 791–795.

Baker, J.C. (1998). Burden of proof in detection of submaximal effort. *Work*, **10**, 63–70.

Burdorf, A., Naaktgeboren, B. and Post, W. (1996). Prognostic factors for musculoskeletal sickness absence and return to work among welders and metal workers. *Occupational and Environmental Medicine*, **55** (7), 490–495.

Carosella, A.M. (1994). Factors associated with early discharge from a multidisciplinary work rehabilitation program for chronic low back pain. *Pain*, **57** (1), 69–76.

Clark, W.L., Haldeman, S., Johnson, P. et al. (1988). Back impairment and disability determination: another attempt at objective, reliable rating. *Spine*, **13** (3), 332–341.

Croft, P.R., Macfarlane, G.J., Papageorgiou, A.C. et al. (1998). Outcome of low back pain in general practice: a prospective study. *BMJ*, **316** (7141), 1356–1359.

de Kort, W.L., Uiterweer, H.W. and van Dijk, F.J. (1992). Agreement on medical fitness for a job. *Scandinavian Journal of Work, Environment and Health*, **18** (4), 246–251.

D'Orazio, B.P. (1993). *Back Pain Rehabilitation*. Andover Medical Publishers.

Dusick, L.A., Menard, M.R., Cooke, C. et al. (1993). Concurrent validity of the ERGOS work simulator versus conventional, functional capacity evaluation techniques in a workers' compensation population. *JOM*, **35** (8), 759–767.

Ehrmann-Feldman, D., Rossignol, M., Abenhaim, L. et al. (1996). Physician referral to physical therapy in a cohort of workers compensated for low back pain. *Physical Therapy*, **76** (2), 150–157.

Engel, C.C., Von Korff, M. and Katon, W.J. (1990). Back pain in primary care: Predictors of high health-care costs. *Pain*, **65** (2–3), 197–204.

Estlander, A.M., Takala, E.P. and Viikari-Juntura, E. (1998). Do psychological factors predict changes in musculoskeletal pain? A prospective, two-year follow-up study of a working population. *Journal of Occupational and Environmental Medicine*, **40** (5), 445–453.

Fishbain, D.A., Abdel-Moty, E., Cutler, R. et al. (1994). Measuring residual functional capacity in chronic low back pain patients based on the Dictionary of Occupational Titles. *Spine*, **19** (8), 872–880.

Fishbain, D.A., Cutler, R.B., Rosomoff, H.L. et al. (1997). Impact of chronic pain patients' job perception variables on actual return to work. *Clinical Journal of Pain*, **13** (3), 197–206.

Fordyce, W.E. (1995). *Back pain in the workplace. Management of disability in nonspecific conditions*. Seattle, Washington, IASP Press.

Grellman, R.J. (1997). Inquiry into Workers' Compensation System in NSW. Sydney, KPMG.

Haldeman, S. (1990). Failure of the pathology model to predict back pain. *Spine*, **15** (7), 718 –723.

Hamilton-Fairfax, A., Balnave, R. and Adams, R.D. (1995). Variability of grip strength during isometric contraction. *Ergonomics*, **38** (9), 1819–1830.

Hazard, R.G., Reeves, V., Weisman, G. et al. (1991). Dynamic lifting capacity: The relationship between peak force and weight as an indicator of effort. *Journal of Spinal Disorders*, **4** (1), 63–67.

Infante-Rivard, C. and Lortie, M. (1998). Prognostic factors for return to work after a first compensated episode of back pain. *Occupational and Environmental Medicine*, **53** (7), 488–494.

Isernhagen, S.J. (1992). Return to work testing. Functional capacity and work capacity evaluation. *Orthopaedic Physical Therapy Clinics*, **1** (1), 83–98.

Kennedy, L.E. and Bhambhani, Y.N. (1991). The Baltimore Therapeutic Equipment Work Simulator: reliability and validity at three work intensities. *Archives of Physical Medicine and Rehabilitation*, **72** (7), 511–516.

Kenny, D. (1994). Barriers to occupational rehabilitation in New South Wales. Presented at Faculty Research Day 1994.

King, P.M., Tuckwell, N. and Barrett, T.E. (1998). A critical review of functional capacity evaluations. *Physical Therapy*, **78** (8), 852–866.

Krause, N., Dasinger, L.K., and Neuhauser, F. (1998). Modified work and return to work: A review of the literature. *Journal of Occupational Rehabilitation*, **8** (2), 113–139.

Lechner, D.E., Jackson, R.D.L. and Straaton, K.V. (1994). Reliability and validity of a newly developed test of physical work performance (PWPE). *JOM*, **36** (9), 997–1004.

Lechner, D., Roth, D. and Straaton, K. (1991). Functional capacity evaluation in work disability. *Work*, **1** (3), 37–47.

Magee, D.J. (1997). *Orthopedic Physical Assessment* (3rd edn). W.B. Saunders.

Maher, C., Latimer, J. and Refshauge, K. (1999). Atlas of clinical tests and measures for low back pain. Student manual. School of Physiotherapy, Faculty of Health Sciences, University of Sydney.

Matheson, L.N., Mooney, V., Grant J.E., et al. (1995). A test to measure lift capacity of physically impaired adults. Part 1 – Development and reliability testing. *Spine*, **20** (19), 2119–2129.

May, V.R., Taylor, D., Brigham, C. et al. (1998). Functional capacity evaluation, impairment rating, and applied certification processes. *Neurorehabilitation*, **11** (1), 13–27.

Mayer, T.G., Barnes, D., Nichols, G. et al. (1988). Progressive isoinertial lifting evaluation II. A comparison with isokinetic lifting in a disabled chronic low-back pain industrial population. *Spine*, **13** (9), 998–1002.

Papageorgiou, A.C., Croft, P.R., Thomas, E. et al. (1996). Influence of previous pain experience on the episode incidence of low back pain: Results from the South Manchester back pain study. *Pain*, **66** (2–3), 181–185.

Pfingsten, M., Hildebrandt J., Leibing, E. et al. (1997). Effectiveness of a multimodal treatment program for chronic low-back pain. *Pain*, **73** (1), 77–85.

Shervington, J. and Balla, J. (1996). WorkAbility Mark III: Functional assessment of workplace capabilities. *Work*, **7** (3), 191–202.

Simonsen, J.C. (1995) Coefficient of variation as a measure of subject effort. *Arch. Phys. Med. Rehabil.* **76** (6) (Jun), 516–520.

Smith, R.L. (1994). Therapists' ability to identify safe maximum lifting in low back pain patients during functional capacity evaluation. *Journal of Orthopaedic and Sports Physical Therapy*, **19** (5) (May), 277–281.

Symonds, T.L., Burton, A.K., Tillotson, K.M. et al. (1995). Absence resulting from low back trouble can be reduced by psychosocial intervention in the workplace. *Spine*, **20** (24) 2738–2745.

Talo, S., Rytokoski, U., Hamalainen, A. et al. (1996). The biopsychosocial disease consequence model in rehabilitation: model development in the Finnish 'work hardening' programme for chronic pain. *International Journal of Rehabilitation Research*, **19** (2), 93–109.

Tan, V. (1997). RTW goal is the single best predictor of RTW. *International Journal of Neuroscience*, **92** (1–2), 161–170.

Thorbjornsson, C.O., Alfredsson, L., Fredriksson, K. et al. (1998). Psychosocial and physical risk factors associated with low back pain: a 24 year follow up among women and men in a broad range of occupations. *Occupational and Environmental Medicine*, **55** (2), 84–90.

Tramposh, A.K. (1992). The functional capacity evaluation: measuring maximal work abilities. *Occupational Medicine: State of the Art Reviews*, **7** (1), 113–124.

Unsworth, C.A. (1993). The concept of function. *British Journal of Occupational Therapy*, **56** (8), 287–292.

van den Hoogen, H., J.M., Koes, B.W. et al. (1998). On the course of low back pain in general practice: a one year follow up study. *Annals of the Rheumatic Diseases*, **57** (1), 13–19.

Voaklander, D.C., Beaulne, A.P. and Lessard, R.A. (1995). Factors related to outcome following a work hardening program. *Journal of Occupational Rehabilitation*, **5** (2), 71–85.

Von Korff, M. and Saunders, K. (1996). The course of back pain in primary care. *Spine*, **21** (24), 2833–2837.

Van Poppel, M.N.M., Koes, B.W., Deville, W. et al. (1998). Risk factors for back pain incidence in industry: A prospective study. *Pain*, **77** (1), 81–86.

Waddell, G. and Main, C.J. (1984). Assessment of severity in low-back disorders. *Spine*, **9** (2), 204–208.

Chapter 9

Interpretation of capacity to work

The relationship between functional capacity and job demands

Robyn Rankin

There are many ways in which information about a person's ability to work can be determined and represented. Job demands fall into various categories and the tools we use to measure those demands are many and varied.

What do non-injured job seekers do when looking for a job? Job seekers consider their knowledge and/or education, interests, ability, skills and perhaps their physical ability to do the job. Many work through Centrelink, which has a tool at its disposal, namely the Australian Standard Classification of Occupations (ASCO).

In the second edition of ASCO (1997) it is stated that 'ASCO is the specified standard for the reporting of workplace accidents under the revised Regulations of the Occupational Health and Safety (Commonwealth Employment) Act 1991'. ASCO classifies jobs into various groups and provides generic job descriptions and also lists jobs that can be included under that generic description. The reason that the American Department of Labor's Dictionary of Occupational Titles is not appropriate for use in Australia is that many of the educational standards and certainly the job demands differ significantly for jobs of the same title in Australia.

It is unfortunate that in ASCO the actual 'job content factors', that is the measurements of the physical and non-physical demands of jobs, are not published. These job content factors were published in the original draft of the pilot study for ASCO in 1983. Without such measurements the job descriptions are quite nebulous, although they may offer a baseline from which to begin when job matching.

The job content factors include worker components such as: formal preparation regarding education and training; informal preparation including experience and on the job training; Holland category regarding worker interests; special requirements including specific job requirements such as personal dedication, upgrading knowledge and a number of other specifics. The second category is materials, which includes subject matter relating to the requirement to work with data, ideas, people or things. This category also delineates the equipment one must be able to use in the job. The third category is functions and includes:

mental and related activities comprising such areas as integrating, analysing, planning, decision making, reasoning, mathematical competence and the use of English language at various levels; physical activities, classifying the level of competence required in hand function, co-ordination, handling, sitting, walking, standing, running and balance, and the level of effort required specifically related to lifting; and social activities indicating whether the worker is required to work alone or in groups and levels of responsibility. The fourth group relates to context, including environmental location and conditions, time constraints and rewards. The final category is indicators which includes labour market size and industry codes.

In job matching a large number of these categories are highly relevant, particularly where a worker can no longer return to their previous job and their previous employer has no work within their capacity. The job content factors are relevant even in determining whether in fact their employer has work within their capacity.

These are the factors that should also be addressed in job or task analysis for matching a worker to their previous job or identifying a range of jobs within their safe capacities.

Critical in any assessment of an injured worker in considering job matching is an interview including their employment history, relevant social factors and the history of their injury, in order to identify non-physical factors that may impact a return to work and/or selection of a new job. This requires an appropriate approach to mediation where there may be industrial and/or psychosocial factors involved.

However, functional capacity assessment is the tool that will provide measurements of the person's physical capacities to meet the physical demands of the job, and an appropriate and detailed job analysis is needed to enable a comparison of functional capacities and physical demands of a job. From such a comparison, it is then possible to: set goals for a graduated return to normal duties; set goals for further interventions including medical management; determine what modifications to process methods or equipment may enable the worker to undertake a specific job safely; and identify a range of jobs within a worker's safe capacities.

References

Australian Standard Classification of Occupations, 2nd edn. Department of Employment, Education, Training and Youth Affairs and The Australian Bureau of Statistics (1997).

Australian Standard Classification of Occupations: Occupational Dictionary. Department of Employment and Industrial Relations and The Australian Bureau of Statistics (1983).

Capacity and job matching

Mark McKie

For rehabilitation providers, this area of capacity is the most important to consider and yet ten years' practical experience in the provider network indicates it is most often the least understood. This seems to be based upon a lack of understanding of the real purpose for establishing capacity, the inability to question results and then a limited understanding of what to do with the information gathered.

Like so many things, the real or 'true purpose' for determining capacity is not usually immediately obvious but is generally the most powerful factor in the process of achieving an outcome. Why do we want to determine capacity, and who cares anyway? Determining capacity is aimed at getting the issue of capacity out of the way, to then deal with the real reasons why the claimant is not returning to work.

Providers become involved in the more difficult workers' compensation cases. In these situations, each of the key parties – claimant, employer, treating practitioner(s), claims agent/insurer and rehabilitation provider – has an opinion regarding the worker's capacity, and these opinions are most often at odds with each other. These opinions are not always free of other influencing factors. The use of capacity can often be the 'red herring' in the story of a worker's return to work, drawing the focus of attention away from other issues, including industrial relations issues, previous work performance difficulties, conflict with supervisors, personal difficulties, and psychological and social difficulties.

In fact, most often what individuals refer to as 'capacity' is the 'incapacity' of the individual, rather than the capacity. The claimant's ability to undertake activities is most often framed in terms of what they can't do. Most medical certificates document: 'to lift no more than 5 kg, and avoid overhead lifting' – these terms develop and maintain a negative narrative that prevents parties from exploring possibilities, whilst focusing on areas of inability. The power of language is not to be abused in the process of return to work, and the 'reframing' of such phrases can refocus individuals – moving from the glass being half empty to being half full. Such medical certificates can set an occupational rehabilitation provider up to be arguing against one 'reality' in which the claimant and often the medical practitioner have a vested interest. In this 'story' maintaining the employment relationship can become difficult and, without an employment relationship, any return to work becomes increasingly difficult and potentially costly for the individual, the workers' compensation schemes and the community.

At the same time this perspective can often keep the key parties in the return to work process involved in adversarial roles and disputes regarding 'true' capacity. Given enough time, and enough medical experts, any range of opinions can be offered regarding an individual's ability to return to work. The rehabilitation provider should not be interested in what individuals cannot do, but in what areas of functioning they do have ability.

If returning individuals to work were as simple as determining capacity and job matching, there would be very little need for occupational rehabilitation consultants. The process would simply require a medical expert to clearly and objectively measure capacity, assess the job demands and implement an appropriate return to work plan.

However, in more complex situations, determining capacity is a tool to enable to rehabilitation provider to deal with the 'real' issues preventing a return to work. As long as the individual's capacity remains unclear, this can be the 'red herring' in the process and prevent the occupational rehabilitation provider from dealing with the range of issues impacting on the return to work, during the 'to and fro' of managing each person's reaction.

Occupational rehabilitation providers should prefer to be able to have capacity clearly determined by the treating medical practitioner – more specifically the individual who is taking responsibility for signing the medical certificates. This is one of the most significant responsibilities in the process. Should this individual provide limited information, which from experience is often the situation, then an objective and sustainable assessment of capacity should be sought, conducted by an appropriately qualified professional who will stand by their assessment. An assessment that says that an individual is capable of lifting 5 kg today, but that this could change tomorrow, is of no value. One is looking for an assessment that relates to the relevant legislation, that provides clear and reputable information, and that understands the psychological and social importance of focusing individuals on their capacity and ability to return to work.

An occupational rehabilitation provider is interested in capacity assessments in order to create a narrative, or story, that helps individuals to participate in the workforce and the community. Such providers are not usually medical practitioners or those trained in the assessment of capacity; however, a provider's job is to co-ordinate and to create a reality that supports a return to work, and to ensure that the legislative responsibility of a return to work is implemented.

To this end, capacity information needs to be effectively matched to job demands, again providing objective data regarding recommended 'suitable employment'. This activity needs to be aimed at taking the responsibility for job matching out of the hands of treating practitioners, who are often family general medical practitioners with little direct knowledge of work sites and even less of industrial relations issues and the workers' compensation arena. Medical certificates frequently document 'light duties' or 'clerical duties' as capacity assessments. Such comments do not appear to provide data regarding capacity, but opinions regarding employment options. This is of particular concern when most often the medical practitioner has not assessed the duties, and is basing recommendations upon a ten or fifteen minute consultation in their room with the claimant and no contact at all with the employment site. Occupational rehabilitation providers do not wish to become involved in medical or treatment issues, and do not have training in this area. It is of concern when medical practitioners become involved in legal, industrial and employment matters with little or limited experience.

Capacity assessments enable job matching, providing treating practitioners with information regarding the workplace, and ensuring each 'player' in the process keeps their expertise specific to their training.

For occupational rehabilitation providers, the process of assessing capacity and job matching is aimed at creating a 'story' that ensures a return to suitable employment as a favourable outcome. The aim is to take elements of the responsibility away from the treating practitioners, enabling them to 'save face' with their patient, and yet support a return to work. To this end, appropriately trained and experienced experts who can provide clear, objective assessments of capacity and job demands, and who are clear regarding the bounds of their role, are invaluable to the return to work process.

This merely provides a baseline and, in a sense, gets the issue out of the way to deal with other issues that impact upon a claimant's ability to return to work. This is based upon the belief that our lives are not based upon what we can get out of the world, but what we can put back in, and that the most important element is to be able to contribute and belong.

Interpretation of capacity to work

Ruth Mitchell

This is probably the most complex issue in the workers' compensation arena; however, it is possible that an understanding of the concept of an 'outcome' will simplify this issue.

An outcome is a worker no longer on workers' compensation benefits, either full or partial payments. The most acceptable social outcome is a return to fully productive employment. This, however, is not the only outcome.

The first question to be posed in relation to this subject is 'what is capacity?'. The reality of workers' compensation is that at least 80 per cent of workers return to fully productive work with or without intervention. Therefore, when discussing this subject, we are predominantly dealing with the 20 per cent who are or who become difficult to return to work.

Lets look at the word 'capacity': what does it mean? There are alternatives to the word capacity, such as potential, competence and capability, as well as readiness and inclination, according to a thesaurus.

Considering that we are particularly looking at the 20 per cent of workers who have difficulty in returning to work, we should not only be looking at the physical aspects that have so far precluded a return to work, but also the mental or emotional aspects (i.e. the readiness or inclination) contributing to why workers have not returned to work. Unfortunately, frequently the physical aspects of the injury continue to remain the focus of the return to work, and this in itself often sabotages a successful and sustainable return to work.

To really understand this philosophy, it may be helpful to go back to the beginning of the injury. The point of view to commence with is:

ALL INJURIES ARE GENUINE

From this point of view, all workers are then given an equal opportunity for treatment and return to work. The legislation, after all, implies that once two points are agreed, i.e. the worker is a worker, and the injury occurred in the course of employment, or out of the course of employment, then a claim exists. Once this statement is understood the next step is to acknowledge that:

ALL INCIDENTS RESULT FROM A SYSTEM BREAKDOWN

It is out of this acknowledgement that proactivity evolves, as part of an occupational health and safety system. Injury management is just one of the components. It is also this philosophy that enables no blame, just solutions.

One of the areas which causes confusion is disability versus capacity. These terms may, in fact, differ between various legislations. There can be a disability without an incapacity 'to do'. Some workers, and indeed others, believe that if they have capacity 'to do', then it will not be believed that they have a compensable disability. This fear can influence the worker's ability to return to work. It is important to educate workers on the difference between the two. From experience, this basic lack of understanding can be the difference between a return and a non-return to work.

Identifying capacity is about not only identifying the worker's physical ability to undertake a task, but also the emotional ability to return to work. All too often workers who have been 'tested' and found to be able to undertake the physical demands of a job, sabotage the return to work in other ways as their emotional needs have not been addressed. Therefore the co-ordinator of the return to work process needs to ensure they have an understanding of the complete picture. Concentration on just the physical aspects will more than likely result in a frustrated, often long and unsuccessful process, the outcome being case closure with a partial or non-return to work.

Chapter 10

Job analysis

Job analysis research: what has been done and what needs to be done?

Åsa Kilbom

Job analysis can be performed for several purposes. The main purpose is for the design of production systems with the aim of improving work organisation, i.e. the balance between work operations, and between machines and humans, thereby influencing productivity. Job analysis systems such as methods time management (MTM) have been and are still widely used for this purpose, although their reputation is not the best due to linkages with Taylorism and its potential exploitation of human resources. Even though such systems have been widely criticised, we must recognise that unless the employer targets productivity, jobs will vanish. Thus it is a perfectly legitimate goal to seek improved productivity. The other main purpose of a job analysis system is to produce data that can be used to analyse the risk of injury and reduced well-being. Such systems have a humanistic purpose and may well clash with the goal of increasing productivity. However, the aim of ergonomics is to optimise the balance between humanistic and productivity purposes. Therefore we need to develop job analysis systems that simultaneously record work output, work organisation and injury risks. No such systems exist yet, to the author's knowledge, although efforts are being made, in one of the research programmes at the Swedish Institute for Working Life, to develop them.

The purpose of this paper is to present and discuss methods for objective, external assessment of work and work tasks. Admittedly, when trying to understand occupational injury and when undertaking ergonomic improvements, there is also a need to record people's subjective, self-rated assessment of their work. Such investigations are usually in the form of questionnaires or rating scales, and will add valuable information about the worker's own perceptions of effort, fatigue and frustrations (Borg, 1990). They provide valuable additional information, but they carry less credibility among employers and authorities. Therefore the aim of this presentation is to describe existing job analysis programmes in ergonomics, mainly focusing on physical workload and the identification and quantifying of the risk for musculoskeletal injury.

METHODS FOR ASSESSING WORKERS' COMPENSATION CLAIMS

Methods for this purpose should have clear cut-off levels of acceptability. Background data for such assessments are numerous, ranging from existing standards and guidelines to scientific reports. There is an ongoing discussion about the scientific support for highly quantitative standards in terms of forces, distances and repetition rates (Kilbom, 1999), and it appears that most standards are poorly substantiated by research. A comparison between different national standards demonstrates relatively large differences and supports the conclusion that there is no consensus among scientists about appropriate cut-off levels. Probably the best documented guideline is the National Institute for Occupational Safety and Health (NIOSH) lifting equation (Waters et al., 1993), although it has not been accepted by OSHA as a standard. The European Union standards under the Machinery Directive (1989) for manual handling, forces and repetition are still not approved but exist in preliminary versions. They are highly quantitative and some doubts have been raised by researchers about their applicability.

Obviously there is a clash of methodological requirements between ergonomists, who know the background and can interpret qualitative standards sensibly, and the practitioner without background knowledge in ergonomics who may need quantitative data. The proposed OSHA ergonomics standard (Silverstein, 1997), available on the Web, is a good example of a mix of a few quantitative recommendations based on a more qualitative umbrella text. Only recently the OSHA has proposed a revised version of this standard, which makes considerably fewer demands on the employer. The Swedish ergonomics standard (Swedish Board of Occupational Health and Safety, 1998) and a similar Norwegian standard are other examples of successful mixes of mainly qualitative texts with additional recommendations of a more quantitative character. These standards apply for manual handling, repetitive work and postures, and the recommendations are subdivided into three levels: not acceptable, conditionally acceptable and acceptable. The application of these standards is fairly simple for trained ergonomists in occupational health services or at the Nordic labour inspectorates, but may prove difficult for the naive user.

METHODS FOR ERGONOMIC INTERVENTIONS

A common task faced by many ergonomists is to analyse the injury risk in a particular work setting as a basis for improvements. The analysis must be sufficiently sensitive to identify changes and therefore needs to be quantitative or at least semi-quantitative, but on the other hand it does not have to have definite cut-off levels. Usually it is not sufficient to analyse only one risk factor, even though the intervention is mainly aimed at one particular risk, as the changes may introduce other risks that must be assessed. Thus the common classification of risks into manual handling, postures, repetition and vibration should be used and all potential risk factors assessed. Ideally, the duration and distribution of risk factors should also be assessed; it is well recognised that long-lasting awkward postures and movements have a considerable importance for injury risk whereas occasional high loads are unimportant.

A number of techniques exist for observation or measurement of postures, manual handling, repetition and vibration. In the last few years interview techniques have also been developed and they can be designed so as not to ask for subjective views but for objective data on work tasks. In the interview method developed by Wiktorin et al. (1996), the subject is asked first about each work task and its duration, and then the frequency and duration of postures (hands above shoulder level and below knee level, as proxies for raised arms and bent back) and repetitions are asked about. Forces exerted in manual handling are recorded on an adjustable force gauge where the subject is asked to reproduce the forces he or she usually exerts at work. The results of these interviews are reliable and valid.

Usually the cost of interview methods are lowest, whilst the cost of observations is higher and direct measurements are the most expensive. On the other hand, the accuracy is highest for direct measurements. With modern monitoring techniques it has become possible to record joint angles, postures and EMGs without disturbing the subject (Wells et al., 1997; Hansson et al., 1996). However, these direct measurements produce an immense amount of data that must be reduced at a high cost in terms of time and for which no consensus of interpretation exists.

Systematic observation techniques may offer the best compromise between accuracy and cost (Kilbom, 1994). A number of observation methods are now available, the simplest being PLIBEL (Kemmlert, 1995) and the most used being OWAS (Karhu et al., 1981). One advantage of observational methods is that they are versatile; a decision on the most appropriate variables/body parts can be made for each individual case. Moreover, work tasks can be observed in parallel with postures/manual handling/repetition, which is necessary for the linking of workloads to work tasks. A computerised, flexible observational method, PEO-flex, has recently been developed (Fredriksson et al., 1999) which has been used for a number of studies in the last few years with reliable results.

Recently some indices for risk assessment by observation have been presented (McAtamney, 1994; Occhipinti, 1998) which consider different risk factors simultaneously and add (or multiply) them into an index. Their value for ergonomic purposes needs further evaluation, and it is necessary to consider not only the concise index but also the magnitude of the individual risk factors.

METHODS FOR EXPOSURE–RESPONSE EVALUATIONS

As a basis for standard setting it is necessary to investigate the exposure–response relationships for musculoskeletal disorders. Is it linear, positively accelerating or U-shaped? What is an acceptable risk? This is a difficult task that can only be analysed by using epidemiological methods (see the paper by Kilbom in Chapter 3), and which requires at least systematic observations or direct measurements (see above).

NEED FOR FURTHER DEVELOPMENT OF JOB ANALYSIS METHODS

Over time, job analysis methods have become more and more sophisticated, requiring either long observation periods or sophisticated instrumentation. This development may not, in the long run, serve ergonomics. We should develop and validate simple and easy to use job analysis methods and spend more effort and time on validating them and on reaching consensus concerning definitions, interpretations and risk levels. No more smart methods should be developed until we know how available methods perform in the assessment of risk. The only area where there seems to be a great need for further methodological development is in establishing links between workload and work organisation/productivity.

References

Borg, G. (1990). Psychophysical scaling with applications in physical work and the perception of exertion. *Scandinavian Journal of Work and Environmental Health*, **16**, 55–58.

European Union (1989). *Machinery Directive 89/392.*

Fredriksson, K., Hägg, G., Kilbom, Å. et al. (1999). PEOflex – a versatile and effective instrument for workload assessment. Example from an auto manufacturing plant intervention. *Proceedings of International Conference on Computer-Aided Ergonomics and Safety*, Barcelona.

Hansson, G-Å, Balogh, I., Ohlsson, K. et al. (1996). Goniometer measurement and computer analysis of wrist angles and movements applied to occupational repetitive work. *Journal of Electromyography and Kinesiology*, **6**, 23–35.

Karhu, O., Härkönen, R., Sorvali, P. et al. (1981). Observing working postures in industry: Examples of OWAS application. *Applied Ergonomics*, **8**, 13–17.

Kemmlert, K. (1995). A method assigned for the identification of ergonomic hazards – PLIBEL. *Applied Ergonomics*, **26**, 199–211.

Kilbom. Å. (1994). Assessment of physical exposure in relation to work-related musculoskeletal disorders – what information can be obtained from systematic observations? *Scandinavian Journal of Work and Environmental Health*, **20**, 30–45.

Kilbom. Å. (1999). Possibilities of regulatory actions in prevention of musculoskeletal disorders. *Scandinavian Journal of Work and Environmental Health.*

McAtamney, L. (1994). *The inter-relationship of risk factors associated with upper limb disorders in VDU users*. PhD thesis, University of Nottingham.

Occhipinti, E. (1998). OCRA: a concise index for the assessment of exposure to repetitive movements of the upper limbs. *Ergonomics*, **41**, 1290–1311.

Silverstein, B. (1997). OSHA efforts to develop standards and guidelines to prevent work-related musculoskeletal disorders. *Proceedings of IEA Conference*, Tampere, Finland, pp. 577–579.

Swedish Board of Occupational Health and Safety (1998). *Ergonomics for the prevention of musculoskeletal disorders*. Statute No. 1998;1, National Board of Occupational Health and Safety.

Waters, T.W., Putz-Anderson, V., Garg, A. et al. (1993). Revised NIOSH equation for the design and evaluation of manual lifting tasks. *Ergonomics*, **36**, 749–776.

Wells, R., Norman, R., Neumann, P. et al. (1997). Assessment of physical workload in epidemiologic studies: common measurement metrics for exposure assessment. *Ergonomics*, **40**, 51–61.

Wiktorin, C., Selin, K., Ekenvall, L. et al. (1996). An interview technique for recording of work postures in epidemiological studies. *International Journal of Epidemiology*, **19**, 171–180.

Job analysis

Barbara McPhee

INTRODUCTION

There are several major hazards which must be considered in the development of work-related musculoskeletal disorders. These include job demands that fall into two main categories of factors.

1. Physical:

   physiological loads including heavy or repetitive muscle work;

   biomechanical loads including stressful work postures.

2. Psychological:

   mental workloads including meeting work targets, control over workload and support in the workplace.

It is now recognised that mental stress may increase the detrimental impact of physical problems and therefore psychological factors must be considered along with physical factors when analysing a job. Inadequate consideration of people in work systems often underlies complaints of physical problems. If for any reason the physical and/or psychological demands of the job exceed the individual's capacity to meet them, either in the short or long term, errors, fatigue, stress or injuries may result.

In most jobs the psychological stresses are much less obvious but they lead to tension and overload. These stresses develop from the organisational aspects of work, which may make simple tasks unnecessarily difficult, impose unrealistic demands or give the employee no control over the way the work is done. Combine these organisational difficulties with physical workload and problems are likely to occur. Therefore an analysis of these factors must go further than the individual job.

ORGANISATIONAL FACTORS NEEDING CONSIDERATION IN JOB ANALYSIS

Task design

What is the employee required to do? This is usually referred to as a job description and outlines the job content. If the job is largely repetitive with little variation or physically very demanding without appropriate rest breaks, overload on certain parts of the body such as the arms and shoulders can occur.

However, the real work demands may differ substantially from job to job, even though they may appear to be similar in nature. Different circumstances change how work is done and problems may be hidden. These can include physical or organisational restrictions; different equipment, furniture or tools; or conflicting requirements from supervisors, managers or clients. There may be time restrictions (deadlines etc.), problems working with other employees, or varying responsibilities for the job.

Work organisation

How are the tasks in a particular job sequenced? Are there peaks and troughs in workload, inefficiencies or organisational difficulties? To whom does the employee report? How is the work organised and why? How much control does the individual have over how and when the work is done, particularly if there are heavy work demands? What is the nature of the organisation and its clients, and the ensuing problems? There are so many potential problems in this area that most jobs need a separate analysis if they are to be identified. Needless to say, most employees know where these problems lie and consultation usually reveals them.

Control and work load

The so-called Karasek model proposes that people become stressed and perhaps ill when the demands made on them at work are not matched with a certain degree of control over how the work will be done. Those employees who have high demands placed on them but who have little say in how and when the work will be completed are the most likely to be at risk of injury or ill health (Figure 10.1).

A modifying influence in the demands versus control theory can be support (at work and/or at home). It is argued that support, or the lack of it, can either reduce or magnify the effects of problems at work.

Support for people at work

How much actual support do employees get from supervisors, senior managers and fellow workers? Supporting people at work by developing their skills, minimising their weaknesses and helping them to cope with life stresses is now considered to be a normal part of good management. Managers need to understand the strengths and limitations of different types of technology and workplace design and how the limitations of some systems may cause problems for users. This requires full consultation with the people who will be doing the work from the start of the design phase through to the ongoing management and evaluation of the system.

Are managers making the right decisions in the purchase of tools, equipment, furniture, hardware and software? Apparently subtle changes in technology or the way the work is organised or managed may lead to significant changes in the way

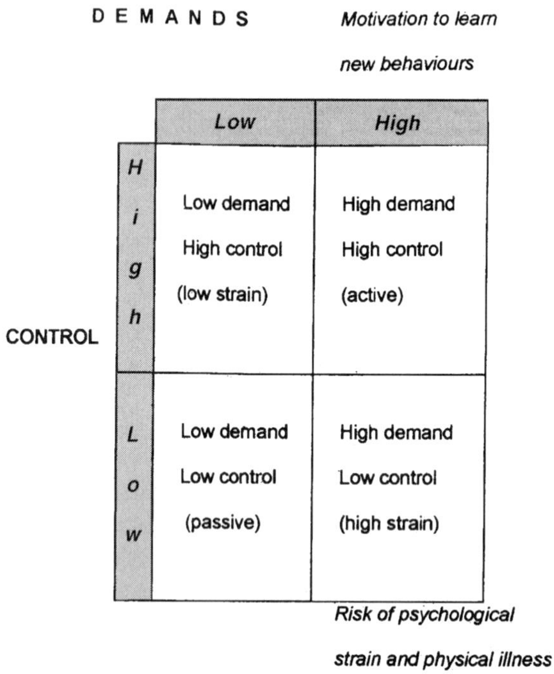

Figure 10.1 The Karasek model, showing the relationship between work demands, worker control and risk of injury or ill health (adapted from Karasek and Theorell, 1990)

the work is performed. Employees may be left trying to make an inappropriate or inadequate system work.

Does each manager understand exactly how much work can be delivered by his/her employees under normal conditions? People often work under undue pressure when it is not necessary. Goodwill from employees is not automatic – it must be earned. Managers can then ask for, and expect, superior effort when it is really needed. Everybody has 'off' days and employees need to be able to ease off occasionally.

Are employees supported consistently and fully through any period of change? Is their full participation and input encouraged and are real 'help' services provided with the introduction of new technology? Are people allowed time to 'learn by doing' and to gain confidence with new systems? Do managers keep a user focus and continually reappraise and fine tune? The support must be continued when the system is up and running especially for crisis times – either at work or in individuals' personal lives.

References

Karasek, R.A. and Theorell, T. (1990). *Healthy Work – Stress, Productivity and the Reconstruction of Working Life*. Basic Books.

Chapter 11

Manual handling

Measuring manual handling injury prevention

Leon M. Straker

INTRODUCTION

Manual handling injuries form a large proportion of occupational injuries and attempts to reduce their incidence and prevalence have been a major focus of occupational health activity for decades.

As an example, the latest available figures from Western Australia (WorkSafe Western Australia 1998; 1995/6 data) show that manual handling injuries account for 30 per cent of all reported injuries. The average duration of lost time due to manual handling injuries is greater than other injuries. In Western Australia in 1994/95 the average number of days lost with a manual handling injury was thirty for males and forty-two for females, compared respectively with twenty and twenty-five for non-manual handling injuries. Thus although manual handling injuries accounted for 30 per cent of incidence, they accounted for 39 per cent of lost days.

Australia has had a national strategy for reducing manual handling injuries since 1989 (WorkSafe Australia, 1989) and a national standard and code of practice since 1990 (WorkSafe Australia, 1990). Victoria led the introduction of new general duty of care and manual handling regulations in 1988 (Victorian Department of Labour, 1988). Whilst conservative political forces refused to pass legislation for manual handling regulations in Western Australia, a code of practice was adopted in 1991 (WorkSafe Western Australia, 1991).

Whether by fortunate coincidence or effect, Western Australia has seen a decline in manual handling injuries since the introduction of the code of practice in 1991, as shown in Figure 11.1.

LACK OF EVIDENCE

Despite what has just been stated, there is no evidence that the decline in reports of manual handling injuries was due to preventive interventions in Western

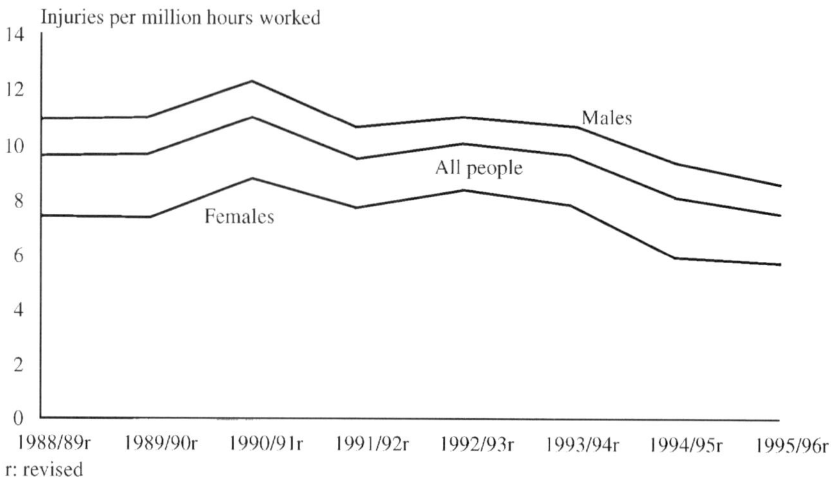

Figure 11.1 Western Australian manual handling injury frequency rates

Australian organisations. Other plausible reasons for the decline include:

- Workers being more reluctant to report injury during economic downturn.
- Reduction in unionisation has made workers feel more vulnerable and more reluctant to report injury.
- Increased mechanisation of manual handling.
- Organisations 'managing' injuries by keeping a worker at work and thus not sustaining a lost time injury.

The Western Australian data presented cover a large geographical area, the full spectrum of industries and the whole gamut of organisations in terms of size, culture and commitment to prevention of manual handling injures. It is therefore perhaps unrealistic to expect this data to provide evidence for the effectiveness of interventions.

To provide reasonable evidence of effectiveness, analysis really needs to be at an organisational level. However, as outlined in Chapter 6; pp. 108–124 evidence is also limited at the organisational level. Therefore, despite considerable well-intentioned activity, we have very little evidence available that any of our prevention strategies are effective in significantly reducing manual handling injuries.

Reasons for this lack of evidence include: we may have been wrong in what we teach and the changes we make to reduce risk; the gradual onset and multifactorial aetiology of many important work-related musculoskeletal disorders may mask any short-term intervention; and difficulty in measuring outcomes may mask the effects of intervention. The last factor is the focus of this paper.

MANUAL HANDLING INJURY OUTCOMES

The most obvious outcome measure to evaluate the effect of intervention is manual handling injury reports.

Manual handling injury reporting in Australia is governed by state legislation. Thus, depending on which state the organisation is in, a manual handling injury resulting in three days' lost time may or may not be reportable. Currently requirements vary from one to seven days' lost time before the injury is notifiable. This diversity is also shown in other countries and is one of the factors which makes international comparisons of manual handling injury data of little meaning.

Despite the quirks of the various systems, lost time injury reports are highly valued by organisations as they directly relate to costs. However, there are a number of difficulties with this measure, which may explain why it rarely provides a clear picture of intervention effectiveness.

1. Perhaps the major difficulty with manual handling injury as an outcome measure is the lack of knowledge about the aetiology of the major manual handling injury, work-related low back pain. In a recent review on what we know about work-related low back pain, Frank et al. (1996, p. 2908) state that: 'Current knowledge does not allow us to determine . . . the exact medical cause of occupational low back pain in most patients. Indeed, 97 per cent of low back pain is called "non-specific" or "strain/sprain" by doctors precisely because the source of the pain is unknown. Uncertainties about the pathology translate directly into uncertainties about causation and work-relatedness.'

   There is a widely held belief in the community that low back pain is due to lifting. Thus, when a warehouse worker notices back pain they are likely to attribute the pain to manual handling tasks and not the sitting aspects of their job. Health professionals may reinforce this causal attribution, despite the lack of evidence. Thus low back pain may be reported as a manual handling injury when it is actually caused by other factors.

   A further implication of this lack of understanding about what causes work-related low back pain is that interventions may be misdirected.

2. A related difficulty with manual handing injury is the bias in the reporting systems towards some specific incident. It is much easier for a worker to claim a sudden onset of pain related to a particular lift. However, this probably does not accurately represent cumulative onset cases.

3. Associated with the aetiological difficulties is the definition of manual handling. In Western Australia manual handling injuries include work-related neck and upper limb disorders associated with prolonged and repeated poor postures in light industry. Thus, interventions directed at box lifting will be

unlikely to have a significant impact on manual handling injury rates in data processing, clothes fabrication, food processing and electronic assembly organisations with a high prevalence of RSI type pathology.

4. As injury rates rely on worker reports, they are only ever an estimate of true injury rate. If there is a large hidden injury component in a workforce, intervention may change the organisation's culture and encourage less hiding of injury. This would result in an apparent increase in injuries. Potentially useful interventions have been terminated by managers seeing this increase in injuries.
5. For most organisations manual handling injuries are fairly rare, and thus the random noise of unpreventable injuries may hide any reduction in preventable injuries.
6. A final difficulty associated with use of manual handling injury as an outcome measure, is that the risk of low back pain is only partly due to current work conditions. Ergonomic interventions in a typical organisation with adult workers will not change the degeneration and susceptibility to injury of the musculoskeletal systems of the workforce.

Thus risk of manual handling injury may be reduced with interventions, but reported injury rates may still increase for some considerable period of time.

Manual handling injury reports are therefore limited in their ability to provide evidence of effectiveness of interventions. Whilst it is an outcome measure that must be monitored due to its impact on cost, other outcome measures should also be used.

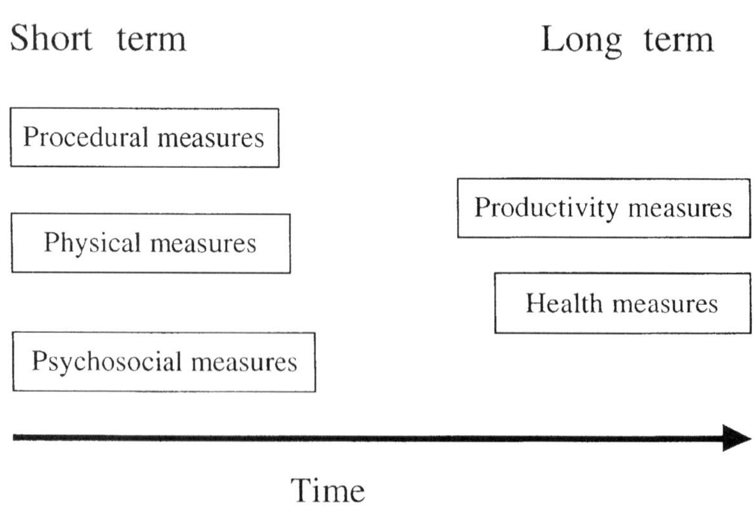

Figure 11.2 Classification of manual handling outcome measures

OUTCOME CLASSIFICATION SYSTEM

A potentially useful classification system for available outcome measures is to separate them into short and long term, as shown in Figure 11.2.

Long-term outcome measures

Long-term outcome measures include health outcomes such as lost time injuries. Incidence rates, prevalence rates and average durations are useful indicators, as are associated costs. Other long-term outcome measures are productivity outcomes such as absenteeism and work group output.

Whilst lost time injury and productivity outcomes can be monitored in monthly time frames, they are probably better when assessed over a minimum of several years. Productivity in many organisations fluctuates (e.g. is seasonal) and the placebo effect of any intervention probably needs a year to fade.

Long-term health and productivity measures will eventually be the criteria organisations will judge interventions with; however, most organisations will not be prepared to wait several years for intervention evaluation. Therefore shorter term outcome measures are required.

Short-term outcome measures

Shorter term measures can be grouped into measures of activity and estimates of risk.

Procedural outcomes such as the number of hazards addressed and the number of risk control options trialled are useful measures of activity. This provides the organisation with an indication of what is being done, and enables them to document attempts at duty of care. It could be argued that the more hazards that are addressed the less workers will be exposed to hazards, and that this should result in favourable longer term health and productivity outcomes.

All the longer term health and productivity and shorter term procedural outcome measures described so far require no specialist knowledge. Perhaps the most valuable outcome measures are the estimates of risk. These should give early indications of longer term health and productivity outcomes in a more detailed manner than procedural outcomes. However, they do require specific expertise and still lack convincing validation.

Measures of physical outcomes such as risk assessment measures like heart rate and estimates of lumbar biomechanical stresses are perhaps the most highly valued short-term measures. Reductions in relative risk are fairly easy to document using these measures. For example, a redesigned task may result in an average heart rate of 100 bpm rather than 120 bpm, or an estimated lumbar compression force of 3000 N rather than 4000 N.

Whether such reductions have a significant effect on absolute risk is less clear. There is very little evidence of what significant thresholds should be for physical measures. Whilst biomechanical measures are perhaps the most researched, and give satisfying quantitative results, their validity is largely unknown. For example, static analysis may significantly underestimate moments and forces, suggesting dynamic analysis. However, even if the technical difficulties of dynamic analysis could be overcome, there is minimal information on what an acceptable threshold should be. Further, whilst most studies have focused on peak stresses, the risk of injury may be more related to the pattern of stresses (average, peak, integral, variability, duration etc.).

Psychosocial outcomes such as maximum acceptable weight, discomfort and satisfaction of workers may also be useful in providing an estimate of risk reduction. Again relative risk reduction is fairly easy to document using these measures, but how these relate to absolute risk is unclear.

CONCLUSIONS

As health professionals, insurers, management, workers and the community at large demand more evidence of effectiveness, the development and use of appropriate outcome measures to evaluate intervention effectiveness becomes critical.

Whilst long-term health and productivity outcomes will be the ‘gold standard’ for evaluating interventions aimed at preventing manual handling injuries, the validation and use of shorter term physical and psychosocial measures as estimates of risk are required to enable timely evaluation.

References

Straker, L.M. (1997). *A Critical Appraisal of Manual Handling Risk Assessment Literature*. International Ergonomics Association Press.

Victorian Department of Labour (1988). *Manual Handling Regulations and Code of Practice*. Government of Victoria Department of Labour.

WorkSafe Australia (1989). *National Strategy for the Prevention of Occupational Back Pain*. Australian Government Publishing Service.

Pilot investigation of the effects of a harness-type external lumbar support during manual handling activities in airline baggage handlers

S. Milanese, K. Grimmer and P. Trott

INTRODUCTION

Despite many years of ergonomic research and intervention, low back pain (LBP) remains a serious problem in industry. Tasks associated with a high incidence of low back pain are characterised by significant levels of manual handling (Garg, 1982). Airline baggage handlers, for whom load handling forms an integral part of the required duties, are an example of workers in an occupation with a significant incidence of LBP (Reddell et al., 1992). In one large Australian airline, low back injuries to airport baggage handlers have been reported to cost approximately $2 million annually (personal communication).

The current recommended approach of risk control for manual handling injuries involves a hierarchy of controls (Hopkins, 1995), ordered in terms of the greatest effect, ranging from elimination of the risk and implementation of engineering controls, through to administrative controls such as training and personal protective equipment.

The ability to successfully perform appropriate manual handling techniques is influenced by the physical nature of the task and the physical work space in which the task is performed. This is particularly appropriate for airline baggage handlers, as they need to perform manual handling activities in the confined space of airplane luggage holds. Lifting in such an environment severely limits the ability to perform tasks utilising an upright posture (Stalhammar et al., 1986), significantly affecting the lifting capacity of the worker, and continually putting the spine at risk.

The use of an external lumbar support (ELS) as personal protective equipment (PPE) for workers involved in manual handling tasks where a significant risk for the development of LBP exists has been advocated (Walsh and Schwartz, 1990) as a risk control measure.

Significant research has been undertaken into the effects of ELSs (Buchalter et al., 1989; Fidler and Plasmans, 1983; Lander et al., 1990; McGill et al., 1990; Magnusson et al., 1996; Marley and Duggasani, 1996; Milanese, 1993; Morris et al., 1961; Reddell et al., 1992; Walsh and Schwartz, 1990; Waters and Morris, 1970). Most studies have involved corset-type supports, for example braces with rigid spinal supports, or abdominal belts as used in weight lifting. There remains a wide scope of opinion regarding the use of the ELS as a preventive measure, ranging from promotion (Walsh and Schwartz, 1990) to demotion (Marley and Duggasani, 1996; NIOSH, 1994) or a more cautious approach (Magnusson et al., 1996; Reddell et al., 1992).

HARNESS-TYPE SUPPORTS

A different style of ELS has recently been promoted in rehabilitation medicine. This device is significantly different in structure to the corset-type lumbar supports previously researched. These ELSs are based on a harness structure, incorporating fixation of the support at the hip/pelvis and at the thoracic spine, with an elastic strap connected between the two fixed points. The 'Tolai' back support (Tolai Pty Ltd, Gawler, South Australia) used in this study is an example of a harness support (Figure 11.3). As harness external lumbar supports (HELSs) are significantly different in structure to corset-type supports, it cannot be assumed that the effects on the wearer are the same.

POTENTIAL BIOMECHANICAL INFLUENCES OF HARNESS-TYPE SUPPORTS

The effects of a HELS on the body mechanics of the wearer can be hypothesised utilising a biomechanical model.

Bending the trunk forwards and lifting a weight involves initial eccentric control of the degree of trunk flexion to access the weight. Sufficient extensor

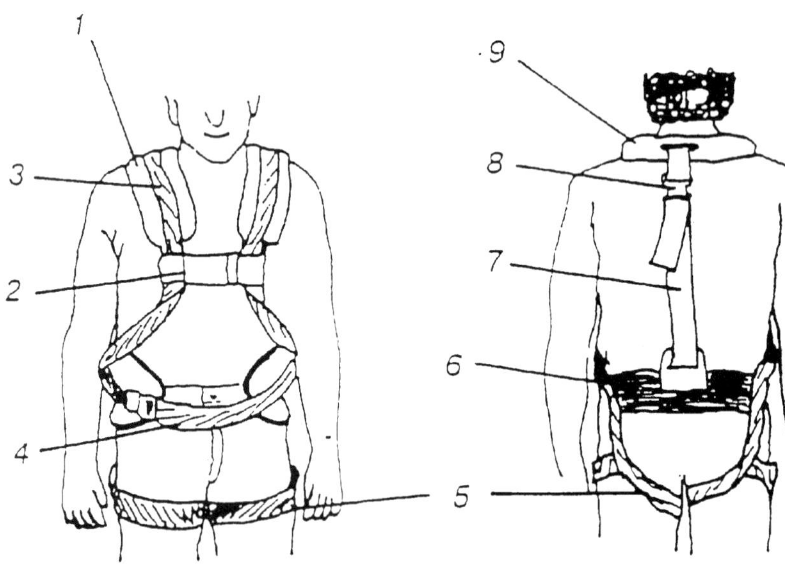

Figure 11.3 Example of a harness support (adapted from Tolai, 1992). 1, lambswool padding; 2, chest straps; 3, shoulder straps; 4, elastic front belt; 5, leg straps; 6, lumbar support belt; 7, posterior elastic strap; 8, tension release slide; 9, neck pad

moment on the spine and hips then needs to be generated to overcome the flexor moment of the trunk and weight, to extend the trunk back to neutral. The total flexor moment acting at the lumbosacral level is the summation of a number of components (Figure 11.4). Normal lifting involves the co-ordinated interplay between the hip and lumbar spine (Farfan, 1978). The extensor moment required to control and overcome this flexor moment is generated by the spinal musculature and passive resistance of the spinal tissue. It has been postulated that there may be an additional effective extensor moment generated by the intra-abdominal pressure mechanism (Bartelink, 1957). The total extensor moment at L5 (TEM) is the sum of extensor moments due to muscle activity of the erector spinae (MA), intra-abdominal pressure (IAP) and passive resistance of the non-contractile spinal tissues (PR).

If a HELS restricts lumbar flexion range during trunk forward bending activities, it must act on the total extensor moment (TEM) at the lumbar spine.

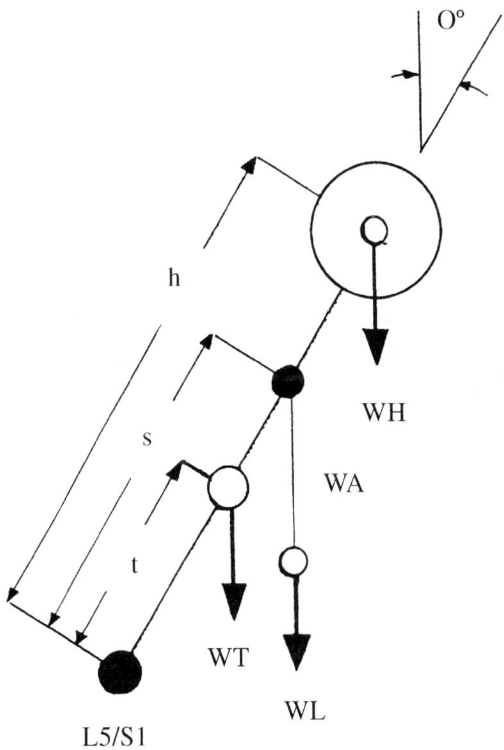

Figure 11.4 Biomechanical model, showing flexor moments acting at the lumbosacral joint (adapted from Lantz and Schultz, 1986). Flexor moment (at L5) = t.WT + s.WA + h.WH + W.H). sin O°, where: t = distance from L5 to trunk; WT = weight of trunk above L5; s = distance from centre of mass of arms to L5; WA = weight of arms; h = distance from L5 to head; WH = weight of head and neck; WL = weight of load; O° = angle of lumbar spine flexion

This influence could be via a direct mechanism, acting as an additional mechanical component to the equation, i.e.: TEM = MA + IAP + PR + ELS.

Alternatively, the HELS may work to indirectly affect the TEM by facilitating the effectiveness of the other components, through proprioceptive influence on erector spinae activity or via increasing intra-abdominal pressure, i.e: TEM = (MA + IAP + PR) × (ELS).

When considering the influence of the HELS on the body mechanics of the wearer, it is also important to consider the effect of the support on other areas of the body. Restriction of movement in the lumbar spine may shunt movement to the hip and thoracic spine, potentially transferring the risk of injury during manual handling to another area of the body.

POTENTIAL PHYSIOLOGICAL EFFECTS

The physiological demands on a person performing physically demanding work while wearing a HELS requires consideration. As a HELS is designed to affect the wearer's movement pattern, it could be expected to influence muscular activity. Changes in muscular activity may affect energy expenditure, and be reflected in altered physiological demands. Robinson (1991) reported a decrease in EMG activity of the superficial erector spinae during forward flexion activities whilst wearing the Tolai HELS. The influence of any ELS on workers' physiological demands has not been clarified and may vary between support types (Kumar and Godfrey, 1986; Marley and Duggasani, 1996).

This paper reports on pilot research into the use of the Tolai HELS during manual handling tasks. Two studies were undertaken: the first (the movement study) assessed changes to range of motion in the hip, lumbar and thoracic spines whilst baggage handlers performed tasks with and without the support; and the second (physiological demand study) assessed the effects of wearing the support on physiological parameters during manual handling tasks.

METHOD

Subjects

Movement study

Ten male volunteer airline baggage handlers in one metropolitan airport, who were currently suffering no symptoms, participated in this study.

Physiological demands study

Three male volunteers were selected on a convenience basis from university staff to participate in this study.

Task standardisation

Movement study

Two tasks, reflecting real life baggage handling activities, were selected for this study, and were standardised with respect to starting position, size and weight of luggage, and the height and distance over which the luggage was lifted.

Task 1

Kneeling subjects, starting in a 'neutral' (upright) position, bent to the left to pick up a 6 kg box from the floor, and then moved the box to the right to place it on a table (height 700 mm). Subjects then moved back to the neutral starting position. This movement took place over a ten second period. A board placed overhead at 1020 mm simulated the confined space of an aeroplane luggage hold.

Task 2

Standing subjects lifted a standard suitcase (weight 23.5 kg) from a table (height 510 mm) to their left, and then turned to the right and placed the suitcase on another table (height 510 mm). A distance of 830 mm separated the tables.

Physiological demands study

Subjects lifted a suitcase (dimensions 670 mm × 450 mm × 180 mm; weight 32 kg) from a table (height 200 mm) and carried it a distance of 950 mm to another table (height 500 mm). Subjects were allowed to lift in their natural manner. Two suitcases were used in this task and the subject was required to lift and carry each suitcase to the second table before reversing the process.

Data collection: equipment

Movement study

The 3 Space Isotrak system (Polhemus Navigational Sciences Division, Kaiser Aerospace, Vermont, USA) was employed to measure (three-dimensionally) the range, timing and pattern of movements of the hip and the thoracic and lumbar spine.

Physiological demands study

The Vista Mini CPX was used to collect data on energy expenditure changes using a breath by breath measuring process during the performance of a task.

Tasks

Movement study

Subjects were familiarised with the tasks prior to data collection. The order of tasks and the use or not of the HELS were randomised. When performing the tasks, subjects were not instructed in speed or pattern of movement, allowing for both within- and between-subject comparisons for repeatability of movement patterns, range and timing.

Physiological demands study

Subjects were instructed in the task until they felt comfortable with the lifting protocol and the testing equipment.

The habituation period was five minutes long and subjects rested for ten minutes following this session. Subjects then undertook the first measurement session, which involved performing the task for five minutes. This was followed by a second rest period of thirty minutes to allow physiological parameters to return to their resting state. A second test also lasting for five minutes was then undertaken.

Data analysis

Movement study

The maximum range of each direction of movement which occurred during the task in the three cardinal planes was described in degrees.

The effect of the support was estimated using multiple repeated analysis of variance (ANOVA) procedures (using a general linear model), which took account of the effects of the HELS and the repeated attempts at the task. In addition, the model took account of the interactive effects of these variables.

A significance level of $p < 0.1$ was set for this investigation, as the multiple components of the general linear model and the small number of subjects reduced the power to detect significant differences. Where a significant overall finding from the ANOVA was supported by a significant independent effect of wearing the HELS, the finding was considered to be truly positive (that is, the HELS exerted an effect that was greater than the between-subject variability). Where only the overall ANOVA finding was significant (that is, there was no significant independent effect of the HELS), this was considered to be a falsely positive result, as the overall significant effect was generated mainly by between-subject variability. A non-significant overall ANOVA finding coupled with a non-significant independent effect of the HELS indicated a truly negative result.

Physiological demands study

Paired *t*-tests were used to compare data from the two measurement sessions.

RESULTS

Movement study

Between- and within-subject variability

For both tasks, there were significant differences between subjects in range of movement at all three anatomical sites, in all directions, of all cardinal plane movements, both supported and unsupported by the HELS. However, generally there was non-significant within-subject variability in each direction of movement in each cardinal plane, suggesting that each subject had stable and repeatable movement patterns.

Table 11.1 *F* values† and degrees of freedom from output of general linear models comparing maximum range of movement with and without TBS, for each direction in each cardinal plane during task 1

	DF	Flexion	Extension	L LATFLEX	R LATFLEX	L ROTN	R ROTN
Lumbar spine							
Overall effect of model	–	**4.1**	**2.9**	0.7	**3.2**	0.9	1.8
Between subjects	9	**11.2**	**9.1**	0.7	**8.7**	1.7	**5.6**
Within subjects (repetitions)	2	0.7	0.1	0.3	0.4	0.4	0.1
Effect of TBS	1	**10.7**	0.1	2.7	**15.5**	**5.8**	0.5
Subject * TBS	18	0.9	0.5	0.7	0.5	0.3	0.3
TBS * repetitions	2	1.1	0.5	0.4	0.2	0.6	0.8
Thoracic spine							
Overall effect of model	–	**2.4**	1.4	**2.9**	**2.9**	1.1	2.1
Between subjects	9	**5.2**	**3.2**	**7.3**	**8.0**	**2.4**	**6.4**
Within subject (repetitions)	2	1.3	0.1	0.9	0.5	0.6	0.3
Effect of TBS	1	**5.1**	**13.0**	**12.5**	**4.1**	**4.5**	0.9
Subject * TBS	18	1.2	1.0	0.6	0.4	0.4	0.4
TBS * repetitions	2	0.9	0.13	0.4	0.2	0.6	0.4
Hip							
Overall effect of model	–	**4.7**	1.1	1.4	3.7	**4.8**	1.5
Between subjects	9	**15.9**	**2.8**	**4.0**	**12.4**	**12.3**	**4.0**
Within subject (repetitions)	2	0.5	0.4	0.2	0.5	1.9	0.7
Effect of TBS	1	2.5	**4.4**	**1.5**	0.01	**9.8**	0.3
Subject * TBS	18	0.2	0.3	0.3	0.2	1.1	0.4
TBS * repetitions	2	0.3	0.7	0.05	0.4	3.7	0.8

† *F* values significant at $p < 0.1$ are presented in **bold** type
TBS = Tolai back support; DF = degrees of freedom; L LATFLEX = left lateral flexion; R LATFLEX = right lateral flexion; L ROTN = left rotation; R ROTN = right rotation; asterisk (*) signifies **30a.

Table 11.2 *F* values[†] and degrees of freedom from output of general linear models comparing maximum range of movement with and without TBS, for each direction in each cardinal plane during task 2

	DF	Flexion	Extension	L LATFLEX	R LATFLEX	L ROTN	R ROTN
Lumbar spine							
Overall effect of model	–	**3.3**	**3.5**	**2.2**	0.9	1.5	0.5
Between subjects	9	**9.3**	**9.9**	**6.6**	1.7	3.3	1.1
Within subjects (repetitions)	2	1.0	0.2	0.01	0.3	0.1	0.1
Effect of TBS	1	**4.6**	**3.3**	0.2	**4.9**	**6.2**	0.6
Subject * TBS	18	0.8	0.9	0.6	0.4	0.6	0.2
TBS * repetitions	2	1.3	1.2	0.5	0.1	0.5	0.1
Thoracic spine							
Overall effect of model	–	**2.5**	**1.8**	**2.3**	**1.9**	**3.2**	**2.0**
Between subjects	9	**7.2**	**2.6**	**4.9**	**4.3**	**9.3**	**6.1**
Within subject (repetitions)	2	1.0	2.3	1.0	2.0	0.6	1.0
Effect of TBS	1	1.8	**17.4**	**4.3**	2.7	1.5	0.1
Subject * TBS	18	0.6	0.3	1.2	0.7	0.7	0.2
TBS * repetitions	2	0.6	**3.8**	0.8	1.3	1.1	1.6
Hip							
Overall effect of model	–	1.4	**3.4**	1.6	0.9	1.4	1.1
Between subjects	9	1.7	3.0	**4.4**	1.5	**2.4**	2.1
Within subject (repetitions)	2	0.1	0.3	0.04	0.2	0.9	0.2
Effect of TBS	1	**5.6**	**72.5**	**3.9**	**8.4**	1.3	0.6
Subject * TBS	18	1.1	0.4	0.4	0.3	0.9	0.8
TBS * repetitions	2	1.1	0.1	0.1	1.3	**1.3**	0.9

[†] *F* values significant at $p < 0.1$ are presented in **bold** type
See footnotes to Table 11.1 for key to abbreviations.

Effect of the harness support

Data on the effects of the HELS on movement patterns are presented in Tables 11.1 and 11.2.

Flexion

There were true positive findings, which supported the effect of the HELS on decreasing the range of flexion at the lumbar spine in both task 1 and task 2, and at the thoracic spine in task 2. During task 1, mean lumbar spine flexion decreased from 9.4° to 6.2°, and thoracic spine flexion decreased from 10.3° to 6.2°. During task 2, lumbar spine flexion decreased from 22.9° to 19.2°. These changes are illustrated by a significant overall finding from the ANOVA models and significant findings for the independent effect of the HELS.

Extension

There was a true positive finding which supported the effect of the HELS on decreasing the range of extension at the lumbar spine during task 2. Mean extension range decreased from 4.1° to 2.2°. This is illustrated by a significant overall finding from the ANOVA model, and a significant finding for the independent effect of the HELS.

Lateral flexion

There were true positive decreases in range of right lateral flexion of the lumbar spine (8.1° to 4.6°) and right and left lateral flexion of the thoracic spine (21.7° to 11.2°, and 40.6° to 25.6° respectively) for task 1. During task 2, left lateral flexion of the thoracic spine demonstrated a true positive decrease in range from 10.9° to 8.8°.

Rotation

There was a significant decrease in lumbar spine rotation during task 2. Mean lumbar left rotation decreased from 6.7° to 4.9°.

Physiological demands

All subjects were considered to have reached steady physiological state after the first two minutes of the task, and for the purpose of this study the data from the third minute to the end of each session were analysed. These results are presented in Table 11.3.

Tidal volume

All subjects demonstrated decreases in tidal volume when wearing the support, with two subjects demonstrating significant decreases.

Heart rate

There was a variable change in heart rate when wearing the HELS for the three subjects. Only one subject had a significant effect, showing a decrease in heart rate.

Table 11.3 Physiological testing data

	Subject braced mean	Subject unbraced mean	*F* value	*P* value
Heart rate (bpm)				
1	139	127	2.7	0.12
2	137	128	3.0	0.09
3	101	115	5.2	0.03
Tidal volume				
1	1.37	1.42	1.1	0.9
2	1.22	1.59	53.7	0.001
3	1.42	1.63	11.7	0.001
Total energy expenditure				
1	0.76	0.83	11.7	0.001
2	0.78	1.21	135.7	0.001
3	1.32	1.45	3.7	0.05

Total energy expenditure

There was a significant decrease in total energy expenditure in all subjects while wearing the HELS.

DISCUSSION

Effects of the harness-type support

Biomechanical

The findings of this pilot study provide evidence to support the usefulness of the harness support as personal protective equipment (PPE) for workers involved in baggage handling tasks. The need to perform repetitive and heavy manual load handling activities, in addition to the constraints imposed by confined spaces, significantly increase the risk of LBP for airline baggage handlers. The use of the harness support, as reported in this study, appears to reduce the amount of lumbar flexion and rotation required for the tasks, without significantly affecting the physiological demands on the worker. The findings of this study suggest no concomitant increase in the other planes of movement of the lumbar spine, and no increase in movement at the thoracic spine during supported activity. There was movement 'shunting' into flexion at the hip, a joint that appears to be biomechanically suited to sustaining force and movement associated with lifting.

The reduction in lumbar flexion range of motion during manual handling activities reflected the findings of previous studies. Milanese (1993) demonstrated that the harness support used in this study restricted lumbar flexion in the order of 17 to 21 per cent during trunk flexion activity, with the greatest reduction in lumbar range occurring in the low lumbar spine (L3–S1).

The observed reduction of lumbar flexion range of motion suggests that the harness support exerts a positive effect on the TEM acting on the lumbar spine during forward trunk flexion. As illustrated in the formulae describing the effect of the support on the total extensor moment, this may occur via direct or indirect mechanisms. Milanese (1993) examined the specific influence of the posterior elastic strap (PES) on lumbar range of motion and found no effect with the PES untensioned compared to not wearing the support. This suggests that the factor responsible for the extensor moment effect on the lumbar spine is the PES.

Robinson (1991), in an EMG study of erector spinae activity in a group of subjects flexing forwards with and without a harness support, found significantly decreased EMG activity in the superficial erector spinae muscles whilst wearing the harness support. This suggests that the harness support acts directly on the TEM equation with the PES acting as an additional component, reducing the contributions required from other components in the equation.

The relative importance of each component to the TEM will alter as the spine passes through its range of movement (i.e. as the spine flexes). As described by Farfan (1978), the lumbar spine flexes approximately 60° with the posterior elements of the spine, at the level of the facet joints, elongating by 20–25 per cent. The last 5–6 per cent of extensor moment is due to the passive support of the ligamentous tissues. Full lumbar flexion is limited by tension of the apophyseal capsular ligaments, intervertebral discs, the supraspinous and intra-spinous ligaments and the ligamentum flavum (Adams, 1980). Towards the end of the lumbar flexion range there is a period of erector spinae muscle silence on EMG readings, termed the 'critical point', and a marked decrease in intra-abdominal pressure (Genaidy et al., 1995), indicating that the TEM is being generated predominantly by non-contractile spinal tissue. As the harness support reduces the degree of flexion of the lumbar spine, it may reduce the role of the non-contractile spinal tissue structures in resisting the flexor moment acting on the spine.

When the worker is required to sustain a position of half trunk flexion during manual handling activities, e.g. working in a confined space such as an aircraft hold, the erector spinae are continually active. As fatigue reduces the ability of the active muscular components to generate an extensor moment, the spine becomes reliant on non-contractile spinal tissue to generate sufficient TEM. By acting as a passive constraint to further lumbar flexion, the harness support may reduce the stress on the non-contractile tissues during sustained half trunk flexion.

Whilst the PES acts mechanically as a relatively non-contractile structure, functioning only when stretched, the elastic nature of the PES material and the ability to alter tension in the PES through altering its length, allows some flexibility in its influence on the spine. The ability to alter the tension in the PES facilitates the effectiveness in generating an effective extensor moment during half flexion activities (Milanese, 1993).

Although the true positive findings consistently provided support for the hypothesis that the harness support reduced lumbar spine range of motion with no concomitant increase in thoracic spine movement, these findings relate to only two baggage handling tasks, involving mainly flexion and rotation. The findings, whilst supportive of a positive effect of the harness support, are therefore not definitive. Further testing of other baggage handling tasks is required before use of the support can be recommended, as are tests on more subjects.

Physiological demands

There was no indication from the physiological demand study that there was any increased physiological load on the wearer of a HELS whilst performing manual handling activity. There were clear trends across all subjects to indicate that wearing the harness support while undertaking the task decreased both tidal volume and total energy expenditure.

As with the use of all PPEs, consideration must be given to the effect of the device on special populations of workers to identify possible contraindications to their use. Concerns have been raised in the literature about the possible effects of abdominal belts on hypertensive workers or those with breathing problems, due to the effect on increasing intra-abdominal pressure, and hence blood pressure. Studies have reported an increase in heart rate with the use of these supports during aerobic activity (Genaidy et al., 1995). However, the findings of this study indicate that the harness-type support does not have as dramatic an effect on the cardiovascular system as abdominal belts. This may be secondary to the absence of significant passive abdominal compression in this type of support compared to corset-type supports. Heart rate changes in this study were variable, with the only significant finding being a decrease in heart rate in one subject whilst wearing the support.

CONCLUSIONS

Further studies of the harness support are required with respect to other baggage handling tasks. Should the findings be similarly positive, a major trial of the support in the workplace is indicated as a means of decreasing the incidence and severity of LBP. The cost of back pain to Australian workers is high. If a non-invasive ELS is found to be effective in reducing reported injury to the lumbar spine in work situations where ergonomic intervention is not feasible, it may assist in minimising the workers' compensation costs in both the long and short term.

REFERENCES

Adams, M.A., Hutton, W.C. and Stott, J.R.R. (1980). The resistance to flexion of the lumbar intervertebral joint. *Spine*, **5** (3), 245–253.

Bartelink, D.L. (1957). The role of abdominal pressure in relieving the pressure on the lumbar intervertebral discs. *The Journal of Bone and Joint Surgery*, **39B** (4), 718–725.

Buchalter, D., Kahanovitz, N., Viola, K. et al. (1989). Three-dimensional spinal motion measurements. Part 2: A non-invasive assessment of lumbar brace immobilisation of the spine. *Journal of Spinal Disorders*, **1** (4), 284–286.

Farfan, H.F. (1978). The biomechanical advantage of lordosis and hip extension for upright activity. *Spine*, **3** (4), 336–342.

Fidler, M.W. and Plasmans, C.M.T. (1983). The effect of four types of support on the segmental mobility of the lumbosacral spine. *The Journal of Bone and Joint Surgery*, **65A** (7), 943–947.

Garg, A. (1982). Lifting and back injuries: a review of the causes of this industrial health problem, and the major methods to combat it. *Plant Engineer*, **36**, 89–93.

Genaidy, A.M., Simmons, R.J. and Christensen, D.M. (1995). Can back supports relieve the load on the lumbar spine for employees engaged in industrial operations? *Ergonomics*, **38** (5), 996–1010.

Hopkins, A. (1995). *Making Safety Work: Getting Management Commitment to Occupational Health and Safety.* Allen and Unwin.

Kumar, S. and Godfrey, C.M. (1986). Spinal braces and abdominal support. In *Trends in Ergonomics/Human Factors III* (W. Karkowski, ed.), pp. 717–726. Elsevier.

Lander, J.E., Simonton, R.L. and Giacobbe, J.K.F. (1990). The effectiveness of weight-belts during the squat exercise. *Medicine and Science in Sports and Exercise*, **22** (1), 117–126.

Lantz, S.A. and Schultz, A.B. (1986). Lumbar spine orthosis wearing: 1. Restriction of gross body motions. *Spine*, **11** (8), 834–837.

Magnusson, M., Pope, M.H. and Hansson, T. (1996). Does a back support have a positive biomechanical effect? *Applied Ergonomics*, **27** (3), 201–205.

Marley, R.J. and Duggasani, A.R. (1996). Effects of industrial back supports on physiological demand, lifting style and perceived exertion. *International Journal of Industrial Ergonomics*, **17**, 445–453.

McGill, S.M., Norman, R.W. and Sharratt, M.T. (1990). The role of an abdominal belt on trunk muscle activity and intra-abdominal pressure during squat lifts. *Ergonomics*, **33** (2), 147–160.

Milanese, S. (1993). The effect of the 'Tolai' back support on lumbar flexion. Masters thesis, University of South Australia (unpublished).

Morris, J.M., Lucas, D.B. and Bresler, B. (1961). The role of the trunk in stability of the spine. *The Journal of Bone and Joint Surgery*, **43A** (3), 327–352.

NIOSH (1994). Workplace use of back belts: Review and recommendations. *DHHS/NIOSH Technical Publications* No. 94–122. National Institute for Occupational Safety and Health, Cincinnati.

Reddell, C.R., Congleton, J.J. and Huchingson, R.D. (1992). An evaluation of a weightlifting belt and back injury prevention training class for airline baggage handlers. *Applied Ergonomics*, **25** (3), 319–329.

Robinson, A. (1991). A study of the effectiveness of the 'Tolai' back support. Research thesis, Department of Mechanical Engineering, University of Adelaide (unpublished).

Stalhammar, H.R., Leskinen, T.P.J., Kuorinka, I.A.A. et al. (1986). Postural, epidemiological and biomechanical analysis of luggage handling in an aircraft luggage compartment. *Applied Ergonomics*, **17** (3), 177–183.

Walsh, N.E. and Schwartz, R.K. (1990). The influence of prophylactic orthoses on abdominal strength and low back injury in the workplace. *The American Journal of Physical Medicine and Rehabilitation*, **69** (5), 245–250.

Waters, R.L. and Morris, J.M. (1970). Effect of spinal supports on the electrical activity of muscles of the trunk. *The Journal of Bone and Joint Surgery*, **52A** (1), 51–60.

Worksafe Australia (1990). *National Standard for Manual Handling and National Code of Practice for Manual Handling*. Australian Government Publishing Service.

WorkSafe Western Australia (1991). *Manual Handling: A Code of Practice*. Occupational Health, Safety and Welfare Commission of Western Australia.

WorkSafe Western Australia (1998). *State of the Work Environment No. 31: Manual Handling Injuries and Diseases, Western Australia 1995/96.*

WorkSafe Western Australia and WorkCover Western Australia (also available at URL http://sage.wt.com.au/safetyline/sowe/sowe31/s31_ind.htm).

A study of manual handling injury among nurses in divisions of medicine at two teaching hospitals

P. Rothmore, G. Elix, D. Ben-Tovim, H. Messenger, S. Pearce and P. Hakendorf

INTRODUCTION

Manual handling injuries among nursing staff comprise the largest proportion of workplace injuries and associated costs in the health care industry. In Australia, the hospital and nursing home industry experiences 30 per cent more injuries per 1000 employees than the overall Australian industries rate (Worksafe, 1995). Nearly 40 per cent of these injuries affect the lower back. A point prevalence of back pain among nursing staff of 17 per cent (compared to 12.5 per cent for the general population) has been reported by Pheasant and Stubbs (1992), while estimates of one year prevalence range from 43 per cent (Pheasant and Stubbs, 1992) to 70 per cent (Yung-Hui and Wen-Ko, 1994). In 1986, Stubbs et al. reported that 12.5 per cent of nurses intending to leave the profession cited back pain as the main factor influencing their decision. In addition, under-reporting of back injury is a recognised problem in the nursing profession. Pheasant and Stubbs (1992) found that, despite having 30 per cent more sick days due to back pain, nurses have 40 per cent less sick days per year when compared with the general population.

A previous history of back pain has been cited as a predictor of back injury. Smedley et al. (1997), in a prospective cohort study of back pain in nurses, found that risk increased with the total duration of previous episodes of back pain and was greatest where pain had been reported during the year prior to their study.

The aetiology of back pain in nursing staff is complex and multifactorial. An association with patient handling has been made in several studies (Arad and Ryan, 1986; Harber et al., 1988; Smedley et al., 1997; Stubbs et al., 1980; Venning et al., 1987). Clinically, episodes of back pain are frequently attributed to a specific patient-handling incident. Jensen (1986) reported that 75 per cent of nurses submitting a compensation claim for back injury cite a specific patient-handling incident as the cause. Other studies (Arad and Ryan, 1986; Garrett et al., 1992; Kumar, 1990; Venning et al., 1987), however, have suggested that lifting exposure (both within a shift and over the total duration of an individual's nursing experience) is a better predictor of back pain. Larese and Fiorito (1994), commenting on the presence of significant differences between the rates of musculoskeletal disorders amongst nurses at two hospitals, attributed the observed differences to discrepancies in the frequency of provision of patient care assistance. Cumulative lifting exposure has been suggested as the link between employment in medical (geriatric, neurology and extended care) wards and back injury.

At two major public hospitals in South Australia, the high rate of manual handling injuries among nurses in medical wards became a source of concern. This was despite the allocation of resources to improve work practices through training, programmes for behavioural change and the provision of equipment. A collaborative approach to injury analysis was undertaken by these two hospitals in order to more fully understand the factors contributing to manual handling injuries among medical ward nurses.

An exploratory study was carried out, with the following aims:

- To examine injury patterns among Medical Division nursing staff and test the influence of nurse-related (intrinsic) and institution-related (extrinsic) factors on injury causation.
- To determine the validity of widely held beliefs regarding the cause of manual handling injuries among nurses.
- To more effectively target future injury prevention initiatives.
- To determine which factors merit further investigation.

METHODOLOGY

Information relating to compensable manual handling injuries among Medical Division nursing staff was collected retrospectively from incident report and WorkCover claim forms, personal interview and a variety of other hospital management information systems. Incidents in which no claim was lodged by a nurse were excluded from this study. Data were collated under the headings listed below.

- Intrinsic characteristics.
- Personal characteristics: age, gender, body mass index (BMI), history of similar injury (see Table 11.4).
- Occupational characteristics: nursing classification (enrolled nurse/registered nurse), employment status (full-time/part-time), years of nursing experience (at the institution/in total since qualification) (see Table 11.5).
- Extrinsic characteristics.
- Injury characteristics: location, mechanism and agency of injury; body part injured (see Table 11.6).
- Organisational characteristics: day, shift and time of injury; proportion of shift worked (shift quartile at time of injury); historical data on number of consecutive shifts worked and type of shift preceding injury, staffing levels on shift of injury (see Table 11.7).

Table 11.4 Personal characteristics

	Total		Hosp. A		Hosp. B	
	Mean	SD	Mean	SD	Mean	SD
Age**	36.8	10.5	40.6	10.2	32.15	9.0
BMI	25.5	5.9	25.6	6.06	25.34	5.9

	Total	Hosp. A	Hosp. B
History of similar injury:			
No	32	17	15
Unknown	11	4	7
Yes	29	19	10

** Difference between Hospital A and Hospital B ($p < 0.001$).

Table 11.5 Occupational characteristics

	Total	Hosp. A	Hosp. B
Classification:			
Enrolled Nurse	22	11	11
Registered Nurse	50	29	21
Employment status:			
< 0.5 part-time	4	3	1
> 0.5 part-time	25	17	8
Full-time	43	20	23

	Total		Hosp. A		Hosp. B	
	Mean	SD	Mean	SD	Mean	SD
Nursing experience:						
Years at current institution	5.3	4.8	6.1	4.8	4.3	4.6
Total years experience**	11.42	7.8	12.7	8.3	9.8	6.8

** Difference between Hospital A and Hospital B ($p < 0.001$).

- Work outcome: days lost, cost of claim and rehabilitation outcome. (Due to a difference in claims management systems, work outcomes will not be discussed further in this paper.)

Where relevant, normative data were obtained across the entire cohort of Medical Division nursing staff for the two institutions, to allow comparison of personal and occupational characteristics of the injured nurses with their cohort. Normative data for staffing levels on the shift equivalent to that when an injury

Table 11.6 Injury characteristics

	Total	Hosp. A	Hosp. B
Location of injury:			
Bedside	59	34	25
Other	10	3	7
Agent:			
Patient	57	33	24
Other	15	7	8
Mechanism:			
Handling object	7	4	3
Push/pull	2	2	0
Lift patient	27	13	14
Collapse patient	11	7	4
Non-specific	16	10	6
Other	9	4	5
Body part injured:			
Neck/shoulder	18	9	9
Low back	41	24	17
Lower limb	3	3	0
Upper back	4	2	2
Upper limb	6	2	4

occurred, one and two weeks prior to the shift of injury, were also obtained, in order to assess the likely contribution of staffing level to the occurrence of injury.

Inclusion criteria

Nursing staff employed by Medical Division at the two hospitals. Both hospitals are general teaching hospitals serving a heterogeneous metropolitan population. One hospital has a dedicated rehabilitation service. The cross-institutional approach allowed not only for the collection of data on a greater number of cases (necessary for statistical validity) but also for the testing of the significance of nurse-related (intrinsic) as opposed to institutional (extrinsic) factors in injury causation. Workers' compensation claims lodged for a manual handling injury suffered between 1 January 1997 and 31 December 1998. It was decided to concentrate on compensable injuries, as opposed to all manual handling incidents, due to the increased rigor with which compensable claims are examined. Exempt employer status under the South Australian Workers' Compensation system made information on compensable claims readily available.

Table 11.7 Organisational characteristics

	Total	Hosp. A	Hosp. B
Previous shift:			
Day off	17	11	6
Early	22	13	9
Late	15	9	6
Night	7	3	4
Other	3	3	0
Number of consecutive shifts (including shift of injury):			
1	18	11	7
2	18	14	4
3	11	6	5
4	6	4	2
5	11	3	8
6	1	1	0
7	1	0	1
Late/early shift:			
No	64	36	28
Yes	7	3	4
Start time of shift of injury:			
Morning	41	26	15
Afternoon	18	8	10
Night	10	3	7
Other	2	2	0
Shift quartile at time of injury:			
1	8	3	5
2	9	6	3
3	19	9	10
4	28	16	12

Exclusion criteria

1. Nurses employed in other hospital divisions.
2. Compensable claims not resulting from manual handling incidents.
3. Manual handling injuries that did not result in workers' compensation claims.

Descriptive information was generated and data analysis was performed using the STATA statistical package (StataCorp, 1999). Categorical data were tabulated and significant difference determined using chi-square analysis. Continuous data were compared and significance determined using Student's *t*-test.

RESULTS

In the period of review, there was a total of seventy-two compensable manual handling injuries experienced by the nurses working in the respective Divisions of Medicine. Eleven of the nurses were male and gender differences were not further explored. Injuries were evenly distributed across the week. In relation to shift worked prior to the shift of injury, the factor of interest was the frequency of a late/early combination, which is widely assumed to predispose to risk of injury. The results for this are included in the tables. The staffing levels during the shifts in which an injury occurred were compared to the levels for identical shifts one and two weeks prior to the shift of injury. No differences were seen. Other results of interest are included in the tables, and some findings that justify specific comment are given below.

There was a significant difference ($p < 0.01$) in the age of injured workers at the two institutions. They did not, however, differ significantly from their cohorts.

There was a significant difference ($p < 0.001$) in the total years of nursing experience between injured staff at the two institutions (12.7 years versus 9.8 years). However, these injured workers did not differ significantly from their cohort.

The majority of injured nurses cited a specific patient-handling incident as having caused their injury (but this was less than the 75 per cent cited in the literature). The second most common reported cause of injury was described as 'no specific incident'. In these reports, the onset of discomfort was described as insidious in nature and attributed to cumulative onset over several shifts or worsening towards the end of a particular shift.

Increased number of consecutive shifts worked was not a predictor of injury. The majority of injuries (71 per cent) occurred within three shifts of beginning a work cycle.

No link to working a late/early shift combination was identified. Only 10 per cent of injuries were reported by staff who had worked a late/early shift combination.

It was particularly noteworthy that 73 per cent of injuries occurred in the last two shift quartiles, with 44 per cent occurring in the last quartile.

DISCUSSION

The personal profiles (intrinsic factors) of injured nurses at the two institutions differed somewhat. Injured nurses at one institution were older, had more years of experience in the workforce, and appeared to have had a more frequent history of similar injury (48 per cent) compared to the injured nurses at the second institution (40 per cent). The present study was based on compensable injuries rather than all musculoskeletal injuries, and consequently the rate of reporting of previous injury may be expected to be somewhat reduced. Differences in data sources utilised by the two institutions to assess previous history mean that caution is needed in the interpretation of this observation.

No significant difference in the mean age of the injured nurses compared to the entire cohort of Medical Division nurses was identified. Years of nursing experience was not found to be a predictor of likelihood of injury: 51 per cent of injured staff had more than 10 years of experience while only 16 per cent of injuries were reported by staff with less than three years' nursing experience. Previous research (Garrett, 1992; Videman, 1989) has suggested that the risk of back injury is highest amongst recently qualified nursing staff.

When employment status (full-time/part-time) of the injured group was compared to that of the entire cohort, it was evident that there was a significantly increased risk of injury to full-time staff as compared to part-time staff. This supports the findings of Waersted and Westaard (1991), who found that sick leave due to musculoskeletal disorders was higher for full-time workers (eight hours/day) than part-time workers (five hours/day). Further information about absolute numbers of staff at risk would be required in order to accurately interpret this observation.

Despite some differences between the workforces at the two hospitals, the patterns of injury were very similar. As would be expected, the majority of injuries at both institutions occurred at the bedside, with the patient as the prime agency of injury. While the locations in which the injuries occurred were scattered throughout both hospital Medical Divisions, one or two locations seemed prominent in injury occurrence. These areas were considered to be those where the most dependent patients, requiring the 'heaviest' manual handling, were located. Further information on relative units of nursing care across these areas would be required in order to confirm that this pattern represented a higher than expected rate of injury for these locations.

When mechanism of injury was evaluated, 38 per cent of injuries were directly attributed to assisting the patient, particularly to move in bed or transfer between bed and another surface. An additional 15 per cent of injuries were associated with the collapse of a patient. Patient handling entails lifting, pushing and pulling movements in adverse ergonomic situations. When a nurse lifts rather than slides the patient, the load lifted may be greater than 35 per cent of their body weight. Substituting a pulling force for lifting (Garg et al., 1991) may significantly reduce the compression and shear forces exerted on the lumbar spine. However, exertion of force horizontally, such as turning a patient in bed, may still be associated with significant spinal loading (Gagnon et al., 1987) and the potential transfer of force to the neck and shoulders. The present study observed a relatively high rate of injury to the neck/shoulder complex – 25 per cent of all injuries.

Approximately 22 per cent of injuries were attributed to 'no specific incident' and may be interpreted as arising from cumulative loading. The authors suggest that this may be an under-estimate, reflecting the injury compensation system rather than injury aetiology. While injuries may result from application of a single load that exceeds tissue failure tolerance (Kumar, 1990; McGill, 1997), this would be expected to occur rarely in the workplace. Single, traumatic events involving an extremely high level of spinal loading could potentially result from catching a falling patient with the spine fully flexed and rotated. While 15 per cent of injuries in this study resulted from patient collapse, the precise mechanism of injury could not be accurately determined. It is suggested that many injuries attributed to specific incidents involve much lower levels of spinal loading than that required to traumatise previously healthy tissues (McGill, 1997).

It is likely that the onset of occupational low back pain involves accumulated trauma from the performance of repetitive tasks at sub-failure loads. Over time, tissue failure tolerance may slowly degrade to a point where a safety margin for an activity no longer exists (McGill, 1997). Furthermore, Mostardi et al. (1992) suggest that continued minor injuries may compromise the muscle force generating mechanisms of the low back, resulting in a situation of increasing weakness and susceptibility to injury. In the health care industry, repeated and sustained loading frequently results from postural compromises contributed to by space restrictions and poor design characteristics or lack of adjustability of equipment and furniture. For example, nursing staff may spend a considerable proportion of their shift in positions of sustained or repeated lumbar flexion. Several studies (Baty and Stubbs, 1987; Engels et al., 1994; Hignett, 1996) have attempted to quantify the postural load of nursing tasks. They have indicated that harmful postures, particularly the flexed/twisted back positions required for patient care and administration activities, may be present for over 20 per cent of a shift.

Evidence in the literature therefore suggests that many injuries attributed to a single event may, in fact, be the result of repeated or prolonged exposure to submaximal loads over a period of time. Focusing on a single event during incident investigation, without recognition of the importance of cumulative load, may therefore be misleading and result in the misdirection of preventive measures (McGill, 1997).

One striking and rather unexpected observation from this study related to the shift quartile during which injury occurred (first 25 per cent of the shift, second 25 per cent etc.). There was a distinct aggregation of injuries in the last quartile of the shifts. Where a quartile could be identified, 43 per cent of injuries occurred in the last quartile, and 30 per cent in the third quartile. Some inter-institutional differences in the prominence of this effect were evident. Further, prospective, investigation with a larger number of subjects would be necessary to substantiate the last quartile effect. However, the possibility of a last quartile effect is clearly a matter of some interest, as the authors are unaware of previous reports of such an effect in hospitals.

There are three main possibilities to explain this observation:

1. The effect may be an artefact due to reporting bias. Verification of the exactness with which time of injury was reported would be necessary before this possibility could be excluded, but error because of this appears unlikely given the consistency of the effect across institutions, clinical units and staff types.

2. It may be a work pattern effect: work that places staff at increased risk may be concentrated at the end of shifts.

3. It may be a within-shift fatigue effect.

While the postural load of nursing duties has been examined previously (Engels et al., 1994; Hignett, 1996), variation across the duration of a work shift has not. Such an examination may determine the relevance of the work pattern effect suggested by the authors. It is further hypothesised that manual handling practices during a shift are influenced by within-shift muscular fatigue. This may lead to the performance of manual handling tasks in an energy conserving but more hazardous manner towards the end of a shift. These energy saving strategies include the adoption of flexed or stooped postures (Garg and Herin, 1979) which, if sustained or repeated, may lead to the progressive deformation of the passive, supporting structures of the spine. This is known as the 'flexion creep' response. A loss of passive restraint to hyperflexion movements may therefore lead to an increased risk of injury to other spinal structures (McGill, 1997). Whilst the flexion creep response has been studied in the laboratory (McGill and Brown, 1992), relevant observations have not been replicated in work settings.

The study was limited in a number of ways. Retrospective studies involving the use of archival information necessitate the analysis and manipulation of data for purposes other than those for which the data were originally intended, introducing the possibility of bias. Such studies do, however, provide a valuable, long-term picture of injuries within a workplace. Clearly, there is a continuing need for an active programme of research into injury aetiology to accompany existing prevention strategies.

ACKNOWLEDGEMENTS

The authors wish to acknowledge the support provided by the Divisions of Medicine, Nursing Information Systems, Occupational Health, Risk Management and Workers' Compensation Services at both institutions, which enabled the study to be conducted.

References

Arad, D. and Ryan, M. (1986). The incidence and prevalence in nurses of low back pain. A definitive survey exposes the hazards. *Australian Nurses' Journal*, **16** (1), 44–48.

Baty, D. and Stubbs, D.A. (1987). Postural stress in geriatric nursing. *International Journal of Nursing Studies*, **24**, 339–344.

Engels, J., Landeweerd, J. and Kant, Y. (1994). An OWAS-based analysis of nurses' working postures. *Ergonomics*, **37** (5), 909–919.

Gagnon, M., Chehade, A., Kemp, F. et al. (1987). Lumbo-sacral loads and selected muscle activity while turning patients in bed. *Ergonomics*, **30** (7), 1013–1032.

Garg, A. and Herrin, G. (1979). Stoop or squat: a biomechanical and metabolic evaluation. *American Institute of Industry and Engineering Transactions*, **11**, 293–302.

Garg, A., Owen, B., Beller, D. et al. (1991). A biomechanical and ergonomic evaluation of patient transferring tasks: bed to wheelchair and wheelchair to bed. *Ergonomics*, **34** (3), 289–312.

Garrett, B., Singiser, D. and Banks, S. (1992). Back injuries among nursing personnel. *American Association of Occupational Health Nurses' Journal*, **40** (11), 510–516.

Harber, P., Billet, E., Vojtecky, M. et al. (1988). Nurses' beliefs about cause and prevention of occupational back pain. *Journal of Occupational Medicine*, **30** (10), 797–800.

Hignett, S. and Richardson, B. (1995). Manual handling human loads in a hospital: An exploratory study to identify nurses' perceptions. *Applied Ergonomics*, **26** (3), 221–226.

Jensen, R. (1986). Disabling back injuries among nursing personnel in New York. *Proceedings of the Human Factors Society 30th Annual Meeting, Santa Monica, California*, pp. 244–248.

Kumar, S. (1990). Cumulative load as a risk factor for back pain. *Spine*, **15** (12), 1311–1316.

Larese, F. and Fiorito, A. (1994). Musculoskeletal disorders in hospital nurses: a comparison between two hospitals. *Ergonomics*, **37** (7), 1205–1211.

McGill, S. (1997). Biomechanics of low back injury. *Journal of Biomechanics*, **30** (5), 465–475.

McGill, S. and Brown, S. (1992). Creep response of the lumbar spine to prolonged lumbar flexion. *Clinical Biomechanics*, **7**, 43–46.

Mostardi, R.A., Noe, D.A., Kovacik, M.W. et al. (1992). Isokinetic lifting strength and occupational injury. A prospective study. *Spine*, **17** (2), 189–193.

Pheasant, S. and Stubbs, D (1992). Back pain in nurses: epidemiology and risk assessment. *Applied Ergonomics*, **23** (4), 226–231.

Smedley, J., Egger, P., Cooper, C. et al. (1997). Prospective cohort study of predictors of incident low back pain in nurses. *British Medical Journal*, **314**, 1225–1228.

StataCorp (1999). Stata statistical software: release 6.0. Stata Corporation, College Station, Texas.

Stubbs, D.A., Rivers, P.M., Hudson, M.P. et al. (1980). Patient handling and back pain in nurses. *DHSS Interim Report* J1/R195/120.

Stubbs, D.A., Buckle, P. and Hudson, M. (1986). Backing out: nurse wastage associated with back pain. *International Journal of Nursing Studies*, **23**, 325–336.

Venning, P., Walter, S. and Stitt, L. (1987). Personal and job-related factors as determinants of incidence of back injuries among nursing personnel. *Journal of Occupational Medicine*, **29** (10), 820–825.

Videman, T., Rauhala, S., Asp, K. et al. (1989). Patient-handling skill, back injuries and back pain: An intervention study in nursing. *Spine*, **14** (2), 148–156.

Waersted, M. and Westgaard, R. (1991). Working hours as a risk factor in the development of musculoskeletal complaints. *Ergonomics*, **34** (3), 265–276.

Worksafe Australia (1995). *Occupational Health and Safety Performance Overviews. Issue 7: Hospitals, Nursing Homes and Related Industries.* Australian Government Publishing Service.

Yung-Hui Lee and Wen-Ko Chiou (1994). Risk factors for low back pain and patient handling capacity of nursing personnel. *Journal of Safety Research*, **25** (3), 135–145.

Development of a manual handling risk assessment tool for community-based nursing care

Narelle Sulley

INTRODUCTION

Manual handling risks to nurses have been well documented over many decades. Community nursing presents additional risk factors with the work environment not designed for the performance of nursing tasks. Small bathrooms, low double beds, carpeted floors and dimly lit, poorly ventilated rooms are often the norm. This is inconsistent with the provision of an ergonomically designed workplace, where the aim is 'to improve efficiency, safety and ... well-being' (Clark and Corlett, 1984).

Despite changes to legislation and the development of Codes of Practice and Regulations in this area during the 1980s and 1990s, injury rates in nursing and other human services remain unacceptable. Owen and Moss (1988) suggest that, as part of their legal responsibilities, 'employers are required to take reasonable steps to protect nurses from injury', which requires 'a combined approach, incorporating risk assessment, provision of equipment and staff training'. The ageing of the population and increased demand for home-based care will place greater demands on organisations and on individual staff members who work for them. The value of staff, and their right to a safe and efficient working environment, is a crucial component of any quality management programme, and it is one of the core values of the Royal District Nursing Service (Royal District Nursing Service, 1998).

The Royal District Nursing Service (RDNS) in Victoria is Australia's largest and oldest independent provider of community-based professional nursing and allied health care services. It provides home nursing for highly dependent and frail aged people, post-acute care such as wound management and intravenous therapies, palliative care and postnatal care for mothers and babies. The service has a well-established reputation as Australia's leading home nursing and health care provider. It currently employs over 1200 staff, based at twenty-one work sites. Last year, care was provided to almost 34,000 clients, with more than one million visits to homes across Melbourne and the Mornington Peninsula in Victoria.

Physiotherapists are employed by the RDNS to provide a consultancy service to nursing staff. A primary function is to act as a resource to maximise staff safety, particularly pertaining to work postures and client transfers. The six physiotherapists (4.2 FTE) have opportunity to observe manual handling practices of nurses working in the community. Through this role, it has been possible to observe work postures and manual handling practices that have been recognised as high risk, such as frequent or sustained bending, and lifting from either awkward positions or in positions of extreme lumbar flexion. Kumar (1990) reported on the association between cumulative load and back pain, a factor that also appears relevant in community nursing. Garg and Owen (1992) concluded that 'an appropriate ergonomic intervention programme offers great promise in reducing physical stress and low back pain in nursing personnel'.

The RDNS in Victoria, through the Occupational Health and Safety (OHS) Co-ordinator, had identified risk factors and the need for appropriate intervention. In 1995, the General Risk Identification Checklist from the Department of Labour Manual Handling Code of Practice (1988) was introduced for nurses to use in the field. However, it was not widely accepted by nursing staff due to its lack of relevance to health services and the care of people. Consequently the process of risk assessment and control was unsatisfactory with a resultant breakdown in the system.

DEVELOPMENT

The need to define a workable system to identify, assess and control manual handling risks became clear to the physiotherapists within the RDNS. To initiate the process, the physiotherapists proposed to the regional OHS committees that an alternative tool be drafted. This was supported by the OHS Co-ordinator, OHS representatives and senior management.

An original draft was produced utilising the Victorian Department of Labour OHS (Manual Handling) Regulations (1988) as the foundation, and incorporating the generally accepted hierarchy of risk control strategies. This was expanded upon using the physiotherapists' intimate knowledge of manual handling hazards in community nursing. Specific examples include poor balance during transfers, performing more than one task at a time (e.g. supporting the client's weight whilst adjusting clothing), transferring clients with impaired weight bearing ability; and handling of unco-operative or resisting clients. In addition, the risk associated with providing care for consecutive complex clients with high level needs was identified. The draft Manual Handling Risk Assessment Tool (RAT) was presented to regional OHS representatives for approval prior to extensive field trials. At all times senior management were advised of progress and continued to demonstrate support of the project, including provision of administrative services.

With minor adjustments, trials of the draft tool were undertaken agency wide, which included multiple clients from over twenty work sites. During the trial period an article was placed in the RDNS internal newsletter Grapevine, to ensure that as many staff as possible were aware of the trial and had the opportunity to provide input if desired.

IMPLEMENTATION

Resulting from positive feedback of the trial, senior management supported a prompt implementation of the new RAT. The tool was launched in March 1998, at a twice-yearly meeting of all OHS representatives. Coincidentally, the Australian Nursing Federation (ANF) Victorian Branch launched their No Lifting Policy at the same time. The RDNS has subsequently adopted the ANF No Lifting Policy, and has operationalised this through the use of the RAT, which supports all of the No Lifting Policy principles.

OHS representatives along with physiotherapists introduced the new tool to all nursing staff at individual work sites, providing appropriate training in its use. Guidelines for its use were provided, including criteria for client selection. A RAT was to be completed on clients identified as high risk, such as those:

- requiring lifting,
- requiring assistance with transfers,
- requiring assistance with repositioning,
- requiring the use of a hoist,
- where staff is doubled to provide care.

In addition, the RAT was to be completed on any client where staff perceived a potential risk, or experienced discomfort during or after care.

A pocket-sized cue card (Figure 11.5), designed by a physiotherapist, was provided to all field staff as a prompt for risk assessment and control when using the tool. Training in use of the RAT and the cue card is now provided as an important part of the client care staff orientation programme.

EVALUATION

Six months following the introduction of the RAT, several strategies were used to monitor its effective use. These strategies included an audit of randomly selected client care records, both at the work site and in client homes using a standardised checklist ($n = 114$). In addition, the physiotherapists conducted audits of client care records during scheduled visits. This review identified some inconsistencies in appropriate application, particularly with transfer of risk control strategies to the nursing care plan. At the conclusion of the formal evaluation period, feedback was provided to nursing staff covering both positive and negative factors identified by the audit.

Ongoing monitoring by the physiotherapists in their role as consultants to the nurses has shown increased effective use of the RAT. In addition, informal feedback received from field staff has been positive and indicates a growing level of comfort in using the RAT to focus on staff safety during manual handling.

Preliminary incident, injury and time lost data indicate a trend towards declining manual handling incidents and related soft tissue injuries (Table 11.8). Twelve-month comparative figures for before and after the March 1998

By J Smith RDNS Physio

Cuecard for RISK ASSESSMENT IN MANUAL HANDLING
- IN CARING IN THE HOME

Risk	*Example*	*Suggested Modifications*
Stooping	Bed height too high/low dressing client - socks/shoes Dropping equipment	Modify work height. Kneel on bed modify client's position pre-plan equipment position
Reaching Above head forward sideways	Toiletries on high shelf Reaching to turn off taps Opening shower curtains	Modify storage of toiletries Modify own position * Modify position nearer to curtain
Twisting	Transferring clients from chair to chair	Modify environment * Modify own position
Unbalanced Transfers	Moving client over shower step. Raise transfer over long distance	Consider possible shower modification. Modify environment *

Home Healthcare
Royal District Nursing Service

By J Smith RDNS Physio

Risk	*Example*	*Suggested Modifications*
Consecutive "Heavy" Clients	2 or 3 clients in a row who need prolonged similar care	Modify workflow - alternate with "lighter" clients
Excessive Manual Handling	Client requires lift, or is unable to participate in transfer, may really need 2 to safely transfer	Modify task - Hoist - use of mechanical assistance - use of Team lifting *
Environmental Risks	Too much furniture unsafe furniture, ie. rugs, mats etc. Awkward furniture position. Slippery/wet surfaces. Poorly lit area.	Modify workplace layout Discuss possible alterations
Personal Limitations	Individual skills may not allow safe transfer of procedure. Personal physical capacity is ?, ie. injury/Pregnancy Personal fitness	Training in principles of safe people handling. Specific training for individual client needs. * Gain assistance to look at personal fitness *
Client Lack of Co-operation	Dementing, resistant, unco-operative client	Modify approach to client. Modify presentation of client

*** CONSIDER PHYSIOTHERAPY REFERRAL**

Home Healthcare
Royal District Nursing Service

Figure 11.5 Pocket-sized cue card

introduction of the RAT were not complete at the time of writing this paper. Nursing Managers at each work site ($n = 16$) were surveyed by questionnaire, utilising e-mail, ten months after the introduction of the RAT. Opinions were sought on prevalence of use, efficacy in assessing and controlling manual handling risks, and general feedback regarding the tool. This feedback was also predominantly positive, with Nurse Managers reporting that most staff used the RAT effectively, and felt that it was a good decision making tool.

DISCUSSION

The aim was to develop a tool which was relevant to community nursing and which would lead the user toward appropriate risk control strategies. Straker (1997), in the summary of his book *A Critical Appraisal of Manual Handling Risk Assessment Literature*, writes that 'participative approaches to risk assessment are probably more appropriate than expert judgement in many situations' – a concept it was hoped the RAT would embrace.

A flow chart format was chosen, providing initial risk assessment, followed by identification of preliminary risk control strategies and then risk re-evaluation. If a risk is still evident, the flow chart directs the user to consult the physiotherapist, OHS representative or relevant senior nursing staff, who, with the primary user, will undertake a further, more detailed analysis. Once additional risk control strategies have been identified and implemented, a further re-evaluation of risk is undertaken. Where no acceptable risk control strategies can be identified or implemented, care can be ceased until a satisfactory resolution can be achieved (Figure 11.6). The tool has been invaluable in objectifying issues during conciliation between a client/family and the RDNS where ongoing care was in question.

In addition to the flow chart format, a crucial component of the new risk assessment and control process was the introduction of detailed documentation of identified risk control strategies in the nursing care plan. This ensures that safe manual handling practices would begin to be integrated into standard nursing practice. In itself, this necessitated a cultural shift within the agency, where previously manual handling issues were often considered separately rather than integrally with nursing care. This is quite different from, for example, infection control practices in nursing, where standard precautions and the wearing of gloves have for a long time been completely integrated.

Another factor believed to be crucial to the long-term acceptance and usage of the tool was the autonomy given to individual OHS representatives. During the trial period, OHS representatives chose a trial method appropriate to their work site, which ensured ownership of the process.

Table 11.8 Preliminary incident, injury and time lost data (excluding those related to motor vehicle accidents, slips/trips/falls, blood and body fluids)

	July '96–June '97	July '97–June '98	July '98–Feb. '99
Staff incidents	189	179	61
Staff injuries	180	146	25
Time lost (days)	1693	1838	170

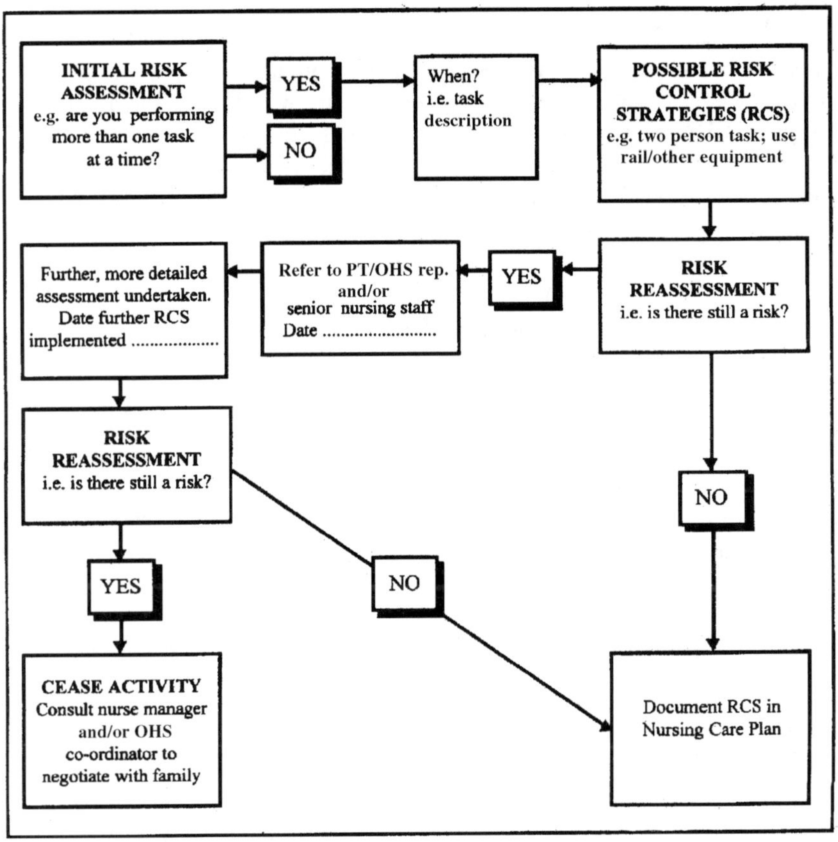

Figure 11.6 Flow chart format

The tool has resulted in significant changes in the way RDNS nurses have approached manual handling issues. There are, however, factors that impact upon its use on an individual basis and, therefore, its effectiveness. With clear policies, procedures and documentation in nursing care plans (NCP), community nurses essentially work alone with minimal day to day supervision. Inevitably, there remain variances in individual application of sound working practices. The physiotherapists in their role as consultants are one method of monitoring the recommended risk control strategies and of providing reinforcement of the No Lifting Policy. With continued reinforcement of the risk identification, assessment and control process, along with the support of senior management and the new practices put into operation through relevant policies, procedures and performance appraisal processes, it is hoped that the cultural shift achieved so far will be consolidated.

This tool provides a system where the risk of injury related to manual handling can be appropriately managed. It also has potential for more widespread application in other community agencies where personal care is a core service.

CONCLUSIONS

The risk assessment tool designed for use in community nursing has allowed the RDNS to focus on manual handling risk assessment and control in a meaningful way. This has enabled, for the first time, integration of manual handling risk control into daily nursing practices. Whilst concrete measures of its usefulness in injury prevention are not yet complete, the process has been useful within the agency in clarifying and objectifying risks inherent in community nursing. The resultant raised profile of OHS issues, combined with the ANF No Lifting Policy, has led to a cultural shift allowing RDNS nurses to no longer just accept lifting and other sustained and awkward postures as part of their job.

ACKNOWLEDGEMENTS

The authors would like to thank the RDNS and the following colleagues for their support in the preparation of this paper: Gabrielle Bortoluzzi, Christina Cooper, Libby Crowe, Jackie Hattam, Bronwen Roberts, Lesley Sulley and Pam Wright.

References

Annual Report (1998). Royal District Nursing Service, Victoria.

Australian Nursing Federation (1998). *No Lifting Policy.* Victorian Branch.

Clark, T. and Corlett, E. (1984). *The Ergonomics of Workspaces and Machines: A Design Manual.* Taylor and Francis.

Garg, A. and Owen, B. (1992). Reducing back stress to nursing personnel: an ergonomic intervention in a nursing home. *Ergonomics*, **35** (11), 1353–1375.

Kumar, S. (1990). Cumulative load as a risk factor for back pain. *Spine*, **15** (12), 1311–1316.

Manual Handling Code of Practice (1985). Department of Labour.

Occupational Health and Safety (Manual Handling) Regulations (1988). Department of Labour.

Owen, A. and Moss. M. (1998). Implementing a safer patient-handling policy. *Professional Nurse*, **13** (10), 681–684.

Straker. L. (1997). *A Critical Appraisal of Manual Handling Risk Assessment Literature.* The International Ergonomics Association Press.

Chapter 12

Functional restoration

Effectiveness of a physiotherapy functional restoration programme compared to patient-selected treatment on chronic compensable low back pain

Jon J. Ford and Kim Bennell

INTRODUCTION

The study described in this paper evaluated the effectiveness of a physiotherapy functional restoration programme on chronic compensable low back pain. It was a pilot project aiming to evaluate whether a randomised controlled trial of the programme would be justified.

The extent of the problem of low back pain (LBP) has been extensively studied in high income earning countries (Waddell, 1987). There is a large variation in reported incidence and prevalence of LBP possibly due to variations in the populations studied and methodological issues (Abenhaim and Suissa, 1987; Burton et al., 1989; Cunningham and Kelsey, 1984; Riihimški et al., 1994; Skovron et al., 1994; Volinn, 1997; Walsh et al., 1992). Despite the variability in results, LBP appears to be a common problem in high income earning countries.

Low back pain is often described as having a favourable natural history, and whereby 80 and 90 per cent of individuals will recover in six weeks (Waddell, 1987). However, other studies show the natural history of LBP to be a recurrent one (Hides et al., 1995; Von Korff et al., 1988 and 1990). Recent studies have shown that recovery from acute LBP may not be as rapid as first thought (Cherkin et al., 1996; Von Korff et al., 1993). Although methodological problems exist with many studies, it appears that recovery from acute LBP is not necessarily rapid, and that recurrence is common.

The cost of compensable LBP in Victoria is relatively high and increasing. In 1996/97 the Victorian WorkCover Authority calculated the average cost of a LBP compensation claim to be $19,000. This compares to $13,500 for other work-related illness. The cost of lump sum payments for LBP has increased from $21 million in 1995/96 to $31 million in 1996/97 (Victorian WorkCover Authority, 1997). Chronic compensable LBP accounts for a large percentage of costs from LBP (Abenhaim and Suissa, 1987). Sufferers of chronic compensable

LBP may also be affected by factors such as depression, anxiety and family stress due to financial, social and emotional stresses (Katon et al., 1985; Naliboff et al., 1985). Clearly, any intervention that might lessen the cost to society and the individual with LBP would be of great value.

THE NATURE OF LOW BACK PAIN

It appears that LBP may be more than a physical phenomenon. Engel (1982) hypothesised that a medical model did not account for the psychological and social aspects of the individual's disease. He proposed a new model that encompassed the physical, psychological and social aspects of disease called the biopsychosocial model of illness.

There are a number of prospective studies examining the validity of the biopsychosocial model of illness in relation to LBP. Psychological factors such as depression and intelligence, as well as social factors such as education have demonstrated an ability to predict onset of acute LBP (Bergenudd and Nilsson, 1988; Bigos et al., 1992; Croft et al., 1996; Viikari-Juntura et al., 1991). In addition, a number of studies have shown that psychosocial factors are able to predict poor outcome following onset of acute LBP (Burton et al., 1995; Klenerman et al., 1995; Lacroix et al., 1990; Milhous et al., 1989). Although some methodological problems exist in the above literature, sufficient evidence is available to justify assessment and intervention strategies addressing the psychosocial as well as the physical aspects of LBP. If the LBP involves a compensation claim, then the negative effect of psychosocial factors on prognosis has been observed to be greater than for non-compensable subjects (Block et al., 1980; Hayes et al., 1993; Rainville et al., 1997).

THE LITERATURE JUSTIFYING A PHYSIOTHERAPY FUNCTIONAL RESTORATION PROGRAMME

Functional restoration (FR) was first defined as 'a multimodal pain management programme that employs a comprehensive cognitive-behavioural treatment orientation to help patients better cope with, and manage, their pain ... while undergoing the sports medicine physical approach to correct functional deficits' (Mayer et al., 1985, p. 483). This approach utilised intensive aerobic, mobilising and strengthening exercise for the spine and whole body. The aim was to restore lost function to the patient through functional exercise, as was widely practised by sports medicine practitioners on peripheral joint injuries. In addition, the cognitive behavioural aspect of function restoration aimed to positively affect the psychosocial component of chronic LBP. Although Mayer and colleagues initially described the approach as multidisciplinary, there have been no conclusive studies validating this claim. The intervention being evaluated in the present study is a physiotherapist-conducted FR programme.

Four randomised controlled trials (RCTs) have evaluated the effect of FR on chronic LBP (Aberg, 1984; Alaranta et al., 1994; Frost et al., 1995; Linström et al., 1992). The details of these studies can be seen in Table 12.1. All studies

Table 12.1 Randomised controlled trials of functional restoration compared to other forms of intervention

Author	Intervention	Comparison	*n*	Outcome measure	Follow-up	Results	Methodological issues
Lindstrom et al. (1992)	Physiotherapy-based functional restoration	Medical management including physiotherapy	105	WS	2 years	Significant difference favouring functional restoration	No assessor blinding No placebo group No reliability of outcome measures
Alaranta et al. (1994)	Functional restoration	Standard physiotherapy	152	WS Psych ROM Strength Other	12 months	Significant difference favouring functional restoration	Poor baseline comparison for clinical/demographic criteria No assessor blinding Poor description of drop-out No placebo group No intention to treat analysis
Frost et al. (1995)	Physiotherapy-based functional restoration	Back school programme	81	ODQ GHP Pain diary Psych	6 months	Significant difference favouring functional restoration	Poor intervention description Poor description of drop-out and no intention to treat analysis No baseline comparison for clinical criteria No placebo group
Aberg (1984)	Functional restoration	Waiting list	353	WS Other	8 months	Significant difference favouring functional restoration	No evaluation sample homogeneity No baseline comparison for clinical/demographic criteria Poor intervention description No assessor blinding No reliability of measures No placebo

ROM, range of movement; Strength, trunk strength; WS, work status; ODQ, Oswestry Low Back Pain Disability Questionnaire; GHP, any general health profile; Psych, a psychological profile; Other, other measures.

reported significant differences favouring the FR group as measured by work status, physical and psychosocial variables. The study by Aberg et al. (1984) had poor methodology. Two of the three trials with acceptable methodology (Frost et al., 1995; Lindström et al., 1992) were physiotherapy-based FR programmes as opposed to the multidisciplinary approach advocated by Mayer et al. (1985).

The components of FR in these studies were variable. The RCTs evaluating isolated exercise approaches have been of varying methodological quality. Intensive trunk extensor training has been shown to be effective in improving chronic LBP (Hansen et al., 1993; Manniche et al., 1991). Lumbar stabilisation exercises, facilitating the lumbar multifidus and transverses abdominus, have also been shown to be effective in chronic spondylolisthesis subjects (O'Sullivan et al., 1997). In addition, there is a significant body of literature that validates the importance of these stabilising muscles for normal lumbar function (Bermark, 1989; Cresswell et al., 1992; Hides et al., 1995; Hodges and Richardson, 1997; Mattila et al., 1986; Panjabi et al., 1989; Rantanen et al., 1993; Wilke et al., 1995; Wohlfahrt et al., 1993; Zetterberg et al., 1987).

Other exercise approaches such as mobilising exercises and trunk flexor strength training have not demonstrated efficacy, although the methodological quality of the RCTs in these areas is poor (Bentsen et al., 1997; Coxhead et al., 1981; Davies et al., 1979; Elnaggar et al., 1991; Johannsen et al., 1995; Spratt et al., 1993). A study by Deyo et al. (1990) examined the efficacy of mobilising exercises and was of acceptable methodological quality. It showed no effect of the exercises after follow-up three months post baseline. Including stabilisation training and intensive erector spinae training in a FR programme is justified by the literature; however, this is not the case with mobilising exercise and trunk flexor training.

Functional and aerobic exercise has not been evaluated in RCTs aside from being part of a FR programme. Psychological interventions have not been shown to be effective for chronic LBP in methodologically sound RCTs (Altmaier et al., 1992; Nicholas et al., 1991). However, both these approaches have a strong theoretical construct justifying their incorporation into a FR programme. FR may positively affect tissue healing of injured structures and reverse the deconditioning effects of excessive rest (MacFarlane et al., 1989; Salter, 1990). Functional exercise in normal movement patterns may also reverse the plastic changes associated with the pathophysiologic pain mechanism (Wall, 1995). In addition, functional exercise provides an appropriate progression whereby lumbar stabilisation exercises can be more intensively and functionally built into training (O'Sullivan et al., 1997). If the biopsychosocial model of illness is accepted, then some form of psychological component to the intervention would be necessary. The theoretical construct underpinning the aims of FR is so dependent on the components of functional exercise and psychological intervention that, by definition, they must be included as part of any FR programme.

This study aimed to evaluate the effectiveness of a physiotherapist-conducted FR programme incorporating lumbar stabilisation, intensive trunk extensor exercises and a cognitive behavioural approach, compared to subject-selected intervention for chronic compensable LBP. The secondary aim of this study was to evaluate the feasibility of conducting a formal RCT in individuals with chronic compensable LBP.

METHODS

A non-randomised quasi-experimental design was used, where subjects received either self-selected medical and paramedical treatment (control group) or a four month physiotherapy FR programme (intervention group). This study was approved by the University of Melbourne Human Research Ethics Committee. All subjects provided written informed consent prior to participating.

The subjects were recruited from Royal and Sun Alliance, an approved WorkCover insurer via postal request for participation. Additional subjects were recruited from referrals to spinal management (SM) clinics in Victoria. Subjects were offered a physiotherapy FR programme at one of five SM clinics. Those subjects who declined the offer were then invited to participate as part of the control group.

The *inclusion criteria* were that the subjects should: (1) have LBP of 12–104 weeks' duration; (2) be off work or on restricted hours; and (3) be between 18 and 65 years of age.

The *exclusion criteria* were: (1) consistent symptoms of progressive nerve root or cauda equina compression; (2) symptoms of non-mechanical pathology such as a history of neoplasms, a history of serious trauma or a history of fever and neurological symptoms, as per Quebec Task Force (1987) recommendations; and (3) lumbar surgery in the previous three months.

All data for the intervention group were gathered whilst attending one of the SM clinics. All control group data were gathered either by telephone or postal questionnaire. Baseline data were gathered from both groups after informed consent was granted. Baseline demographic data for both groups comprised: weight, height, age, sex, years of education and ethnicity. Baseline clinical data for both groups comprised: presence of leg symptoms, presence of distal paraesthesia, pain drawing score, past lumbar surgery and duration of LBP. Measurement of demographic and clinical characteristics was adapted from Deyo et al. (1990). Baseline outcome measures were also recorded at this time.

The intervention consisted of a two week period of home stabilisation training in the most appropriate position for recruitment of the transversus abdominis and lumbar multifidus (Richardson and Jull, 1995). This was followed by a four week, five day per week, supervised exercise programme where the stabilisation muscles were trained to be constantly active in functional aerobic and resistance training. Functional exercise was devised according to the subject's normal pre-injury work and non-work related activity. The physical aims of the programme were to improve functional activation of the stabilisation muscles, work capacity, general fitness and strength. In addition, correct postural and manual handling principles were reinforced. Following the supervised programme, a three month home or gym-based programme was instituted aiming to continue the rehabilitation process more independently. During this time the subjects were monitored to ensure that the FR principles were being maintained. Throughout the FR programme, a number of systematised intervention strategies aiming to affect psychosocial factors were implemented. These strategies consisted of a cognitive behavioural approach to exercise and facilitation of return to work

Cognitive behavioural training

A cognitive behavioural component of FR has been described as the most effective method of addressing the psychosocial aspects of chronic LBP (Alaranta et al., 1994). Cognitive behavioural training is a combination of two psychological approaches, namely cognitive therapy and behavioural therapy. Behavioural or operant behavioural therapy was initially described in relation to long-standing injury by Fordyce et al. (1973), and can be defined as 'attempts to increase the response rate of adaptive well behaviours, and to eliminate maladaptive behaviours' (Lockwood, 1996, p. 14). Cognitive therapy focuses on the nature and modification of a patient's thoughts, feelings and beliefs (Turk and Meichenbaum, 1989).

Changing non-organic and inappropriate pain behaviour, as well as maladaptive cognitions, was one of the primary goals of the FR programme. Basic cognitive behavioural principles were applied in the context of a supervised progressive exercise programme by physiotherapists with specific training. It was not the intention of the programme to engage in formal cognitive behavioural therapy.

The progressive exercise programme aimed to teach the subject that it was safe to move within the limits of their capacity (Fordyce et al., 1981). Other pain behaviours such as grimacing, guarded movement patterns and limitations in activity greater than accounted for by the degree of injury were not reinforced by the physiotherapist (Fordyce et al., 1981). Positive behaviours such as adherence to correct posture/manual handling recommendations, progression in exercise intensity/duration and gradual returning to normal function including work were positively reinforced (Fordyce et al., 1981; Fordyce et al., 1986).

Pacing teaches the individual to learn the extent of their functional limitations and to base their behaviour consistently around those limitations, rather than around their level of pain (Harding and Williams, 1995). The concept of pacing was fundamental to facilitating self-management in the intervention group. Pacing also provided structure to the exercise programme where small but regular increases in exercise intensity and duration were made that did not aggravate the pain.

Cognitive restructuring involves identification and modification of thoughts and beliefs that underpin maladaptive behaviours (Turk and Meichenbaum, 1989). Such counter-productive thoughts were challenged and modified through discussion and education during the FR programme. A typical example of a counter-productive cognition by the intervention group was 'rest will fix my back'.

Generalisation and maintenance empowers the individual to maintain the improvements gained during a cognitive behavioural oriented FR programme into the long term. In maximising the individual's self-efficacy, optimal generalisation and maintenance will be attained (Turk and Meichenbaum, 1989). This was achieved by continued but progressively decreasing monitoring of the subject for utilisation of the FR principles.

Return to work

Formulation of a return to work programme by the SM clinic practitioner in conjunction with the rehabilitation provider, employer, insurer and local doctor was undertaken where physical capacity was adequate. The return to work programme encouraged the subject to return to work within his/her capacity, and to set goals regarding returning to normal hours and duties. The subject was encouraged to apply the self-management and postural principles taught during the FR programme to work. Return to work was implemented at any time during the four month rehabilitation programme, depending on the subject's capacity and work availability. Ongoing communication between all parties was essential in optimising return to work outcomes.

Control group treatment

The control group subjects were instructed that they were free to pursue any form of intervention at their own discretion. Such treatment may have included physiotherapy, chiropractic, massage, acupuncture or other FR programmes. At six months post baseline, a telephone interview was completed to record the nature of treatment received.

After six months, all intervention and control subjects were re-evaluated for all outcome measures. The Oswestry Low Back Pain Disability Questionnaire (ODQ) and Quebec Back Pain Disability Scale (QDS) are two self-administered questionnaires that have demonstrated acceptable reliability and validity (Fairbank et al., 1980; Kopec et al., 1996). Work status (WS) was also measured on a five-point scale following recommendations by Fishbain et al. (1993). Although there are problems with the validity of WS as an outcome measure, it is seen by many as essential in outcome studies due to its relevance in the 'real world' (Cutler et al., 1994; Flores et al., 1997).

Data analysis

The intervention and control groups were examined for demographic and clinical comparability at baseline using independent *t*-tests, Mann-Whitney U tests or chi square tests as appropriate. The differences in ODQ and QDS scores (six month score minus baseline score) were compared between control and intervention groups using an independent *t*-test. A one-way analysis of covariance was performed to assess the influence of differing baseline variables on the differences in ODQ and QDS scores. Baseline WS scores were tested for comparability between the groups using the Mann-Whitney U test. Final WS scores were also compared between control and intervention groups using the Mann-Whitney U test. A two-tailed significance level was set for all tests at alpha = 0.05.

RESULTS

In total, thirty-eight subjects (fifteen control and twenty-three intervention) were recruited into the study. Thirty-two subjects (thirteen control and nineteen intervention) were included in the final analyses. Two control group subjects withdrew, one reporting the questionnaire was 'too much effort' and the other suffering a heart attack. Two intervention subjects withdrew, one reporting travel difficulties and the other due to poor compliance with the programme. Due to an administrative error, data were unavailable from a further two intervention subjects.

The groups were well matched at baseline for demographic and clinical characteristics apart from a significantly greater proportion of the control subjects having leg symptoms, distal paraesthesia and previous lumbar surgery compared with the intervention group (Tables 12.2 and 12.3). The control group also had a significantly longer duration of LBP than the intervention group.

There were no co-interventions for the intervention group. The majority of the control group subjects received physiotherapy, exercise and medication from their doctor as treatment.

The means (and standard deviations) of the baseline and final ODQ and QDS scores are shown in Table 12.4. An independent *t*-test showed a significant difference between the groups with regard to the change in the ODQ ($p = 0.002$) and the QDS scores ($p = 0.03$). In a one-way analysis of covariance comparing the difference in the ODQ and QDS between groups, leg pain, distal paraesthesia, past history of surgery and duration of LBP were included as covariates. For the change in ODQ, there was still a significant difference between groups after adjusting for the influence of these covariates ($F(1,29) = 4.94$, $p = 0.04$). For the

Table 12.2 Demographic characteristics for each group at baseline given as the mean (SD) or the number (%)

Characteristic	Control ($n = 13$)	Intervention ($n = 19$)	Statistics
Height (cm)	170 (9)	174 (11)	$t(27) = -1.12$, $p = 0.27$
Weight (kg)	77 (13)	83 (14)	$t(27) = -1.04$, $p = 0.31$
Age (years)	44 (12)	39 (9)	$t(29) = 1.39$, $p = 0.16$
Sex			
Male	6 (50 %)	5 (26 %)	
Female	6 (50 %)	14 (74 %)	$\chi^2 = 1.35$, $p = 0.29$
Education*	10 (2)	10 (2)	$t(25) = -0.24$, $p = 0.81$
Ethnicity†			
Australian	9 (69 %)	10 (53 %)	
Ethnic	4 (31 %)	9 (47 %)	$\chi^2 = 2.56$, $p = 0.14$

*Number of years of education comprising primary, secondary and tertiary.
†Both parents of ethnic origin = ethnic; one or both parents of Australian origin = Australian.

Table 12.3 Clinical characteristics for each group at baseline given as the mean (SD) or the number (%)

	Control ($n = 13$)	Intervention ($n = 19$)	Statistics
Presence of leg symptoms (n)	11 (85 %)	8 (42 %)	$\chi^2 = 5.80$, $p = 0.02$*
Presence of distal paraesthesia (n)	9 (69 %)	6 (32 %)	$\chi^2 = 4.40$, $p = 0.04$*
Pain drawing score	29 (15)	18 (17)	$t(30) = 1.74$, $p = 0.09$
Past lumbar surgery (n)	5 (45 %)	0 (0 %)	$\chi^2 = 9.90$, $p = 0.001$*
Medical specialist† (n)	13 (100 %)	19 (100 %)	$\chi^2 = 0.00$, $p = 1.00$
Duration of LBP (months)	12 (6 %)	8 (3 %)	$t(30) = 2.62$, $p = 0.01$*

*Significant difference between groups, $p < 0.05$.
†Those who have seen a medical specialist for their current episode of LBP.

Table 12.4 The mean (SD) of baseline and final ODQ and QDS scores

Dependent variable	Control group		Intervention group	
	Baseline	Final	Baseline	Final
ODQ	47.9 (13.6)	50.0 (14.0)	42.4 (15.0)	34.4 (19.5)
QDS	63.2 (15.5)	60.3 (17.3)	51.7 (18.2)	40.8 (24.7)

ODQ, Oswestry Low Back Pain Disability Questionnaire; QDS, Quebec Back Pain Disability Scale.

change in the QDS, there was no longer a significant difference between groups after adjusting for the influence of the covariates ($F(1,29) = 2.63$, $p = 0.12$).

The baseline and final median (interquartile range) scores of WS are presented in Table 12.5. There was no significant difference in baseline WS. However, a significant between-group difference favouring the intervention group was observed with final WS scores ($p = 0.003$).

Table 12.5 Baseline and final median (interquartile range) scores of work status

	Control	Intervention	Test
Baseline	5 (5–5)	5 (5–5)	$U = 114$, $p = 0.59$
Final	5 (4.8–5)	2 (1–5)	$U = 60$, $p = 0.003$*

*Significant difference between groups, $p < 0.05$ using the Mann-Whitney U test.

DISCUSSION

The results suggest a physiotherapy FR programme may be more effective in chronic compensable low back pain than patient-selected medical and paramedical treatment. These findings support other studies demonstrating that a physiotherapist-conducted FR is effective in reducing chronic LBP and disability (Frost et al., 1995; Lindström et al., 1992). Whilst some authors have found that with acute LBP a minimalist approach, where general practitioners encourage early return to function, is more effective than physiotherapy (Malmivaara et al., 1995), it appears that in chronic LBP a physiotherapy FR programme may result in superior outcomes compared to medical and paramedical management.

The current study supports other papers that demonstrate effective FR is not exclusively the domain of a multidisciplinary team (Frost et al., 1995; Lindström et al., 1992). Medical researchers continue to describe FR as being exclusively multidisciplinary (Hazard, 1995); however, this view is not justified in the literature or by the current study. It may be that a physiotherapy-based FR programme is a cost-effective option for individuals identified early as being at risk for development of chronicity (Frank et al., 1996).

The effect of the intervention on WS was comparable with other FR RCTs that showed a positive effect on vocational factors (Aberg, 1984; Lindström et al., 1992). In both of these studies, as well as the current study, generalisation of the positive effect of the FR programme to return to work was attempted. In other RCTs on FR a vocational focus was not mentioned. In these studies WS was not measured (Frost et al., 1995) or was not affected by the intervention (Alaranta et al., 1994). It appears that for WS to be affected by FR, a directive approach is necessary where return to work is supported and facilitated (Catchlove and Cohen, 1982).

There are significant methodological limitations in the present study. Due to the non-randomised nature of the study, subject characteristics not measured may have been unevenly distributed between the groups and may thus have affected the outcome. However, analysis of covariance did not affect the significance of the change in ODQ scores between the groups. The analysis of covariance did affect the significance of the change in QDS scores. However, given that there were four covariates included in the analysis, it is possible that the response of the QDS to covariate analysis was due to low sample size and resultant low power. In addition, each covariate was not related to the change in QDS scores. The literature was reviewed with regard to predictive ability of the clinical characteristics that were different between the groups. When examined in the context of the complete subject baseline profile, no evidence was found in the literature that suggested the differences between groups at baseline would have affected outcome (Burke et al., 1994; Cheadle et al., 1994; Dionne et al., 1997; Frymoyer, 1992; McCulloch, 1977; Wahlgren et al., 1997).

There were six subjects who withdrew from the study and for which final data were not available, and four of these were from the intervention group. In all but one of the subjects, the reason for withdrawal from the intervention group was not related to compliance or potential to respond to the intervention. It is therefore unlikely that withdrawal rates affected the outcome.

This study was designed as a pilot with a view to commencing a RCT on the physiotherapy FR programme. The results support the view that the cost of a large multi-centre RCT would be justified with the intervention described. Effect sizes were calculated for the ODQ and QDS and seen to be moderate in magnitude as defined by Cohen (1977). The QDS had a slightly higher effect size (0.50) compared to the ODQ (0.46). For future studies to have 80 per cent power to detect an effect size of this magnitude using two-tailed *t*-tests, approximately 60 subjects would be required in each group (Portney and Watkins, 1993).

Further research is required regarding diagnosis and classification of LBP. Whilst classification based on observable physical and psychosocial criteria allows meaningful sub-groups to be formed for clinical and research purposes, a more accurate identification of the physical and psychosocial nature of LBP would be useful. In this study it was anecdotally observed that certain subjects did not improve with the physiotherapy FR programme. Some of these subjects appeared to have severe internal disc disruption (Bogduk and Twommey, 1997), while others demonstrated overt inorganic behaviour and pain behaviour that limited their participation in the programme. Accurate identification of these subjects by physical pathology and/or non-physical screening tests would lead to more accurate identification of subject classifications specific for an intervention.

Further research needs to be completed regarding the optimal components of FR. This should be in the form of continued research regarding each component in isolation, as well as trials where the effect of each component and its interaction with other components are analysed. Components that do not have support from the outcome study literature or that do not have a theoretical rationale for their inclusion should be eliminated to simplify further research. Components included in this study include: aerobic and resistance exercise of a functional nature, lumbar stabilisation exercises, intensive erector spinae strength exercises, and cognitive behavioural principles. The question of which professionals are most suitable and cost-effective for conducting FR programmes also needs evaluation.

CONCLUSIONS

This study supports other research suggesting that a physiotherapy FR programme is more effective than patient-selected medical and paramedical treatment for chronic compensable LBP. Clinically and statistically, the difference between the groups, particularly in WS and ODQ, was highly significant. In addition, this study provides important information which might be used in planning a RCT evaluating a physiotherapist-conducted FR programme. The findings of this study should, however, be interpreted with caution due to the non-randomised quasi-experimental research design and potential for sampling bias. Additional questions requiring further research include the efficacy of the individual components of FR in isolation and in interaction trials and the efficacy of physiotherapy versus multidisciplinary FR.

References

Abenhaim, L. and Suissa, S. (1987). Importance and economic burden of occupational back pain: a study of 2,500 cases representative of Quebec. *Journal of Occupational Medicine*, **29**, 670–674.

Aberg, J. (1984). Evaluation of an advance back pain rehabilitation program. *Spine*, **9**, 317–318.

Alaranta, H., Rytokoski, U., Rissanen, A. et al. (1994). Intensive physical and psychosocial training program for patients with chronic low back pain. A controlled clinical trial. *Spine*, **19**, 1339–1349.

Altmaier, E.M., Lehmann, T.R., Russell, D.W., Weinstein, J.N. and Kao, C.F. (1992). The effectiveness of psychological interventions for the rehabilitation of low back pain: a randomised controlled trial evaluation. *Pain*, **49**, 329–335.

Bentsen, H., Lindgärde, F. and Manthorpe, R. (1997). The effect of dynamic strength back exercise and/or a home training program in 57-year-old women with chronic low back pain. *Spine*, **22**, 1494–1500.

Bergenudd, H. and Nilsson, B. (1988). Back pain in middle age; occupational workload and psychologic factors: an epidemiologic survey. *Spine*, **13**, 58–60.

Bermark, A. (1989). Stability of the lumbar spine; a study in mechanical engineering. *Acta Orthopaedica Scandinavica*, **230**, 20–24.

Bigos, S., Battie, M., Spengler, D. et al. (1992). A longitudinal, prospective study of industrial back injury reporting. *Clinical Orthopaedics and Related Research*, **279**, 21–34.

Block, A., Kremer, E. and Gaylor, M. (1980). Behavioural treatment of chronic pain: variables affecting treatment efficacy. *Pain*, **8**, 367–375.

Bogduk, N, and Twommey, L. (1997). *Clinical Anatomy of the Lumbar Spine and Sacrum*, 3rd edn. Churchill Livingstone.

Burke, S.A., Harms-Constas, K. and Aden, P.S. (1994). Return to work/work retention outcomes of a functional restoration program. A multi-center, prospective study with a comparison group. *Spine*, **19**, 1880–1886.

Burton, A., Tillotson, K. and Troup, J. (1989). Prediction of low back trouble frequency in a working population. *Spine*, **14**, 939–946.

Burton, A.K., Tillotson, K.M., Main, C.J. and Hollis, S. (1995). Psychosocial predictors of outcome in acute and subchronic low back trouble. *Spine*, **20**, 772–778.

Cheadle, A., Franklin, G., Wilfhagen, C. et al. (1994). Factors influencing the duration of work-related disability: a population-based study of Washington State workers' compensation. *American Journal of Public Health*, **84**, 190–196.

Cohen, J. (1977). Statistical Power for the Behavioral Sciences. Academic Press.

Coxhead, C., Inskip, H., Meade, T. and North, W. (1981). Multicentre trial of physiotherapy in the management of sciatic symptoms. *The Lancet*, **May 16**, 1965–1968.

Cresswell, A., Grundstrom, H. and Thorstensson, A. (1992). Observations on intra-abdominal pressure and patterns of abdominal intra-muscular activity in man. *Acta Physiology Scandinavia*, **144**, 409–418.

Croft, P.R., Papageorgiou, A.C., Ferry, S. et al. (1996). Psychologic distress and low back pain. Evidence from a prospective study in the general population. *Spine*, **20**, 2731–2737.

Cunningham, L. and Kelsey, J. (1984). Epidemiology of musculoskeletal impairments and associated disability. *American Journal of Public Health*, **74**, 574–579.

Cutler, R.B., Fishbain, D.A., Rosomoff, H.L. et al. (1994). Does nonsurgical pain center treatment of chronic pain return patients to work? A review and meta-analysis of the literature. *Spine*, **19**, 643–652.

Davies, J., Gibson, T. and Tester, L. (1979). The value of exercises in the treatment of low back pain. *Rheumatology and Rehabilitation*, **18**, 243–247.

Deyo, R., Walsh, N., Martin, D., Schoenfeld, L. and Ramamurthy, S. (1990). A controlled trial of transcutaneous electrical nerve stimulation (TENS) and exercise for chronic low back pain. *The New England Journal of Medicine*, **322**, 1627–1634.

Difabio, R., Mackey, G. and Holte, J. (1996). Physical therapy outcomes for patients receiving workers' compensation following treatment for herniated lumbar disc and mechanical low back pain syndrome. *Journal of Orthopedic and Sports Physical Therapy*, **32**, 180–187.

Dionne, C., Koepsel, T., Von Korff, M. et al. (1997). Predicting long-term functional limitations among back pain patients in primary care settings. *Journal of Clinical Epidemiology*, **50**, 31–43.

Elnaggar, I.M., Nordin, M., Sheikhzadeh, A., Parnianpour, M. and Kahanovitz, N. (1991). Effects of spinal flexion and extension exercises on low back pain and spinal mobility in chronic mechanical low back pain patients. *Spine*, **16**, 967–972.

Engel, G. (1982). The biopsychosocial model and medical education. *New England Journal of Medicine*, **306**, 802–805.

Fairbank, J., Couper, J., Davies, J. and O'Brien, J. (1980). The Oswestry Low Back Pain Disability Questionnaire. *Physiotherapy*, **66**, 271–273.

Fishbain, D., Cutler, R., Rosomoff, H. et al. (1996). "Movement" in work status after pain facility treatment. *Spine*, **21**, 2662–2669.

Fishbain, D., Rosomoff, H., Goldberg, M. et al. (1993). The prediction of return to the workplace after multidisciplinary pain center treatment. *The Clinical Journal of Pain*, **9**, 3–15.

Flores, L., Gatchel, R. and Polatin, B. (1997). Objectification of functional improvement after non-operative care. *Spine*, **22**, 1622–1633.

Fordyce, W., Brockway, J., Bergman, J. and Spengler, D. (1986). Acute back pain: a control-group comparison of behavioral vs traditional management methods. *Journal of Behavioral Medicine*, **9**, 127–140.

Fordyce, W., Fowler, R., Lehmann, J. et al. (1973). Operant conditioning in the treatment of chronic pain. *Archives of Physical Medicine and Rehabilitation*, **54**, 399–408.

Fordyce, W., McMahon, R., Rainwater, G. et al. (1981). Pain complaint: exercise performance relationship in chronic pain. *Pain*, **10**, 311–321.

Frost, H., Klaber Moffett, J.A., Moser, J.S. and Fairbank, J.C. (1995). Randomised controlled trial for evaluation of fitness programme for patients with chronic low back pain. *British Medical Journal*, **310**, 151–154.

Frank, J.W., Brooker, A., DeMaio, S.E. et al. (1996). Disability resulting from occupational low back pain. *Spine*, **21**, 2918–2929.

Frymoyer, J.W. (1992). Predicting disability from low back pain. *Clinical Orthopaedics and Related Research*, **279**, 101–109.

Hansen, F., Bendix, T., Skov, P. et al. (1993). Intensive, dynamic back-muscle exercises, conventional physiotherapy, or placebo-control treatment of low-back pain. *Spine*, **18**, 98–108.

Harding, V. and C de C Williams, A. (1995). Extending physiotherapy skills using a psychological approach: cognitive behavioural management of chronic pain. *Physiotherapy*, **81**, 681–688.

Hayes, B., Solyom, C., Wing, P. and Berkowitz, J. (1993). Use of psychometric measures and nonorganic signs testing in detecting nomogenic disorders in low back pain patients. *Spine*, **18**, 1254–1262.

Hazard, R. (1995). Spinal update functional restoration. *Spine*, **20**, 2345–2348.

Hides, J., Richardson, C. and Jull, G. (1995). The effect of specific postural holding exercises on lumbar multifidus muscle recovery in acute low back pain patients. *Proceedings of the World Confederation of Physical Therapists*, Washington, p. 984.

Hodges, P.W. and Richardson, C.A. (1997). Feed forward contraction of transversus abdominis is not influenced by the direction of arm movement. *Experimental Brain Research*, **114**, 362–370.

Johannsen, F., Remvig, L., Kryger, P. et al. (1995). Exercises for chronic low back pain: a clinical trial. *Journal of Orthopedic and Sports Physical Therapy*, **22**, 52–59.

Katon, W., Egan, K. and Miller, D. (1985). Chronic pain: lifetime psychiatric diagnoses and family history. *American Journal of Psychiatry*, **142**, 1156–1160.

Klenerman, L., Slade, P.D., Stanley, I.M. et al. (1995). The prediction of chronicity in patients with an acute attack of low back pain in a general practice setting. *Spine*, **20**, 478–484.

Kopec, J., Esdaile, J., Abrahamowicz, M. et al. (1995). The Quebec back pain disability scale. *Spine*, **20**, 141–152.

Lacroix, J.M., Powell, J., Lloyd, G.J. et al. (1990). Low back pain. Factors of value in predicting outcome. *Spine*, **15**, 495–499.

Lindström, I., Ohlund, C., Wallin, L., Peterson, L. and Nachemson, A. (1992). The effect of graded activity on patients with subacute low back pain : a randomised prospective clinical study with an operant-conditioning behavioral approach. *Physical Therapy*, **72**, 279–293.

Lockwood, S. (1996). How can physiotherapists influence chronic pain behaviour: negatively and positively. *New Zealand Journal of Physiotherapy*, **April**, 13–16.

MacFarlane, B., Edwards, P., Frank, C., Rangayyan, B. and Liu, Z.-Q. (1989). Quantification of collagen remodelling in healing non-immobilised and immobilised ligaments. *Transactions of Orthopaedic Research Society*, **14**, 300.

Malmivaara, A., Hakkinen, U., Aro, T. et al. (1995). The treatment of acute low back pain – bed rest, exercise, or ordinary activitiy? *The New England Journal of Medicine*, **332**, 351–355.

Manniche, C., Lundberg, E., Christensen, J., Bentzen, L. and Hesselsoe, G. (1991). Intensive dynamic back exercises for chronic low back pain: a clinical trial. *Pain*, **47**, 53–63.

Mattila, M., Hurm, M., Alaranta, H. et al. (1986). The multifidus muscle in patients with lumbar disc herniation: a histochemical and morphometric analysis of intraoperative biopsies. *Spine*, **11**, 732–738.

Mayer, T.G., Gatchel, R.J., Kishino, N. et al. (1985). Objective assessment of spine function following industrial injury; a prospective study with comparison group and one-year follow up. *Spine*, **10**, 482–493.

McCulloch, J. (1977). Chemonucleolysis. *Journal of Bone and Joint Surgery*, **59B**, 45–52.

Milhous, R.L., Haugh, L.D., Frymoyer, J.W. et al. (1989). Determinants of vocational disability in patients with low back pain. *Archives of Physical Medicine and Rehabilitation*, **70**, 589–593.

Naliboff, B., Cohen, M., Swanson, G., Bonebakker, A. and McArthur, D. (1985). Comprehensive assessment of chronic low back pain patients and controls: physical abilities, level of activity, psychological adjustments and pain perception. *Pain*, **23**, 121–134.

Nicholas, M., Wilson, P. and Goyen, J. (1991). Operant-behavioural and cognitive behavioural treatment for chronic low back pain. *Behavioural Research and Therapy*, **29**, 225–238.

O'Sullivan, P., Twomey, L. and Allison, G. (1997). Evaluation of specific stabilising exercise in the treatment of chronic low back pain with radiologic diagnosis of spondylolysis or spondylolisthesis. *Spine*, **22**, 2959–2967.

Panjabi, M., Abumi, K., Duranceau, J. and Oxland, T. (1989). Spinal stability and intersegmental muscle forces: a biomechanical model. *Spine*, **14**, 194–199.

Portney, L. and Watkins, M. (1993). *Foundations of Clinical Research: Applications to Practice*, 1st edn. Appleton and Lange.

Quebec Task Force (1987). Report of the Quebec Task Force on Spinal Disorders. *Spine*, **12**, European edition supplement 1, S1–S59.

Rainville, J., Sobel, J., Hartigan, C. and Wright, A. (1997). The effect of compensation involvement on the reporting of pain and disability by patients referred for rehabilitation of chronic low back pain. *Spine*, **22**, 2016–2024.

Rantanen, J., Hurme, M., Falck, B. et al. (1993). The lumbar multifidus muscle five years after surgery for a lumbar intervertebral disc herniation. *Spine*, **18**, 568–574.

Richardson, C. and Jull, G. (1995). An historical perspective on the development of clinical techniques to evaluate and treat the active stabilising system of the lumbar spine. *Australian Journal of Physiotherapy Monograph*, **1**, 5–14.

Riihimški, H., Viikari-Juntura, E., Moneta, G. et al. (1994). Incidence of sciatic pain among men in machine operating, dynamic physical work, and sedentary work. *Spine*, **19**, 138–142.

Salter, R. (1990). *The Biological Concept of Continuous Passive Motion of Synovial Joints: The First 18 Years of Basic Research and Its Clinical Application*. Raven Press.

Skovron M., Szpalski, M., Nordin, M., Melot, C. and Cukier, D. (1994). Sociocultural factors and back pain: a population based study in Belgian adults. *Spine*, **19**, 129–137.

Spratt, K.F., Weinstein, J.N., Lehmann, T.R., Woody, J. and Sayre, H. (1993). Efficacy of flexion and extension treatments incorporating braces for low-back pain patients with retrodisplacement, spondylolisthesis, or normal sagittal translation. *Spine*, **18**, 1839–1849.

Statistical Report. (1997). Victorian WorkCover Authority.

Turk, D. and Meichenbaum, D. (1989). A cognitive behavioural approach to pain management. In *Textbook of Pain*, 2nd edn (P. Wall and R. Melzack, eds). Churchill Livingstone.

Viikari-Juntura, E., Vuori, J., Silverstein, B.A. et al. (1991). A life long prospective study on the role of psychosocial factors in neck, shoulder and low back pain. *Spine*, **16**, 1056–1061.

Volinn, E. (1997). The epidemiology of low back pain in the rest of the world. *Spine*, **22**, 1747–1754.

Von Korff, M., Dworkin, S., Le Resche, L. and Kruger, A. (1988). An epidemiologic comparison of pain complaints. *Pain*, **32**, 173–183.

Von Korff, M., Dworkin, S. and Le Resche, L. (1990). Graded chronic pain status: an epidemiologic evaluation. *Pain*, **40**, 279–291.

Von Korff, M., Deyo, R., Cherki, D. and Barlow, W. (1993): Back pain in primary care: outcomes at 1 year. *Spine*, **18**, 855–862.

Waddell, G. (1987). A new clinical model for the treatment of low back pain. *Spine*, **12**, 632–654.

Wahlgren, D., Atkinson, J., Epping-Jordan, J. et al. (1997). One-year follow up of first onset low back pain. *Pain*, **73**, 213–221.

Wall, P. (1995). *Treatment of Pain*. Butterworth-Heinemann.

Walsh, K., Cruddas, M. and Coggon, D. (1992). Low back pain in eight areas of Britain. *Journal of Epidemiology and Community Health*, **46**, 227–230.

Wilke, H., Wolf, S., Claes, L., Arand, M. and Wiesend, A. (1995). Stability increase on the lumbar spine with different muscle groups. *Spine*, **20**, 192–198.

Wohlfahrt, D., Jull, G. and Richardson, C. (1993). The relationship between the dynamic and static function of abdominal muscles. *The Australian Journal of Physiotherapy*, **39**, 9–13.

Zetterberg, C., Gunnar, B., Andersson, J. and Schultz, A. (1987). The activity of individual trunk muscles during heavy physical loading. *Spine*, **12**, 1035–1040.

The effect of a supervised physical activity programme on persons with work-related low back injury

Elfreda D. Marshall, Martin Mackey, Roger Adams and Sandra K. Hunter

INTRODUCTION

Several rehabilitation research groups (Bendix et al., 1997; Burke et al., 1994; Faas et al., 1995; Frost et al., 1995; Hazard et al., 1989; Indahl et al., 1995; Kellett et al., 1991; Lindstrom et al., 1992; Linton et al., 1989; Mayer et al., 1987; Reilly et al., 1989) have independently reported on the efficacy of physical activity in the rehabilitation of patients with low back injury (LBI). These studies have included patients with acute, sub-acute and chronic LBI, and the degree of physical activity involved has ranged from advice (Indahl et al., 1995) to intensive supervision of the rehabilitation programme (Hazard et al., 1989; Mayer et al., 1987). The programmes have also varied in design, frequency and duration. Having reviewed the literature, Koes (1995) and Manniche (1996) have argued that, given the variety of methodologies, it is difficult to determine valid conclusions from the currently available findings. However, they did conclude that chronic LBI sufferers benefited most from a physical activity programme. This beneficial effect is supported by other studies (Berwick et al., 1989; Lindequist et al., 1984) that have reported limited positive effects on the recovery of sub-acute LBI and associated sick leave in patients who undertook a physical activity programme (PAP). The study reported here is the first to investigate the contribution of supervised PAPs to the rehabilitation of people with a work-related, compensable low back injury using an analytical design and within the Australian context.

METHODS

Subjects

The experimental group (EX) comprised fifty-eight volunteers with a non-specific low back injury who were drawn from six rehabilitation programmes in the Sydney metropolitan and Hunter regions of New South Wales (NSW) over a twenty-four month period. All subjects had been referred to an individual PAP supervised by a physiotherapist and funded by the relevant workers' compensation insurer. In order to be accepted for a workers' compensation claim in NSW the injury must be verified by a registered medical practitioner.

Inclusion criteria were: (1) subjects aged between 20 and 45 years; (2) compensable work-related non-specific low back injury; and (3) the injury incurred a minimum of eight weeks prior to inclusion in the study.

Subjects were excluded from the study if they had: (1) a verified herniated disc lesion appropriate for surgery; (2) defined orthopaedic (recent vertebral fracture), medical (tumour, inflammatory disease) or psychiatric disorders; (3) pregnancy; (4) known drug abuse (except nicotine abuse); and (5) time off work associated with back pain in the six months prior to the current injury. These criteria were similar to those reported elsewhere (Lindstrom et al., 1992). Procedures were approved by the University of Sydney Human Ethics Committee and informed consent was received from all subjects prior to participation in the study.

Control subjects (CO) were drawn from insurance company data and were matched with the EX for gender, age (within two years), date of low back injury (within three months) and initial time lost from work.

Physical activity programme

The EX participated in a supervised PAP. The common features of all programmes were that they were designed to improve the participant's flexibility, strength and endurance. The programmes were at least of fifty minutes' duration per session and undertaken for twelve sessions over a four week period. In order to meet the specific physical needs and abilities of the subjects without aggravation of injury, each of the PAPs was individually tailored by a registered physiotherapist. Participants were asked to record the intensity of their exercise using Borg's rate of perceived exertion (RPE) scale (Borg, 1970) and the mode of exercise performed during the supervised PAP in an exercise diary. Exercises performed external to the supervised sessions such as home exercises were also recorded and reported by the subjects.

Evaluation

Prior to participation in the PAP, the EX were interviewed for demographic and background information. This included: age; gender; level of education; current and previous employment; self-reported physical activity levels (National Heart Foundation, 1990); smoking and alcohol consumption history; and history of low back pain.

Self-reported pain and disability experienced by the EX were assessed prior to and at the completion of the programme, using scores compiled from the McGill Pain Questionnaire (Melzack, 1987) and Roland and Morris Questionnaire (RDQ) (Roland and Morris, 1983). The McGill Pain Questionnaire included three indicators of pain: (1) the short-form McGill Pain Questionnaire (SF-MPQ); (2) present pain intensity (PPI); and (3) a visual analogue scale (VAS). Both the McGill Pain Questionnaire and the RDQ have previously been reported as valid and reliable indicators of pain and disability (Beattie and Maher, 1997; Melzack, 1987; Roland and Morris, 1983).

The perceived commitment of each EX subject in the PAP was rated by the programme supervisor on a descriptive scale between 1 and 10. A score of 1 (the subject failed to complete the required sessions with little apparent reason) represented a very low degree of motivation and commitment. A score of 7 was indicative of full attendance but the participant appeared to take no responsibility for their rehabilitation. A score of 10 (total and full commitment to the PAP with completion of regular external exercise sessions; highly motivated) represented a very high commitment.

Twelve month monitoring period for sick leave and utilisation of medical services

The EX were given a data collection sheet and asked to record days off work due to back pain and visits to medical providers (doctors, physiotherapists, chiropractors etc.). Subjects were monitored on a monthly basis during the twelve month period following completion of the PAP to obtain records of sick leave and the utilisation of medical/physiotherapy services associated with recurrence of back pain. Sick leave and utilisation of medical/physiotherapy services were also recorded from insurance data for the matched CO over the same twelve month period.

Statistical analysis

Either an independent Student's *t*-test or a Mann-Whitney U non-parametric test was used to compare the EX and CO for: (1) sick leave; and (2) utilisation of medical services during the twelve month period following completion of the PAP. A Mann-Whitney U non-parametric test was used only in cases when there was non-homogeneous variance as indicated by a significant Levene test ($p < 0.05$). The results from all data are expressed as the mean $\pm$ SE and significance accepted at $p < 0.05$.

A paired *t*-test was used to compare the perceived pain and disability of the EX measured prior to and on completion of the PAP. Pearson-product moment correlations and stepwise linear regression analysis were used to assess the relationships between various independent variables with: (1) the initial time off work after back injury; and (2) return to work (RTW) outcomes, sick leave and utilisation of medical services for the EX.

RESULTS

Subject description

The characteristics of the EX subjects are shown in Table 12.6. Fifteen subjects withdrew during the course of the study: twelve subjects (20.7 per cent) failed to complete the PAP and a further three (5 per cent) withdrew during the twelve month monitoring period. Stepwise multiple regression showed that those subjects who had lower formal education were more likely to drop out during the course of the study ($r = 0.31$, $p < 0.05$).

Severity of injury effect

Severity of injury, as reflected by the initial time lost from work following LBI, was grouped into one of six categories: less than one week; one to two weeks; more than two to four weeks; more than four to thirteen weeks; more than thirteen to twenty-six weeks; and more than twenty-six weeks. Fifty-three per cent ($n = 30$) of the EX subjects had more than four weeks off work after LBI and 16 per cent ($n = 9$) had more than twenty-six weeks off work (Figure 12.1).

Stepwise multiple regression analysis was performed to identify whether any of the following factors were predictive of initial time off work: age; body mass index (BMI); gender; level of education; duration of employment; level of physical activity prior to injury; smoking history; consumption of alcohol; time between injury and rehabilitation; and time spent performing manual handling tasks during a typical work day. Analysis indicated that two factors significantly accounted for the 15 per cent variation in the initial time off work. Firstly, the proportion of time an individual reported performing manual tasks during a typical working day was directly associated with lost time ($p = 0.005$); and secondly, BMI was inversely associated with lost time ($p = 0.045$), in that subjects who were comparatively light for their height had more lost time.

Manual handling demands of employment

The average time EX subjects reported they had been employed in the occupation at the time of LBI was 7.1 ± 0.8 years (range of two months to twenty-eight years). The majority of subjects ($n = 54$; 93 per cent) reported that, prior to injury, they were required to perform some type of manual handling tasks (including pulling, pushing, lifting or carrying) during a typical day of employment (Figure 12.2).

There was a significant association between the per cent duration an EX subject spent performing manual tasks during a typical work day and the initial working days lost after LBI ($r = 0.35$, $p = 0.008$). Further analysis using an independent groups *t*-test indicated that those subjects who spent more than

Table 12.6 Subject characteristics of EX by gender (mean ± SE)

Characteristic	**Females ($n = 19$)**	**Males ($n = 39$)**	**Total ($n = 58$)**
Age (years)	31.0 ± 1.7	31.4 ± 0.9	31.2 ± 0.8
Weight (kg)	68.1 ± 2.7	84.9 ± 2.2	79.4 ± 2.0
Height (cm)	166 ± 0.01	176 ± 0.01	173 ± 0.01
BMI	24.7 ± 0.9	27.2 ± 0.56	26.4 ± 0.5

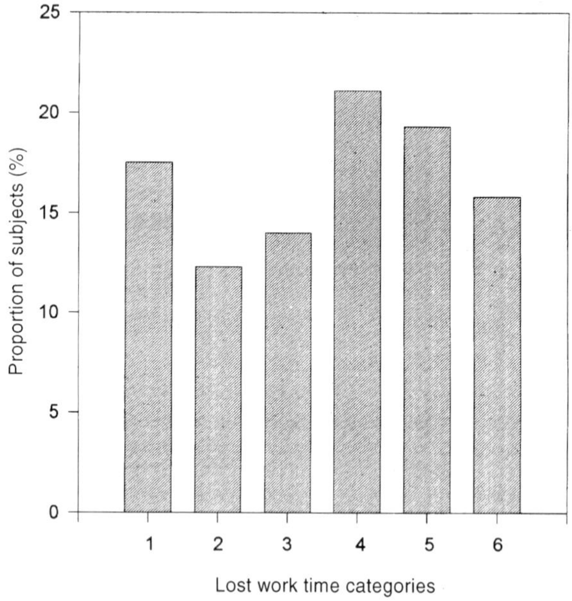

Figure 12.1 The work time initially lost by EX subjects after LBI. The relative numbers of subjects in each work time lost category ($n = 57$) are shown. Categories: 1, <1 week; 2, 1–2 weeks; 3, >2–4 weeks; 4, >4–13 weeks; 5, >13–26 weeks; 6, >26 weeks

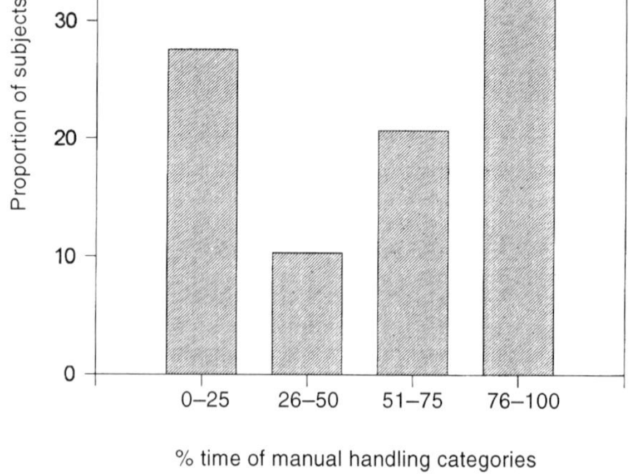

Figure 12.2 Relative time spent performing manual tasks by EX subjects during a typical work day ($n = 58$). The relative proportions of subjects are shown

50 per cent of their working day performing manual tasks ($n = 36$) had significantly more days lost after injury (category 4.1 ± 0.27) compared to those who spent less than 50 per cent of their working day performing manual tasks ($n = 22$, category 2.7 ± 0.34, $t = -3.1$, $p = 0.003$.

The physical activity programme

Twenty-five of the forty-six EX subjects who completed the PAP returned their exercise diaries. The mode and intensity of exercise performed during the PAP was self-reported and recorded in an exercise diary by twenty-one of these subjects. EX subjects exercised, on average, for 4 hours 12 ± 14 minutes per week and the supervised sessions represented 56.5 per cent of this time. Figure 12.3 shows the mean proportion of time and mode of exercise that the subjects performed when exercising at the supervised programme and externally (home). The mean duration of supervised sessions was 1 hour 11 minutes and most (77.5 per cent) of the supervised PAPs were performed at a moderate intensity (Table 12.7).

Commitment to the PAP

A rating of 8 or above, indicating high commitment, was assigned by the supervising physiotherapist to 78 per cent of the subjects (Figure 12.4). There was a moderate but significant association between those subjects who were more

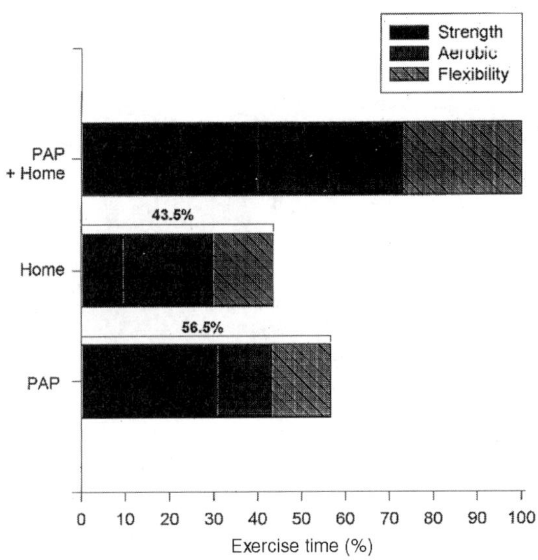

Figure 12.3 The proportional time of exercise mode during the supervised physical activity programme (PAP) and home/external exercises (Home). PAP + Home shows the proportional exercise time of PAP and Home exercises combined ($n = 21$)

Table 12.7 Intensity and proportion of aerobic and strength exercise time performed during the supervised PAP ($n = 21$)*

Intensity of exercise	Proportion of time	
	Aerobic (%)	**Strength** (%)
Low	19	11
Moderate	77	78
High	4	11
Total	100	100

*The intensities of exercises were self-reported using the Borg Scale (rate of perceived exertion scale, RPE) according to the following criteria: low = RPE 6–10; moderate = RPE 11–15; High = RPE 16–20. Flexibility was not assessed according to intensity.

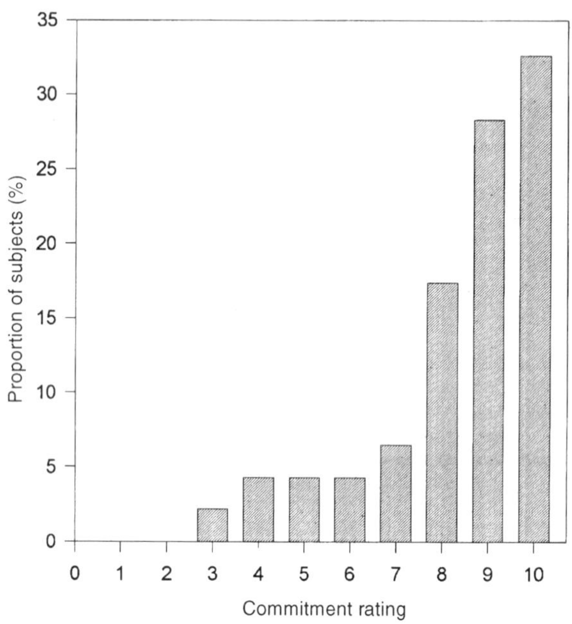

Figure 12.4 Commitment ratings of EX subjects to the PAP ($n = 46$). The relative numbers of subjects that scored in each category are shown

committed to the PAP and those who returned their exercise diary ($r = -0.35$, $p = 0.02$).

Perceived pain and disability pre- and post-PAP

Comparisons of pre- and post-PAP scores from the short-form McGill Pain Questionnaire (SF-MPQ), the visual analogue scale (VAS) and The Roland and

Table 12.8 Pain and disability scores* of EX subjects pre- and post-PAP ($n = 46$) (mean ± SE)

Variable	Pre-PAP	Post-PAP	Mean difference	*p* value
SF-MPQ	12.6 ± 1.3	9.2 ± 1.2	3.4	0.006
PPI	2.01 ± 0.16	1.68 ± 0.12	0.33	0.053
VAS	3.1 ± 0.26	2.3 ± 0.25	0.8	0.002
Disability	11.9 ± 0.74	9.8 ± 0.84	2.1	0.001

*The higher the score, the higher the pain or disability.
SF-MPQ, short-form McGill Pain Questionnaire; PPI, present pain intensity; VAS, visual analogue scale.

Morris Questionnaire (RDQ) using paired *t*-tests indicate that the EX subjects experienced significantly less pain and disability after completion of the PAP (Table 12.8). Present pain intensity (PPI) showed borderline significance.

Return to work (RTW)

On completion of the twelve month follow-up period the EX subjects were grouped into one of five RTW status categories (Figure 12.5). Fifty-one per cent had returned to their original occupation performing normal duties and hours. Only two EX subjects had not returned to work due to back injury.

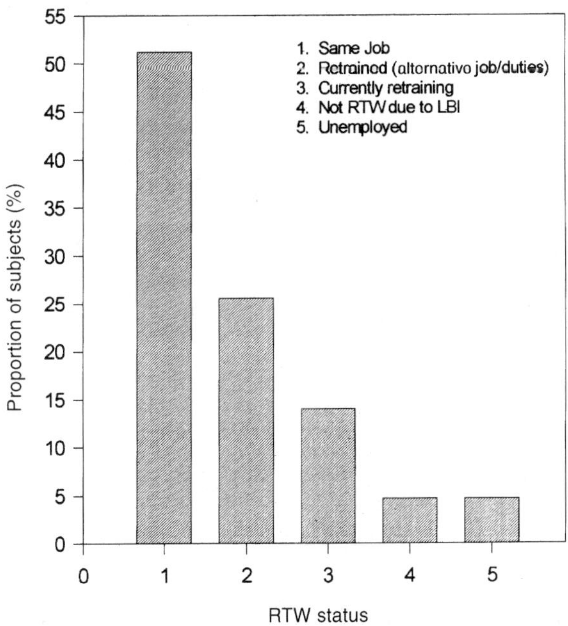

Figure 12.5 Return to work status of EX subjects after the twelve month monitoring period. The relative numbers of subjects ($n = 43$) are shown

There was a significant association between the initial work time lost due to LBI and the RTW status of the subject ($r = 0.37, p = 0.016$). This indicates that those EX subjects who had fewer initial days off work were more likely to return to work in a full-time capacity in the same employment.

Sick leave and utilisation of medical services

Sick leave and the utilisation of medical/physiotherapy services due to recurrence of LBI during the subsequent twelve months following programme completion were compared between the EX and the CO. Forty-three of the fifty-eight EX subjects initially interviewed were followed for twelve months after completing the PAP and twenty-nine of these were successfully matched with one to two control subjects. The EX had significantly less days off work due to back injury in the twelve month follow-up period when compared to CO ($p < 0.05$), but there was no significant difference between the groups on utilisation of medical services ($p = 0.436$) (Figure 12.6). Those EX subjects who had failed to return to work at the time of the twelve month follow-up were not included in the sick leave data.

DISCUSSION

The main findings of this study were that workers with LBI, who had participated in a four week supervised physical activity programme (PAP), had significantly less sick leave in the subsequent twelve month period but no difference in the utilisation of medical services when compared with a matched control group who

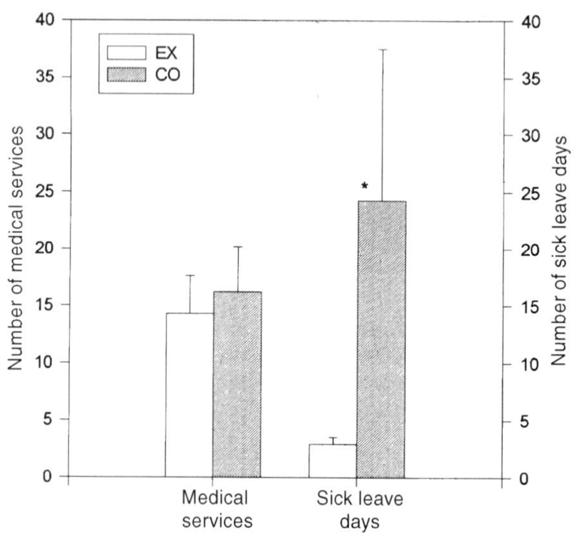

Figure 12.6 The number of medical services utilised and sick days taken due to LBI by EX and CO subjects during the twelve month monitoring period. The means ± SE are shown ($*p = 0 < 0.05$)

did not undertake a PAP. Furthermore, the reported pain and disability of the EX group was significantly less after the four weeks of the PAP.

The sick leave findings are consistent with other studies that implemented a PAP for those with LBI (Burke et al., 1994; Indahl et al., 1995; Lindstrom et al., 1992; Mayer et al., 1987). The reasons for the reduced sick leave cannot be determined but there are a number of possible explanations. Firstly, the LBI subjects who participated in the PAP increased their physical capacity and maintained this increase throughout the twelve month period, resulting in a greater work capacity and thus a reduction in sick leave. A further explanation is of psychological origin, in that the LBI subjects underwent an enhanced perceived coping capacity to work tasks. Thus, the experience of participating in the PAP with a LBI and discomfort shifted the subject's criteria for the amount of discomfort they were able to tolerate before taking sick leave. The marked differences in sick leave between the EX group and CO group may be related to the reduction in disability and perception of pain as reported by the EX group and also reported by other studies (Bendix et al., 1997; Frost et al., 1995). A third possibility is that subjects and controls did not represent the same population despite being matched for age, gender, and severity of injury as determined by the initial lost work time.

The similarity in the utilisation of medical services was consistent with findings for sub-acute LBI (Berwick et al., 1989; Lindequist et al., 1984). In the present study, given that the groups were matched for age, gender and initial time lost, the similar utilisation of medical services may indicate that there was little difference in the degree of pain and discomfort experienced between the EX and CO subjects – though, given the rationale for the sick leave results above, this explanation seems unlikely. Alternatively, it may indicate that the workers' compensation system in NSW demands utilisation of medical services for systematic review and continuation of the compensation benefits. Another study found that, in comparing the results of differing types of physical activity management, only those who undertook a very intensive physical activity programme (135 hours over six weeks) utilised health services less (Bendix et al., 1997). These investigators also showed that their subjects had less back pain and disability, took less analgesics and were more 'work ready', but did not have significantly less days off in the twelve month follow-up period.

Experimental group subjects in the present study demonstrated significant improvements in pain and disability measures at the completion of the PAP. One of these pain measures (PPI) showed only borderline significance and may indicate that it is a less sensitive measure of pain than the SF-MPQ and VAS. The overall findings of less pain and disability following a PAP are consistent with those reported by other investigators (Correy, 1994; Hazard et al., 1989; Kuukkanen and Malkia, 1996; Schofferman and Wasserman, 1994).

Improvements in pain and disability following a PAP may be due to a number of factors. Regular aerobic exercise is associated with increased production of pain-relieving endogenous opiates (Astrand, 1987). Alternatively, participation in regular physical activity may lead to improvement in overall sense of well-being and self-efficacy (Frost et al., 1995). For chronic pain sufferers, the experience of carrying out physical activity, which they previously did not think possible, may help reshape attitudes about their condition (Frost et al., 1995). Furthermore, patients who attribute their improvements to their own efforts are also less likely to relapse (Dolce et al., 1986). The beneficial effects of exercise appear to be augmented by supervision of the exercise process. It has been suggested that the 'exercise leader' plays a crucial role in extinguishing dysfunctional behaviours and provides reinforcement of healthy behaviours (Reilly et al., 1989).

Supervised programmes generally result in higher compliance (Reilly et al., 1989). Supervising physiotherapists in this study rated subjects on their commitment to the PAP. The maximum ranking on the commitment scale reflected not only compliance but also enthusiasm while participating in the programme, and a reported willingness to undertake physical activity in between scheduled sessions. Surprisingly, whilst 78 per cent of participants demonstrated high commitment to the programme only 54 per cent returned their exercise diaries. There may be a number of reasons to explain this apparent discrepancy. These include fear of misuse of documentation in any future legal proceedings, lack of confidence in written expression or non-compliance with external exercise requirements.

Experimental subjects were apparently more willing to do aerobic and flexibility activities than strengthening activities when not supervised. This highlights the need to have supervised programmes if strengthening is considered desirable. The commitment of subjects to their rehabilitation may reflect careful selection for the programme by the referring physiotherapists and/or a skilful ability to motivate on behalf of the programme supervisor.

There was a significant association between the initial time lost and the reported percentage of the working day spent performing manual handling tasks. This may indicate that, for those employed in jobs with high physical demands, the opportunities to return to work on restricted or alternative duties were less (Caruso et al., 1987). A significant association was also found between initial time lost and BMI. Those with lower BMI ratings had greater initial time lost. The average BMI ratings of the subjects investigated in this study fell within the normal Australian BMI range for both men (95 per cent CI 19.98–31.26) and women (95 per cent CI 18.34–32.1) (National Heart Foundation, 1990). If initial time lost is a measure of severity of injury, then the finding in relation to those with lower BMIs may indicate that they are sustaining more severe back injuries. It is hypothesised that severe back injuries may be associated with the performance of manual handling tasks in excess of the physical capacity of the workers.

Twenty-one per cent of the subjects dropped out of the exercise group and an additional three were lost to follow-up. The drop-out rate is similar to that reported by Burke et al. (1994) (20 per cent) and greater than those reported by Bendix et al. (1997) (17 per cent) and Frost et al. (1995) (12.3 per cent). It is probably also important to learn to predict those who will complete an exercise programme. In a multidisciplinary work rehabilitation programme for chronic low back pain, Carosella et al. (1994) found that those who were younger, out of work longer and with lower return to work expectations, and those with increased somatisation, pain intensity and disability, were more likely to drop out of the programme. It has also been reported that drop-out from rehabilitation is a predictor of long term chronicity and lower RTW rates (Snook and Webster, 1992).

This study found that, of the forty-three subjects who completed the twelve month follow-up, only two (4.7 per cent) had not returned to work at twelve months of follow-up due to back pain. Further, the significant association between the RTW status of the subjects twelve months after completion of the PAP and the initial time lost from employment indicates that those with a severe injury were less likely to return to work in their original full-time employment. There are a number of factors reported in the literature which predict successful RTW in LBI workers. Positive individual or demographic factors include workers with less personal and family-related problems (Hazard et al., 1989; Lancourt and Kettelhurt, 1992); those with lower anxiety over their injury (Hazard et al., 1989); those demonstrating greater compliance (Di-Fabio et al., 1995); and positive health beliefs (Szpalski et al., 1995). Job-related factors predictive of successful RTW include less job-related problems (Lancourt and Kettelhurt, 1992); flexible RTW arrangements such as availability of light or alternative duties (Lancourt and Kettelhurt, 1992; Snook and Webster, 1992); less heavy manual handling jobs (Caruso et al., 1987); and good labour relations at work (Padgett et al., 1993). Rehabilitation factors predictive of successful RTW include decreased time off work following injury, which was also found in this study (Dworkin et al., 1985; Lancourt and Kettelhurt, 1992; Robert et al., 1995; Snook and Webster, 1992); early intervention and referral to rehabilitation (Lechner, 1994; Lusted, 1993; Morrison, 1993; Ryan et al., 1995; Strautins and Hall, 1989); setting early RTW goals (Lechner, 1994); and participating in supervised graded physical activity programmes (Hazard et al., 1989; Mayer et al., 1987).

When drawing comparisons between this and other studies, consideration needs to be given to the description of the study populations in terms of such factors as distribution of gender and degree of chronicity in the subjects included and whether or not different studies represent the same group. For example, in the present study the ratio of female to male subjects was 12 (33 per cent female), which is representative of the WorkCover Authority of NSW's statistics (30 per cent female) (WorkCover, 1996). However, Bendix et al. (1997) used subjects with chronic back pain (defined as greater than three months since injury) and the ratio of females to males was 2 : 1 (62 per cent female), which is very different to the WorkCover Authority of NSW's statistics (WorkCover, 1996) or the study population described here. Lindequist et al. (1984) and Berwick et al. (1989) used a study population of subjects with sub-acute low back pain (greater than two weeks' duration), whereas Hazard et al. (1989) used subjects with low back injury of greater than nineteen months' duration. Hence, differing reported results of intervention for LBI may only reflect a lack of clear definition of the study population or a failure to consider this by the reader, rather than ambiguity in the findings.

In a similar vein, any comparison of studies needs to be cognisant of the fact that exercise routines vary enormously from what is essentially advice to 'keep moving' (Indahl et al., 1995) to intensive programmes of thirty-five hours for six weeks (Bendix et al., 1997; Hazard et al., 1989; Mayer et al., 1987). The cost implications of the more intensive programmes are large and such programmes may, with further study, prove to be only necessary in those who represent the small percentage (11 per cent) with compensable low back injury of greater than six months' duration, who also represent the major part (41 per cent) of the cost (WorkCover, 1996). Hence, a supervised PAP such as the type profiled in this study may prove to be all that is necessary for the majority of workers with low back injuries of more than six weeks' and less than six months' duration.

Malkia and Ljunggren (1996) claim a demonstrated beneficial effect of light exercise in those whose LBI has become chronic, but the beneficial effect is not as clearly apparent for those in the acute phase of the injury. Most low back injuries of less than six weeks' duration will recover regardless of the intervention (Plowman, 1992). The challenge presented is being able to accurately identify those that will not spontaneously recover so that early rehabilitation is provided to prevent the development of long-term chronicity.

CONCLUSIONS

The results of this study indicate that those investigated with chronic work-related low back injury obtain benefit from the incorporation of a four week supervised physical activity programme into their overall rehabilitation programme. This study confirms previous ones investigating the effects of exercise in rehabilitation of work-related LBI but is the first to do so in an Australian population. Specifically, this study demonstrated that NSW workers aged between twenty and forty-five years with non-specific LBI acquired a minimum of eight weeks earlier, have significantly less sick leave in the twelve months following programme completion. The study also confirms that the EX group reported significantly less pain and disability following completion of the physical activity programme.

ACKNOWLEDGEMENTS

This study was funded by WorkCover Authority NSW, Australia. The authors thank the MMI Insurance Group, Sydney, NSW for their support and assistance in completing the data collection for the study.

References

Astrand, P.O. (1987). Exercise physiology and its role in disease prevention and in rehabilitation. *Archives of Physical Medicine and Rehabilitation*, **68**, 305–308.

Beattie, P. and Maher, C. (1997). The role of functional status questionnaires for low back pain. *Australian Journal of Physiotherapy*, **43**, 29–38.

Bendix, A.F., Bendix, T., Lund, C. et al. (1997). Comparison of three intensive programs for chronic low back pain patients: a prospective, randomised, observer-blinded study with one year follow-up. *Scandinavian Journal of Rehabilitation Medicine*, **29**, 81–89.

Berwick, D., Budman, S. and Feldstein, M. (1989). No clinical effect of back school in an HMO: a randomised prospective trial. *Spine*, **14**, 338–344.

Borg, G. (1970). Perceived exertion as an indicator of somatic stress. *Scandinavian Journal of Rehabilitation Medicine*, **2**, 92–98.

Burke, S.A., Harms-Constas, C.K. and Aden, P.S. (1994). Return to work/work retention outcomes of a functional restoration program. *Spine*, **19**, 1880–1886.

Carosella, A.M., Lackner, J.M. and Feuerstein, M. (1994). Factors associated with early discharge from a multidisciplinary work rehabilitation program for chronic low back pain. *Pain*, **57**, 69–76.

Caruso, I.A., Chan, D.E. and Chan, A. (1987). The management of work-related back pain. *American Journal of Occupational Therapy*, **41**, 112–117.

Correy, J.R. (1994). Outcomes of a functional restoration program for chronic benign low back pain. *Australian Faculty of Rehabilitation Medicine: Second Annual Scientific Meeting, Adelaide*.

Di-Fabio, R.P., Mackey, G. and Holte, J.B. (1995). Disability and functional status in patients with lower back pain receiving workers' compensation: a descriptive study with implications for the efficacy of physical therapy. *Physical Therapy*, **75**, 180–193.

Dolce, J.J., Croker, M.F., Moletteire, C. et al. (1986). Exercise quotas, anticipatory concern and self efficacy expectations in chronic pain: a preliminary report. *Pain*, **24**, 365–372.

Dworkin, R.H., Handlin, D.S., Richlin, D.M. et al. (1985). Unraveling the effects of compensation, litigation, and employment on treatment response in chronic pain. *Pain*, **23**, 49–59.

Faas, A., Eijk, J.T.Mv., Chavannes, A.W. et al. (1995). A randomised trial of exercise therapy in patients with acute low back pain. *Spine*, **20**, 941–947.

Frost, H., Klaber-Moffet, J.A., Moser, J.S. et al. (1995). Randomised control trial for the evaluation of a fitness program for patients with chronic low back pain. *British Medical Journal*, **310**, 151–154.

Hazard, R.G., Fenwick, J.W., Kalisch, S.M. et al. (1989). Functional restoration with behavioural support. *Spine*, **14**, 157–161.

Indahl, A., Velund, L. and Reikeraas, O. (1995). Good prognosis for low back pain when left untampered: A randomised clinical trial. *Spine*, **20**, 473–477.

Kellett, K.M., Kellett, D.A. and Nordholm, L.A. (1991). Effects of an exercise program on sick leave due to back pain. *Physical Therapy*, **71**, 283–293.

Koes, B.W., Bouter, L.M., Beckerman, H. et al. (1991). Physiotherapy exercises and back pain: a blinded review. *British Medical Journal*, **302**, 1572–1576.

Kuukkanen, T. and Malkia, E. (1996). Muscular performance after a 3 month progressive physical exercise program and 9 month follow-up in subjects with low back pain. *Scandinavian Journal of Medicine and Science in Sports*, **6**, 112–121.

Lancourt, J. and Kettelhurt, M. (1992). Predicting return to work for lower back pain patients receiving workers' compensation. *Spine*, **17**, 629–638.

Lechner, D.E. (1994). Work hardening and work conditioning interventions: Do they affect disability? *Physical Therapy*, **74**, 471–493.

Lindequist, S., Lundberg, B., Wikmark, R. et al. (1984). Information and regime at low back pain. *Scandinavian Journal of Rehabilitation Medicine*, **16**, 113–116.

Lindstrom, I., Ohlund, C., Eek, C. et al. (1992). The effect of graded activity on patients with subacute low back pain: a randomised prospective clinical study with an operant-conditioning behavioural approach. *Physical Therapy*, **72**, 279–293.

Linton, S.J., Bradley, L.A., Jensen, I. et al. (1989). The secondary prevention of low back pain: a controlled study with follow-up. *Pain*, **36**, 197–207.

Lusted, M. (1993). Predicting return to work after rehabilitation for low back injury. *Australian Journal of Physiotherapy*, **39**, 203–210.

Malkia, E. and Ljunggren, A.E. (1996). Exercise programs for subjects with low back disorders. *Scandinavian Journal of Medicine and Science in Sports*, **6**, 73–81.

Manniche, C. (1996). Clinical benefit of intensive dynamic exercises for low back pain. *Scandinavian Journal of Medicine and Science in Sports*, **6**, 82–87.

Mayer, T.G., Gatchel, R.J., Mayer, H. et al. (1987). A prospective two-year study of functional restoration in industrial low back injury. *Journal of the American Medical Association*, **258**, 1763–1767.

Melzack, R. (1987). The short-form McGill Pain Questionnaire. *Pain*, **34**, 191–197.

Morrison, M.H. (1993). Rehabilitation and return to work. Do other countries succeed? *Work*, **3**, 48–54.

National Heart Foundation Risk Prevalence Study (No. 3) (1989). National Heart Foundation.

Padgett, M., Hollander, E.C., Warden, L. et al. (1993). Evaluation of a model return-to-work program in Texas. *Work*, **3**, 21–41.

Plowman, S.A. (1992). Physical activity, physical fitness, and low back pain. In *Exercise and Sport Science Reviews*, Vol. 20 (J.O. Holloszy, ed.), pp. 221–242. Williams and Wilkins.

Reilly, K., Lovejoy, B., Williams, R. et al. (1989). Differences between a supervised and independent strength and conditioning program with chronic low back syndromes. *Journal of Occupational Medicine*, **31**, 547–550.

Robert, J.J., Blide, R.W., McWhorter, K. et al. (1995). The effects of a work hardening program on a cardiovascular fitness and muscular strength. *Spine*, **20**, 1187–1193.

Roland, M. and Morris, R. (1983). A study of the natural history of back pain. Part I: Development of a reliable and sensitive measure of disability in low-back pain. *Spine*, **8**, 141–144.

Ryan, W.E., Krishna, M.K. and Swanson, C.E. (1995). A prospective study evaluating early rehabilitation in preventing back pain chronicity in mine workers. *Spine*, **20**, 489–491.

Schofferman, J. and Wasserman, S. (1994). Successful treatment of low back pain and neck pain after a motor vehicle accident despite litigation. *Spine*, **19**, 1007–1010.

Snook, S.H. and Webster, B.S. (1992). The effectiveness of a standardised treatment protocol in reducing disability from low back pain. *International Scientific Conference of Work-related Musculoskeletal Disorders, Stockholm*.

Strautins, P. and Hall, W. (1989). Does early referral to an on-site rehabilitation program predict an early return to work? *Journal of Occupational Health and Safety*, **5**, 137–143.

Szpalski, M., Nordin, M., Skovron, M.L. et al. (1995). Health care utilization for low back pain in Belgium: Influence of sociocultural factors and health beliefs. *Spine*, **20**, 431–442.

WorkCover Authority (1996). Back injuries: statistical profile 1994/95 for New South Wales Workers' Compensation. WorkCover New South Wales.

Chapter 13

Pre-placement assessments

Appropriateness of pre-placement assessments

David Worth

In any judgement of a person's capacity to work, both the physical and aptitudinal capacities of the person and demands of the job must be taken into consideration. For a person to be judged capable of performing the job safely, the person's capacities must be equal to or greater than the job demands. Sections 19, 20, 21 and 22 of the Occupational Health, Safety and Welfare Act 1986 in South Australia require that an employer shall ensure, so far as is reasonably practical, that each employee whilst at work is safe from injury and risks to health, and in particular shall provide and maintain a safe working environment, safe systems of work and plant and substances in a safe condition. This implies that, so far as is reasonably practicable, there is an obligation on the employer to ensure that the employee under consideration for a job has the capacity to perform the job safely with every effort of the employer to provide a safe working environment.

Premium structures and proposed premium structures for workers' compensation cover in South Australia have resulted in the following employer responses:

- Careful selection of recruits.
- Maintenance of present but ageing workforce.
- Increasing preference for contract labour hire.
- Tendency to reduce recruitment and employment with increasing staff rationalisation.

Employers are, therefore, increasingly using pre-placement assessments which determine a job applicant's capacity to safely perform the job. To fulfil this requirement, pre-placement assessments must contain:

- Analysis of physical and mental job demands.
- Interview and analysis of general health and medical history.
- Measurement of physical capacity.
- Clinical examination of neuromusculoskeletal systems, including special job-specific tests.

- General health assessment.
- Comparison of capacity to job demands.

The Rankin occupational safety and health (ROSH) pre-placement assessment consists of three parts:

1. A Key Method job placement assessment, which involves a number of physical functional activity tasks – within the person's own capacity, by a ROSH physiotherapist.
2. A ROSH clinical pre-placement assessment involving a short physical examination and review of medical and health details by a physiotherapist.
3. Assessment of hearing (in a sound-proof booth), vision (using a vision screening machine) and blood pressure, and urinalysis by registered occupational health nurses.

A person's perceived capacity to perform the job depends upon the assessor having access to and detailed knowledge of all of the job demands of the specific job for which the applicant is applying.

The results of the pre-placement assessment of the applicant are then matched against the job demands using the same range of values on the same range of variables.

Pre-placement assessment outcomes fall into three categories, namely red, yellow and green, as described below:

- Red: Candidate demonstrated unsafe postures, weights, elevated heart rates or physical capacities less than the job demands.
- Yellow: Candidate intermittently demonstrated unsafe postures, weights or elevated heart rates.
- Green: Candidate demonstrated safe postures, weights and heart rates and met job demands.

This form of assessment is more expensive than the traditional pre-employment medical as it takes longer to perform and contains a greater number and variety of tests and assessment protocols. However, initial results indicate a high level of cost effectiveness with significant reduction in the number of injuries and incidents in new employees in the first twelve months of employment.

RESULTS

In a fortuitous retrospective study by Key International, reported at the World Congress of Physical Therapy (WCPT), Washington in 1995, a total of 226 employees of the Minnesota Department of Transport were studied. Each subject had undergone a Key Method job placement assessment and, despite the results of the assessment, for unknown reasons all applicants had been employed. Of the 226 subjects, twenty-four (10.6 per cent) were assessed in the red group, ninety-four (41.6 per cent) in the yellow group and 108 (47.8 per cent) in the green group. Of those assessed in the red group, 41.7 per cent sustained an injury, in the yellow group 13.8 per cent sustained an injury and in the green group only 10.2 per cent sustained an injury. The differences between the three groups were statistically significant.

In a study of seventy-five applicants who undertook the ROSH pre-placement assessment under instructions from a single employer, forty-nine were employed, fourteen were not employed and twelve were hired but left employment shortly after they had started. After seven months of employment, two of the forty-nine reported an injury (4.1 per cent of employed applicants). Only the applicants who were classified in the green group were hired by this employer.

In the case of the second employer, 105 applicants who were assessed in the green group were hired and none of these employees reported injuries in the first eight months of their employment.

Comparisons between the fortuitous study of employees at the Minnesota Department of Transport and the two employee groups who underwent the ROSH pre-placement assessment indicate similar results, confirming a reasonable level of reliability and predictability in this form of assessment.

CONCLUSIONS

Injuries occur at the place of interaction between workers who sustain the injuries and the work hardware and environment. There is a contribution from both sides of this interaction and it is appropriate to consider the person's capacity and ways in which the work hardware and environment may be modified when considering this capacity to safely perform the job. If this is considered equitably along with the specific job demands, it is unlikely that a person considered not to possess the capacity to safely perform the job despite every possible job adaptation will be considered discriminated against. Therefore it is essential that the pre-placement assessment is always directed towards the person's capacity to perform a specific job safely and is not used to test a person's maximum capacity or any other capacity other than that to perform the specific job for which the person is applying.

This form of assessment is, therefore, cost effective and protects an applicant from potential injury. This form of assessment assists an employer in recognising where it is reasonable to modify jobs and adapt them to the specific requirements of workers.

References

Key, G.L. (1995). *The Productive Ability of a Job Placement Assessment.* WCPT.

The role of aerobic and general fitness in pre-placement assessment

Janet Baines

INTRODUCTION

A review of the literature has revealed a large number of articles written on the use of pre-placement assessment in the screening for potential low back problems but nothing as to its use for screening of other musculoskeletal problems.

Pre-placement assessment has been used in industry in an attempt to lessen the problems due to back injuries. Back problems are a major health and economic concern in the industrialised nations of the world. Accumulated losses to industry are huge in terms of lost production time, decreased output, increased insurance premiums, reduced efficiency and the indirect costs of rehabilitation, retraining and restaffing. In addition, of course, there is the cost to the individual. Battie et al. (1989a) stated that back problems are the most expensive health problem in the thirty to fifty age group and the leading cause of activity limitation in adults under forty-five years. Back pain has become a very expensive workers' compensation problem.

Yu et al. (1984), in a review of the literature, stated that there were two options for the prevention of back injuries in industry: medical screening and ergonomic intervention at the work site – to this can be added training and education.

A review of the epidemiological research on the risk factors of low back pain by Hildebrant in 1987 concluded that the following factors are of importance as individual risk factors:

- Age and its associated degenerative changes in the tissues.
- Relative muscle strength.
- Physical fitness.
- Low back complaints in the past.
- Psychological problems.
- Work experience.

PHYSICAL FITNESS

In the pre-placement assessment we can look at the health-related components of physical fitness:

- cardiorespiratory function

- body composition
- strength
- flexibility.

CARDIOVASCULAR FITNESS

Aerobic fitness is determined by VO_2max, which is the maximum rate at which the body can use oxygen during exercise. For practical purposes, the maximum test is not always appropriate and sub-maximal tests are used. The subject is exercised at a pre-set level and extrapolations are made from normative tables to estimate oxygen uptake.

Pope et al. (1996), in a study involving army personnel, found that aerobic fitness was a strong indicator of injury risk. Those who enter training programmes with low level fitness have much higher injury rates than fitter people.

Bigos and Battie (1987), in a prospective study involving 3020 aircraft manufacturing employees, found that there was a statistically significant lower fitness level in subjects who developed chronic disabling back pain as compared with age- and sex-matched controls. Battie et al. (1989a), in a further analysis of this same worker group, found that men with a history of back pain were more likely to have been excluded from cardiovascular testing due to characteristics that may have put them at risk. Cady et al. (1979) reported on a prospective study of fitness and subsequent back problems in fire-fighters. They found that those with greater fitness were at less risk of back problems, had fewer recurrences and less costly claims. The fittest group had one-tenth the injury rate of the least fit group. Fitness was defined by a composite score of strength, flexibility and cardiovascular fitness measures. Cady, in a follow-up study reporting on the results of fourteen years' experience with a fitness programme, reported a 25 per cent decrease in workers' compensation costs, with the greatest decrease in the number of disabling injuries. This result was predominantly due to improved cardiovascular fitness, as there were only very slight changes in flexibility and strength.

While a poor cardiovascular fitness level may not be a stand-alone risk factor for having an episode of back pain, it may affect the response and recovery time.

SMOKING

Battie et al. (1989b) found that workers who smoked were significantly more likely to subsequently suffer a low back problem than non-smokers. The relative risk for a smoker to report a back injury was 1.4 times that of a non-smoker in the follow-up period. They also found that smoking was a risk factor for chronic back pain disability.

Boshuizen et al. (1992), in a study involving 4054 male blue collar workers, aged twenty-five to fifty-five years, found a causal relationship between smoking and pain in all joints, not just to pain in the back. Frymoyer et al. (1983), in a survey of 1221 men, found that those with severe back pain were more likely to be smokers and had a greater tobacco consumption as measured by the number of cigarettes smoked per day and the number of years of exposure.

FLEXIBILITY

Troup et al. (1987) studied 2500 British workers and reported a statistically significant difference between lesser spinal flexibility in the sagittal plane (flexion less than extension) and reports of back problems in a follow-up year. Biering-Sorensen (1984) found that reduced spinal flexibility was more pronounced in subjects who experienced a recurrence of back pain in the year following examination. Contrary to Troup et al., he found that flexion was the most restricted movement. Cady, in his study, also reported an association between reduced flexibility and subsequent work-related back injury reports.

Battie et al. (1990) reported that subjects who had received prior treatment for back problems or had current symptoms on examination had less flexibility. They stated that flexibility measures by themselves do not affect the risk of future industrial back pain, but are related to prior back problems.

LIFTING STRENGTH

A large number of studies report a positive relationship between back strength and low back pain. Greater strength had been associated with greater physical ability and a reduced tendency for low back problems. Isometric strength testing has proved to be of value in job simulation. Chaffin (1978) tested 551 employees prior to their assignment to new jobs. He found that a worker's likelihood of sustaining a back injury increased when the job lifting requirements approached or exceeded the worker's strength capability as demonstrated on isometric simulation of the job. Snook (1987) states that the probability of a musculoskeletal disorder is up to three times greater when the lifting requirements of the job approach or exceed the worker's isometric strength capability. Battie et al. (1989b) examined isometric lifting strength in 2178 subjects in three standard lifting positions. They found that strength values decreased with age in both males and females in torso and leg lifts, and for men only in the arm lift. In this study they found that general isometric lifting strength testing was ineffective in identifying individuals at risk of industrial back problems. However, the authors acknowledge that their testing was not related to a specific job and state that a mismatch between strength and job demands may be a factor in back pain complaints.

Biering-Sorensen (1984), in a study of 449 men and 479 women, showed that men who experienced low back pain for the first time had lower isometric endurance of their back muscles when measured up to one year before the episode of pain. This trend was not repeated in women. He concluded that good isometric endurance of the back musculature seemed to prevent low back pain in men. Snook also stated that high isometric trunk strength and endurance are related to lower levels of musculoskeletal injury.

Jorgensen and Nicolaisen (1987) examined a group of fifty-three male postal workers and concluded that back extensor muscle strength was of no prognostic value for the subsequent development of back pain, but that those with earlier attacks of back pain had less endurance on isometric testing.

GENERAL FITNESS

Battie et al. (1990) found that a history of back symptoms requiring treatment in the previous ten years was a significant predictor of future back pain and that straight leg raise reproducing back pain was the best predictor. They also stated that height, weight (body mass index) and scoliosis displayed tendencies of being risk factors of low back pain. Bigos et al. (1987) also stated that the strongest variable for predicting subsequent back injury was previous or current back problems. Troup et al. (1987) found prior back pain to be the best predictor of future problems but that its predictive value was enhanced by other test results of reduced flexibility, reduced cardiovascular fitness and reduced lifting strength, both static and dynamic.

Fuortes et al. (1994), reviewing 100 back injury workers' compensation records from a large hospital, of which 90 per cent were women, found obesity (BMI > 25) to be a risk factor for back injury. They also stated that previous back injury was a significant risk factor and that any previous occupational injury was a risk factor for subsequently developing a low back injury.

Orvieto et al. (1994) examined the association between body mass index and the prevalence of low back pain in a quarter of a million male army recruits aged seventeen to eighteen years. They found a statistically significant association between low back pain and increased body mass index.

Bigos et al. (1990), in their long-term study of employees at the Boeing Company, found a statistically significant difference in fitness levels between subjects who developed disabling back problems of at least three months' duration and their sex- and age-matched controls.

CONCLUSIONS

To be used effectively, pre-placement testing must be related to a specific job. The testing should cover medical history, a full musculoskeletal examination, cardiovascular fitness, body composition, flexibility and strength to give an overall picture as to the worker's ability to perform a specific job. Pre-placement testing has a role in detecting individuals who are grossly mismatched to the work duties involved.

Low back injuries in the workplace are a major economic and health concern in industrialised countries. A comprehensive programme is required to control these injuries. This should encompass pre-placement testing, training and ergonomics – no single component will solve the problem. Pre-placement testing can contribute to reducing low back injury in industry by its use in the selection of workers for jobs that are difficult to design and control. However, it must not be used as a replacement for training and ergonomic intervention at the work site.

References

Battie, M., Bigos, S., Fisher, L. et al. (1989a). A prospective study of the role of cardiovascular risk factors and fitness in industrial back pain. *Spine*, **14** (2), 141–147.

Battie, M., Bigos, S., Fisher, L. et al. (1989b). Isometric lifting strength as a predictor of industrial back pain reports. *Spine*, **14** (8), 851–856.

Battie, M., Bigos, S., Fisher, L. et al. (1990). Anthropometric and clinical measures as predictors of back pain complaints in industry. *Journal of Spinal Disorders*, **3** (3), 195–204.

Biering-Sorensen, F. (1984). Physical measurements as risk indicators for low back trouble over a one year period. *Spine*, **9**, 106–119.

Bigos, S. and Battie, M. (1987). Preplacement worker testing and selection considerations. *Ergonomics*, **30** (2), 249–251.

Boshuizen, H., Verbeek, J., Broesen, J. et al. (1992). Do smokers get more back pain? *Spine*, **18** (1), 35–40.

Cady, L., Bischoff, D., O'Connell, E. et al. (1979). Strength and fitness and subsequent back injuries in firefighters. *Journal of Occupational Medicine*, **21** (4), 269–272.

Chaffin, D., Herrin, G. and Keyserling, W. (1978). Pre-employment strength testing. *Journal of Occupational Medicine*, **20** (6), 403–408.

Frymoyer, J., Pope, M., Clements, J. et al. (1983). Risk factors in low-back pain. *Journal of Bone and Joint Surgery*, **65A** (2), 213–218.

Fuortes, L., Shi, Y., Zhang, M. et al. (1994). Epidemiology of back injury in university hospital nurses from review of workers' compensation records and a case-control survey. *Journal of Occupational Medicine*, **36** (9), 1022–1026.

Hildebrant, V. (1987). A review of epidemiological research on risk factors of low back pain. In *Musculoskeletal Disorders at Work* (P. Buckle, ed.), pp. 9–16. Taylor and Francis.

Jorgensen, K. and Nicolaisen, T. (1987). Trunk extensor endurance: determination and relation to low-back trouble. *Ergonomics*, **30** (2), 259–267.

Orvieto, R., Rand, N., Lev, B. et al. (1994). Low back pain and body mass index. *Military Medicine*, **159**, 37–39.

Pope, R., Herbert, R., Kirwan, J. et al. (1996). A randomised trial to determine whether pre-exercise stretching prevents injury. In *Proceedings of the 1996 National Physiotherapy Congress*, p. 193.

Snook, S. (1987). Approaches to preplacement testing and selection of workers. *Ergonomics*, **30** (2), 241–247.

Troup, J., Foreman. T., Baxter, C. et al. (1987). The perception of back pain and the role of psychological tests of lifting capacity. *Spine*, **12** (7), 645–657.

Yu, T., Roht, L., Wise, R. et al. (1984). Low-back pain in industry. *Journal of Occupational Medicine*, **26** (7), 517–524.

Chapter 14

On-site injury management

On-site injury management and prevention

David Worth

ABILITY MANAGEMENT: PLACEMENT AND PREVENTION

Prevention commences with a detailed knowledge of jobs performed at an enterprise and the physical, aptitudinal and psychological demands of those jobs prior to a job offer being made to an applicant. In order to maximise safety and prevention, it is then essential that both the job applicant and the enterprise itself are fully aware that the applicant is safely capable of performing all tasks within the job and all elements of the tasks. Therefore, an appropriate pre-placement assessment is conducted as the first part of primary prevention of occupational injury and illness. Pre-placement assessment of applicants for jobs must be performed strictly in accordance with the requirements of all equal opportunity and discrimination legislation. The purpose of such a pre-placement assessment is only to determine whether or not the applicant possesses the physical, psychological and aptitudinal abilities to meet the job demands.

Once the job offer is accepted following the pre-placement assessment, recommendations arising from the pre-placement assessment, such as the need for intensive training in safe manual handling skills and safe use of body mechanics, will be made. This may be part of induction training and/or further ongoing education and training, requiring the enterprise to have a well-developed education and training programme, managed by skilled trainers.

Many jobs have high levels of physical demand in terms of the intensity of the loads handled, and the frequency and/or duration of task performance, and the job may be performed at a rate driven by the production through-put. Therefore, the enterprise should introduce a new worker to the job on a graduated basis, allowing ability management work conditioning.

In cases where the applicant may not be able to safely perform the job because of specific impairments, job method and process modifications will be made by the enterprise to ensure that the applicant may perform the task with minimal, if any, risk of aggravating the symptoms or exacerbating the condition related to the impairment.

ON-SITE PROGRAMMES

Programmes for injury and illness management and prevention commence with hazard identification both before and after recruitment. Before recruitment an 'occupational dictionary', consisting of job descriptions including the results of job analysis and listing all of the physical, aptitudinal and psychological demands of all the jobs at the enterprise, is created. Pre-placement assessment of all applicants takes place, measuring the capacity of the applicant to meet the job demands. The occupational dictionary is revised every six months or when it is known that a specific job has been altered. Induction training, health promotion, fitness and job performance training is undertaken, leading to safe workers and a safe workplace.

Hazard identification is undertaken by industrial physiotherapists with qualifications, skills and experience in ergonomics, biomechanics, sports medicine and manipulative physiotherapy. Recommendations on hazard controls, ergonomics, occupational safety, health and hygiene and job method and process modifications are made and followed through with ongoing contact with the enterprise's occupational safety, health and welfare management team. The physiotherapist attends the work site on a regular basis and maintains continuous surveillance and training programmes regarding control of all identified hazards.

The physiotherapist is skilled and experienced in identification of hazards in movements and postures, personal factors, loads and work organisation. Risk controls therefore include ergonomic interventions such as: job method and process modifications; workplace layout modifications; modifications to work and materials flow; instruction in actions, movements and forces; mechanical assistance; team lifting; and manual handling equipment.

PLACEMENT SUSTAINABILITY

There are two major parties contributing to a sustainable placement: the person on the one hand and the job on the other hand. For there to be a sustainable placement, the worker's capacities must be equal to or greater than the demands of the job. This may sound obvious, but it is not simple. Satisfaction of this equation depends on the reliability and validity of all the data collected when measuring a worker's capacities and the demands of the job. Therefore, it is essential that the assessments of a worker's functional capabilities are precise and accurate, whether performed by the treating doctor, an independent clinical assessment or a functional capacity assessment. Equally important is the accuracy and precision of the data collected as a result of analysing the job, whether by somebody at the enterprise, work site assessment by a medical expert or a detailed job analysis by a medical expert experienced in job analysis techniques. Put simply, the equation depends upon the accuracy of measurement of values for variables which are the same on either side of the equation. An example might be in respect of lifting, where the person's capacity to lift a certain load through a certain distance a certain number of times for a certain length of time needs to be equally and realistically measured when analysing the demands of the job. This includes how much weight is lifted through what distance how many times and for what duration in order to validly compare the person's capacities to the job demands.

Job analysis consists of a job description of all the functions of the job, a checklist of all the demands of the job, a detailed inventory of the frequency, duration, forces and distances through which the forces are moved to meet the demands of the job, and an ergonomic evaluation of the physical aspects of the job to discover hazards for which appropriate modifications should be made.

PRE-CLAIM MANAGEMENT

Pre-claim management commences with a pre-placement assessment of all applicants with respect to the demands of the job. This consists of a Key Method job placement assessment, which involves a number of physical functional activity tasks by a trained physiotherapist, a clinical pre-placement assessment involving a short physical examination and review of medical and health details, and an employee health check including instrumented hearing tests in a sound-proof booth, vision tests using a vision screening machine, blood pressure measurement and urinalysis by registered occupational health nurses. The employee health checks may be extended in accordance with the requirements of the enterprise.

Depending upon the size and scale of the enterprise, the occupational health, safety and welfare (OHSW) infrastructure may include:

- OHSW manager
- OHSW supervisor
- workers trained in first aid and certificated accordingly
- occupational health nurse
- occupational health and safety officer
- training officers
- workers' compensation officer
- internal rehabilitation consultant
- visiting medical practitioner
- arrangements with an external medical clinic
- on-site physiotherapist.

IMMEDIATE RESPONSE MODEL – PRE-CLAIM

Programmes which have been analysed for outcomes in enterprises justifying a full infrastructure will immediately respond to the report of a pre-claim incident or symptoms in the following manner:

- First aid given by either the occupational health nurse or another worker trained in first aid.
- Triage to immediately determine the most appropriate direction for the injured worker to obtain immediate management either by a worker trained in first aid, the occupational health nurse or the on-site physiotherapist.
- Immediate assessment by the on-site physiotherapist to assess the condition and commence immediate treatment, assess the worker's capacities, the job demands and jobs within the worker's capacity, and modify the job method or processes.
- If appropriate, placement in suitable duties.
- Refer the worker for appropriate management.
- Review progress.
- Return the worker to normal duties and close the case.

This follows the sports medicine model, where immediate response is required and delivered and the earliest possible safe return to competitive sport is achieved.

Identifying hazards and making appropriate job method and process changes may be regarded as secondary prevention, as not only will such modifications assist the injured worker, but also all other workers in that job.

POST-CLAIM MANAGEMENT

The immediate response model again applies once a claim has been made and the on-site members of the team, especially the on-site physiotherapist, collaborates with the treating medical experts, rehabilitation consultants, WorkCover agent, union and family. The physiotherapist conducts a job match, again in order to provide work within capacity so as to satisfy the equation for a sustainable placement. On-site physiotherapy treatment and management is offered, as is on-site internal rehabilitation management. Job method and process modifications are undertaken in order to ensure a sustainable placement, and progress is reviewed frequently until the person has returned to fully productive duties and the case is closed. Again, secondary prevention occurs as a result of identification of hazards and appropriate job method and process modifications. To assist in post-claim management, a method of enhancing the prevention of aggravation of symptoms or exacerbation of a condition during a return to work programme is implemented. This may be regarded as tertiary prevention. The fail-safe immediate response system (ROSH, 1998) is implemented. The aims of this system are to:

- Prevent aggravation of symptoms and exacerbation of pathology.
- To assist the worker to remain at work by preventing re-aggravation of symptoms.
- To assist in the graduated increase of workday and work week duration to achieve sustainable placement in new normal duties.

The objectives in order to achieve these aims are as follows:

- Early identification of latent and immediate symptom aggravation.
- Teach on-site method and process modifications.
- Resolve psychosocial problems as far as is possible.
- Increase worker endurance.
- Liaise with treating and certifying general medical practitioner or specialist.
- Create and/or restore motivation to return to normal duties and close the worker's compensation claim.
- Build sound and durable relationships between worker and employer.

This tool has been shown to be effective in identifying blocks in the return to work process, which may include physical blocks such as job method and process, or psychosocial blocks such as attitudes and behaviours of both workers, co-workers and management. Prevention of psychosocial problems and psychological and psychiatric diseases may be achieved by the use of this tool.

ON-SITE MANAGEMENT OUTCOME MEASURES AND RESULTS

It is difficult to establish the exact level of contribution the programmes described in this paper make to the total outcome as far as prevention and reduction of cost of work-related injuries are concerned, for the following reasons:

- An enterprise willing to invest in such an active programme is likely to be implementing other activities designed to achieve the same outcomes.
- The measures in the outcome statistics are not exclusively attributable to any one intervention.
- External factors, such as changes in the workers' compensation system, health, safety and welfare legislation, Australian Standards and safety technology, also affect the outcomes that may be changed by these interventions.

However, it is appropriate to take a baseline on the following outcome measures and to make comparisons after a suitable period of time of intervention to establish possible value added results:

- Reduction in total number of open claims.
- Reduction in lost time incidents.

- Reduction in total cost of all claims.
- Reduction in hours lost due to workplace injury.
- Reduction in hours lost as a percentage of hours worked.

In a review of the results of these interventions at one enterprise over a twelve month period, the results were as follows:

- Open claims had dropped by 44 per cent.
- Lost time claims had dropped by 50 per cent.
- Hours lost had dropped by 61 per cent.
- Hours lost as a percentage of hours worked had dropped by 73 per cent.
- Total cost of all claims had dropped by 33 per cent.

COST EFFECTIVENESS

The above results demonstrate significant reductions in the number of incidents, time loss and the cost of workers' compensation, which in part must be attributed to the programmes referred to in this paper. Most particularly, the programmes aimed at the prevention of workplace accident and illness described in this paper have contributed to a demonstrable reduction in the incidence of work-related injury and illness. The cost of the service to the enterprise whose results are referred to above was less than 10 per cent of the reduction in the cost of all claims for the twelve months in which the results were obtained. Allowing for the fact that not all of this reduction was due to the programme described above, a substantial amount, well in excess of the cost of the programme, could be explained by its introduction.

Thus, the occupational health and safety services instigated to provide a safe and healthy work environment at any enterprise must be paid for directly by the employer and must be substantially less costly than the value of their liability reduction. The results of these services must be accountable to both the workers and the employer.

Prevention is the best form of rehabilitation and is best undertaken at the work site by an on-site team providing continuous hazard identification, assessment, control, ergonomics, pre-placement assessment, job analysis, training and on-site physiotherapy management.

References

ROSH Pty Ltd (1998). ROSH fail-safe immediate response system. Rankin Occupational Safety and Health, South Australia.

An example of on-site physiotherapy services in industry

Kerry L. Butler

Physiotherapists working in industry, particularly in an on-site capacity, are still somewhat of a rarity. As a consequence, the considerable benefits of the inclusion of physiotherapists in industry are not widely appreciated. An example of an on-site physiotherapy service is that which has now been in place for some ten years at the Swan Brewery in Western Australia. The service consists of a once weekly on-site visit to provide physiotherapy-based and supplementary services, and additional visits on an as-required basis for additional services such as specific training programmes.

Swan Brewery is a manufacturing company which currently has some 300 employees including contractors. There are 150 shop floor employees and fifty in sales and marketing, with the remainder being office-based staff.

In 1988 the safety and health programme was in its infancy and was essentially a reactive process with two full-time on-site nurses who were involved largely in treating injuries as they occurred. At that point in time the Lost Time Injury Frequency Rate was 90 and the workers' compensation premium was $1 million with a similar amount in incurred costs. In 1988 a safety and health practitioner was employed on a full-time basis and a consultant physiotherapist was hired for half a day per week.

Following the safety practitioner's direction, a new approach to safety and health was instigated. The aim was to reduce both the exorbitant costs of work-related injuries and the number of injuries occurring. To do this, case management, on-site treatment and injury prevention and training programmes were required. To achieve such a system, a multidisciplinary approach including the safety practitioner, nurse and physiotherapist was utilised. Considerable involvement of the insurance company was also required and this involved a new approach on their part and a degree of risk taking because of the new and untried methods that were to be incorporated. The amalgamation of their expertise permitted a planned, proactive programme and the results have been astounding. A significant drop has been seen in both the number and severity of injuries occurring on site. This is demonstrated by a reduction of lost time resulting from injury of over 80 per cent.

As a result, the company has made considerable financial savings, including a large decrease in the workers' compensation premium – now down to $250,000 – with incurred costs of some $15,000 per annum.

While financial savings to the company were seen within the first year of instigation of this programme, to achieve maximum results, involvement is required over a period of years, since it takes time for changes to be implemented and aims to be achieved.

The thrust of occupational health and safety for this employer is awareness and communication. Any injury, whether work-related or not, can be reported to the Occupational Health Centre. While it is mandatory to report work-related injuries, there is an encouragement to seek appropriate treatment for non-work-related injuries as well.

The philosophy is that an employee is always more productive when they are at work than when they are not. Therefore, if basic treatment can be given on-site, then the employee is at work and productive. Injuries that are musculoskeletal in nature are referred to the physiotherapist during the once-weekly on-site sessions and treatment is available for both work- and non-work-related injuries, again to increase productivity. Initial diagnosis and treatment is performed by the physiotherapist. Simple ongoing treatment such as heat, ice packs and ultrasound can then be performed on a daily basis by the full-time occupational health nurse, as directed by the physiotherapist. Although employees must be referred off-site if more comprehensive treatment is required, it has been found that many injuries can be treated on-site as described. In addition to treatment, regular meetings are held with the workers' compensation insurer, the insurance broker, the occupational health nurse and the physiotherapist to discuss current compensable cases. Most of the case management is conducted jointly by the occupational health nurse and the physiotherapist.

While the original role of the physiotherapist for the Swan Brewery consisted largely of hands-on treatment and a small amount of rehabilitation work, the success of the programme has resulted in an evolution and broadening of the role over time, to include treatment, prevention, rehabilitation and consultancy aspects on a scheduled basis.

Specific training programmes have been developed for musculoskeletal risk management, manual handling, office ergonomics and occupational overuse syndrome prevention. All shop floor jobs have been assessed and physical job descriptions developed for use in determining pre-employment appropriateness for the work or for doctors to have a good précis of the exact physical parameters involved in a particular job for workers' compensation claims. In addition, ergonomic consultancy is given on an as-required basis, e.g. with the implementation of different work practices where musculoskeletal problems develop, or where an individual has begun to develop symptoms of some description. Also, assessments are undertaken with individuals who have some form of physical restriction/s in their work duties. The physiotherapist is also an accredited rehabilitation provider and, as such, has an additional task of undertaking in-house rehabilitation programmes as required. This entails communication between the occupational health nurse, the treating medical practitioner, and the relevant departmental supervisor or manager at the Brewery.

Unfortunately, the benefits associated with having physiotherapists on-site are not widely appreciated. This is due, at least in part, to physiotherapists not having put forward relevant data, anecdotal or otherwise, relating to their achievements or that the achievements have been couched in more 'medical' terms than "business" terms. Working in an industry-based health field, those aims that might be promoted in the medical model of health and injury care often become inappropriate. The medical model is poorly understood and is of little direct influence or interest to those in industry. The aims put forward, therefore, must reflect those that directly relate to 'business'. It is, however, possible to marry the aims of both the medical model and business and achieve satisfactory outcomes for both.

The aims for on-site physiotherapy services in industry might then include decreasing the costs to industry and the specific company in particular. This would involve:

- Workers' compensation premiums.
- Non-compensable costs such as down time, replacement staff, administration costs, processing of the claim, training of other staff to take the place of the injured person etc.
- Decreasing the number of lost time injuries.
- Decreasing absenteeism, i.e. keeping people at work who are carrying non-work-related injuries.
- Increasing productivity due to decreasing the number of injuries at work and the absenteeism associated with off-site injury occurrences.
- Improved case management.
- Social benefits for injured employees as a consequence of being kept at work.

From the medical model point of view, the aims might include:

- Decreasing the costs to the employee, e.g. avoiding lost benefits or penalty rates due to being off work, maintaining the role of being the breadwinner, or being able to have treatment at work at reduced or no cost to the patient.
- Increasing the convenience to the employee – no need to go off site for appointments.
- Dealing with injury complaints at an earlier stage in many instances, resulting in more effective recovery from injuries.

On-site physiotherapy services need not, and arguably should not, be confined to hands-on treatment. The expertise of the physiotherapist is such that additional services can be extensive, including pre-employment physical assessments; assessment, diagnosis and treatment of work- and non-work-related injuries; assessment of job performance criteria (i.e. the physical parameters or requirements of any job classification for assistance in employment selection or for rehabilitation after injury); injury prevention through ergonomic assessment and/or development of training programmes; and case management and rehabilitation of work-related injury.

Of course, the physiotherapist should not work alone in terms of achieving the company's aims. A multidisciplinary approach is required for best effect. In the example described here, this included a safety practitioner and an experienced occupational health nurse. There must then be overlap between the roles of the players, but areas of single expertise. Further, there must be a sharing of information, regular communication and a team approach to solving the problems and achieving the aims. Each person adds to the breadth of the approach, resulting in the achievement of sound occupational safety and health goals (the result is the sum of the composite parts).

Interestingly, a number of representatives of other companies have visited or contacted Swan Brewery over the years to find out how they approach occupational safety and health. Information regarding Swan's methodology is freely discussed yet, despite the positive opinions of Swan's insurers and insurance brokers, no other company has followed in its footsteps. Typically companies continue to use only a safety practitioner, or an occupational health nurse, or a company doctor, rather than utilising the skills of a number of individuals as has been undertaken by Swan, and arguably the results are not as good. Unfortunately, this approach is not going to be possible in all companies, as a certain economy of scale is required. Such an approach would probably not be possible for employee numbers of less than 100–150. Nevertheless, for companies in which size makes this approach feasible, the benefits have been clearly demonstrated.

Chapter 15

Chronic pain

Overcoming the return to work barrier of poorly managed pain

N. Ayers and L. Tonkin

INTRODUCTION AND BACKGROUND

The longer injured workers are off work, the less likely they are to return to work (Rosen, 1994). Persisting pain is one reason that a large proportion of injured workers give for their delayed return to work (Grellman, 1997). The data available indicate that about 10 per cent of injured workers develop chronic pain and this group contributes disproportionately to the costs of workers' compensation in industrialised countries. They not only take much longer to return to work but also consume considerably more health services than those who do not develop chronic pain (Frymoyer and Cats-Baril, 1991; Grellman, 1997; Rosen, 1994).

Injured workers who develop chronic pain and do not return to work also tend to suffer excessively from disability and depression. Sanderson et al. (1995), for example, found that injured workers with persisting back pain who remained at work were significantly less disabled generally compared to those with similar injuries who had not returned to work. Similarly, Cohen et al. (1997), in a study of injured workers in New South Wales, found that of the most disabled cases (none of whom had returned to work within two years post injury) over 50 per cent were thought by their medical carers to be depressed – which was significantly more than the figures for those who had returned to work. These figures may not appear that surprising, but what is more remarkable is that the same study found that treatment or help for the identified depression was instituted in less than half the cases. These findings are not alone. A British study by Cornes and Aitken (1992), based on an audit of medical reports on people claiming compensation for personal injury, found that, while medical aspects of the reports were covered to a high standard, this was not the case in relation to functional, psychosocial and occupational topics – areas which are known predictors of disability and poor adjustment in those with injuries (e.g. Sanders, 1994). Similarly, a large US study revealed that the longer injured workers are off work, the more physical investigations and treatments (mostly of dubious value) they received, to the virtual exclusion of attention to the psychosocial domain (Williams et al., 1998).

Such findings suggest that medical services and other somatic modalities, like physiotherapy, are not only overlooking psychological and social aspects of patients in persisting pain but, even when these issues are identified, relatively few are referred to psychological services for assessment and intervention.

These findings are of particular concern when it is considered that there is accumulating evidence that psychological and social (or environmental) factors can be of greater import for pain-related disability than physical findings. A report by an international, multidisciplinary task force of the International Association for the Study of Pain (IASP) on disability attributed to work-related back pain found no medical distinction between those with a diagnosis of non-specific back pain who were functioning despite pain and those who were unable to work because of the pain (Fordyce, 1995). The difference was attributed to psychosocial, fear avoidance and work-related factors. Burton et al. (1995), for example, in a longitudinal study of back pain from initial presentation, found that psychological factors, especially distorted, catastrophic thinking in reaction to pain, accounted for more pain-related disability in people than conventional physical findings such as straight leg raising. Similarly, Waddell et al. (1984) found that heightened distress and illness behaviour, rather than physical pathology, were associated with greater amounts of medical treatment in people with back pain lasting more than three months. More recently, Gaines and Hegmann (1999) found that patients exhibiting overt, inappropriate behaviour or responses during physical examination (which are believed to reflect psychological distress, especially anxiety) took four times as long to return to unrestricted regular work than those who did not display these responses. Relative to the inappropriate behaviour group, those exhibiting less of this behaviour also made significantly less use of physiotherapy and CT scans.

In relation to likely environmental variables that could interfere with return to work, the most obvious in the injured workers group are compensation and work issues. Certainly, there is evidence that those receiving workers' compensation payments can take longer to recover than those who don't (e.g. Sander and Meyer, 1986). However, this is not a simple, clear-cut conclusion to make, as the results are conflicting and different countries and even states within countries have different workers' compensation legislation, making firm conclusions across countries difficult. Guest and Drummond (1992), for example, in an Australian study found that those injured workers who were receiving compensation payments were more distressed and disabled than those who had had their claims settled. However, all members of both groups were unemployed. In other Australian studies (Mendelson, 1993), compensation recipients were not found to exaggerate their symptoms any more than those patients with similar physical problems. However, as Guest and Drummond (1992) pointed out, employment status, sex and length of pain history could have been confounding variables in these studies. In the UK study referred to earlier by Sanderson et al. (1995), injured workers with persisting back pain who remained at work were significantly less disabled generally compared to those with similar injuries who had not returned to work, yet both groups had pending compensation claims, suggesting that work status was a critical factor in the difference found.

The reporting of pain and return to work has also been found to be associated with work-related factors. For example, a longitudinal prospective study of 3020 employees at the Boeing Company (Bigos et al., 1991) found that, other than a history of current or recurrent back problems, work perceptions and certain psychosocial responses were most predictive of subsequent reports of acute back pain. Workers who stated that they 'hardly ever' enjoyed their jobs were 2.5 times as likely to report a back injury as those who 'almost always' enjoyed their jobs. In a study of employer practices, Hunt and Habeck (1993) found that employers with policies which facilitated return to work after injury had fewer lost work days among their injured employees relative to those employers who did not. Naturally, the nature of the work (e.g. heavy manual versus light clerical), the skill repertoire (or transferable skills) and the nature of the injuries of the injured worker are also likely to contribute to the return to work outcome (e.g. Daltroy et al., 1991; Tsai et al., 1992).

Thus, it would seem that achieving improved return to work rates amongst injured workers with persisting pain is unlikely to depend totally on the effectiveness of a particular treatment. Rather, type of treatment, the behaviour and psychological state of the injured worker, and the behaviour of the employer would all seem to be important in influencing return to work outcomes. Failure to address any one of these domains could place achieving return to work outcomes at risk.

This paper describes a cognitive behavioural approach to the management of pain in injured workers. This approach attempts to address the issues identified in the literature above, with a view to achieving improved return to work outcomes amongst injured workers with persisting pain, traditionally a group associated with poor outcomes. Firstly, the programme and its background will be outlined and secondly, to illustrate how the approach can work in some detail, two case studies will be described and the implications they raise will be discussed.

THE ADAPT PROGRAMME

Utilising a conceptualisation of chronic pain as a complex, multidimensional experience comprising physical, psychological and environmental factors, cognitive behavioural pain management programmes (and variants of them) have attempted to modify the psychological and environmental elements. Patients who are not progressing (i.e. still reporting pain, disability and distress) and are not considered suitable for specific evidence-based treatments that are associated with pain reduction (e.g. Lord et al., 1996; McQuay et al., 1997) are suitable for assessment for treatment in a cognitive behavioural pain management programme. There is level 1 evidence (meta-analyses and systematic reviews of a large number of published studies) (Flor et al., 1992; McQuay et al., 1997; Morley et al., 1999) that good quality programmes (e.g. Williams et al., 1996) can achieve lasting improvements in mood, function and quality of life and reduced use of health resources despite persisting pain.

The ADAPT programme at the University of Sydney Pain Management and Research Centre at the Royal North Shore Hospital in Sydney is directly based on the programme at St Thomas' Hospital in London (see Williams et al., 1996). The director of the ADAPT programme (MKN) was the original director of the St Thomas' programme and ADAPT uses the same patient manual, the same group methodology (with individualised goals and sessions), a similar daily schedule, and an intensity similar to the St Thomas' programme (9.00 a.m. to 5.00 p.m., Monday to Friday, for three weeks at ADAPT versus 9.00 a.m. to 5.00 p.m., Monday to Friday lunchtime, for four weeks at St Thomas'). Both programmes include a four-week home phase (where the patients are expected to apply the programme at home in a planned way) after the initial hospital attendance, and this is reviewed at a return visit to the hospital after that period. The St Thomas' programme involves patients staying at the hospital, but in hostel-style accommodation, whereas the ADAPT programme entails patients travelling to the hospital either from home or from local motel accommodation. Like the St Thomas' programme, ADAPT employs a multidisciplinary staff who work in a highly focused, collaborative manner. In ADAPT's case, the staff includes clinical psychologists, medical pain specialists, physiotherapists, nurses and a rehabilitation counsellor. All staff, regardless of discipline, employ the same cognitive behavioural principles in their work with the patients (see Nicholas and Sharp, 1997, for a fuller description). Outcome data from both programmes indicate that similar gains are achieved by both programmes in terms of improved function, self-efficacy and mood and reduced use of medication.

Rather than continuing to target the pain for treatment in those cases where there is no realistic cure available, cognitive behavioural treatments like ADAPT are targeted at each specific problem area (e.g. behavioural deficits and excesses such as resting too much, taking too many drugs, not engaging in daily household chores, depressed mood, unhelpful beliefs etc.) identified in the assessment process. From this perspective, it is expected that if these problems could be greatly reduced, the person would suffer less and, while not cured, should find that his/her pain did not trouble them nearly as much as before. They should then be much more capable of resuming a more active and fulfilling lifestyle which is less constrained by the pain. Reduction in pain severity is usually seen as an indirect outcome, but it is often reported (Morley et al., 1999). Once these gains (goals) have been achieved, the option of return to work, at least in a graduated manner, should become more feasible than is usually the case beforehand.

As indicated in the literature cited earlier, work-related factors will also influence matters at this stage; for example, whether or not the injured worker has a job to return to and the degree to which the employer is willing to facilitate a return to work programme (as opposed to saying 'no light duties available') (e.g. Hunt and Habeck, 1993). This is an area that often appears to be overlooked in the treatment outcome literature in the pain field, yet it can have a critical influence on the outcomes achieved. Of similar importance is the degree of reinforcement the pain management approach of the cognitive behavioural programme receives from the patient's other health care and rehabilitation advisers. It is not difficult to imagine that, if the self-reliant approach fostered by the pain management programme is not supported by these other health care professionals (who then re-institute the same passive modalities which didn't work previously, usually on the basis that the patient continues to report persisting pain), then the gains achieved in the programme could be rapidly eroded. However, identifying these potential problem areas is one thing; doing something about them is another.

What happens to a patient after he or she leaves a programme is, to a large extent, beyond the power of programme staff to influence. However, in an attempt to improve adherence to the principles of the ADAPT programme by the patients and their rehabilitation providers and other health care providers after discharge, a rehabilitation counsellor was employed. The focus of this person was to act in a liaison role between the programme staff and the rehabilitation providers responsible for assisting the injured workers in the next phase of their rehabilitation process. The rehabilitation counsellor was also expected to identify potential barriers to successful rehabilitation following the programme and to alert both the patient and their rehabilitation provider to these issues.

In the two years that a rehabilitation counsellor has been part of the ADAPT team, a number of recurring barriers to return to work for ADAPT graduates have been identified. These include: physical and cognitive limitations (including fear of further damage associated with pain, leading to avoidance of activities which aggravate pain); continued treatment seeking by the patient and treatment provision by their doctors and other health care providers; requirements for equipment; adjustments required to the job; limited transferable skills; literacy level; degree of vocational experience; possible financial disincentives; unrealistic wage expectations; length of time out of employment; mood; substance abuse; and ability to travel.

As mentioned earlier, the behaviours of the rehabilitation provider and other health care providers can also have a significant impact on the outcomes achieved. Thus, part of the ADAPT rehabilitation counsellor's role is to support and inform the rehabilitation providers in their work with the injured worker following the ADAPT programme. In particular, it was felt that the rehabilitation provider should endeavour to maintain contact with the programme staff both during the patient's attendance at the programme and following it, to ensure they had: an up-to-date understanding of chronic pain and its effective management (especially a cognitive behavioural perspective); skills in applying a cognitive behavioural approach to chronic pain (including the ability to deal with common problems such as flare-ups in pain or expressed desire by the injured worker to resume medication or further investigations); skills in dealing with the injured worker's doctor (to encourage effective communication and consistency of approach); and skills in providing education to the workplace in relation to developing appropriate expectations and adjustments with respect to the return to work plans.

OUTCOMES FOLLOWING ADAPT

Based on 308 patients who attended ADAPT between 1994 and 1998, the average length of time in pain before attending the programme was 5.2 years. Ninety-two per cent of this group were taking medication for their pain on admission to the programme, 55 per cent were significantly depressed (a Beck Depression Inventory score of greater than twenty-one) (Beck and Beamsderfer, 1974), and 52 per cent were significantly disabled by their pain (a Roland and Morris Disability Questionnaire score of greater than fifteen) (Roland and Morris, 1983). At the completion of the three week intensive phase, 92 per cent of patients had completed the programme (i.e. only an 8 per cent drop-out rate), 90 per cent were taking no medication for their pain (versus 8 per cent before) and 75 per cent were not significantly disabled by their pain (versus 48 per cent before). Thus, 92 per cent of those who attended demonstrated that they could attend an intensive programme which ran from 9.00 a.m. to 5.00 p.m. each weekday for three weeks. During this time they participated in a programme of exercise comprising two one-hour sessions each day (including walking, stair climbing, lifting small weights to different heights, using a walking machine, and performing exercises on a floor mat). They also participated daily in pain management skills training sessions, relaxation training and an educational group. Much of the day was spent either sitting or standing and moving about. In other words, the patients were active throughout the day and gradually increased their level of activity in most areas over the three week period. At the end of this process it could be claimed that at least 75–90 per cent of those who completed the programme demonstrated the capacity for at least part-time work (depending on skills, type of work etc.).

Interestingly, despite the clear increase in activity levels and markedly reduced use of analgesic medication, the patients' average pain severity ratings did not change significantly. This would suggest that medication was producing little of the desired effects and that persisting pain does not have to stop physical upgrading.

By the time of the first follow-up review, one month after the initial three week intensive phase of the programme, the mood ratings of 70 per cent of the patients were within normal limits for chronic pain patients (a Beck Depression Inventory score of less than thirteen) (versus 45 per cent before ADAPT).

Within six months of leaving the programme, of the ninety-eight patients of working age and eligible for work (e.g. not on home duties or retired) who returned for the six month follow-up, 63 per cent were either working in some capacity or retraining for return to work (versus 28 per cent in this group before the programme). Whilst this figure may be biased by the number of patients who did not return for review at six months (about 50 per cent), it does indicate that amongst this group (acting as their own control) there was a 50 per cent improvement in work status within six months of discharge from the programme, despite persisting pain.

Overall, it can be concluded that by the end of the programme at least 75 per cent of the patients had improved enough to start active rehabilitation. At this stage they should no longer require 'unfit for work' certificates and, given the assessment process they underwent before admission to the programme (which specifically ruled out their appropriateness for further medical or surgical treatment), the patients should no longer require ongoing medical or other passive treatments. It is in this context that the rehabilitation counsellor operates to facilitate the next phase of the patient's rehabilitation. Two case studies will be briefly described to illustrate the types of issues typically encountered in this period.

CASE STUDY 1

L presented to RNSH Pain Centre with a nine month history of persistent pain as the result of a motor vehicle accident whilst at work. She reported neck pain, lower back pain and intermittent sensory loss to her hands. She had continued to work (as a general duties police officer) for a month post injury, but had ceased her duties due to her pain and immobility in her neck. She reported significant interference in home activities due to her pain, but excellent support from her husband and family.

At initial assessment she presented as depressed, with sleep problems, and exhibited a great deal of fear in relation to movement and the possibility of further damage.

L attended the three week ADAPT programme, staying each night in a nearby motel as she lived too far from the hospital to commute every day. At the end of Week 1 she was progressing well with an increased range of movement and increased confidence. She returned home for the weekend, but on returning for Week 2 she had regressed significantly. However, she persisted with the programme, but later that week became sick (flu) and went home early for the weekend. She returned in Week 3, feeling a little better, and a significant improvement occurred again, until her husband attended for the day and she regressed once more.

Concerns were raised about her husband's over-solicitousness, and he attended a session with the clinical psychologist to address this. The importance of allowing (and encouraging) his wife to regain her independence was stressed. This proved to be a turning point in her treatment. By the end of the programme her depression level had been substantially reduced but was still higher than desirable. Her level of disability had also been significantly reduced, along with her use of medication (ceased). However, her sense of self-efficacy (confidence in being able to engage in normal activities despite her pain) was still very low and this was of considerable concern as we would expect it to be closer to 40–60 (on the PSEQ) by the end of the programme to have a reasonable chance of RTW. L's RTW was also complicated by the need for a high level of physical fitness to function in her normal duties.

Prior to discharge from ADAPT, a meeting was held at the hospital with the workplace rehabilitation staff and plans were developed for L's RTW, which was to be monitored by them. She did return to work after the programme (in a limited capacity and for restricted hours). Unfortunately, due to lack of available time for one-on-one monitoring, and inconsistencies in the workplace itself, progress was poor. Progress was also hampered due to lack of liaison by the initial rehabilitation provider, his lack of knowledge with respect to chronic pain and appropriate treatment, and his ongoing reinforcement of pain behaviour exhibited by L. Eventually, due to her lack of progress, he appeared to try to put pressure on her to increase her duties at work too quickly. This resulted in L becoming distressed again and the RTW plan was placed in jeopardy, effectively undermining the gains she had made at ADAPT. As an interim measure, the rehabilitation counsellor at ADAPT monitored her progress with RTW, until a suitable external rehabilitation provider was located.

Many trips were made by the ADAPT rehabilitation counsellor to both the workplace and the new rehabilitation provider to provide education on appropriate management of chronic pain.

L returned for her six month follow-up at ADAPT and was continuing to gradually increase her hours and her duties, in the hope that she could still resume working on her pre-injury general duties. While she reported frustration at her inability to increase her hours more, she also reported more confidence overall and less fear with respect to further damage.

More than a year later, she is working in a permanent part-time position on restricted duties with the police force, and has accepted her situation. She reports an improvement in mood, an ability to function at a far higher level *despite* her pain, an overall increase in activity and a significant weight loss as a result. The results achieved in this case are summarised in Table 15.1.

Table 15.1 Summary of Case 1 results

Age:	27 years
Sex:	Female
Marital status:	Married
Site of injury:	Neck/back
Date of injury:	09/08/96
Admitted to ADAPT:	September 1998
Treatment before ADAPT:	Passive physiotherapy, swimming, medication

	Pre-ADAPT	**Post-ADAPT**	**6 month follow-up**
Medication	Panadeine Forte Panadol Ceclor	Nil	Nil
BDI (depression) (0–63)	41	16	22
PSEQ (self-efficacy) (0–60)	2	6	24
DQ (disability) (0–24)	20	13	13
RTW status	Off	2 hrs × 2 days	4 hrs × 4 days

BDI, Beck Depression Inventory (Beck and Beamsderfer, 1974); PSEQ, Pain Self-Efficacy Questionnaire (Nicholas et al., 1992); DQ, Disability Questionnaire (Roland and Morris, 1984).

CASE STUDY 2

T presented at RNSH Pain Centre with an eight year history of chronic lower back pain and raised leg pain following a motor vehicle accident in 1990. She presented as extremely depressed, very passive in the management of her pain, and extremely fearful of causing further damage due to movement. She reported sleep problems and extreme marital problems. T was taking 450 mg of morphine (MS Contin) and was admitted as an in-patient at RNSH for one week prior to the ADAPT programme to 'detox' under the cover of a ketamine infusion. She commenced ADAPT the following week on 120 mg (per day) of MS Contin, plus temazepam for sleep and Panadeine.

During Week 1 of ADAPT she continued to experience withdrawal symptoms as the medication was further reduced, and she exhibited extreme pain behaviours, seeking attention frequently about her symptoms. These behaviours were ignored by the staff (after explanation of the reason for this and reassurance by the staff that the symptoms she was experiencing were related to withdrawal effects and to disuse effects, rather than to more damage). The pain behaviours subsequently subsided in frequency.

T made minimal physical gains during the first three weeks of the programme, which she attributed to her medication withdrawal, but she was clearly looking much better, as well as walking and moving more freely. Her husband attended during the programme, and after some joint sessions with the clinical psychologist, some improvement was reported in their relationship. During her attendance at ADAPT a rehabilitation meeting was conducted between clinic staff and the workplace rehabilitation co-ordinator and plans were developed for a graduated RTW programme.

Unfortunately, the rehabilitation co-ordinator had little understanding of chronic pain and was not confident that T could return to work until she was reporting less pain. A recommendation was made by the ADAPT rehabilitation counsellor for an external rehabilitation provider (one who was conversant with the ADAPT approach and would agree to implement it) to be allocated to her case and assist in her RTW. Another rehabilitation meeting was conducted with the new rehabilitation provider and clinic staff to develop the RTW plan. At the meeting T demonstrated no pain behaviours, reported that she was taking no medication and was extremely motivated to implement the RTW plan (despite her pain).

Meetings and education sessions were conducted at the workplace by the new rehabilitation provider and regular monitoring occurred, with frequent liaison with the Pain Centre. The employer made considerable efforts to facilitate the RTW plan and was very accommodating and patient.

T had many difficulties following completion of the programme, especially early on. She asked her husband to leave when she returned home (something that could be seen as indicative of her regaining her self-respect, as she had previously been blaming herself for his infidelities). She resumed taking MS Contin on an irregular basis (though in greatly reduced doses). Fortunately, her local doctor assisted the management plan by not prescribing more medication. She commenced abusing alcohol as a means of coping, and had many 'flare-ups' in pain. Unfortunately, due to her high medication level early in the programme the staff felt that she had had difficulty in absorbing the cognitive coping strategies taught during ADAPT. As a result she was not able to implement these strategies as well as required and thus suffered more than necessary from her increased pain (and hence her tendency to fall back on her old stand-bys of MS-Contin and alcohol). Despite all of this, however, T has remained at work, gradually increasing her hours, and has commenced local psychological therapy for a limited period, aimed at improving her skills in applying the strategies taught at ADAPT, free of the medication 'haze'.

Within six months of completing ADAPT, T's husband had returned home, she had ceased all medication and alcohol consumption, and her overall function and activity levels had improved dramatically, as well as her mood. She began attending the local gym on a regular basis. One year after the programme she is working five hours per day, five days per week in her old position as a supervisor in her workplace. Outside work, she reports that she has increased her activity level and is much happier with her new lifestyle. She continues to keep in touch with her rehabilitation provider from time to time. She is also continuing to apply the pain management strategies taught at ADAPT – to the extent that recently she had her wisdom teeth removed and declined the offer of Panadeine Forte for the pain, preferring instead to use her own strategies. The results achieved in this case are summarised in Table 15.2.

Table 15.2 Summary of Case 2 results

Age:	25 years
Sex:	Female
Marital status:	Married
Site of injury:	Back
Date of injury:	06/10/90
Admitted to ADAPT:	March 1998
Treatment prior to ADAPT:	Acupuncture, medication, scans, hospitalisation

	Pre-ADAPT	Post-ADAPT	6 month follow-up	12 month follow-up
Medication (per day)	450 mg morphine	Nil	Nil	Nil
BDI (depression)	52	23	42	'Much improved'
PSEQ (self-efficacy)	3	30	20	'Much better'
DQ (disability)	21	14	21	'Much reduced'
RTW status	Off	4 hrs×2 days	4 hrs×5 days	5 hrs×5 days

See footnote to Table 15.1 for key to abbreviations.

WHAT CAN WE LEARN FROM THESE CASES?

These two cases graphically illustrate the conclusions that can be drawn from the literature in this area. Specifically, injured workers who develop chronic pain and do not have a speedy return to work can rapidly become very complex cases, making return to work progressively less likely. Not surprisingly, complex cases usually require complex solutions, and no simple intervention (e.g. a drug, a nerve block or an exercise regime) is likely to adequately address all the factors involved in the case. As a result, lasting restoration of function, let alone return to work, is unlikely to be achieved by such means. Any intervention in such cases, even attending a comprehensive pain management programme like ADAPT, no matter how well-founded, is unlikely to be sufficient to guarantee lasting improvement unless the other factors identified (e.g. in the home, other clinical inputs and the workplace) are also addressed. In the face of strong reinforcement (e.g. by the family, the treating doctor/therapist or the workplace) for increased disability or unrealistic demands (e.g. expecting too much too soon), relapse following initial success in a pain management programme is very likely.

Clearly, achieving a successful outcome in this group of chronically disabled, distressed and often medication-dependent patients will also depend upon the patients themselves implementing the new pain management strategies they have learnt, as well as making changes in the home and work environments. Specifically, the injured worker must persist with the strategies that helped them to improve at ADAPT, and key people in their environments, such as spouses, doctors, rehabilitation providers and employers, must adhere to the principles underpinning ADAPT in their dealings with the injured worker with chronic pain. The two cases cited here indicate how difficult this can be. Yet even quite unpromising cases can be turned around with the methods described, despite pessimistic expectations and persisting pain. Rehabilitation providers are in an ideal position to facilitate this process, but they can also be a hindrance if they are not familiar with effective pain management principles. Clearly, persisting pain does not have to be a barrier to successful RTW outcomes. However, earlier intervention in cases like those described here could have made the RTW task considerably easier. Early identification and appropriate management of cases where pain is limiting restoration of function could also help to prevent the development of many of the complex problems associated with chronic pain.

References

Beck, A.T. and Beamesderfer, A. (1974). Assessment of depression: The Depression Inventory. In *Psychological Measurements in Psychopharmacology* (P. Pichot, ed.), pp. 151–169. Karger Press.

Bigos, S.J. Battie, M.C., Spengler, D.M. et al. (1991). A prospective study of work perceptions and psychosocial factors affecting the report of back injury. *Spine*, **16**, 1–6.

Burton, A.K., Tillotson, K.M., Main, C.J. et al. (1995). Psychosocial predictors of outcome in acute and subchronic low back trouble. *Spine*, **20** (6), 722–728.

Cohen, M., Nicholas, M.K. and Blanch, A. (1997). Identification of medical factors influencing return to work following low back or cervicobrachial pain. Final Report for WorkCover New South Wales.

Cornes, P. and Aitken, R.C.B. (1992). Medical reports on persons claiming compensation for personal injury. *Journal of the Royal Society of Medicine*, **85**, 329–333.

Daltroy, L.H., Larson, M.G., Wright, E.A. et al. (1991). A case-control study of risk factors for industrial low back injury: Implications for primary and secondary prevention programs. *American Journal of Industrial Medicine*, **20**, 505–515.

Flor, H., Feydricht, T. and Turk, D.C. (1992). Efficacy of multidisciplinary pain treatment centres: a meta-analytic review. *Pain*, **49**, 221–230.

Fordyce, W.E. (ed.) (1995). Back Pain in the Workplace: Management of Disability in Nonspecific Conditions. IASP Press.

Frymoyer, J.W. and Cats-Baril, W. (1991). An overview of the incidences and costs of low back pain. *Orthopaedic Clinics of North America*, **22**, 263–271.

Gaines, W.G. and Hegmann, K.T. (1999). Effectiveness of Waddell's nonorganic signs in predicting a delayed return to regular work in patients experiencing acute occupational low back pain. *Spine*, **24**, 396–401.

Grellman, R.G. (1997). Final Report: Inquiry into Workers' Compensation System in NSW. Department of the NSW Attorney-General.

Guest, G.H. and Drummond, P.D. (1992). Effect of compensation on emotional state and disability in chronic back pain. *Pain*, **48**, 125–130.

Hunt, A. and Habeck, R. (1993). The Michigan Disability Prevention Study. Michigan: W.E. Upjohn Institute for Employment Research.

Lord, S.M., Barnsley, L., Wallis, B.J. et al. (1996). Percutaneous radiofrequency neurotomy for chronic cervical zygapophyseal joint pain. *New England Journal of Medicine*, **335**, 1721–1726.

Mendelson, G. (1993). Compensation and motivation in relation to musculoskeletal pain. In *Progress in Fibromyalgia and Myofascial Pain* (H. Voerey and H. Merskey, eds), pp. 101–112. Elsevier Science Publishers.

McQuay, H.J., Moore, R.A., Eccleston, C. et al. (1997). Systematic review of outpatient services for chronic pain patient control. *Health Technology Assessment*, **1** (6), 1–135.

Morley, S., Eccleston, C. and Williams, A. (1999). Systematic review and meta-analysis of randomized controlled trials of cognitive behaviour therapy and behaviour therapy for chronic pain in adults, excluding headache. *Pain*, **80**, 1–13.

Nicholas, M.K. and Sharp, T.J. (1997). Cognitive-behavioural programs: Theory and application. In Acute and Chronic Pain (A.R. Molloy and I. Power, eds). *International Anesthesiology Clinics*, **35**, 155–170.

Nicholas, M.K., Wilson, P.H. and Goyen, J. (1992). Comparison of cognitive-behavioural group treatment and an alternative non-psychological treatment for chronic low back pain. *Pain*, **48**, 339–347.

Roland, M. and Morris, R. (1983). A study of the natural history of back pain: Part 1. Development of a reliable and sensitive measure of disability in low back pain. *Spine*, **8**, 141–144.

Rosen, M. (Chairman) (1994). Report of a Clinical Standards Advisory Group Committee on Back Pain for UK Health Ministers. HMSO.

Sander, R.A. and Meyer, J.E. (1986). The relationship of disability to compensation status in railway workers. *Spine*, **11**, 141–143.

Sanders, S.H. (1995). Risk factors for the occurrence of low back pain and chronic disability. *American Pain Society Bulletin*, **5**, 1–6.

Sanderson, P.L., Todd, B.D., Holt, G.R. et al. (1995). Compensation, work status, and disability in low back pain patients. *Spine*, **20**, 554–556.

Tsai, S.P., Gilstrap, E.L., Cowles, S.R. et al. (1992). Personal and job characteristics of musculoskeletal injuries in an industrial population. *Journal of Occupational Medicine*, **34**, 606–612.

Waddell, G., Main, C.J., Morris, E.W. et al. (1984). Chronic low back pain, psychological distress and illness behavior. *Spine*, **9**, 209–213.

Williams, A. Cde C., Richardson, P.H., Nicholas, M.K. et al. (1996). Inpatient vs. outpatient pain management: results of a randomised controlled trial. *Pain*, **66**, 13–22.

Williams, D.A., Feuerstein, M., Durbin, D. et al. (1998). Health care and indemnity costs across the natural history of disability in occupational low back pain. *Spine*, **23**, 2329–2336.

Chapter 16

Conflict mediation

Moving in on conflict: the role of mediation in occupational injury

Pat Smart

In many cases of occupational injury, workplace conflict is an underlying issue, colouring the attitudes of employer and employee and often hindering the return to work process. Relentless focusing on the compensable injury or illness often results in collusion in the process of keeping the real issues hidden and unaddressed, and encourages the key parties to use the injury as the means to deal with unresolved conflict.

Mediation provides neutral ground and neutral people to assist participants to communicate and negotiate more effectively and to resolve conflict. Mediation not only assists parties to resolve the dispute but also provides an example and an experience of a format and structure to help them in future conflicts.

DEFINITION

Mediation is the process through 'which the participants, together with the assistance of a neutral third person or persons, systematically isolate the dispute issues in order to develop options, consider alternatives and reach consensual agreement that will accommodate the participants' needs. Mediation is a process which emphasises the participants' own responsibility for making decisions that affect their lives' (Folberg and Taylor, 1986).

Using this definition, the key elements of mediation can be isolated.

- Participants are responsible for their own decision making. Mediators do not impose solutions or opinions and must ensure that parties negotiate from equal power bases.
- Mediators must be neutral and impartial and be trusted by the participants to remain so.
- Mediators control the process and participants control the content. It is the mediator's role to set guidelines for communication and how participants behave during the mediation.
- Mediation requires both confidentiality and open, frank communication.

- Mediation focuses on the future, not past events, and on needs and interests, not on positions.

WORKPLACE MEDIATION

In Australia, workplace mediation is in an embryonic stage of development. At Resolutions, the focus is given to continually working on and developing effective mediation strategies and processes for Australia's diverse workplace environments.

The majority of workplace mediations have the main aim of reaching agreements about ways for the participants to improve or repair their continued working relationship. If the participants are able to effect a shift to a more empowered, problem solving style that can then be transposed to the workplace, the mediation has a therapeutic and transformative purpose, regardless of the outcome. It is therefore helpful in workplace mediation if mediators make a clear distinction between process and outcome in their opening statements.

Some mediations are more focused on settlement involving agreement by the parties not to continue working together, and in these cases amicable separation is the outcome worked towards by the participants.

There are two categories of workplace mediation: industrial disputes and interpersonal disputes.

Industrial disputes

These include:

- Enterprise bargaining/workplace agreements.
- Employment contracts.
- Conditions of employment.
- Classification structures.
- Demarcation disputes.

Interpersonal disputes

These include:

- Interpersonal conflicts (style or communication differences, role conflicts, power imbalances).
- Performance review disputes.
- Retrenchment/redundancy.
- Grievances and disciplinary procedures.

- Unfair dismissals.
- Personal injury (workers' compensation, motor vehicle accident, income protection).

This paper deals with the second of these categories and discussion will focus on mediation in occupational injury or illness. It might be argued, though, that effective mediation, provided early in many instances of workplace conflict, could prevent the lodgement of a workers' compensation claim.

STUDY OF OUTCOMES

A retrospective, qualitative study of mediation outcomes in cases involving occupational injury was carried out on twenty-two randomly selected mediations conducted by staff at Resolutions in the period from March 1998 to March 1999. All mediations were conducted by formally trained mediators who are also accredited providers of occupational rehabilitation services under both State and Commonwealth jurisdictions.

Outcome durability and effectiveness was ascertained through contact with the referrer to assess whether there was:

- Separation without further conflict.
- An ongoing, effective working relationship.

A standardised participant satisfaction questionnaire surveyed:

- Effectiveness of the mediation process.
- Implementation of outcome agreements.
- Usefulness and transference of learned skills such as listening, assertiveness, issue identification, problem solving skills, style awareness and flexibility.
- Well-being of participants.
- Durability of outcome over a twelve month period.

The basis for referral of the cases included in the study was unresolved conflict between parties in the workplace which was impeding progress in return to work and resolution of the claim.

Of the cases studied, the following outcomes were reported at twelve months after mediation:

- In seven cases the participants had achieved separation without further conflict.
- In eleven cases the participants were continuing to work together without exacerbation of the issues leading to mediation.
- In three cases the participants continued to work together but implementation of the agreements had not been sustained.

- In one case the mediation was stopped by the mediator and the case proceeded to a court hearing.

There were eleven cases where a total of twenty-eight participants continued to work effectively alongside people with whom they had previously experienced conflict. Here the following was reported:

- Twenty-three participants felt a greater sense of work satisfaction and increased feelings of well-being at work.
- Twenty-two participants reported they were aware of and using the skills they had acquired during the mediation process.
- Seven participants experienced the process of mediation as 'uncomfortable'.
- Twenty-five participants reported feeling pleased that they had participated in the process and said that they would recommend mediation to other colleagues if the need arose.

THE MEDIATION PROCESS

Pre-mediation phase

In workplace mediation, it is worth taking time before the mediation to ensure that:

- The mediation process and the role of the mediator are clearly outlined.
- Issues are identified and clarified.
- The ability of parties to participate in the process is ascertained.
- Agreement to mediate is secured.
- Commitment and willingness to proceed in good faith is gauged.
- Reassurance is given that the mediator will manage/control the process.
- Debriefing/counselling/skills training can be engaged in when required.

At Resolutions it has been found that these points can be covered by the rehabilitation consultant responsible for the case. This professional would not be involved in both the delivery of rehabilitation services and conducting a mediation in the same case.

In addition to the above, the mediator may request an intake session or sessions with the participants. The necessity for these sessions is largely dictated by the complexity of the case, the number of participants and the mediator's sense of the level of conflict and possible power imbalances. Participants can be directed by the mediator to obtain further details about substantive issues such as medical information, financial factors, workplace agreements and other information which may be relevant to the mediation. It is important that the mediator ascertains that decision makers at the appropriate level will be present to ratify any agreements reached.

Mediators should also ensure that there is time to prepare themselves and the room before the mediation, with a view to creating a calm and positive atmosphere. Physical comfort helps people feel at ease and enhances concentration.

Mediator's opening and introduction

The mediator begins by introducing the parties to the process of mediation. This includes congratulating the parties on reaching agreement to participate in mediation. Recognition of the work already undertaken to reach this point can assist the mediator to build rapport with the parties. Roles are clarified and guidelines explained. Many mediators find it helpful to write the guidelines on a whiteboard, so that they can be easily referred to if anybody 'strays off the track'. Any queries that have arisen for the parties can be answered and practicalities addressed.

The parties' presentations

The parties present their concerns and the mediator observes the dynamic of any interaction, works to engage the parties and develop their trust, and asks questions to elicit further background information.

The main issues

The mediator organises the presented conflicts into manageable portions and works to neutralise and mutualise the issues. This means separating the people from the problem and identifying the areas where there is agreement. In many situations it comes as a surprise to the parties that there are any points of agreement and it is important to highlight these. The mediator assists the parties to decide on the order of addressing the issues identified.

Seeking options, negotiating and decision making

This is usually the longest phase of the mediation process and requires a determined effort on the part of the mediator to control the process while keeping 'hands off' the content. Co-operative decision making between the parties is encouraged and the mediator can assist them to test their decisions by asking questions using the pattern: 'If ... then what ... '. Parties will need varying amounts of assistance to understand each other's point of view and will be encouraged to air their feelings and use creative ways of exploring options to achieve consensus. The mediator provides a structure for this future-oriented problem solving, maintains order in the process, reflects, reframes and summarises.

In addition, the mediator needs to be analysing what is happening in terms of:

- Each of the parties.
- The mediation itself.
- Him or herself.

Private sessions

Private or separate sessions are an optional step in mediation, although many mediators regard them as a significant and even essential feature of the process. Private sessions provide opportunities for the parties to meet separately with the mediator, either accompanied by a legal adviser or other support person or alone. The session may be called by the mediator or requested by either party. It is essential to give equal time to both parties in private session, no matter who initiated the request. The mediator's objectives in calling for a private session are:

- To enable parties to move beyond a block or impasse by changing the dynamic of the process or engaging in reality testing with a party adopting a positional stance.
- To give time and opportunity to reflect, recover and speak more freely, especially if one party is disempowered.
- To elicit further concerns which may not have been raised but will contribute to the resolution of the dispute.
- To build trust in or re-educate the parties about the mediation process.
- To avoid negative or destructive communication styles which cannot be remedied in joint sessions.

One of the main concerns about private sessions is that confidentiality may be breached. Another is that the mediator's relationship with a party may be altered and doubts about mediator impartiality may arise. The mediator must continue to manage the process with an awareness of these concerns, checking at the beginning of a private session that the party is happy for all information from the session to be shared unless the party indicates otherwise. Another check is made at the end of the session, reiterating the same understanding. Constant vigilance on the part of the mediator to ensure that the defined role is maintained will minimise these concerns.

Shuttle mediation is the term given to mediations which consist entirely of private sessions, with the mediator moving between the parties. The shortcomings of this style of mediation are that opportunities for the parties to observe and practise more effective communication and conflict resolution are missed, and the process can become unwieldy and costly because of the extra time required. However, where parties aren't willing to approach normal mediation, such shuttle mediation may be better than to deny them access to the process altogether.

Agreement preparation and writing

This phase marks the culmination of the negotiation and the written agreement is the tangible outcome of the mediation. The parties have reached a point where they are able to settle on an option or options for dealing with issues in a mutually acceptable way which is different from what has been used in the past. The mediator needs to ensure that all agreements made are recorded in the parties' own words, and needs to check the wording for understanding and acceptability.

It is important to remember that parties may reach agreements that do not appear fair or reasonable to the mediator. Other than checking to ensure each party's satisfaction that they have been heard, considered and included in the agreement, the mediator has no arbitrating role with regard to the agreements themselves. Parties may wish to have legal validation of their agreement but, from experience, this is rare. Without court sanction, mediated agreements have the same status as any other agreement.

Closing the mediation

It is appropriate for the mediator to formalise the closure of the mediation, not least because this provides a demarcation point for the cessation of the confidentiality requirements. It is also an opportunity to congratulate the parties on their achievements, and this applies even when agreements have not been reached.

CONCLUSIONS

At present, the lack of information and understanding on the part of stakeholders in occupational rehabilitation about the process of mediation means it is under-utilised as a tool. Its application at various stages in the management of occupational injury will assist in addressing underlying conflicts which may impede return to work and efficient resolution of a claim. It is important to see mediation not as a cure-all for perceived complexities, but as a cost-effective tool which, judiciously applied, can provide the means for parties in dispute to move from a fearful, defensive and self-focused state to one where they can take a more assertive, open and empathic approach to issues.

ACKNOWLEDGEMENTS

The author gratefully acknowledges the assistance provided by Ms Di McDonald, Managing Director of Resolutions Pty Ltd, in her role as mentor, guide and coach to a neophyte mediator.

References

Acland, A. (1990). *A Sudden Outbreak of Commonsense: Managing Conflict through Mediation*. Hutchinson.

Astor, H. and Chinkin, C. (1992). *Dispute Resolution in Australia*. Butterworths.

Boulle, L. (1996). *Mediation: Principles, Process, Practice*. Butterworths.

Folberg, J. and Taylor, A. (1984). *Mediation: A Comprehensive Guide to Resolving Conflicts Without Litigation*. Jossey-Bass.

Index